Beginning VB 2008

From Novice to Professional

Christian Gross

Apress®

Beginning VB 2008: From Novice to Professional

Copyright © 2008 by Christian Gross

ISBN-13 (pbk): 978-1-59059-938-9

ISBN-10 (pbk): 1-59059-938-1

ISBN-13 (electronic): 978-1-4302-0542-5

ISBN-10 (electronic): 1-4302-0542-3

Printed and bound in the United States of America 9 8 7 6 5 4 3 2 1

Lead Editor: Matthew Moodie
Technical Reviewer: Andy Olsen
Editorial Board: Clay Andres, Steve Anglin, Ewan Buckingham, Tony Campbell, Gary Cornell, Jonathan Gennick, Kevin Goff, Matthew Moodie, Joseph Ottinger, Jeffrey Pepper, Frank Pohlmann, Ben Renow-Clarke, Dominic Shakeshaft, Matt Wade, Tom Welsh
Project Manager: Sofia Marchant
Copy Editor: Marilyn Smith
Associate Production Director: Kari Brooks-Copony
Production Editor: Laura Esterman
Compositor: Susan Glinert Stevens
Proofreader: Nancy Riddiough
Indexer: Broccoli Information Management
Artist: Kinetic Publishing Services, LLC
Cover Designer: Kurt Krames
Manufacturing Director: Tom Debolski

Distributed to the book trade worldwide by Springer-Verlag New York, Inc., 233 Spring Street, 6th Floor, New York, NY 10013. Phone 1-800-SPRINGER, fax 201-348-4505, e-mail orders-ny@springer-sbm.com, or visit http://www.springeronline.com.

For information on translations, please contact Apress directly at 2855 Telegraph Avenue, Suite 600, Berkeley, CA 94705. Phone 510-549-5930, fax 510-549-5939, e-mail info@apress.com, or visit http://www.apress.com.

Apress and friends of ED books may be purchased in bulk for academic, corporate, or promotional use. eBook versions and licenses are also available for most titles. For more information, reference our Special Bulk Sales–eBook Licensing web page at http://www.apress.com/info/bulksales.

The source code for this book is available to readers at http://www.apress.com.

Some food for thought when writing software:

"A common mistake that people make when trying to design something completely foolproof is to underestimate the ingenuity of complete fools."

"The major difference between a thing that might go wrong and a thing that cannot possibly go wrong is that when a thing that cannot possibly go wrong goes wrong it usually turns out to be impossible to get at or repair."

—Douglas Adams, Mostly Harmless

Contents at a Glance

Contents

About the Author

 Many people say that by looking at a person's dog, you can tell what the person is like. Well, the picture is of my dog Louys, an English bulldog. And yes, my English bulldog and I have many common characteristics. But what about the biography of the author, **CHRISTIAN GROSS**? It's pretty simple: I'm a guy who has spent oodles of time strapped to a chair debugging and taking apart code. In fact, I really enjoy this business we call software development. I have loved it ever since I learned how to peek and poke my first bytes. I have written various books, including *Ajax and REST Recipes: A Problem-Solution Approach*, *Foundations of Object-Oriented Programming Using .NET 2.0 Patterns*, *A Programmer's Introduction to Windows DNA*, and *Beginning C#: From Novice to Professional*, all available from Apress.

These days, I enjoy coding and experimenting with .NET, as it is a fascinating environment. .NET makes me feel like a kid opening a present on Christmas morning. You had an idea what the gift was, but you were not completely sure. And with .NET, there is no relative giving you socks or a sweater. It's excitement all the way!

About the Technical Reviewer

ANDY OLSEN is a freelance developer and consultant based in the UK. Andy has been working with .NET since beta 1 days, and has coauthored and reviewed several books for Apress, covering C#, Visual Basic, ASP.NET, and other topics.

Andy is a keen football and rugby fan, and enjoys running and skiing (badly). He lives by the seaside in Swansea with his wife, Jayne, and children, Emily and Thomas, who have just discovered the thrills of surfing and look much cooler than he ever will!

Introduction

The first computer programming book I read was titled *Programming Windows 3.0* by Charles Petzold. This was around the time when Microsoft Windows 3.0 (circa 1992) once and for all showed the industry that Microsoft was a company with a future. Writing code for Windows back then was complicated by many things: lack of documentation, 16-bit architecture, and the necessity of buying a compiler separate from the software development kit (SDK). Charles's book tied everything together and solved the problem of how to write a program for Windows.

Now the problems are quite the opposite: we have too much documentation, we have 64-bit architectures, and everything including the kitchen sink is thrown into a development environment. Now we need to figure out what we actually need. We have too many options—too many ways to solve the same problem. What I am trying to do with this book is the same thing that Charles did for me when I first started out, and that was to help me figure out what I needed to write code.

This book is about explaining the Visual Basic programming language in the context of solving problems. Visual Basic has become a sophisticated programming language that can achieve many goals, but you are left wondering what techniques to use when. This book is here to answer your questions.

This book is not a reference to all of the features of the Visual Basic programming language. I don't explain the esoteric Visual Basic features. I stick to the Visual Basic programming features that you will use day in and day out. That does not mean that you will be missing certain Visual Basic programming language constructs, because I have covered all of the major features.

To get the full benefit of this book, I suggest that you do the exercises at the end of the chapters. The answers are available on the Apress web site (http://www.apress.com), and you can cheat and not do the exercises, but I advise against that.

If you are a beginning programmer who has no clue about Visual Basic, and you read this book and do the exercises, I believe that you will be a solid and knowledgeable Visual Basic programmer by the end of the book. If that sounds like a big promise, well, yes it is. The chapter text is intended to get you acquainted with the Visual Basic programming language and how to apply its features. The exercises are intended to make sure you actually understand the Visual Basic programming language and its features.

The chapter exercises are challenging. They cannot be solved within a few minutes. In fact, when I did all of the exercises, it took me five working-hour days to do all of them!

If you have any questions, such as, "So what was he trying to get at with that exercise?" I am available on Skype with the user ID christianhgross. Please don't just ring me. First chat using text, and if necessary, we can have a voice conversation. Also, you can send e-mail to me at christianhgross@gmail.com.

Thanks and good luck.

CHAPTER 1

■ ■ ■

Ready, Steady, Go!

This book is about the Visual Basic programming language first and foremost. It is about becoming a proficient Visual Basic programmer. Reading this book from cover to cover will not make you a superstar, but it will make you a programmer who understands what needs to be done when writing robust, stable, and maintainable Visual Basic applications.

In this chapter, you'll get started by acquiring the tools you need to develop Visual Basic applications and taking those tools for a test spin. Along the way, you'll create a couple Visual Basic applications.

Downloading and Installing the Tools

Getting started with Visual Basic 2008, you're probably really excited about writing some code that does something. It's like getting your driver's license and wanting to drive a car without even thinking about where you want to go. You just want to drive. The great part of .NET is that you can start writing some code after you have installed either the .NET software development kit (.NET SDK) or a Visual Studio integrated development environment (IDE). Downloading and installing the right environment is critical to taking your first step toward an enjoyable coding experience.

■**Note** Software version numbers, product descriptions, and technologies can be confusing. Having used Microsoft technologies for over a decade, I can say that naming a technology or product has never been Microsoft's strong point. The technologies have been great (for the most part), but product classification and identification have not been so great. Thus, this book covers the Visual Basic 2008 programming language that is used to write applications for the .NET Framework. With Visual Basic 2008, the .NET 3.0 and 3.5 Frameworks are used. .NET 3.0 gives you all of the essentials, and .NET 3.5 gives you the extras.

For the examples in this book, you'll be using Visual Basic 2008 Express Edition, because it's freely available and has everything you need to get started with Visual Basic 2008. The other Express Edition IDEs available from Microsoft are tailored to different languages (C# and C++) or, in the case of Visual Web Developer Express, specific functionality that is too restrictive for our purposes.

Microsoft also offers full versions of the Visual Studio IDE, such as the Standard, Professional, and Team editions. Each of these editions has different features and different price tags. See the Microsoft Visual Studio web site (http://msdn2.microsoft.com/en-us/vstudio/default.aspx) for more information. If you already have Visual Studio 2008 Professional, you can use that for the examples in this book. That edition can do everything that Visual Basic 2008 Express can do, and in fact, has many more options.

Note I personally use Visual Studio Standard or Professional in combination with other tools such as X-develop and JustCode! from Omnicore (http://www.omnicore.com), TestDriven.NET (http://www.testdriven.net/), and NUnit (http://www.nunit.org). The Visual Studio products are very good, but others are available. Being a good developer means knowing which tools work best for you.

Installing and downloading Visual Basic Express from the Microsoft web site involves the transfer of large files. If you do not have a broadband connection, I suggest that you install the IDE from a CD instead.

Downloading Visual Basic Express

The following is the procedure for downloading Visual Basic Express from the Microsoft web site. By the time you are reading this book, the procedure may be a bit different, but it will be similar enough that you'll be able to find and download the IDE package.

1. Go to http://www.microsoft.com/express/.

2. Select the Download Now! link.

3. Scroll down to the Visual Basic 2008 Express Edition section, as shown in Figure 1-1.

4. Click the Download link.

5. A dialog box appears, asking where you want to store the downloaded file. The file that you are downloading is a small bootstrap file, which you'll use to begin the actual installation of the Visual Basic Express IDE. Choose to save the file on the desktop.

These steps can be carried out very quickly—probably within a few minutes. Do not mistake this procedure for downloading the complete Visual Basic Express application, because that's not what happened. The installation procedure will download the vast majority of the IDE.

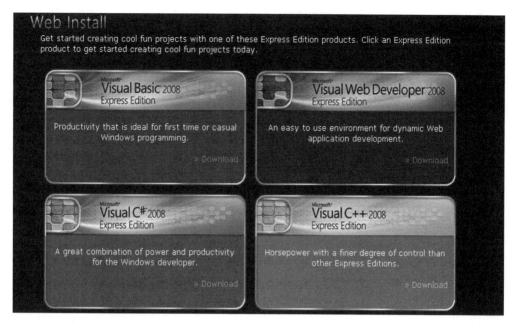

Figure 1-1. *Selecting Visual Basic 2008 Express Edition*

Installing Visual Basic Express

After you've downloaded the setup file, you can start the Visual Basic Express installation. During this process, all the pieces of the IDE—about 300MB—are downloaded and installed. Follow these steps:

1. On your desktop, double-click the vbsetup.exe file. Wait while the setup program loads all the required components.

2. Click Next on the initial setup screen.

3. A series of dialog boxes will appear. Select the defaults and click Next to continue through the setup program. In the final dialog box, click Install.

4. After all the elements have been downloaded and installed, you may need to restart your computer.

After Visual Basic Express is installed, you can start it by selecting it from the Start menu.

Choosing the Application Type

With Visual Basic Express running, you're ready to write your first .NET application. However, first you need to make a choice: what type of application will you write? Broadly speaking, in .NET, you can develop three main types of programs:

- A *console application* is designed to run at the command line with no graphical user interface (GUI).

- A *Windows application* is designed to run on a user's desktop and has a GUI.

- A *class library* holds reusable functionality that can be used by console and Windows applications. It cannot be run by itself.

So that you know what each type of program is about, in this chapter, you will code all three. They are all variations of the Hello, World example, which displays the text "hello, world" on the screen. Hello, World programs have been used for decades to demonstrate programming languages.

Creating Projects and Solutions

Regardless of which program type you are going to code, when using the Visual Studio line of products, you will create projects and solutions:

- A *project* is a classification used to describe a type of .NET application.

- A *solution* is a classification used to describe multiple .NET applications that most likely relate to each other.

Imagine building a car. A project could be the steering wheel, engine, or car body. Putting all of the car projects together creates a complete solution called the car.

A solution contains projects. For the examples in this chapter, our solution will contain three projects representing each of the three different program types.

When using Visual Basic Express, creating a project implies creating a solution, because creating an empty solution without a project does not make sense. It's like building a car with no parts. When I say "project" or "application" in this book, from a workspace organization perspective, it means the same thing. *Solution* is an explicit reference to one or more projects or applications.

Our plan of action in terms of projects and solutions in this chapter is as follows:

- Create the .NET solution by creating a Windows application called WindowsApplication (creating this application also creates a solution).

- Add to the created solution a console application called ConsoleApplication.

- Add to the created solution a class library project called ClassLibrary.

Creating the Windows Application

We'll dive right in and start with the Windows application. With Visual Basic Express running, follow these steps to create the Windows application:

1. Select File ➤ New Project from the menu.

2. Select the Windows Forms Application icon. This represents a project style based on a predefined template called Windows Forms Application.

3. Change the default name to `WindowsApplication`.

4. Click OK.

These steps create a new project and solution at the same time: Visual Basic Express will display only the complete project, as shown in Figure 1-2.

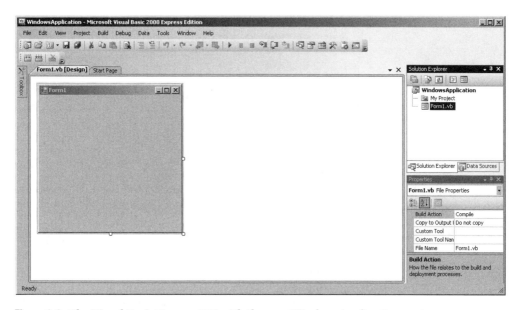

Figure 1-2. *The Visual Basic Express IDE with the new WindowsApplication project*

Viewing the Source Code

When you create a new application, Visual Basic Express automatically generates some source code for it. Right-click the `Form1.vb` item in the Solution Explorer and select View Code from the context menu. The following source code will appear in the area to the left of the Solution Explorer.

■**Note** To shift between the user interface and generated code, right-click `Form1.vb` in the Solution Explorer. A submenu appears with the options View Code (to see the code) or View Designer (to see the user interface).

```
Public Class Form1

End Class
```

In Visual Basic, the source code is spartan because Visual Basic is what was once called a rapid application development (RAD) environment. The idea at the core of Visual Basic is the ability to develop an application as quickly as possible without the esoteric details of the language getting in your way. This legacy is both good and bad. Figure 1-2 shows a simple project with a single file, but another file exists at the hard disk level, as shown in Figure 1-3 (you can see this file by clicking the Show All Files icon in the Solution Explorer and expanding the Form1.vb node).

Figure 1-3. *All files that make up the WindowsApplication project*

In previous versions, the Form1.Designer.vb file used to be a binary file that you could not edit. Now it is a text file that you can edit, but you should not make any changes to this file because it is maintained by the IDE. Contained within the Form1.Designer.vb file are the details of how to construct Form1, as is shown in Figure 1-2. At this point, Form1 does not contain anything noteworthy, and neither does the text file. However, if you were to add a button or text box to the form, those details would be added to the text file Form1.Designer.vb.

Visual Basic is a complete programming language that still adheres to the RAD model. For example, the following code creates a user-defined type (which you'll learn about throughout the rest of the book).

```
Public Class Example
    Public Sub Empty()
    End Sub
End Class
```

The main elements to note are as follows:

Class: An organizational unit that groups related code together. This grouping is much more specific than a solution or a project. To use the car analogy again, if a project is a car engine, then a class can be the carburetor. In other words, projects are made up of multiple classes.

Sub: A set of instructions that carry out a task. Also called a *method*, a sub is analogous to a function in many other languages. The Empty() method can be called by another piece of code to carry out some type of action.

Saving the Project

After you've renamed the solution, it's good practice to save your changes. To save the project, follow these steps:

1. Highlight the project name in the Solution Explorer.

2. Select File ➤ Save WindowsApplication.

3. Notice that Visual Basic Express wants to save the solution using the WindowsApplication name, which isn't ideal. (We're using three projects in this solution, of which one is a Windows Forms application.) To save the solution with a new name, you need to change the WindowsApplication solution name to ThreeExamples (make sure you leave the WindowsApplication project name as it is). Note the path of where Visual Basic Express saves your projects, as you will need to know it from time to time.

4. Click the Save button.

When the solution and project are successfully saved, you'll see the message "Item(s) Saved" in the status bar in the lower-left corner of the window.

In the future, whenever you want to save the solution and project, you can use the keyboard shortcut: Ctrl+S.

■**Note** If you have not saved your changes and choose to exit Visual Basic Express, you will be asked if you want to save or discard the solution and project.

To open a solution you have previously saved, you can choose File ➤ Open Project at any time and navigate to the solution file. You can also select the solution from the Recent Projects window when you first start Visual Basic Express. The Recent Projects window is always available on the Start Page tab of the main Visual Basic Express window as well (and the File menu contains a list, too).

Running the Windows Application

The source code generated by Visual Basic Express is a basic application that contains an empty window with no functionality. The source code gives you a starting point where you can add more source code, debug the source code, and run the application.

To run the application, select Debug ➤ Start Debugging. Alternatively, use the keyboard shortcut F5. You'll see a window representing the WindowsApplication application. You can exit the application by clicking the window's close button. Figure 1-4 illustrates the process. (Debugging is covered in Chapter 5.)

Running the application enables you to see what it does. When you run an application though the IDE, it is identical to a user clicking to start the application from the desktop. In this example, WindowsApplication displays an empty window without any controls or functionality. The source code's functionality is to display an empty window when started and provide a button to end the application (and buttons to maximize and minimize the window). Close the application now.

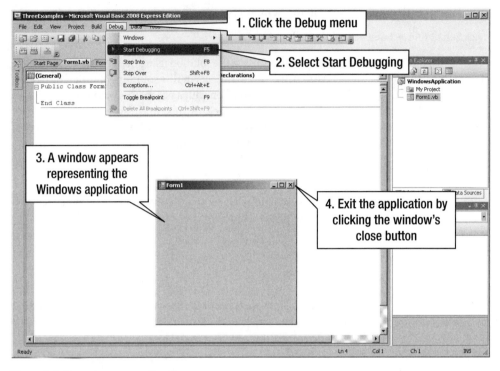

Figure 1-4. *Running an application*

You have not written a single line of code, yet you have created an application and something actually happened, and all because Visual Basic Express generates some boilerplate Visual Basic code that works straight out of the box.

You have created an application, seen its source code, and run it. You did all of this in the context of a comfortable, do-it-all-for-you development environment called Visual Basic Express. Visual Basic Express is both a good thing and a bad thing. Visual Basic Express is good because it hides the messy details, but it is bad because the messy details are hidden. Imagine being a car mechanic. It is good that car manufacturers produce dashboards that have little lights that go on when something is wrong. But it would be bad if the mechanic had to rely on the little lights to fix problems in a car.

Making the Windows Application Say Hello

The Windows application does nothing other than appear with a blank window that you can close. To make the application do something, you need to add user interface elements or add some code. Adding code without adding user interface elements will make the program do something, but it's not as exciting. So, we'll add a button that, when clicked, will display "hello, world" in a text box.

First, you need to add the Button control to the form. Double-click Form1.vb in the Solution Explorer to display a blank form. Then click the Toolbox tab to access the controls and open the Common Controls tab (click the pin icon on the Toolbox to leave the Toolbox tab open if you like). Click Button, and then click the form to place the button on the form. These steps are illustrated in Figure 1-5.

Figure 1-5. *Adding a button to the form*

Next, add a TextBox control using the same basic procedure. Finally, align the button and text box as shown in Figure 1-6. To move a control, use the handles that appear when you highlight the control. Visual Basic Express will align the edge of a control to nearby edges as you drag it, so that you can align controls accurately.

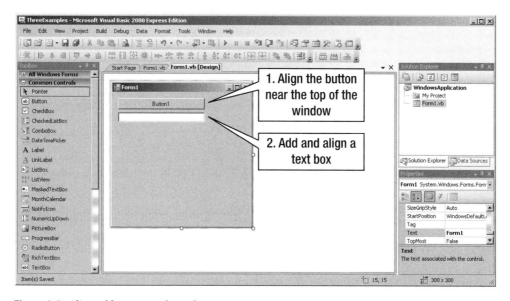

Figure 1-6. *Aligned button and text box*

If you now executed WindowsApplication by pressing Ctrl+F5 (Ctrl+F5 starts the application without debugging), you would see a window with a button and a text box. You can click the button and add or delete text from the text box. But whatever you do has no effect, because neither control has been associated with any code.

To make the application do something, you need to think in terms of *events*. For example, if you have a garage with an automatic door opener, you would expect that pressing the remote control button would open the garage door when it's closed and close the door when it's open. The automatic garage door manufacturer associated the event of pushing the remote control button with the action of either opening or closing the garage door. In WindowsApplication, we'll associate the clicking of the button with the action of showing text in the text box.

Select the button on the form in Visual Basic Express and double-click it. The work area changes to source code, with the cursor in the Button1_Click() function. Add this source code to the function:

```
TextBox1.text = "hello, world"
```

Figure 1-7 illustrates the procedure for associating an event with an action.

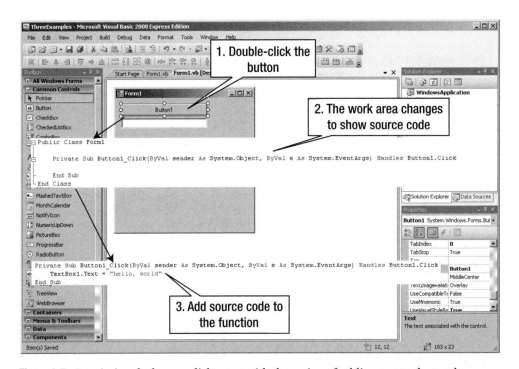

Figure 1-7. *Associating the button click event with the action of adding text to the text box*

Note that TextBox1 is the name of the text box you added to the form. This name is generated by Visual Basic Express, just as it generated a default name for the button. You can change the default names (through each control's Properties window), but we've left the default for this example.

Adding an action to an event is very simple when following the instructions shown in Figure 1-7. The simplicity is due to Visual Basic Express, and not because the event or action is simple. Visual Basic Express makes the assumption that when you double-click a control, you want to modify the *default event* of the control, and as such, automatically generates the code in step 3 of Figure 1-7. In the case of a button, the default event is the click event; that is, the event that corresponds to a user clicking the button. The assumption of the click event being the default event for a button is logical. Other controls have different default events. For example, double-clicking a TextBox control will generate the code for the text-changed event.

Run the application by pressing Ctrl+F5, and then click the button. The text box fills with the text "hello, world." Congratulations, you've just finished your first Visual Basic application.

You have associated an event with an action: the button click with the text display. Associating events with actions is the basis of all Windows applications.

Adding Comments to the Application

Now that you have a working program, it would be good to document what it does, right there in the source code. Then if you come back to the application in the future, you won't be puzzled by your previous work. In fact, you may not even be the person who maintains your code, so leaving comments in the code to help explain it is definitely good practice. Even if you know you will be maintaining the code forever, treat your future self as a stranger. You may be surprised how long it takes to decipher code you have written when revisited months or years later.

To add a single-line comment, use the following syntax:

```
' A single-line comment
```

Anything after the ' on the same line is ignored by the compiler and is not included in the final application. Let's document our Windows application:

```
' When the user clicks the button, we display text in the text box
    Private Sub Button1_Click(ByVal sender As System.Object,
ByVal e As System.EventArgs) Handles Button1.Click
        TextBox1.Text = "hello, world"
    End Sub
```

The Visual Basic language is a single-line language. This means that a statement must be part of a single line. Let's look at a single statement:

```
    TextBox1.Text = "hello, world"
```

This line of code is a single statement because it is considered an assignment of one variable by another piece of source code. You could not write the statement as follows:

```
    TextBox1.Text =
            "hello, world"
```

When the statement is broken into two lines of source code, the Visual Basic compiler sees it as two statements. Since those two statements are not complete, a compilation error will result. If you need to break a single statement over two lines, you must let the compiler know by adding the line-continuation character—an underscore (_)—at the end of the continued code, as follows:

```
    TextBox1.Text = _
            "hello, world"
```

Navigating the User Controls of the Solution

When you are writing your code, your most important form of navigation is the Solution Explorer. The Solution Explorer is the tree control that contains the references to your solutions and projects. Consider the Solution Explorer as your developer dashboard, which you can use to fine-tune how your .NET application is assembled and executed.

I suggest that you take a moment to click around the Solution Explorer. Try some right-clicks on various elements. The context-sensitive click is a fast way of fine-tuning particular aspects of your solution and project. However, when clicking, please do not click OK in any dialog box; for now, click Cancel so that any changes you may have made are not saved.

To the right of the Solution Explorer is your work area. The work area is where you write your code or edit your user interface. The work area will display only a single piece of information, which could be some code, a user interface, or a project. As you saw earlier, when you double-click Form1.vb in the Solution Explorer, the work area displays the form related to the Form1.vb file.

Now that you have an idea of how the IDE works, let's continue with our examples. Next up is the console application.

Creating the Console Application

A console application is a text-based application. This means that rather than displaying a GUI, it uses a command-line interface.

The console has a very long history because the console was the first way to interact with a computer. Consoles are not very user-friendly and become very tedious for any complex operations, yet some people claim that a console is all you need. (See http://en.wikipedia.org/wiki/Command_line_interface for more information about the console.)

Writing to the console works only if the currently running application has a console. To open the console in Windows, select Start ➤ Run and type cmd in the dialog box. When you test a console application, Visual Basic Express opens a console for you.

Visual Basic Express can create, build, and manage console applications.

Adding a Console Application Project to the Solution

We will now create an application that outputs the text "hello, world" to the console. Follow these steps to add the new project to the ThreeExamples solution:

1. Choose File ➤ Add ➤ New Project.

2. Make sure the location is the same as that of WindowsApplication.

3. Select Console Application and change the name to ConsoleApplication.

The Solution Explorer changes to show the additional project and now also shows the solution. The work area displays the source code.

Notice the simplicity of the console application. It contains a single, plain-vanilla source code file, called Module1.vb. Console applications typically do not have any specialized groupings and do not have any events.

Making the Console Application Say Hello

To make the console application do something, you need to add some source code to the Main() method, as follows:

```
Module Module1

    Sub Main()
        Console.WriteLine("hello, world")
        Console.ReadKey()
    End Sub

End Module
```

The bolded line writes the text "hello, world" to the console.

If you tried to run the console application by pressing Ctrl+F5, you would instead cause the Windows application, WindowsApplication, to run. Let's change that next.

Setting the Startup Project

To execute the console application, you need to set the console application as the *startup project*. Did you notice how the WindowsApplication project is in bold in the Solution Explorer? That means WindowsApplication is the startup project. Whenever you run or debug an application, the startup project is executed or debugged.

To switch the startup project to ConsoleApplication, right-click the ConsoleApplication project and select Set As StartUp Project. ConsoleApplication will now be in bold, meaning it is the startup project of the ThreeExamples solution.

Running the Console Project

With ConsoleApplication set as the startup project, you can now press Ctrl+F5 to run the console application. The output is as follows:

```
hello, world
```

Executing the console application does not generate a window, as you saw with the Windows application. Instead, a command prompt is started with ConsoleApplication as the application to execute. Executing that application generates the text "hello, world." You will also see that you can press any key to close the command prompt window. Visual Basic Express automatically generated the code to show this output and execute this action.

In general, the console application is limited, but it's an easy way to run specific tasks. Now let's move on to the next example.

Creating the Class Library

The third example in this chapter is not a .NET application; rather, it is a shareable piece of functionality, typically called a *class library*. Windows applications and console applications are programs that you can execute from a command prompt or Windows Explorer. A class library cannot be executed by the user, but needs to be accessed by a Windows application or console application. It is a convenient place to put code that can be used by more than one application.

Adding a Class Library Project to the Solution

We will now create a class library for the Windows application and console application to share. Follow these steps to add the new project to the ThreeExamples solution:

1. Right-click the solution name, ThreeExamples, in the Solution Explorer.

2. Select Add ➤ New Project.

3. Select Class Library and change the name to ClassLibrary.

The resulting solution project should look like Figure 1-8.

Figure 1-8. *Updated solution structure that contains three projects*

The added ClassLibrary project has a single file called Class1.vb, which is a plain-vanilla source code file.

Moving Functionality

Now we will move the code used to say "hello, world" from ConsoleApplication to ClassLibrary. Add the code to Class1.vb as follows (the bolded code):

```
Public Class Class1
    Public Shared Sub HelloWorld()
        Console.WriteLine("hello, world")
    End Sub
End Class
```

The modified code contains a method called HelloWorld(). When called, this method will output the text "hello, world." As mentioned earlier in the chapter, a method is a set of instructions that carry out a task. Methods are discussed in more detail in Chapter 2.

In order for applications to actually share the code that's in a class library, you must make the projects aware of each other's existence. You do that through references.

Defining References

To make one project aware of definitions in another project, you need to define a *reference*. The idea behind a reference is to indicate that a project knows about another piece of functionality.

■**Note** The project only knows about the functionality that has been declared as being public. Public functionality, or what Visual Basic programmers call *public scope*, is when you declare a type with the Public keyword. You will learn about public and other scopes throughout this book.

To make ConsoleApplication aware of the functionality in the ClassLibrary project, you need to set a physical reference, as follows:

1. In the Solution Explorer, click ConsoleApplication.

2. Right-click and select Add Reference.

3. Click the Projects tab.

4. Select ClassLibrary, and then click OK. ClassLibrary will be added to ConsoleApplication's references.

Once the reference has been assigned, ConsoleApplication can call the functionality in ClassLibrary.

To know which references your application or class library has, you need to look in the project settings. To do so, right-click the project name, ConsoleApplication, in the Solution Explorer and select Properties. In the Properties window, select the References tab, as shown in Figure 1-9.

Figure 1-9. *References used by the Visual Basic project*

Calling Class Library Functionality

Now we need to change ConsoleApplication so that it calls the function in ClassLibrary. Modify the Module1.vb file in ConsoleApplication as follows:

```
Module Module1

    Sub Main()
        Console.WriteLine("hello, world")
        ClassLibrary.Class1.HelloWorld()
        Console.ReadKey()
    End Sub

End Module
```

Run ConsoleApplication by pressing Ctrl+F5. A command prompt window should appear and generate the "hello, world" text twice. The first "hello, world" is generated by the code Console.WriteLine(). Calling the function ClassLibrary.Class1.HelloWorld() generates the second "hello, world."

USING REFERENCE SHORTHAND

ClassLibrary.Class1.HelloWorld() is the longhand way to use a reference. If we were to use long-hand for the Console.WriteLine() call, we would write System.Console.WriteLine(), because the Console.WriteLine() method is defined in the System reference. However, Visual Basic Express includes the System reference by default, so we don't need to do it this way.

To use shorthand for the ClassLibrary call, we would include an Imports line at the beginning of Module1.vb in ConsoleApplication and change the call to Class1's HelloWorld() method:

```
Imports ClassLibrary
Module Module1

    Sub Main()
        Console.WriteLine("hello, world")
        Class1.HelloWorld()
        Console.ReadKey()
    End Sub

End Module
```

But shorthand like this has a downside. What if we had many references, each containing a class called Class1? In this case, Visual Basic Express wouldn't know which Class1 to use without the help of longhand. Granted, you are not likely to name multiple classes Class1, but even sensible names can be duplicated in a collection of references. And if you are using someone else's code as a reference, the possibility of duplicate names becomes higher. Therefore, you're better off using longhand in this case.

Using Variables and Constants

One of the core concepts in a Visual Basic program is to use variables. Think of a variable as a block of memory where you can store data for later use. This allows you to pass data around within your program very easily.

In our ClassLibrary project, it would make life easier if we could define the message to display at the beginning of the method. That way, if we decide to change the message, we can get at it much more easily. As it stands, if we were to add more code before the Console.WriteLine() call, we would need to scroll through the text to find the message to change. A variable is perfect for this, as we can define some data (the message to print), and then use it later in our program.

```
Public Class Class1
    Public Shared Sub HelloWorld()
        Dim message As String = "hello, world"
        Console.WriteLine(message)
    End Sub
End Class
```

Here, we've defined a variable called message of type String (a String is a length of text). We can then refer to the message variable later when we want to place its contents into the code. In the example, we place its contents into the Console.WriteLine() call, which works as before. This time, however, we have set the message to display in a separate statement.

This is very useful for us, but there is more to variables. They have something that is called *scope*. The message variable has method-level scope, which means it is available only in the method in which it is defined. Consider this code:

```
    Public Shared Sub HelloWorld()
        Dim message As String = "hello, world"
        Console.WriteLine(message)
    End Sub

    Public Shared Sub DisplayeMessageText()
        Console.WriteLine("hello, world")
        Console.WriteLine(message)
    End Sub
```

The DisplayMessageText() method prints two lines of text to tell us what the message text should be. However, this doesn't compile, because the compiler knows that the variable message is not available to the DisplayMessageText() method because of its method-level scope.

To fix this, we need to give message class-level scope by moving it to the beginning of the class definition (as it is used by methods marked Shared, it must also be Shared):

```
Public Class Class1
    Shared Dim message As String = "hello, world"
    Public Shared Sub HelloWorld()
        Console.WriteLine(message)
    End Sub

    Public Shared Sub DisplayeMessageText()
        Console.WriteLine("hello, world")
        Console.WriteLine(message)
    End Sub
End Class
```

Now the variable message is shared by all the methods of Class1. You'll learn much more about method-level and class-level scopes, as well as the Public and Shared keywords, throughout this book.

Sharing a variable among methods of a class can be useful, but it's sometimes not wise to do this. That's because methods can change variables as they carry out their tasks, which can produce unpredictable results further down the line. We can lock the value by using a *constant* instead of a variable. The Const keyword denotes the constant:

```
Public Class Class1
    Const MESSAGE As String = "hello, world"
    Public Shared Sub HelloWorld()
        Console.WriteLine(MESSAGE)
    End Sub

    Public Shared Sub DisplayeMessageText()
        Console.WriteLine("hello, world")
        Console.WriteLine(MESSAGE)
    End Sub
End Class
```

Constant names are usually all uppercase. The contents of a constant cannot be changed at any point. The following would not compile, for instance.

```
Public Class Class1
    Const MESSAGE As String = "hello, world"

    Public Shared Sub DisplayeMessageText()
        MESSAGE = "another text that cannot be assigned"
        Console.WriteLine(MESSAGE)
    End Sub
End Class
```

Now that you've worked through this chapter's examples, let's talk a bit about how your Visual Basic code in Visual Basic Express actually turns into a program that can run on an operating system like Windows.

Understanding How the .NET Framework Works

When you write Visual Basic source code, you are creating instructions for the program to follow. The instructions are defined using the Visual Basic programming language, which is useful for you, but not useful for the computer. The computer does not understand pieces of text; it understands ones and zeros. To feed instructions to the computer, developers have created a higher-level instruction mechanism that converts your instructions into something that the computer can understand. The conversion utility is called a *compiler*.

The twist with .NET, in contrast to traditional programming languages such as C++ and C, is that the compiler generates a binary-based intermediate language called Common Intermediate Language (CIL). The .NET Framework then converts the CIL into the binary instructions required by the computer's processor.

You might think converting the source code into an intermediate language is inefficient, but it is a good approach. Let's use an analogy. There are dogs that learn quickly and those that take a while to learn. For example, German shepherds tend to learn quickly and don't require much repetition of lessons. On the other hand, bullmastiffs need quite a bit of patience, as they tend to be stubborn. Now imagine being a trainer who has created instructions on how to teach things specifically geared toward the bullmastiff. If those same instructions are used on the German shepherd, you end up boring the German shepherd and possibly failing to teach that dog what you wanted him to learn.

The problem with the instructions is that they are specifically tuned for a single dog. If you want to teach both dogs, you need two sets of instructions. To solve this problem, the instructions should be general, with added interpretation notes saying things like, "If dog is stubborn, repeat."

Converting this into computer-speak, the two sets of instructions are for two different processors or processors used in specific situations. For example, there are server computers and client computers. Each type of computer has different requirements. A server computer needs to process data as quickly as possible, whereas a client computer needs to show data on the screen as quickly as possible. There are compilers for each context, but to have the developer create multiple distributions with different compiler(s) or setting(s) is inefficient. The solution is to create a set of instructions that are general, but have associated interpretation notes. The .NET Framework then applies these instructions using the interpretation notes.

The .NET Framework compiles to instructions (CIL) that are then converted into processor-specific instructions using notes embedded in the .NET Framework. The .NET architecture is illustrated in Figure 1-10.

Figure 1-10. *.NET architecture*

In Figure 1-10, Visual Basic Express is responsible for converting the Visual Basic source code into a CIL package. The converted CIL package is a binary file that, when executed, requires a common language runtime (CLR). Without a CLR installed on your computer, you cannot run the CIL package. When you installed Visual Basic Express, you installed the CLR in the background as a separate package. Visual Basic Express is an application that allows you to develop for the CLR, but it also uses the CLR.

The CLR has the ability to transform your instructions in the CIL package into something that the operating system and processor can understand. If you look at the syntax of .NET-compatible languages, such as Visual Basic, C#, and Eiffel.NET, you will see that they are not similar. Yet the CLR can process the CIL package generated by one of those languages because a .NET compiler, regardless of programming language, generates a set of instructions common to the CLR.

When using the .NET Framework, you are writing for the CLR, and everything you do must be understood by the CLR. Generally speaking, this is not a problem if you are writing code in Visual Basic. The following are some advantages of writing code targeted to the CLR:

Memory and garbage collection: Programs use resources such as memory, files, and so on. In traditional programming languages, such as C and C++, you are expected to open and close a file, and allocate and free memory. With .NET, you don't need to worry about closing files or freeing memory. The CLR knows when a file or memory is not in use and will automatically close the file or free the memory.

■**Note** Some programmers may think that the CLR promotes sloppy programming behavior, as you don't need to clean up after yourself. However, practice has shown that for any complex application, you will waste time and resources figuring out where memory has not been freed.

Custom optimization: Some programs need to process large amounts of data, such as that from a database, or display a complex user interface. The performance focus for each is on a different piece of code. The CLR has the ability to optimize the CIL package and decide how to run it as quickly and efficiently as possible.

Common Type System (CTS): A string in Visual Basic is a string in C#. This ensures that when a CIL package generated by Visual Basic talks to a CIL package generated by C#, there will be no data type misrepresentations.

Safe code: When writing programs that interact with files or memory, there is a possibility that a program error can cause security problems. Hackers will make use of that security error to run their own programs and potentially cause financial disaster. The CLR cannot stop application-defined errors, but it can stop and rein in a program that generates an error due to incorrect file or memory access.

The benefit of the CLR is allowing developers to focus on application-related problems, because they do not need to worry about infrastructure-related problems. With the CLR, you focus on the application code that reads and processes the content of a file. Without the CLR, you would need to also come up with the code that uses the content in the file and the code that is responsible for opening, reading, and closing the file.

The Important Stuff to Remember

This chapter got you started working with Visual Basic in an IDE. Here are the key points to remember:

- There are three major types of Visual Basic programs: Windows applications, console applications, and class libraries.

- A Windows application has a user interface and behaves like other Windows applications (such as Notepad and Calculator). For Windows applications, you associate events with actions.

- A console application is simpler than a Windows application and has no events. It is used to process data. Console applications generate and accept data from the command line.

- You will want to use an IDE to manage your development cycle of coding, debugging, and application execution.

- Among other things, IDEs manage the organization of your source code using projects and solutions.

- In an IDE, keyboard shortcuts make it easier for you to perform operations that you will do repeatedly. For example, in Visual Basic Express, use Ctrl+S to save your work and Ctrl+F5 to run your application without debugging.

- Visual Basic Express projects contain plain-vanilla files and specialized groupings. When dealing with specialized groupings, make sure that you understand how the groupings function and modify only those files that you are meant to modify.

Some Things for You to Do

The following are some questions related to what you've learned in this chapter. Answering them will help you to get started developing your projects in the IDE.

■**Note** The answers/solutions to the questions/exercises included at the end of each chapter are available with this book's downloadable code, found in the Source Code/Download section of the Apress web site (http:// www.apress.com). Additionally, you can send me an e-mail message at christianhgross@gmail.com.

---

1. In an IDE, solutions and projects are used to classify related pieces of functionality. The analogy I used talked about cars and car pieces. Would you ever create a solution that contained unrelated pieces of functionality? For example, would you create an airplane solution that contained car pieces?

2. Projects are based on templates created by Microsoft. Can you think of a situation where you would create your own template and add it to Visual Basic Express?

3. In the Solution Explorer, each item in the tree control represents a single item (such as a file, user interface control, and so on). If you were to double-click a .vb file, you would be manipulating a Visual Basic file that would contain Visual Basic code. Should a single Visual Basic file reference a single Visual Basic class or namespace? And if not, how would you organize your Visual Basic code with respect to Visual Basic files?

4. You have learned about how a .NET application can generate an executable file. Let's say that you take the generated application and execute it on another Windows computer. Will the generated application run? Let's say that you take the executable file to a Macintosh OS X or Linux computer, will the application run? Why will it run or not run?

5. You are not happy with the naming of the element TextBox1, and want to rename it to TxtOutput. How do you go about renaming TextBox1?

6. ClassLibrary has embedded logic that assumes the caller of the method is a console application. Is it good to assume a specific application type or logic of the caller in a library? If yes, why? If no, why not?

CHAPTER 2

■■■

Learning About .NET Number and Value Types

In the previous chapter, you learned how to use Visual Basic Express, and what .NET is in terms of the CIL and CLR. In this chapter, we are going to roll up our sleeves and begin writing real Visual Basic code—specifically, a calculator.

A calculator is an ideal example to start with, because it allows you to focus on the application without having to deal with all the nasty details that are normally associated with programs. In a programming language like Visual Basic, adding two numbers is trivial. What is not trivial is how to put the operation of adding two numbers into a program.

This chapter focuses on the mechanics of writing a program in Visual Basic—taking an idea and converting it into a Visual Basic program that can execute your intentions. You'll learn how to organize your development and implement a Visual Basic class library, as well as how the .NET CLR manages number types.

Focusing and Organizing Your Development

When you develop software, you will split your work into two main tasks: organizing and implementing. Organizing your development involves figuring out what features and libraries you are going to define, how many people are going to be developing the features, and so on.

Organizing your development is one of the most important tasks when writing code, and it is also typically the most confusing for new developers. Professional developers seem to organize their work instinctively, but it only appears that way because they have done it so many times that the process has become automatic.

When developers are tasked with creating a program, they are asked to write software that implements a set of features. Features could include calculating daily interest payments, automatically generating letters indicating the acceptance or rejection of a loan, and so on. A feature always relates to performing some task that is determined by some process. You could say that feature implementation is the direct implementation of a task.

When defining the features, two major steps are involved:

- Gain an understanding of the features. You can't implement something that you don't understand. To be able to write the source code for a feature, you need to know the whys and whats of a feature.

- Describe the features using structured design methods. Simply organizing your thoughts may be enough if you are the only person working on a program; however, more often than not, you will be part of a team. You need to use a structured design method so that you and your team members can communicate the thoughts related to program development.

One common structured design method is the Unified Modeling Language (UML). UML is used to organize the features into units that correspond to programming language constructs, such as classes. Think of UML as software developer-specific lingo used to describe the various aspects of a programming environment at a higher level of abstraction. UML allows you to get an overall understanding of the architecture without having to read the source code. Think of UML as the structured doodle on the napkin of software programming.

Along with UML, there are other ways of structuring your development process. For example, another technique is called agile software development. The idea with agile software development is to use a whiteboard and develop your own structured communication mechanism.

The choice of UML, agile software development, or another structured design method is up to you and your team members. But you will need to organize your thoughts and have a structured communication technique. If you don't, your software will be late, buggy, too expensive, or incomplete. It is not an understatement to say that organization is half the battle.

In this chapter, I am going to give you a taste of a simplified structured development technique, so that you at least have an idea of how structured development works.

Organizing the Calculator

To begin this chapter's example, get a piece of paper and a pen or pencil, or you can use a tablet PC for writing, if you have one. Next, in the center of the paper (or virtual paper), draw a circle and in it write the word *Calculator*. Now stop and think about what a calculator means with respect to the software that you will be writing. Write those ideas on the paper surrounding the circle. My thoughts are shown in Figure 2-1.

Your thoughts and my thoughts may or may not be the same, but what our results will have in common is a hodgepodge of ideas everywhere. Figure 2-1 illustrates that one of the biggest problems software developers face is lack of focus and organization. It is not that developers can't focus or organize, but that developers are bombarded by information, and it is a Herculean task to keep track of, let alone organize, all of that information. But software projects that are successful must remain focused and organized. Therefore, the next step is to focus and organize your thoughts, which results in something like Figure 2-2.

In Figure 2-2, the ideas are organized by classification. As this is book is about a programming language, the only relevant ideas are those related to source code functionality. Roughly speaking, in the source code category, each thought corresponds to a feature to implement.

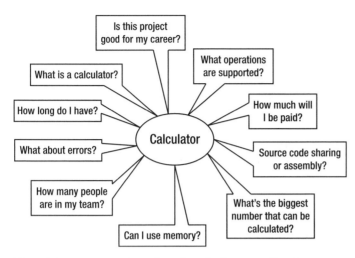

Figure 2-1. *Brainstorming what the calculator application represents*

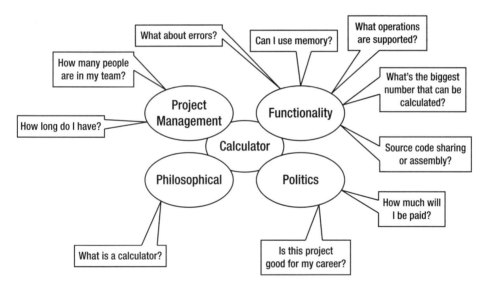

Figure 2-2. *Focused and organized brainstorming*

Focusing the Calculator

To implement a feature, you need source code, which means a file, project, and other programming techniques. The following two levels of organization are defined in Visual Basic:

- *File level*: At the file level, you are organizing what kinds of projects and solutions you will be creating.

- *Source code level*: At the source code level, you are organizing the namespaces, modules, class names, and other identifiers that are referenced throughout the source code.

For the most part, Visual Basic developers do not concern themselves too much with the file organization. A common practice is to consider a class or module as a single file.

When implementing an application, you will begin by deciding whether you will use a console application, a Windows application, or a class library.

If the calculator were a Windows application, it could look like Figure 2-3. A calculator implemented as a Windows application allows users to perform calculations by clicking the appropriate buttons. For example, to add two numbers, the user clicks the appropriate buttons to key in the first number, then an operation, then the second number, and finally, the equal sign to perform the calculation. The equal sign is a signal to the calculator application to process the data that has been entered and generate a result. The text box would display the results.

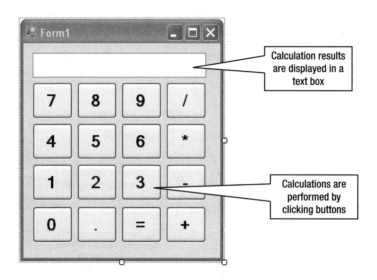

Figure 2-3. *A calculator implemented as a Windows application*

The second choice is to implement a calculator using a console application, where the numbers are entered as text, as illustrated in Figure 2-4. The calculator does not expect users to click buttons; rather, they press the appropriate keyboard keys to enter the appropriate number at the appropriate time with the appropriate operation. Typically, an Enter key will serve as an equal sign button and perform a calculation, which is output to the console. Once one calculation has completed, the cycle starts again.

If you had to choose between a Windows or console application for the calculator, you would choose the Windows application because it looks better and is easier to use. In the focused thoughts of Figure 2-2, ease of use was not defined as a feature. Should the user interface type have been a feature? Normally, yes it should be a feature, but for the scope of this chapter, it is not.

The user interaction between the two types of applications is dramatically different, and implies two different programs, even though they implement the same features. The focus is not on creating a particular program type, but on the overall programming structure.

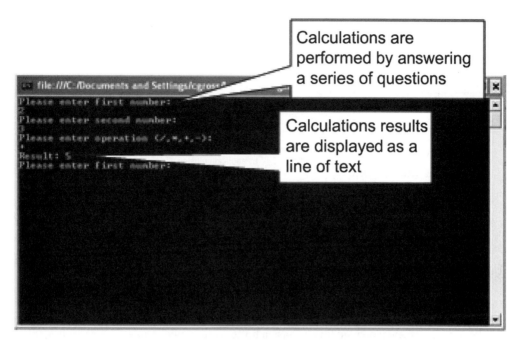

Figure 2-4. *A calculator implemented as a console application*

Let's step back and think about this abstractly. You are a programmer and have been charged with the task of implementing the calculator for both user interfaces. Again, thinking abstractly, would you implement all the functionality twice, or would you try to think about which parts of the calculator could be reused for both user interfaces? Most likely, your answer will be that you want to reuse parts of the calculator so that you have less work. But you also want to reuse parts so that you can avoid additional maintenance and program extension problems.

So, for software development, you need to think of the software as pieces that are assembled into a program. Some pieces can be reused, and other pieces cannot be reused. Therefore, think of the calculator application as two pieces: the user interface and the piece that performs calculations based on data delivered by the user interface. From an organizational perspective, or in developer lingo, from an architectural perspective, the calculator pieces would be arranged as shown in Figure 2-5.

The individual pieces in Figure 2-5 are called *components*. (Some individuals might even call the pieces *modules*, but I personally prefer the term *components*, and in a Visual Basic book, calling them modules could lead to confusion). The components are arranged from the lower-level functionality at the bottom of the picture to the higher-level functionality near the top of the picture.

Each component fulfills a particular task, and the higher-level components use those tasks implemented at a lower level. The idea is that each level is responsible for certain functionality, and other levels do not duplicate efforts by reimplementing certain functionality. The higher-level functionality does have a lower-level dependency, but the lower level does not have a higher-level dependency.

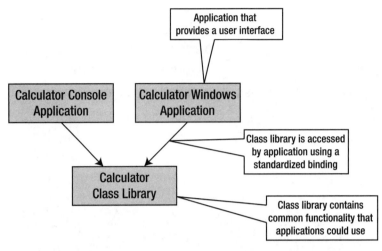

Figure 2-5. *Arrangement of calculator pieces*

Applications are realized using either top-down or bottom-up architecture. A top-down methodology means creating the higher-level components and then implementing the lower-level components when needed. In contrast, a bottom-up methodology means creating the bottom components first.

A bottom-up approach is useful when you know clearly which features need to be implemented. A top-down approach is better when you have a rough idea of what features need to be implemented, but don't want to stray too far from the goal of the application. The focus of this chapter is to develop the Calculator class library, shown at the bottom of Figure 2-5, so we will take the bottom-up approach in this chapter.

Implementing the Class Library

The creation of a class library is a form of file organization. The next step is to create some source code for the class library. The source code is implemented in two steps:

- Define the class and methods.

- Implement the methods.

One of the biggest problems when learning a new language is understanding what the language can and cannot do. You can't write source code that the language does not understand. So it is extremely important to know the programming language, because it determines how your thoughts will be structured.

You will write two types of source code: source code that organizes and source code that does something. Organizational source code is like a filing system with folders. Source code that does something is like a folder with stuff in it. When you are creating the filing system, you don't care about the contents of the folder. And when you fill the folder, you generally don't care about the filing system.

Modules, classes, namespaces, and methods are all concepts used to organize source code. A method is filled with source code and does something like add numbers or create a textual string.

One of the most common things that you will do when filling a method with source code is reference other pieces of organized source code. Think of referencing as putting a sticky note in a folder with the text, "Please also look in folder B."

Following is a piece of source code that is 100% organizational and does nothing.

```
Namespace MyMainTypes
    Public Class AType
        Public Shared Sub DoSomething()
        End Sub
    End Class
End Namespace


Module AnotherType
    Public Function DoSomething() As Integer
    End Function
End Module
```

The source code has three levels of organization. A namespace (MyMainTypes in the example) encapsulates types like classes (AType in the example). Classes and modules (like AnotherType in the example) encapsulate methods (DoSomething() in the example) or properties. Within a namespace, all types must be unique. You can have two types with the same identifier in different namespaces. Within a type, you cannot have identical identifiers with identical parameters. (This will be clearer as you learn more about Visual Basic in the upcoming chapters.)

Visual Basic has the additional rule that classes and modules (like AType and AnotherType) are in the namespace of the Visual Basic project. That namespace is not explicitly defined, but it is identified by the project, as shown in Figure 2-6.

In Figure 2-6, the Root Namespace text box shows the root namespace of all types in a Visual Basic project. So if both AType and AnotherType were part of the project, the full-length identifiers would be Calculator.MyMainTypes.AType and Calculator.AnotherType.

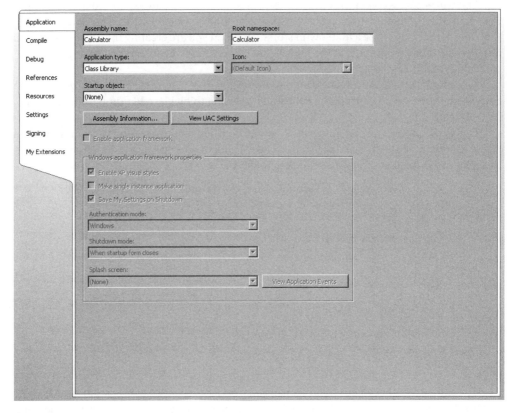

Figure 2-6. *Default root namespace of project*

Following is the same organizational code with some source code added to do something (shown in boldface).

```
Namespace MyMainTypes
    Public Class AType
        Public Shared Sub DoSomething()
        End Sub
    End Class
End Namespace

Module AnotherType
    Public Function DoSomething() as Integer
        MyMainTypes.AType.DoSomething()
    End Function
End Module
```

In the bolded code, there is a reference to another namespace, type, and method with a pair of parentheses. This makes a method call on a shared class and shared method. It says that the implementation of the method is the calling of another method.

Notice how the other method is referenced using both namespace and type identifiers. Also notice how there is no reference to the `Calculator` namespace. This is not necessary because, from the perspective of `AnotherType`, `Calculator` is implied. This is how all types and methods are always referenced. A namespace identifier is necessary only if the type (for example, class) is not defined in the current namespace.

If you have namespaces with long names, this referencing can get tedious. As an alternative, you can add an `Imports` statement to reference the namespace, similar to the following.

```
Imports Calculator.MyMainTypes
Module AnotherType
    Public Function DoSomething() as Integer
        AType.DoSomething()
    End Function
End Module
```

The `Imports` statement says that if the code references any types that are not defined locally, look in this namespace (`Calculator.MyMainTypes` in the example) to find the type. When using the `Imports` statement, you need to specify the full namespace of `Calculator.MyMainTypes`. Note that if you use two namespaces that have identically named types, you will get a compiler failure, because the compiler won't know which type to reference.

This covers the absolute basics of writing some code, and we are ready to use Visual Basic to do something.

Writing the Add() Method

We'll write the code to add two numbers. To begin, create a new project in Visual Basic:

1. Open Visual Basic Express. (If Visual Basic Express is open, choose File ➤ Close Project to ensure you have a clean slate.)

2. Click File ➤ New Project or choose Create: Project from the Start Page tab.

3. Choose Class Library, name it `Calculator`, and click OK.

4. Rename `Class1.vb` to `Operations.vb`.

5. Save the solution.

We can now write the `Add()` method. Add the bolded code to the `Operations.vb` file.

```
Public Class Operations
    Public Shared Function Add(ByVal number1 As Integer, ByVal number2 As _
Integer) As Integer
        Return number1 + number2
    End Function
End Class
```

This simple code actually has many different pieces that fit together. The type `Operations` is implied to be in the namespace `Calculator` because the default root namespace is the same as the project. Defined within `Operations` is a method that is both `Public` and `Shared`. Using the

Function declaration implies that the caller expects to get a value back from the method. The data type of the returned value is specified by the As Integer keywords—this particular function will return an Integer value. (If you want to define a method that does not return a value, use Sub rather than Function.)

Methods and parameters must be associated with a type, as Visual Basic is a type-safe programming language. *Type-safe* means that when you write code, you know what you are manipulating.

Suppose that you are writing code and are confronted with the numbers 1, 1.0, and "1.0". To you, these three numbers are identical. But in the context of the source code, they are not identical. The 1 is an integer, the 1.0 is a double, and the "1.0" is a string. When you want to add, subtract, or otherwise manipulate pieces of data, they should be the same types; otherwise, you might run into consistency errors. Type-safe programming languages help avoid such problems. The .NET number types are discussed in more detail in the "Understanding the CLR Numeric Types" section later in this chapter.

The declaration of Add() says that we need to pass in two integer-based numeric values, and the method returns an integer-based numeric value. The combination of parameters and a return type is a *method signature*. The method signature becomes important when another piece of code calls the Add() method. The other piece of code must use the same types as the declaration. Figure 2-7 shows a piece of code that calls the Add() method, which we'll do from another application in the next section.

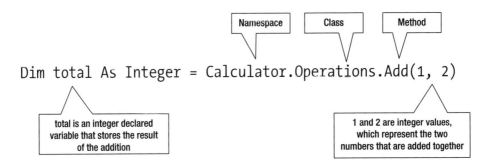

Figure 2-7. *The Add() method is called by referencing the namespace and class containing the method. A period is used to separate the identifiers.*

The caller must do two things:

- Reference the correct combination of namespace, class, and method identifiers.

- Pass the correct types into the method, as specified by the method signature.

In the example, the addition of 1 and 2 results in 3, and therefore the variable total should contain the value 3 (the equal sign assigns the value returned from the method to the variable on its left). I say "should contain the value," because when writing code, you are not always sure. Sometimes the code you write will be wrong because you overlooked something or forgot to reference something.

Look at the calling code, and ask yourself if you are guaranteed that calling Add() with 1 and 2 will result in 3. The answer is that, as a caller, you cannot be 100% sure that the total variable will contain 3. Just because a box has the label "Dishes" does not necessarily mean that dishes are in the box. You think you know the contents, but you cannot be 100% sure until you open the box. Likewise, in code, you need to look at how the Add() method is implemented to be sure of the contents of the total variable.

In a production coding session, looking at the implementation code to verify it is doing what you expect is not a feasible solution, because that would take too much time and be completely unreliable. The only real solution is to write test code.

Writing Code to Test the Add() Method

Test code is caller code that passes parameters with targeted values and expects a targeted answer. If the caller does not get the targeted answer, then the implementation of the tested method is wrong. Figure 2-8 shows sample caller code that tests the Add() operation (we'll add this to a project next).

Figure 2-8. *Testing the Add() method*

The calling code of the test bears an uncanny resemblance to the code you saw in the previous section. The difference is that the test code uses targeted variables and values, whereas the other code could contain any variables and values. Another requirement of test code is to verify the answers returned by the method with targeted responses. The If statement is used to check whether the value of the variable total is equal to 3.

When writing test code, the way the Add() method is used must be the same way the console or Windows application uses the method. Otherwise, it would be like testing a winter tire in the middle of the Sahara—fun to do but irrelevant.

Another question related to testing has to do with the timing of tests. Do you create the tests before or after implementing the Add() method? To get a clear understanding of the problem, imagine the development of a tire. Do you define the tests for the tire before or after the tire has been developed? Most likely, the answer is before, during, and after development. This is an important consideration when developing software. Tests are written before, during, and after implementation, as follows:

- You develop tests before implementing the Add() method to get an idea of what namespaces, classes, and methods you will be defining. The definition of the different items gives the developer an idea of how the items will be used.

- You develop tests during the implementation of the Add() method to verify that your source code implementation is on the right track.

- You develop tests after the implementation of the Add() method as an exhaustive measure to make sure you've dotted the i's and crossed the t's in the implementation.

Adding a Test Project to Your Solution

When writing test routines, you will need to organize the source code, and that means figuring out to which project the tests are added. For the calculator application, you could place the test routines within the Calculator class library. However, doing that is not the proper approach due to distribution of the class library and correct testing context. Remember that the test routines must be identical to how the code will be used. Thus, the appropriate place for the test routines is in their own application.

The ideal approach is to create another application that represents the tests. Figure 2-5 illustrated how a Windows and console application could use the Calculator class library. Figure 2-9 adds the testing console application that also uses the class library.

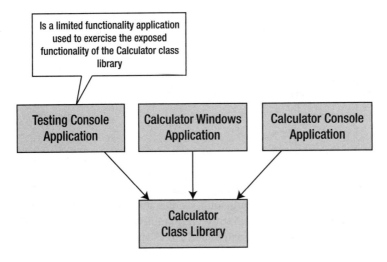

Figure 2-9. *Adding the testing console application*

The testing console application is like the console application created in Chapter 1, and it references the Calculator class library. Both projects should be part of the Calculator solution.

Go ahead and add the TestCalculator project to the Calculator solution. Remember to add a reference to the Calculator class library (right-click TestCalculator and choose Add Reference ➤ Projects ➤ Calculator). Remember to set TestCalculator as the startup project for debugging purposes. Figure 2-10 shows the TestCalculator and Calculator projects in the Solution Explorer.

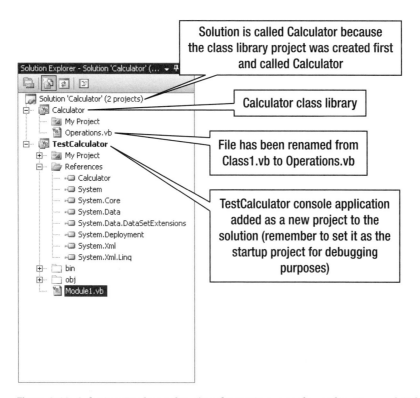

Figure 2-10. *Solution Explorer showing the testing console application and Calculator class library*

Testing Simple Addition

Add the boldfaced code to Module1.vb in the testing console project to verify the addition of 1 and 2 (the <> operator means is not equal to):

```
Imports Calculator

Module Module1
    Public Sub TestSimpleAddition()
        Dim result As Integer = Operations.Add(1, 2)

        If (total <> 3) Then
            Console.WriteLine("Oops 1 and 2 does not equal 3")
        End If
    End Sub

    Sub Main()
        TestSimpleAddition()
        Console.ReadKey()
    End Sub

End Module
```

Press Ctrl+F5 to test the calculation. When executed, the testing console application calls the test method TestSimpleAddition(), which calls and verifies the functionality of the Calculator class library. If everything works, the message will not appear.

Note Recall that the Main() method is where a project begins its operation. To make an application do something, you must add code to its Main() method.

To see that the test also fails, change the Add() method as follows:

```
Public Shared Function Add(ByVal number1 As Integer, ByVal number2 As _
Integer) As Integer
        Return number1 * number2
    End Function
```

Now rerun the program, and you'll see the failure message.

THE DEVELOPMENT CYCLE

So far in this chapter, we've dealt with three pieces of code:

- The code segment that implements the Add() method performs the calculation operation.

- The code that represents a caller, which could be either the Windows application or the console application, is considered production code.

- The code that contains the production code with some verification routines represents testing code. The testing code is important because, if the component implementation is altered, you need to rerun only the testing code to make sure everything works as it should.

These three pieces of code have demonstrated a complete development cycle.

Testing the Addition of Two Very Large Numbers

The code and projects have been organized, but we're missing some tests. The current test adds two simple numbers. Another test could be to add two really big numbers, such as 2 billion and 2 billion.

The code to test the addition of two really big numbers is shown in Figure 2-11. Add this to Module1.vb in the TestCalculator project.

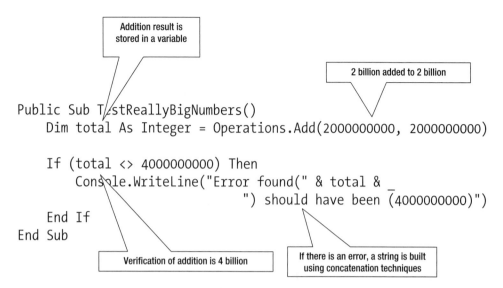

Figure 2-11. *Testing the addition of two large numbers*

The test to add two very large numbers is identical to the test to add two simple numbers, except for the numbers themselves. The error message is handled a bit differently than in the previous code, in that it is built using concatenation techniques. In the example, a string is concatenated with an integer with a string. Visual Basic will automatically convert the integer into a string.

Often, you will write tests where the only real difference is the data itself, not the ramifications of the data. Do you think of adding two very large numbers (such as 2 billion plus 2 billion) and two smaller numbers (such as 2 plus 2) as different? No, because to humans, the major difference between 2 billion and 2 is a bunch of zeros; the result is either 4 billion or 4, which seems very trivial. Yet with respect to a computer, 4 billion is very different from 4, as you'll soon see.

Before you run the test, you need to add a call to it in the Main() method:

```
Sub Main()
    TestSimpleAddition()
    TestReallyBigNumbers()
    Console.ReadKey()
End Sub
```

Now run the very large number test. You will see the output shown in Figure 2-12.

What happened? The problem has to do with the addition of very large numbers that cause an *overflow*, which is a computer construct.

Figure 2-12. *Visual Basic Express highlighting the overflow error*

Understanding Problems with Numeric Numbers

What you understand as numbers and what the computer understands as numbers are two completely different things. As a child, you learn to count starting at 1 and ending at 100, which you thought was a gargantuan number. As you grew up, you learned about zero and numbers less than zero. Later, you advanced to studying fractions and decimal values.

Throughout all of this learning about numbers, you considered the number 1 and the number 1.5 to be the same kind of thing—that is, numbers. Yet to the computer, they are not the same type of values.

The reason numbers are different to computers has to do with computer efficiency and how the computer stores numbers. For those who have learned the decimal system with place-holders, you start counting at 0, continue to 9, and then the next number is a decimal increment called 10. The decimal system is originally accredited to the Babylonians, but they used a decimal system that was sexagesimal (60 unique identifiers versus our decimal 10 unique identifiers). The computer has a similar counting scheme, except it is binary with only two unique identi-fiers: 1 and 0. Computers have two unique identifiers because they signify two unique states: on and off. At the heart of a computer is a transistor that has the ability to distinguish between on and off; there are no "sort of" on and "sort of" off states.

Figure 2-13 shows an example of how a computer would count to 7 using the binary system.

In theory, you could count until you die. You have that ability because you are human and have no limits on how high you can count. A computer does have limits, such as random-access memory (RAM), hard disk, and so on. Specific numeric data types on a computer also have limits on how high they can count. For example, the Integer data type that we have been using can count to only a specific number and can store only whole numbers.

Think of the different numeric data types as odometers. Most car odometers have upper limits of 1 million miles/kilometers. Imagine adding 900,000 and 200,000 using an odometer. The result would be 100,000, and not the 1.1 million that you expected. This is exactly the problem that we encountered when adding 2 billion and 2 billion.

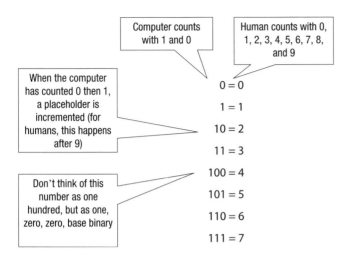

Figure 2-13. *How a computer counts to 7*

The bad part of an odometer is that you don't know when the odometer has been wrapped around. You could end up with a car whose odometer read 100,000 miles/kilometers, but actually had driven 1.1 million. Fortunately, .NET knows when the number type has been wrapped around. The technical jargon for this situation is *overflow* or *underflow*. Overflow is when the odometer wraps over in the positive direction (900,000 to 1.1 million), and underflow is when the odometer wraps around in the negative direction (0 to –100,000). Detection of either situation is activated as a project property. Follow these steps to deactivate overflow/underflow detection for the Calculator class library:

1. Right-click the Calculator project in the Calculator solution and select Properties.

2. Click Compile, and then click Advanced Compile Options.

3. Check "Remove integer overflow tests" to remove the test for overflow situations.

4. Click OK to finish.

Rerun the test console application, and you will get an exception indicating that an overflow has occurred.

```
Error found(-294967296) should have been (4000000000)
```

Having an overflow situation is a problem, and the fact that .NET can catch it is a good thing. But at the end of the day, our preferred solution is to be able to add 2 billion plus 2 billion. After all, Bill Gates would probably prefer having 4 billion in his bank account instead of the calculated minus value or an error indicating that the bank cannot accept his 4 billion.

Understanding Numeric and Value Data Types

A *data type* is a way of describing a piece of data using a metadescription. For example, if you have a Double type, you know you will have a double number. Many data types are available: Integer, Long, Short, Single, Double, String, Enum, Structure, and so on. You can even define your own data types. Data types are the heart of the CLR and a type-safe programming environment.

Understanding Value and Reference Types

The CLR supports two ways of representing data: value and reference. The major difference between a value and reference type is how the information associated with the type is stored. The problem with value and reference types is that they are a technical invention and can be confusing.

When the CLR runs an application, a thread is executing the Common Language Infrastructure (CLI). Think of a thread as you wandering around a mall buying things. You are an individual and can buy things independently of other people. The store will have many people looking around and buying different things. Likewise, a computer has many threads doing many different independent things. When you look around in a store, you might bump into people and cause them to drop things. While the CLR tries to avoid such problems, if you try hard enough in your code, you can cause other threads to "drop" things.

When it executes, a thread has a local memory pool called a *stack*, which is akin to you carrying a wallet that contains cash and credit cards. You carry the wallet with you from store to store, like a thread carries a stack when calling one method to another. When you enter the store and want to purchase something, you have two major ways of paying for the item: with cash or by using a credit/debit card. However, with a credit/debit card, you can't pay immediately. You need a machine that calls a server to verify that your piece of plastic has enough money to pay for the item. Paying with cash is much faster than paying with a credit card, because you don't need to talk to a remote computer.

Now suppose you and your spouse want to pay for the item. You could use the same credit card account, but you have unique credit cards. But you cannot do the same thing with cash. If you have a $10 bill, your spouse cannot share the $10 with you. Your spouse would need a second $10 bill, and together you would have $20.

The cash and credit card payment methods are analogous to value and reference types. Cash is a value type, and the credit card is a reference type. When the CLR executes, the code dragged from one method call to another method call is the stack that contains a number of value type variables. Value types are stored directly on the stack like cash. Reference types are stored as pointers to memory on the stack, just like a credit/debit card points to cash somewhere else. The reference pointer points to a piece of memory called the *heap*. These concepts are illustrated in Figure 2-14.

With value types, when one value type is assigned to another, the contents are copied. If you modify one of the copies, the original will not be altered. In contrast, when you change the value of a reference type, the values of all the pointers to that reference type change. Going back to the credit card and cash example, if you have $10 and so does your spouse, then when you spend $8, it does not affect the $10 that your spouse has, as befits the value type model. However, if you and your spouse have $10 available with your credit card and you spend $8, only $2 remain, as you would expect with a reference type.

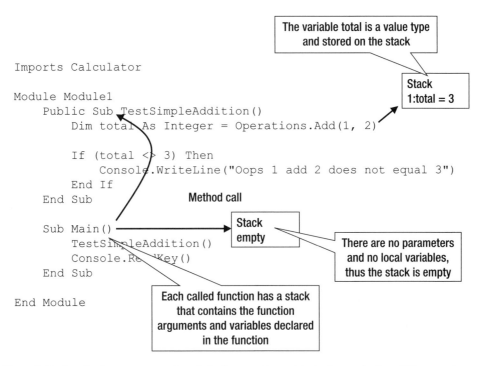

Figure 2-14. *Stacks that are created and the interaction with the heap during CLR execution*

There are times when you use value types and times when you use reference types, just as there are times when you pay for things using cash and times when you use a credit card. Typically though, you use credit cards when you want to pay for expensive things, because you don't want to carry around large amounts of cash. This applies to value and reference types, in that you don't want to keep large footprint value types on the stack.

By knowing the difference between the stack and heap, you automatically know the difference between a value type and a reference type, as they are directly related. Value types are stored on the stack, and the contents of reference types are stored on the heap.

Understanding the CLR Numeric Types

The CLR has two major types of numbers: whole numbers and fractional numbers. Both of these number types are value-based data types, as explained in the previous section. The Add() method used the type Integer, which is a whole number–based value type. As you saw, whole numbers have upper limits, which are set by the space available.

Consider the following number:

```
123456
```

This number takes six spaces of room. For illustrative purposes, imagine that the page you are reading allows only six spaces of room for numerals. Based on that information, the largest number that can be written on this page is 999,999, and the smallest is 0. In a similar manner, specific number types force the CLR to impose restrictions on how many spaces can be used to represent a number. Each space is a 1 or a 0, allowing the CLR to represent numbers in binary notation.

Computers may use binary notations, but humans work better with decimals, so to calculate the largest possible number a data type can store, you use 2 to the power of the number of spaces and then subtract 1. In the case of the Integer type, there are 32 spaces. Before we calculate the biggest number Integer can store, though, we need to consider negative numbers. The upper limit of Integer isn't actually 4,294,967,295 (the result of $2^{32} - 1$), because Integer also stores negative numbers. In other words, it can save a negative whole number, such as –2.

The computer uses a trick in that the first space of the number is reserved for the sign (plus or minus) of the number. In the case of Integer, that means there are only 31 spaces for numbers, so the largest number that can be represented is 2,147,483,647, and the smallest is –2,147,483,648. Going back to our addition example, this fact means that when the result of our addition is 4 billion, which in binary requires 32 spaces, Integer does not have the space to store it.

The .NET environment includes the numeric data types listed in Table 2-1, which have varying sizes and storage capabilities. The following terminology is used to describe numeric data types:

- A *bit* is a space of storage, and 8 bits make a *byte*.

- *Integers* are whole numbers.

- *Floating-point* types are fractional numbers.

- *Signed* means one space in the number is reserved for the plus or negative sign.

Table 2-1. *.NET Numeric Data Types*

Type	Description
Byte	Unsigned 8-bit integer; the smallest value is 0, and the largest value is 255
SByte	Signed 8-bit integer; the smallest value is –128, and the largest value is 127
UShort	Unsigned 16-bit integer; the smallest value is 0, and the largest value is 65535
Short	Signed 16-bit integer; the smallest value is –32768, and the largest value is 32767
UInteger	Unsigned 32-bit integer; the smallest value is 0, and the largest value is 4294967295
Integer	Signed 32-bit integer; the smallest value is –2147483648, and the largest value is 2147483647
ULong	Unsigned 64-bit integer; the smallest value is 0, and the largest value is 18446744073709551615
Long	Signed 64-bit integer; the smallest value is –9223372036854775808, and the largest value is 9223372036854775807
Single	32-bit floating-point number; the smallest value is -3.4×10^{38}, and the largest value is 3.4×10^{38}, with a precision of 7 digits
Double	64-bit floating-point number; the smallest value is -1.7×10^{308}, and the largest value is 1.7×10^{308}, with 15 to 16 digits of precision
Decimal	Special 128-bit data type; the smallest value is 1.0×10^{-28}, and the largest value is 1.0×10^{28}, with at least 28 significant digits of precision[a]

[a] *The Decimal type is often used for financial data because sometimes a calculation will result in one penny less than the correct result (for example, 14.9999, instead of 15.00) due to rounding errors.*

With so many variations of number types available, you may be wondering which ones to use and when. The quick answer is that it depends on your needs. When performing scientific calculations, you probably need to use a Double or Single. If you are calculating mortgages, you probably need to use a Decimal. And if you are performing set calculations, you probably should use an Integer or a Long. It all depends on how accurate you want to be, or how much numeric precision you want.

Numeric precision is an important topic and should never be dealt with lightly. Consider the following example: every country takes a census of its people, and when the census is compiled, we learn some interesting facts. For example, in Canada, 31% of people will divorce. Canada has a population clock that says every minute and 32 seconds, someone is born. At the time of this writing, the population was 32,789,736. Thus, at the time of this writing, 10,164,818 people will divorce. Think a bit about what I just wrote. I said that there is a direct relationship of people who will divorce to the number of births in Canada (31%, in fact). You should be amazed that the births and divorces are timed to the point where 10,164,818—not 10,164,819 nor 10,164,820—people will divorce. Of course, I'm being cynical and just trying to make the point that numbers are just that: numbers that you round off.

I can't say 10,164,818 people will divorce, because I can't be that accurate without performing an actual count. I could probably say 10,164,818 plus or minus 100,000 will divorce. Using the plus or minus, the range is 10,064,818 to 10,264,818, or roughly speaking, 10.2 million people. The number 10.2 million is what a newsperson would report, what literature would say, and what most people would use in conversation. So, if I add 10.2 million and 1,000, can I say that the total is 10,201,000? The 10.2 is a roundoff to the nearest tenth of a million, and adding a thousand means adding a number that is less than the roundoff. The answer is that I cannot add 1,000 to 10.2, because the 1,000 is not significant with respect to the number 10.2. But I can add 1,000 to 10,164,818, to get 10,165,818, because the most significant value is a single whole number.

Relating this back to numeric types, it means integer-based numbers have a most significant single whole number. Adding 1.5 and 1.2 as whole numbers results in 3, as illustrated in Figure 2-15.

Let's extend this concept of significant digits to a floating-point number type, Single, and consider the example shown in Figure 2-16. The {0} construct in the Console.WriteLine() method is replaced by the second argument. If there were a third argument, it would be placed in the resultant string with {1}, a fourth would be replaced with {2}, and so on.

As shown in Figure 2-16, if you want to keep the precision of adding a small number to a large number, you will need to switch number types to Double. But even Double has limits and can remember only 15 to 16 digits of precision.

If you want even more precision, you could use Decimal, but Decimal is more suitable for financial calculations. With financial calculations, you will run into the problem of having very large numbers added to small numbers. Imagine being Bill Gates and having a few billion in your bank account. When the bank calculates the interest, you will want to know how many pennies you have accumulated, because pennies, when added over a long period of time, make a big difference. In fact, some programmers have "stolen" money from banks by collecting the fractional pennies and accumulating them.

Now that you've seen some of the complexities involved when working with numbers, let's finish the calculator.

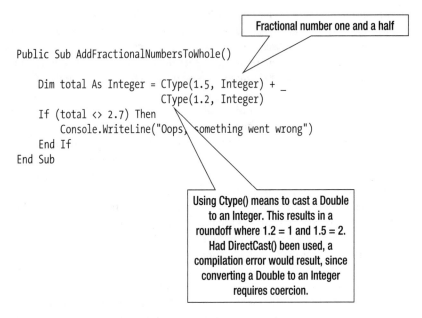

Figure 2-15. *Adding fractions using the Integer data type*

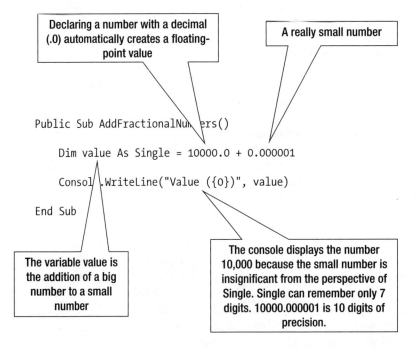

Figure 2-16. *Adding fractions using the Single data type*

Finishing the Calculator

The original declaration of the Add() method for the calculator worked, but had some serious limitations on what kinds of numbers could be added. To finish the calculator, we need to declare the Add() method using a different type, and then add the remaining operations.

We could use one of three types to declare the Add() method:

- Long: Solves the problem of adding two very large numbers like 2 billion, but has the problem that you cannot add fractional numbers like 1.5 plus 1.5.

- Double: Solves the problem of adding two very large or small numbers, and can be used to add fractional numbers. Generally speaking, Double is a good choice, but can suffer from significance problems if a very large number is manipulated by a very small number.

- Decimal: A generally good approach and suitable for all types of precision, but also the slowest when adding, subtracting, or performing other mathematical operations.

The simplest all-around numeric data type to use is Double, as it provides good precision and is relatively fast. The complete implementation of the calculator is as follows:

```
Public Class Operations
    Public Shared Function Add(ByVal number1 As Double, ByVal number2 As _
Double) As Double
        Return number1 + number2
    End Function

    Public Shared Function Divide(ByVal number1 As Double, ByVal number2 As _
Double) As Double
        Return number1 / number2
    End Function

    Public Shared Function Multiply(ByVal number1 As Double, ByVal number2 As _
Double) As Double
        Return number1 * number2
    End Function

    Public Shared Function Subtract(ByVal number1 As Double, ByVal number2 As _
Double) As Double
        Return number1 - number2
    End Function
End Class
```

The four operations are methods with different identifiers, but identical method signatures, making it easy to remember how to use each method. Each of the operations would have an appropriate set of tests verifying the correctness of the implementation. The tests are not reproduced here, but they are implemented in the sample source code. I advise you to take a quick look at the tests to make sure you understand the individual pieces.

The Important Stuff to Remember

In this chapter, you learned about developing a class library that is used to perform some calculations. The following are the key points to remember:

- Organization of your thoughts, projects, and features makes all the difference when writing software.

- When writing software, stay focused. It is very easy to drift around in software development, because software lets you stray easily. A successful developer will always be organized and focused.

- Software is designed using an architecture that could be implemented top-down or bottom-up.

- Within an architecture, individual pieces are called *components*, and they fit together to create a complete application.

- You write tests because you cannot verify the functionality of a component based on its identifier, parameters, or return value.

- When implementing components, you develop tests before, during, and after writing the source code.

- A test is a piece of source code that calls a component using targeted input data, and the results from the component are verified with targeted responses. If the results do not match the targeted responses, the component has failed.

- The CLR offers many different data types, with the major distinction being between value and reference types.

- The CLR has many different number types, but all number types are value types.

- Numbers can overflow or underflow. You should activate a compiler setting to make sure that the CLR will catch those situations.

- When deciding on a specific number type, a large part of the decision is based on how much precision is desired.

Some Things for You to Do

The following are some things to consider related to what you've learned in this chapter:

1. When you write code, how should you organize your code? For example, do you enforce certain naming conventions for your classes? Do you enforce the use of code comments?

2. In the development community, there is a discussion of whether organization of your software should involve formal structures or should be ad hoc. Think about how software should be organized.

3. In general, how would you test whether or not a component that uses a database worked properly? Outline the process with bulleted points.

4. In general, how would you test the correctness of writing data to a file? To help understand the nature of the problem, how do you know that an operating system manipulates files properly?

5. If the CLR did not provide for a mechanism to catch overflow and underflow conditions, how would you ensure that overflow and underflow didn't happen?

6. For a Pentium CPU (32 bits), which number type would result in the fastest calculations?

7. In this chapter's example, the class `Operations` is designed to perform arithmetic using the `Double` type. How would you change this so that the calculations are generic and don't rely on the `Double` type?

CHAPTER 3

■ ■ ■

Learning About String Manipulations

In the previous chapter, you learned the basics of how data is stored and managed by .NET, including the difference between value and reference types. .NET has three major data types: number-related, custom-defined, and String. The previous chapter focused on the number-related types. This chapter will focus on the String type.

As you'll learn in this chapter, the String type has some special characteristics. If you were to look at the bits and bytes of the String type, you would not realize that they were letters. In an abstract description, a String type is a number type with a special grammar. Since a computer understands only numbers, it uses lookup tables that map a set of letters to a set of numbers.

The example in this chapter is a multilingual translation program. The translation program will not be sophisticated, nor will it be capable of much. However, it will illustrate many of the issues that you will be confronted with when working with strings.

Organizing the Translation Application

As emphasized in the previous chapter, the first step in developing an application is to get organized. We need to understand and define the features of the sample application we are going to develop. The multilingual translation program will implement the following features:

- Translate greetings into three different languages: French, German, and English.

- Convert numbers into the three different languages.

- Convert a date into the three different languages.

From a feature perspective, the first feature is logical, but the second and third features are not as obvious. We generally think of translation as translating one word to another word(s). Yet, languages also can represent numbers and dates in different ways. Translation will mean two things: translate a word from one language to another, and translate a number or date from one language to another.

As in Chapter 2, we'll create the solution as components with three pieces: a Windows application, a testing console application, and a class library. After you have created each of the projects, your workspace should look like Figure 3-1. Remember to add a reference to the

LanguageTranslator class library (right-click TestLanguageTranslator and choose Add Reference ➤ Projects ➤ LanguageTranslator). Also remember to set TestLanguageTranslator as the startup project.

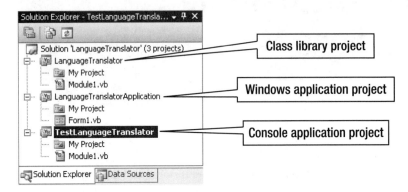

Figure 3-1. *Structure of projects for the translation application in Visual Basic Express Solution Explorer*

Building the Translator Application

The translation application, like the calculator application example in the previous chapter, is built in pieces: the class library that performs translations based on data delivered by the user interface, the tests, and the user interface. The individual pieces are components that can be fit together like a jigsaw puzzle to create an application.

Note Components are a core part of your development toolbox. As you will see throughout the book, components allow you to reuse and modularize functionality. Components result in applications that are maintainable and extendable. Of course, there are limits, and the advantages are not automatic. You will need to properly design your application to benefit from using components.

Creating the Translator Class

When working with Visual Basic Express, or one of the other Visual Studio products, using the default templates for creating a class library results in the creation of a file named Class1.vb. It is good that a default file is created for a class library, but the identifier Class1.vb does not imply much. Therefore, you should go ahead and delete that file from the project (simply renaming the file does not rename the class within it). In its place, create the Translator class, as follows:

1. Right-click the LanguageTranslator project.

2. Click Add ➤ New Item.

3. Select Class.

4. Rename the file Translator.vb.

5. Click Add to create the file and add it to your project.

Notice how quickly you managed to create a Visual Basic class using the IDE. The speed of creating a class file lets you focus on adding source code to the file. But do not be misled into believing that by creating a number of class files, your code will automatically work and be a masterpiece. You still need to think about which files, projects, classes, and tests to create.

Translating Hello

The first feature we will implement is the translation of the text "hello." Since "hello" is English, the first translation will be English to German. The following is the code to implement this feature. It is added to the Translator.vb file in the LanguageTranslator project.

```
Public Class Translator
    Public Shared Function TranslateHello(ByVal input As String) As String
        If (input.CompareTo("hello") = 0) Then
            Return "hallo"
        ElseIf (input.CompareTo("allo") = 0) Then
            Return "hallo"
        End If
        Return
    End Function

End Class
```

Translator is the main class that is exposed to other components or pieces of source code. Think of it as the identifier of the black box. The black box has a single method: TranslateHello(). TranslateHello() is used to convert the French "allo" and the English "hello" to the German "hallo." The method's input is a String type, which is a reference object type.

In the implementation of TranslateHello(), we compare the contents of the input buffer to the parameter "hello". If the comparison is equal, meaning that the strings are equal, 0 is returned. As you'll learn in the "Investigating the String Type" section, String is a class that can be used to create objects, and objects typically have methods. One of the String type's methods is CompareTo(). The caller of TranslateHello does not know how you managed to translate one word to another language. The caller actually does not care; it cares only that the method behaves as expected.

The abstract intent of the TranslateHello() method is to accept some text and, if the text is matched, return a German "hallo."

Creating the Test Application

Without questioning the abstract intent, the written code needs some testing. The test code is added to the test application, which is the project TestLanguageTranslator.

The following code is added to the Module1.vb file. Remember to import the LanguageTranslator namespace; otherwise, the test code will not compile.

```
Imports LanguageTranslator

Module Module1
    Private Sub TestTranslateHello()
        If (Translator.TranslateHello("hello").CompareTo("hallo") <> 0) Then
            Console.WriteLine("hello to hallo test failed")
        End If
        If (Translator.TranslateHello("allo").CompareTo("hallo") <> 0) Then
            Console.WriteLine("allo to hallo test failed")
        End If
        If (Translator.TranslateHello("allosss").CompareTo("") <> 0) Then
            Console.WriteLine("Verify nontranslated word test failed")
        End If
        If (Translator.TranslateHello("  allo").CompareTo("hallo") <> 0) Then
            Console.WriteLine("Extra whitespaces allo to hallo test failed")
        End If
    End Sub

    Sub Main()
        TestTranslateHello()
        Console.ReadKey()
    End Sub

End Module
```

The source code contains four tests. Each calls the method TranslateHello() with some input and receives the output. The test happens when the output is verified against an expected result. The verification tests use the CompareTo() function to test for correct translation.

Notice the third test:

```
If (Translator.TranslateHello("allosss").CompareTo("") <> 0) Then
    Console.WriteLine("Verify nontranslated word test failed")
End If
```

This test expects an explicit failure. You need to write tests that expect to fail. Successful tests that are meant to fail ensure that your code does not generate false positives. A *false positive* is when your code is supposed to fail and it does not.

The tests are within a method that needs to be called from the Main() method, as in the following example:

```
Sub Main()
    TestTranslateHello()
    Console.ReadKey()
End Sub
```

If you compile and run the tests, you will find that one of the tests fails. The failing test is the fourth one, which attempts to translate a word that has whitespace. Whitespace is space that we humans don't notice, but is necessary to distinguish words, sentences, and so on. Before we can solve the whitespace problem, we need to determine which part of the application is not working properly.

Answering the Question of Responsibility

The whitespace problem is an interesting one. The caller explicitly put in the extra spaces, but is the whitespace a bug, or is it data that is passed in incorrectly?

The problem can be defined in the context of reasonable usage. Imagine that you've just bought a car and you're driving it on the highway. If the car breaks down, the warranty will be in effect and cover the costs of the car repair. Now imagine the situation where you think you are one of the Dukes from the *Dukes of Hazzard*. And being a Duke, you drive your new car as fast as you can and then perform a flying jump. The car will jump into air, which looks quite spectacular, but then the car lands. After that, the shocks collapse, and the car cannot be driven any further. Even though the car is brand new, the Duke did not use the car as envisioned by the car manufacturer, and thus invalidates the warranty.

Getting back to the translation component, it exposes the method `TranslateHello()` and has responsibilities. And the caller of `TranslateHello()` has the responsibility of being reasonable about what can be expected to be translated. So, is whitespace sent by the caller reasonable?

If the whitespace is a normal circumstance, then the failed test is a bug in the component. But if the whitespace is not a normal circumstance, the caller is wrong and must be fixed. The answer is that the caller is being reasonable, and the component is not acting properly. We have a bug in the component that needs to be fixed. How do I know that the caller is not being reasonable? I made it up, because that is how I expected the contract to be implemented. The key is in defining a good contract.

The bug in the component relates to the problem of how a word is being translated. We used the `CompareTo()` method, which means that each character is compared, position for position. The test failed because the caller passed in a string with whitespace, and the component expected no whitespace. This bug is not a surprise, because we humans ignore the whitespace, but computers cannot.

Before I explain how to fix the bug, I need to take a step back and talk about what a string is and how you can figure out what a string can do.

Investigating the String Type

`String` is a class type, and thus a reference type. `String` is a type that has methods and properties. Value types like `Double` and `Integer` have methods and properties, but `String` is the first type you are encountering that is a class in its own right (`Double` and `Integer` are not actually classes).

To investigate a type, you can read the documentation, or you can use IntelliSense. Reading the documentation is not a bad idea, but it is the slowest and most cumbersome. IntelliSense is an IDE approach, in which a defined type's methods and properties are presented to you in an easy-to-comprehend manner.

The first time you use IntelliSense, it can be nerve-racking, because it seems like the IDE has a life of its own. There is a convention on how to use IntelliSense, as illustrated in Figure 3-2. I suggest that you take a few moments to experiment with it. I also recommend that you keep IntelliSense active in Visual Basic Express.

Figure 3-2. *Using IntelliSense on a String typed variable*

IntelliSense works on only identified variables that have types. In Figure 3-2, IntelliSense worked because the IDE parsed the code and had the ability to read the metadata associated with the type. *Metadata* is data that describes your source code. Whenever you define a class, methods and properties are associated with it. The method and property descriptions are pieces of metadata that is displayed by IntelliSense. One of the strengths of .NET is that all types have metadata.

The Basis of All Types: Object

By default, everything in .NET is an object with a few basic properties and methods. Four basic methods are associated with every object:

- Equals(): Verifies the equality of two objects (see Figure 3-3).

- GetHashCode(): Retrieves a unique number describing the object (see Figure 3-4). Two objects with the same contents will return the same hash code.

- GetType(): Retrieves the metadata associated with an object (see Figure 3-5). Allows the program to play "Are you a . . . ?" to dynamically determine which methods and properties a type has. It is used by IntelliSense to display a list box.

- ToString(): Converts the contents of the type into a string (see Figure 3-6). Note that the default CLR ToString() implementations work only for value types.

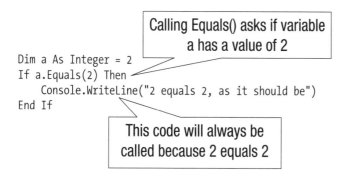

```
Dim a As Integer = 2
If a.Equals(2) Then
    Console.WriteLine("2 equals 2, as it should be")
End If
```

Calling Equals() asks if variable a has a value of 2

This code will always be called because 2 equals 2

Figure 3-3. *Equals() is used to verify the equality of two objects.*

Don't think of a, b, and c as values associated with a variable. Think of a, b, and c as having contents associated with the variables. The contents of a and b match; the contents of c do not match the contents of a and b.

```
Dim a As Integer = 2
Dim b As Integer = 2
Dim c As Integer = 3
```

The contents of a and b are identical; thus, GetHashCode() returns the same number

```
If a.GetHashCode() = b.GetHashCode() Then
    Console.WriteLine("2 equals 2, as it should be")
End If

If c.GetHashCode() <> b.GetHashCode() Then
    Console.WriteLine("3 does not equal 2, as it should be")
End If
```

The contents of c and b are not equal, so GetHashCode() will return two different numbers

Figure 3-4. *GetHashCode() retrieves a number describing the object.*

The four basic methods can be called on every variable that you declare. You will use ToString() when debugging or inspecting the state of an object instance during runtime. ToString() returns a human-readable string that contains the state of the object instance.

You might use the GetType() method occasionally, but your IDE and other tools will use it all the time. Using GetType(), you have the ability to figure out the capabilities of a variable during the execution of a program. In technical terms, GetType() returns the formal metadata description of the type.

From reading the description of Equals() and GetHashCode(), you would get the impression that these two functions serve the same purpose. However, this is not the case.

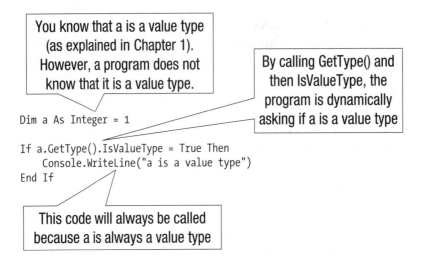

Figure 3-5. *GetType() retrieves the metadata associated with an object.*

Figure 3-6. *ToString() converts the contents of the type into a string.*

Let's say you're moving and you've packed two boxes containing kitchen items. Both boxes contain five red dishes, three silver forks, two copper knives, and two wineglasses. If you compare the boxes, both Equals() and GetHashCode() will return equality, indicating the boxes contain the same number and color of items. It is important to understand that even though the two boxes are unique instances containing unique articles, their contents are identical. When you compare object instances using Equals() or GetHashCode(), you are comparing the metadata and value attributes, not the unique instances.

Now imagine the situation where one of the boxes has wineglasses from IKEA and the other has wineglasses from Pier 1. If you use the Equals() method to compare the boxes, it will return False, because the box content details are not identical. The difference lies in how the glasses are described. In contrast, calling GetHashCode() will indicate that the contents of the boxes are identical. This is because GetHashCode() is doing a quick contents identification.

The difference between the Equals() and GetHashCode() methods is perspective. In the example, from the perspective of the moving company, the boxes are identical because the moving company does not care whether the wineglasses are from IKEA or Pier 1; it will not distinguish wineglasses from different companies.

The fact that GetHashCode() can return identical numbers for what would seem dissimilar object contents can confuse developers. The way to understand GetHashCode() is that, rather than being useful to verify equality, it helps you verify *inequality*. If two objects return dissimilar hash code values, then you know the contents are not identical. The intent of a hash code is to generate a quick fingerprint of the contents of an object. It is not completely reliable, but works for the most part.

WHEN INTELLISENSE IS NOT ENOUGH

IntelliSense is very good and will even display comments that explain what the method does (as illustrated in Figure 3-2). Another place to find answers is the Microsoft documentation itself, which you can access by selecting Help ➤ Index. You can use the Look For box to search for a specific type. For example, if you type "String class" in the Look For box, you will see details of the String class, which you can then filter using the links at the top of the page.

The Microsoft documentation is part of the Microsoft Developer Network (MSDN) (http://msdn.microsoft.com). The MSDN web site contains documentation that helps you figure out the .NET standard software development kit (.NET SDK) application programming interface (API). There are literally thousands of types, with an explosion of methods and properties. You will definitely not use all of them in a single application, but you will always use the .NET SDK.

In most cases, MSDN will be enough to help you figure out when you don't know about a specific type. If you want to learn more about concepts, you can surf to a web site such as Code Project (http://www.codeproject.com). Code Project contains plenty of examples for almost every development topic that suits your fancy.

The Problem: Character-by-Character Comparison

Let's get back to the bug of the whitespace. The method that caused problems was CompareTo(). Looking at the MSDN documentation, you see the following definition for this method (found by scrolling down the String class page and clicking the CompareTo link):

Compares this instance with a specified Object.

This definition does not tell you much, so you will need to go back to the String page and click another method name. Click the Compare link, and then click the Compare(String, String) link. In the explanation of the Compare() method, you find the following text:

The comparison terminates when an inequality is discovered or both strings have been compared. However, if the two strings compare equal to the end of one string, and the other string has characters remaining, then the string with remaining characters is considered greater. The return value is the result of the last comparison performed.

■**Note** Looking up the meaning of a method is not a long process, even though it may seem like that from the description in this section. With experience, you don't even notice the extra clicks.

The CompareTo() method failed because of the character-by-character comparison, which is illustrated in Figure 3-7.

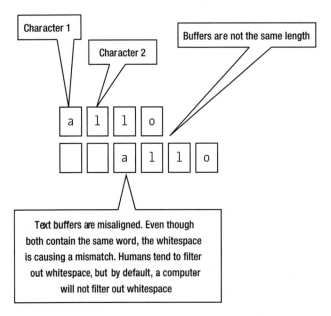

Figure 3-7. *How CompareTo() fails to compare strings that appear identical but have extra characters*

Strings are stored in buffers, with one space in the buffer allocated to one character. As you can see from Figure 3-7, whitespace takes up one space in the buffer. We can take advantage of this sometimes, as you'll see in the next section.

Now that you know what the problem is, the next step is to find a solution.

Solving the Extra Whitespace Problem

You can solve the whitespace problem in multiple ways. Which way you use depends on your needs. Let's look at several solutions and see which works best for our translation program.

Trimming the Whitespace

The first solution we'll look at is to trim the whitespace using a method intended for that purpose. The whitespace problem is not unique and is well known. The String type has a method that can be used to remove, or trim, the whitespace from a buffer. You can remove whitespace at the beginning, end, or both sides of the buffer.

As tempting as it is to change the original implementation of TranslateHello(), don't do that, because you might inadvertently break something that is working just fine. When you develop code, you have multiple possible ways to solve a problem. If you start messing around with the original source code, by the time you reach the third or fourth solution, the code might be a complete mess. Your fixes might make things worse, and trying to backtrack in your source code becomes very difficult.

■**Note** To manage your source code, you should use version control. However, even with version control, when you delete past attempts, ideas get lost. Thus, while your source code will be clean, you might forget something you did three or four hours ago. Trust me, this happens, because developing source code is an intensive thought process.

The solution is to create a shim that calls the TranslateHello() method. The shim is used to fix the bug. The following shim code is a temporary solution:

```
Public Function TrimmingWhitespace(ByVal buffer As String) As String
    Return Translator.TranslateHello(buffer.Trim())
End Function
```

TrimmingWhitespace() is a method that trims whitespace from the string to be translated. buffer.Trim is new functionality that preprocesses the buffer. Finally, we call the original method, TranslateHello(), to perform the translation.

Of course, we need to test the new method to see if it trims the string to be translated. The following is the corresponding test code.

```
Dim verifyValue As String = TrimmingWhitespace("  allo")
If verifyValue.CompareTo("hallo") <> 0 Then
    Console.WriteLine("Extra white spaces allo to hallo test failed")
End If
```

The test calls the work-in-progress method, TrimmingWhitespace(), to see if everything works. The verification code does not change.

So that you get predictable results, remember to call the shim and not the original method. If you run the test code, you'll see that the shim works, and thus we have a solution.

Finding a Substring

Another solution to the whitespace problem is to find a specific substring in a buffer. Think of it as a search solution, where a method iterates over a string and attempts to match elements of a buffer to some text that is being searched. The work-in-progress code is shown in Figure 3-8.

The test code is not shown here, because it is similar to that for the previous solution, with the difference being the method being tested.

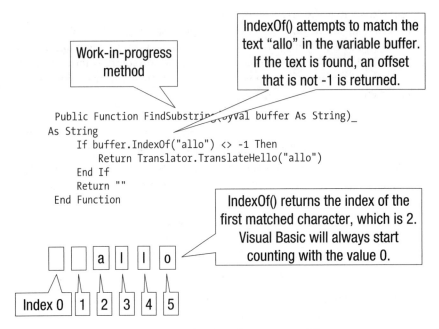

Figure 3-8. *Finding a substring to solve the whitespace problem*

Which Is the Best Solution?

Take a moment to think about which is the best solution: trimming the whitespace or finding a substring. The answer is neither is perfect; each solution has its problems. This is a very common occurrence when you are developing software. You think you have all the corners covered, and then another scenario causes your software to fail.

Again, I want to stress that you need to write more tests to figure out which scenarios might cause your software to fail. For the solution of trimming whitespace, writing another test causes it to fail, as shown in the following code. It cannot be tweaked to make the test succeed.

```
Dim verifyValue As String = TrimmingWhitespace("a  allo")
If verifyValue.CompareTo("hallo") <> 0 Then
    Console.WriteLine("Test failed: cannot parse multiple words")
End If
```

In the test, the leading "a" is considered the first character and is not trimmed. The verification will fail because CompareTo() cannot verify the misaligned buffer caused by the leading "a."

If the new test were executed against the substring solution, it would succeed and find the word "allo." Because the new test caused the first solution to fail, it would seem that solution is a no-go. Our confidence has been increased in the second solution because the old test and the new test did not fail. But don't be too hasty to consider that as the best path. The substring solution fails with the following test.

```
Dim verifyValue As String = FindSubstring("allodium")
If verifyValue.CompareTo("hallo") <> 0 Then
    Console.WriteLine("allodium to hallo test failed")
End If
```

The word tested, "allodium," contains the characters `allo`. The verification will succeed, and this is an example of a false positive.

Note It is important to have many tests that verify a multitude of different scenarios. You should have tests that are supposed to succeed and those that are supposed to fail.

The conclusion is that neither of the solutions works properly. With extended testing, each solution created new problems. We need to find another solution.

DEVELOPMENT FRUSTRATIONS

It would seem that creating solutions and then creating tests that nullify the solution is a lesson in frustration. You create code that does not solve the problems. What you must realize and take to heart is that this is part of the software development process. Yes, some people write code and don't worry about the tests, but those developers give software development a bad name.

You want to be a trustworthy developer who tests your code. I have been, and my wife is, a software development manager. In her words, "I can deal with slow developers, but I cannot deal with developers who I cannot trust to write stable and robust code. The problem with untrustworthy developers is that I cannot let them release code into production and always have to have somebody looking over their shoulders."

Writing the Tests Before Writing the Code

The reason the previous solutions failed is because each solution was a knee-jerk reaction. Knee-jerk reactions are those where when you encounter a bug, you fix the bug—no more and no less. Instead, you should figure out what the bug is trying to tell you. The original bug with the leading whitespace was not a whitespace bug, but a bug that was saying, "Hey, what if my text is not aligned, or part of a sentence, and so on?"

To solve the bug, you don't write code, but you think of all of the tests that your code needs to pass. You need to assign responsibility and define contexts that succeed and fail. In the translation example, the appropriate implementation approach would be to write the tests before writing the code. Table 3-1 shows the contexts that fail and succeed.

Table 3-1. *Appropriate Tests for the Translation Program*

Test	Verification Result
`allo`	Success
`" allo "`	Success
`word allo`	Fail: you can't translate a single word without translating the other words
`word allo word`	Fail: same reason as with word allo
`prefixallo`	Fail: different word

Table 3-1. *Appropriate Tests for the Translation Program (Continued)*

Test	Verification Result
alloappend	Fail: different word
prefixalloappend	Fail: different word

As you can see in the table, most test cases are failures because the translation component is meant to translate single words only. The test cases seem complete, but in fact, we are missing one more set of cases, which are outlined in Table 3-2.

Table 3-2. *The Missing Test Cases for the Translation Program*

Test	Verification Result
Allo	Success
" allo "	Success

Text can contain mixed cases, and from a human perspective, mixed case is still the same word. However, the computer considers mixed case as a completely different buffer, and so we must be able to cope with this situation.

Figure 3-9 shows the working solution.

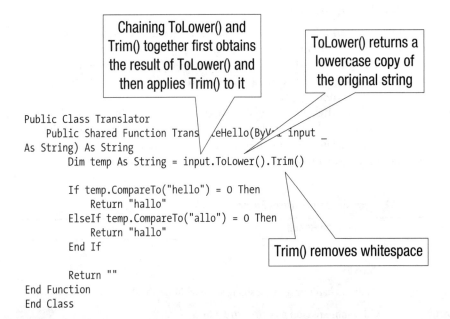

Chaining ToLower() and Trim() together first obtains the result of ToLower() and then applies Trim() to it

ToLower() returns a lowercase copy of the original string

```
Public Class Translator
    Public Shared Function TranslateHello(ByVal input _
As String) As String
        Dim temp As String = input.ToLower().Trim()

        If temp.CompareTo("hello") = 0 Then
            Return "hallo"
        ElseIf temp.CompareTo("allo") = 0 Then
            Return "hallo"
        End If

        Return ""
End Function
End Class
```

Trim() removes whitespace

Figure 3-9. *The final translation solution*

Looking at the solution, you see that there are elements from the first solution, which was discounted because it did not work properly. This is an example of how quickly solving a bug, seeing that code fail, and discounting the solution can be incorrect. You need to think through why something fails, and not just fix the bug to get rid of it.

■**Note** All of the solutions involved use String type methods. The String type is very sophisticated and supports many operations that are commonly performed on text.

At this point, we are finished with the translation of the greeting. Next, I'll point out a couple of additional items that you need to keep in mind when dealing with strings.

Quoting Strings

Along with strings, Visual Basic has the Char type. A Char can be described as a single letter of a sentence. However, it would be more accurate to say that it is a single character. You can assign a string to a Char type, as long as Option Strict is Off (which it is by default). For example, suppose you wrote the following code to assign a string to the variable val.

```
' The Option Strict declaration must come right at the top of your code
Option Strict Off
. . .
Dim val As Char
val = "hello"
```

The example compiles, but you will not get what you want. Because Option Strict is Off, the string is converted to a character. In this conversion, data is lost—specifically, the characters ello are lost. The value stored in the variable val is the single letter h.

If Option Strict were On, the example would not compile. When Option Strict is On, the compiler does not do conversions where data might be lost. If you have code that does attempt a conversion, an error will be flagged by the compiler.

If you really wanted to store the single letter h in the variable val, you would need to explicitly define the character to be assigned to the variable, as follows:

```
Option Strict On
. . .
Dim val As Char
val = "h"c
```

To define a single-character string, you enclose that character in double quotation marks, followed by a lowercase c to indicate that the single-character string is a character.

VISUAL BASIC STRICT AND EXPLICIT

Programming languages have two distinct flavors: *static typed* and *dynamic typed*. Do not get these two terms confused with the terms *strongly typed* and *weakly typed*. Those two sets of terms are orthogonal to each other. A language can be dynamic typed and strongly typed at the same time. For example, the following code is strongly and dynamic typed.

```
Dim a = 10
```

The type is dynamic because I have not declared the variable to be of any type. It is strongly typed because when a is assigned to a value of 10, it is defined to be an Integer. A strongly and dynamic typed language means that variables can be any type, but once they are assigned, their type cannot be changed. Thus, you cannot convert an integer to a string or a string to an integer without some type of failure.

The following code is weakly and static typed.

```
Dim val As Char = "hello"
```

Here, I explicitly say that val is a Char, and I've assigned to it a string. However, because of weak typing, a strong-armed conversion of the string to a Char is made. Think of it as fitting a square peg into a round hole. If the square peg has a diagonal length less than the diameter of the hole, the process works without much effort. But if the square peg's length is the same as the diameter of the hole, you will need to use brute force.

Visual Basic allows you to write all types of code, and the flags Option Strict and Option Explicit relate to what kind of code you want. When you set Option Strict to On, you are saying that you don't want to support weakly typed code. The flag has no effect on dynamic typing. The Option Explicit flag does not affect weakly typed code, but it partially affects dynamic typed code. Consider the following code that compiles when Option Explicit is set to Off.

```
a = 10
```

The code is an assignment, but you don't know if the variable is declared in the file, in the class, or local to the method. The variable could be defined out of the blue and then used. Dynamic typing allows this; but again, after the variable has been assigned, it stays the same type. When you set Option Explicit to On, you are making an explicit declaration of the variable a requirement.

With all of these options, you are left wondering which combination of flags you want. The answer is that it depends on what style of programmer you are. If you want a traditional language (like C#, Java, C++, and so on), then you should have both flags set to On. If you want a more dynamic programming language (like Python, Ruby, PHP, and so on), then you should have both flags set to Off. Unless you have experience in the dynamic programming environment and know what side effects may occur, you should start off taking the traditional language approach. For that reason, the code in this book is written with both flags set to On.

You can define the Option Strict and Option Explicit flags in the source code, as shown in the examples in the previous "Quoting Strings" section, or you can set them in the compile settings of the individual project settings or for the whole of Visual Basic Express. To set them for a project, right-click the project name and select Properties ➤ Compile. The two settings are in the drop-down boxes at the top of the page. To set the options for all projects, select Tools ➤ Options, and then select Projects and Solutions ➤ VB Defaults.

Character Mapping

A single character takes 16 bits of space, and the space that a string consumes depends on the number of characters in a buffer. If a buffer is 10 characters long, then the entire buffer takes up 160 bits of space.

A single character is 16 bits long so that a buffer can store text in a multitude of different formats. The standardized length is due to a standard called Unicode.

Consider the character *a*. Philosophically, how do you know that an *a* is an *a*? For humans, that's easy because our brains are trained to recognize the curve and look of an *a*. Now look at the Russian letter shown in Figure 3-10.

Н

Figure 3-10. *A Russian letter*

What letter does Figure 3-10 show? It looks like an *H*, right? But comparing it to the English language, it is an *N*. The Russian language has its own set of letters, and someone has determined that a Russian *H* is an English *N*. Figure 3-11 is a mapping of the Russian letters to the English letters.

Russian	English transliteration	Russian	English transliteration
а	a	р	r
б	b	с	s
в	v	т	t
г	g	у	u
д	d	ф	f
е / ё	e	х	kh
ж	zh	ц	ts
з	z	ч	ch
и / й	i	ш	sh
к	k	щ	shch
л	l	ъ	''
м	m	ы	y
н	n	ь	'
о	o	э	e
п	p	ю	iu
		я	ia
Sennaya.com			

Figure 3-11. *Mapping of Russian letters to English letters*

If I were learning Russian, I would want the mapping provided in Figure 3-11. The mapping gives me an idea of what each letter in Russian represents. You could think of Figure 3-11 as a lookup table. The computer has the same sort of need, because a computer does not understand letters. A computer understands only numbers and thus uses lookup tables that map a set of letters to a set of numbers.

There are many lookup tables, such as American Standard Code for Information Interchange (ASCII). For example, using ASCII, the letter *a* maps to the number 97. The problem with ASCII is that it works well for English, but works horribly for other languages. ASCII was extended to deal with Western European languages, but still fails for languages such as Chinese, Russian, and Arabic.

The solution chosen by .NET is Unicode. Unicode is the definition of a set of lookup tables that map to letters for all of the languages of the world.

For the most part, you will not have to concern yourself with the Unicode, because .NET manages everything transparently. This was not the case many years ago, when programmers had to manage the lookup tables themselves. So consider yourself lucky that you did not experience this pain in developing multilingual applications.

Dealing with Languages and Cultures

Managing strings in .NET does not stop with Unicode. .NET is very innovative in that it understands concepts such as culture and language, which are a reflection of how humans speak and live. The ideas of culture and language do not exist in other programming environments.

Consider Switzerland as an example. Throughout Switzerland, there are mountains that happen to separate four individual languages: German, Italian, Romansch, and French. Even with the four languages, the Swiss all trade the same currency and write numbers the same way.

In previous programming environments, the language would be tied to a particular country. This works fine for France, Germany, and the United States, but fails miserably for Canada, Switzerland, Belgium, and India. You need to separate language from culture, because multiple languages are used in different cultures. For example, Italian is spoken in Switzerland and Italy. French is spoken in France, Switzerland, Luxembourg, and Canada. German is spoken in Germany, Switzerland, and Austria.

Setting Culture and Language in Windows

The Windows operating system allows you to set the culture and language of your computer, regardless of the language in which Windows is operating. Figure 3-12 shows an example.

The example in Figure 3-12 is running a German version of Windows in Switzerland. The language is English, and the culture is Canada. It would seem that Windows would get confused, but in fact, if you write your .NET application properly, multilanguage support is simple.

Figure 3-12. *Setting the culture and language in Windows*

Parsing and Processing Numbers

The culture and country become important when interacting with numbers and dates that are stored as strings. Imagine retrieving a string buffer with an embedded number and then attempting to perform an addition, as illustrated by Figure 3-13.

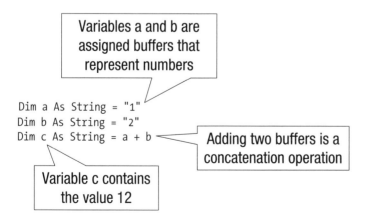

Figure 3-13. *Performing arithmetic on numbers represented as strings can lead to unexpected results.*

Adding numbers is performing a mathematical operation. When the add operation is performed on strings, it always results in a buffer concatenation. The add operation is a very simple way to concatenate string buffers together.

However, concatenation is not the aim of the example. The aim is to treat the strings as numbers and then add the numbers so that c contains the value 3 (1 + 2 = 3). The rewritten version of the example is shown in Figure 3-14. This code parses a string into an integer.

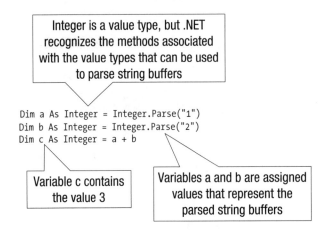

Figure 3-14. *Parsing strings into integers before doing the arithmetic*

The type Integer has a Parse() method that can be used to turn a string into an integer. The parsing works only if the buffer is a valid number. If the buffer contains letters or an invalid number, an error will be generated.

If the code can cope with a failed string conversion, the solution used by the parsing routines is to generate an exception that a program could process. Alternatively, a fail-safe way to parse a number is to use TryParse(), as in the following example.

```
Dim value As Integer
If Integer.TryParse("1", value) Then
    . . .
End If
```

The TryParse() method does not return an integer value, but instead returns a Boolean flag, indicating whether the buffer could be parsed. If the return value is True, then the buffer could be parsed, and the result is stored in the parameter value. You can parse other number types using the same techniques (for example, Single.TryParse()).

There are more variations in how a number can be parsed. For example, how would the number 100 be parsed, if the number 100 is hexadecimal? (Computers use hexadecimal numbers.) Here is an example of hexadecimal conversion:

```
Imports System.Globalization
. . .
Public Sub ParseHexadecimal()
    Dim value As Integer= Integer.Parse("100", NumberStyles.HexNumber)
End Sub
```

This example uses a variant of Parse(), which has an additional second parameter that represents the format of the number. In this case, the second parameter indicates that the format of the number is hexadecimal (NumberStyles.HexNumber, from the System.Globalization namespace).

■**Note** If you are wondering how 100 maps to 256 at the hex level, use the calculator that comes with the Windows operating system. Switch the calculator to scientific view (View ➤ Scientific). Click the Hex radio button, enter the number 100, and then click the Dec radio button.

The enumeration NumberStyles has other values that can be used to parse numbers according to other rules. For example, some rules handle the use of parentheses surrounding a number to indicate a negative value. Other rules deal with whitespace. Here is an example:

```
Public Sub TestParseNegativeValue()
    Dim value As Integer = Integer.Parse( " (10) ", _
    NumberStyles.AllowParentheses Or _
    NumberStyles.AllowLeadingWhite Or _
    NumberStyles.AllowTrailingWhite)
End Sub
```

The number " (10) " in this example is complicated in that it has whitespace and parentheses. Attempting to parse the number using Parse() without using any of the NumberStyles enumerated values will not work. The enumeration AllowParentheses processes the parentheses, AllowLeadingWhite ignores the leading spaces, and AllowTrailingWhite ignores the trailing spaces. Then, when the buffer has been processed, a value of –10 will be stored in the variable value.

Other NumberStyles enumerated values allow you to process decimal points for fractional numbers, positive or negative numbers, and so on. This then raises the topic of processing numbers other than Integer. Each of the base data types, such as Boolean, Byte, and Double, has associated Parse() and TryParse() methods. Additionally, the method TryParse() can use the NumberStyles enumeration. (See the MSDN documentation for details on the NumberStyles enumerated values.)

Parsing integer values is the same, regardless of the country. Parsing double values or dates is not the same. Consider the following example, which tries to parse a buffer that contains decimal values.

```
Public Sub TestDoubleValue()
    Dim value As Double = Double.Parse("1234.56")

    value = Double.Parse("1,234.56")
End Sub
```

In this example, both uses of the Parse() method process the number 1234.56. The first Parse() method is a simple parse, because it contains only a decimal point separating the whole number from the partial number. The second Parse() method is more complicated in that a comma is used to separate the thousands of the whole number. In both cases, the Parse() routines did not fail.

If you test this code, it's possible that an exception will be generated. In this case, the culture of the application is to blame. The numbers presented in the example are encoded using en-CA, which is English-Canadian notation.

Working with Cultures

In .NET, culture information is made up using two identifiers: language and specialization. As I mentioned earlier, in Switzerland, there are four spoken languages, which means that there are four different ways of expressing a date, time, and currency. This does not mean that the date is different for German speakers and French speakers. The date format will be identical, but the words (*Maerz* or *Mars* for the month March) will be different. The words for the date are the same in Austria, Switzerland, and Germany, but the format is not identical. This means multilanguage countries such as Canada (French and English) and Luxembourg (French and German) need to be able to process multiple encodings, hence the need for the two identifiers.

To retrieve the current culture, use the following code:

```
Dim info As System.Globalization.CultureInfo = _
    System.Threading.Thread.CurrentThread.CurrentCulture
Console.WriteLine("Culture (" & info.EnglishName & ")")
```

The property Thread.CurrentThread.CurrentCulture retrieves the culture information associated with the currently executing thread. As a side note, it is possible to associate different threads with different cultural information. The property EnglishName generates an English version of the culture information, which would appear similar to the following:

```
Culture (English (Canada))
```

Consider the following number:

```
1,234
```

The number with an American or Canadian culture is one thousand two hundred thirty-four, but with a German culture, it is one point two three four (for those who do not know about German formatting, a comma is used as a decimal separator, and a period is used as a thousands separator). One way to change the culture is with the dialog box shown earlier in Figure 3-12. The second way to change the culture is at a programmatic level, as in this code:

```
Imports System.Threading
Thread.CurrentThread.CurrentCulture = new CultureInfo("en-CA")
```

In the example, a new instance of CultureInfo is created with the culture information en-CA. Next is an example that processes a double number encoded using German formatting rules:

```
Public Sub TestGermanParseNumber()
    Thread.CurrentThread.CurrentCulture = new CultureInfo("de-DE")
    Dim value As Double = Double.Parse("1,234")
End Sub
```

This example assigns the de-DE culture information to the currently executing thread. Then whenever any parsing routines are used, German from Germany is used as the basis for the formatting rules. Changing the culture information does not affect the formatting rules of the programming language.

It is also possible to parse dates and times using the Parse() and TryParse() routines, as demonstrated by the following examples:

```
Public Sub TestGermanParseDate()
    Dim datetime As Date = Date.Parse("May 10, 2008")
    If 5 = datetime.Month Then
        Console.WriteLine( "correct")
    End If
    Thread.CurrentThread.CurrentCulture = new CultureInfo("de-DE")
    datetime = Date.Parse("10 Mai, 2008")
    If 5 = datetime.Month Then
        Console.WriteLine( "correct")
    End If

End Sub
```

Notice how the first Date.Parse() processed English-Canadian formatted text and knew that the identifier May equaled the fifth month of the year. For the second Date.Parse() method call, the culture was changed to German, and it was possible to process 10 Mai, 2008. In both cases, processing the buffer posed no major problems, as long as you knew that the buffer was a German or English-Canadian date. Where things can go awry is when you have a German date and an English culture.

Converting a data type to a buffer is relatively easy because the ToString() methods have been implemented to generate the desired output. Consider the following example, which generates a buffer from an integer value:

```
Public Sub TestGenerateString()
    Dim iValue As Integer = 123
    Dim buffer As String = iValue.ToString()
    If buffer = "123" Then
        Console.WriteLine( "correct")
    End If
End Sub
```

In the example, the value 123 has been assigned to iValue, which is of type Integer, and then its ToString() method is called, which generates a buffer that contains "123". The same thing can be done to a Double value, as in this example:

```
Dim number As Double = 123.5678
Dim buffer As String = number.ToString("0.00")
```

Here, the number 123.5678 is converted to a buffer using the ToString() method, but ToString() has a parameter, which is a formatting instruction that indicates how the double number should be generated as a buffer. The desired result is a buffer with a maximum of two digits after the decimal point. Because the third digit after the decimal is a 7, the value is rounded up, resulting in the buffer 123.57.

Let's see an example where the culture information also applies to generating a buffer. Here, a Double value is generated in the format of the culture:

```
Public Sub TestGenerateGermanNumber()
    Dim number As Double = 123.5678
    Thread.CurrentThread.CurrentCulture = _
        new CultureInfo("de-DE")
    Dim buffer As String = number.ToString("0.00")
    If buffer = "123,57" Then
        Console.WriteLine( "correct")
    End If
End Sub
```

As in the previous examples, the CurrentCulture property is assigned the desired culture. Then when the Double variable number has its ToString() method called, the buffer "123,57" is generated.

The Important Stuff to Remember

In this chapter, you learned about strings and writing code. Here are the keys points to remember:

- Writing tests is an important part of your development practice. A test is not just a mechanism to catch errors, but also a mechanism used to understand the dynamics of your code.

- The String type is a special reference type that has many methods and properties. You are advised to look at the MSDN documentation to see what a string can do.

- IntelliSense and the MSDN documentation are your best bets when you want to find out about specific methods, properties, or types. Books and web sites such as Code Project are good resources to help you understand concepts.

- All variables and types are based on the object type.

- When writing code, you need to define responsibilities and contexts. Don't fix bugs or write code using knee-jerk reactions.

- All strings are based on Unicode. Each Unicode character is 16 bits wide.

- When translating buffers, you need to deal with the translation of text and the translation of numbers and dates.

- .NET includes sophisticated technology to help you translate numbers and dates using a combination of language and culture information.

Some Things for You to Do

The following are some exercises that relate to what you've learned in this chapter.

1. Finish the application to translate from one language to another language, allowing the user to choose which direction the translation takes.

2. Extend the `LanguageTranslator` component to be able to translate the words *au revoir* and *auf wiedersehen* to *good bye*.

3. You can combine strings by using the plus sign, but doing many additions will slow down your code. Use the `StringBuilder` class to concatenate two buffers together. Hint: you want to convert the code `String c = a + b`, and make a and b use the `StringBuilder` class. The result of the `StringBuilder` is assigned to the variable `c`.

4. Create a test that demonstrates what happens when a number value is added to a string value. Write the appropriate tests to verify your conclusion.

5. Extend the `LanguageTranslator` component to include methods to translate English numbers into German numbers.

6. Extend the `LanguageTranslator` component to include methods to translate dates from American or Canadian dates into German dates. Note that the added wrinkle is that you could input an American or Canadian date.

7. Implement the Windows application that calls the `LanguageTranslator` component.

■■■

Learning About Data Structures, Decisions, and Loops

When you are creating applications, the source code will need to make decisions, such as should you open the file or save the file? And if you open the file, what kind of iterative code is going to read the contents of the file? These sorts of questions are answered by employing data structures, decisions, and loops.

The easiest way to demonstrate how to make a decision is to write a miniature artificial intelligence (AI) system. The AI system will be extremely primitive, but AI is interesting because it makes extensive use of decision and loop constructs. The AI system iterates and makes decisions based on data defined in a neat and orderly custom data structure.

Using the example of creating an algorithm, the following topics will be covered in this chapter:

- Data structures, including custom types

- The restrictions of value types

- Algorithm design

- Class constructors, which allow you to initialize an object

- The For loop, which allows you to iterate over sets of data

- The If statement, which allows you to execute specific code based on logic

Understanding the Depth-First Search Algorithm

AI involves searching for data, and a core algorithm of AI is searching. The search algorithm that we will develop for this chapter's example is a depth-first search system. AI has other types of searches, such as an A* or a breadth-first search, but they are all based on the same idea as the depth-search algorithm. This idea is searching for information that is arranged in a tree structure.

> ■**Note** An *algorithm* is a logical set of finite, repeatable steps for completing a task. The term is usually applied in relation to formal problems such as searching, but most, if not all computer programs, use algorithms of one sort or another.

Before we write any code, you need to understand what the depth-first search algorithm does and why you would use it. The problem to solve is how to get from point A to point B in the most efficient manner. This problem can be stated generally as, "how to solve task A when you have X options."

Imagine you are about to drive to work and you are at the front door of your house. You don't know where your keys are, and thus you begin a search for the keys in the house. Of course, you try to remember, but your memory is not working that early in the morning. You try to retrace your steps, and think of logical places where you could have placed your keys. When you retrace your steps, you follow your memory's logic. Simply put, your search algorithm is based on your memory's suggestion of where the keys might be. The data structure that you are navigating is the rooms of your house. Your brain-based search algorithm could create a search pattern like that shown in Figure 4-1.

Figure 4-1. *A possible search order for your keys*

In Figure 4-1, you found the keys in the hall, but yet your search algorithm led you astray for a while, since you searched the hall last. The cynic could say that you kept walking around the keys without realizing that they were so close to you. But this is the crux of the problem, because you didn't know you developed a search algorithm that would lead you astray this time. And the same algorithm might not lead you astray next time.

Note Searching using different strategies is very similar to how you will write computer algorithms. There is no single best algorithm; there are only good algorithms that have certain compromises. When you implement an algorithm, you need to consider the one that best suits your needs with the least number of compromises that could cause problems.

As Figure 4-1 illustrates, you searched in a counterclockwise manner. Another strategy would have been to go clockwise or even in a zigzag, or you could have searched some rooms multiple times.

Let's convert Figure 4-1 into a program that has a search algorithm and a data structure. The search algorithm will be depth-first, and the data structure will be based on a path between the respective rooms. The data structure representing the house in Figure 4-1 is illustrated in Figure 4-2.

Figure 4-2. *A tree structure illustrates each possible action. Highlighted lines represent a depth-first search, and each circle represents a destination.*

In the tree structure shown in Figure 4-2, each node represents a destination that can be reached from a particular place in the house. From each room, you can reach the other room. But this structure is recursive. From the child bedroom, you can reach the living room, and then you can reach the child bedroom again. Even though you navigated down the tree, you moved from one room to another and back to the original room. This is perfectly acceptable from a data structure perspective, even though you are probably saying, "But that is wrong since rooms will show up multiple times."

Note The tree representation in Figure 4-2 is by no means complete, because from each room you can go to the other room. A full tree representation would be a combinatorial explosion.

The structure is the way it is because the data structure is a representation of the house. If you were searching the house, would you be able to move from one room to another and back again? Sure you would. Would you do it? No, because your search algorithm would say, "Hey dude, you're repeating yourself." And therein lies the trick when writing applications. You have a data structure and an algorithm that operates on the data structure. I call this building an application in layers. You have the lowest level, which is an intelligent data structure, and a higher level that uses the functionality of the intelligent data structure.

By *intelligent data structure*, I mean that the structure is always consistent and does not corrupt itself. In this example, a room will not point to itself, a room will be present in the structure only if it is present in the house, and so on. The higher-level algorithm would be responsible for figuring out how to find information in the tree. It should be smart enough to realize that constantly traveling between two rooms is not going to achieve anything other than wasted time.

The search logic is where you go down the tree traversing one room after another. It is called a *depth-first* search algorithm because you iterate the tree by going down the tree one level after another. You stop traversing down the tree once you reach a room that you have already traversed. Then you go back one level and traverse the room beside the room that you have already traversed. This could mean the search path found by the computer would be similar to Figure 4-1. That's because the computer is as dumb as you are, albeit the computer is not saying to itself, "If only I had started in the hall."

Realize that there is no magic wand to find the keys for you. The technique that you and the computer used is called *brute force*, and it is computationally expensive and typically avoided. In this case though, brute force is the only real solution, because you don't know where the keys are—they could be anywhere in the house. It just happened to be your bad luck that the keys were found in the last place you looked.

Let's try to improve the situation. Imagine for a moment that your keys are tagged with a clapper. The idea is that with your keys going "beep, beep, beep," you will be able to instantly find them and avoid the brute-force searching. But suppose that the keys are in the upper-right corner of the child bedroom. Listening for the beeping, you think that you hear the keys either in the kitchen or the child bedroom. So, where do you go first?

Which path comes first or is the most efficient is a common problem, and you may witness it every day if you have a global positioning system (GPS) for you car. A search algorithm is commonly used in GPS devices. You punch in a set of coordinates, and the GPS device will attempt to find the quickest or shortest way. In the abstract sense, the search algorithm the GPS makers apply is identical to the search algorithm that we are going to develop in this chapter.

Implementing User-Defined Types

The data structure on which the algorithm will operate is a user-defined type. In the examples up to this point, we have been using types like Double and String, which are CLR-provided types. For the example in this chapter, we will define our own type, which we will use to represent a node in the tree.

Declaring Structures and Classes

A user-defined type can be implemented in one of two ways: as a structure or as a class. An example of each is shown in Figure 4-3.

Figure 4-3. *Choices for implementing the Node custom type*

As shown in Figure 4-3, you can choose to create a user-defined type as a value type (Structure) or reference type (Class) type. For the most part, developers use a reference type, because it has fewer constraints and is easiest to use in a general context. A value type has some constraints due its behavior of storing everything on the stack, as discussed in the following sections.

Value Type Constraints

The constraints of using a value type relate to the fact that data is copied. This has an impact on what happens when you embed reference types in value types and use value types as parameters to methods.

The Effects of Copying Data

When one value type is assigned to another value type, the contents of the value types are copied. To see this in action, consider the declarations in Figure 4-4.

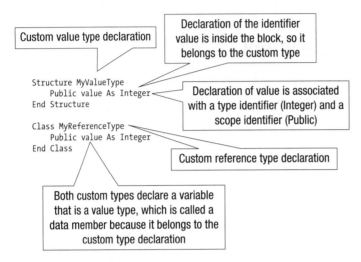

Figure 4-4. *Declaring custom types*

When declaring user-defined types, the data members and methods are declared inside the block of code. You can think of the declaration as the writing on the outside of the box, and anything in the block of code as the contents of the box. The custom types (MyValueType and MyReferenceType) as declared in Figure 4-4 do not have a scope identifier. Think of a scope identifier as defining who has access to your pockets and wallet. In the case of the types in the example, the scope is like saying that your spouse is allowed to peek into your wallet, but strangers cannot. In other words, the types cannot be used outside their own namespace.

If the Public keyword had been in front of the type identifier, then the user-defined type would be exposed like a wallet that is allowed to be peeked into by the general public. This means the types can be used by other code. In the case of the wallet, it's a bad idea to have unfettered public scope, but sometimes public scope is desirable when you are able to control its access. And you do this every time you pay for something by handing a credit card to the cashier. In that case, you are publicly exposing parts of your wallet under your supervision. In code terms, this means making your types public, but not necessarily making the data members public.

Next, consider the code in Figure 4-5. It instantiates MyValueType and assigns it to another variable of the same type.

The example in Figure 4-5 illustrates what happens to two variables when one is instantiated and assigned to the other, and then the other is modified. You want to understand how each data type is modified when an interaction with another type occurs.

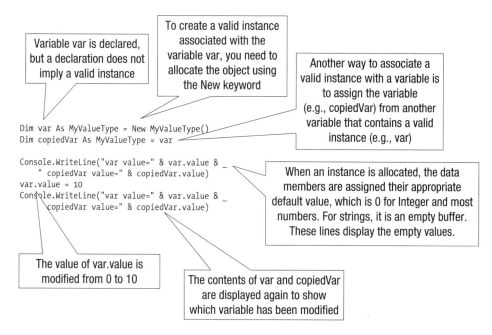

Figure 4-5. *Using a custom value type*

As a comparison, the same operations can be carried out using a reference type, where the reference code is as follows:

```
Dim val As MyReferenceType = New MyReferenceType()
Dim copiedVal As MyReferenceType = val

Console.WriteLine("val value=" & val.value & _
    " copiedVal value=" & copiedVal.value)
val.value = 10
Console.WriteLine("val value=" & val.value & _
    " copiedVal value=" & copiedVal.value)
```

So, if two code pieces are functionally identical, with the single difference being their type (value type versus reference type), will they generate the same results?

Running both code pieces results in the following output:

```
var value=0 copiedVar value=0
var value=10 copiedVar value=0
val value=0 copiedVal value=0
val value=10 copiedVal value=10
```

Looking closely at the results, you see that two functionally identical code pieces that differ only in the variable type they use generate completely different results:

- When you assign and modify a value type, only the contents of the modified variable change.

- When you assign and modify a reference type, the original object changes, so the original variable and assigned variable change because they both point to the same original object.

This example demonstrates that when defining user-defined types, you need to be careful how you treat value and reference types.

As you learned in Chapter 2, a value type is stored on the stack. Thus, declaring a user-defined value type means the full contents of the user-defined type are stored on the stack, and when you assign one value type variable to another value type variable, you are copying the complete contents of the value type. This copying was obvious in our example when we used simple numeric number types (such as Double), but when you copy complete structures with contents, the side effects might not be what you expect.

Value Types That Contain Reference Types

Value types copy the contents when you assign variables, but there is caveat in that this rule does not apply if the value type contains a reference type. Consider the following declaration.

```
Structure MyValueTypeWithReferenceType
    Public value As Integer
    Public reference As MyReferenceType
End Structure
```

The first line in the value type declaration contains a single value type (Integer). The second line is the data member declaration that is a reference type. The declaration implies that the value type is stored on the stack, but the reference type is on the heap.

The value type that contains a reference type is manipulated using the following test code.

```
Dim var As MyValueTypeWithReferenceType = New MyValueTypeWithReferenceType()
var.reference = New MyReferenceType()
Dim copiedVar As MyValueTypeWithReferenceType = var

Console.WriteLine("var value=" & var.reference.value & _
    " copiedVar value=" & copiedVar.reference.value)
var.reference.value = 10
Console.WriteLine("var value=" & var.reference.value & _
    " copiedVar value=" & copiedVar.reference.value)
```

It is important to realize that allocating MyValueTypeWithReferenceType does not imply an allocation of the embedded custom type. In the test code, the allocation of the MyValueTypeWithReferenceType is the same as the previous code examples, but a second allocation of MyReferenceType is required because MyReferenceType is a reference type. Had MyReferenceType been a value type, the allocation would not have been necessary. But if you allocate a value type like a reference type, the compiler will ignore the directive.

Running the test code results in the following:

```
var value=0 copiedVar value=0
var value=10 copiedVar value=10
```

When you assign and modify an embedded reference type, the reference type instance is modified for both variables. In this case, when we assigned the value type, the contents were copied, including the pointer to the reference type.

Table 4-1 summarizes the behavior of types when the allocated variable is assigned to another variable and the data member from the original is modified. For example, if the code is `custom2 = custom1 custom1.member = [new value]`, what's the value of `custom2.member`?

Table 4-1. *Behavior When the Allocated Variable Is Assigned to Another Variable and the Data Member from the Original Is Modified*

Type	Behavior
Value type	Assigned data member is not modified
Reference type	Assigned data member is modified
Value type embedding value type	Assigned embedded data member is not modified
Value type embedding reference type	Assigned embedded data member is modified
Reference type embedding value type	Assigned embedded data member is modified
Reference type embedding reference type	Assigned embedded data member is modified

Value Types and Parameters

Another value type constraint relates to how variables are stored and manipulated when they are passed via a method. Suppose you create a method that has as parameters a value type and a reference type. If in the method the parameters are modified, what modifications does the caller of the method see? Consider the following code:

```
Sub Method(ByVal value As MyValueType, ByVal reference As MyReferenceType)
  value.value = 10
  reference.value = 10
End Sub
```

The caller can pass in instances of a value type and a reference type that are manipulated in the context of the method. Now let's call `Method()` with the following code:

```
Dim value As MyValueType = New MyValueType()
Dim reference As MyReferenceType = New MyReferenceType()
Method(value, reference)
Console.WriteLine("value value=" & value.value & _
    " reference value=" & reference.value)
```

The calling code instantiates the types MyValueType and MyReferenceType, calls the method Method(), and then inspects the value of the data member value from the value and reference types.

Running the code will generate output similar to the following:

```
value value=0 reference value=10
```

The executed code shows that the value type (MyValueType) data member was not altered, whereas the reference type (MyReferenceType) data member was altered. This is correct, and it demonstrates that when you call a method, you are assigning the parameters of the method to variables in the called method. Looking back at Table 4-1, you can see that when you assign a value to a value type, manipulating the assigned instance does not change the original instance.

However, you can gain some control over how parameters are handled. When Method() is declared, the assumption is made that all of the parameters are passed to the method implementation as value types. It is possible to pass the parameters to the method as reference types, as determined by one of the following keywords:

ByVal: When a method has parameters declared with the ByVal keyword, the parameter has its value copied from the caller variable to method implementation variable, even if it is a reference type.

ByRef: When a method has parameters declared with the ByRef keyword, the caller variable is not copied to the parameter variable; rather, the variable used by the caller and the method variable are one and the same. Thus, changes to the method variable, as in the previous example, would be visible to the caller of the method.

Figure 4-6 illustrates how to use the ByRef keyword so that a modified value type will be visible to the caller of the method.

Now that you have an understanding of the depth-first search algorithm and how the data structure will be defined as a user-defined value type, let's get started building the search algorithm.

ByRef is associated with the parameter indicating that the value variable can be modified in the method and the result will be visible to the caller

```
Sub Method(ByRef value As MyValueType, ByVal reference As MyReferenceType)
    value.value = 10
    reference.value = 10
End Sub

Dim value As MyValueType
Dim reference As MyReferenceType = New MyReferenceType()
Method(value, reference)
Console.WriteLine("value value=" & value.value & _
    " reference value=" & reference.value)
```

The variable value.value will contain the value of 10 assigned in the method

Figure 4-6. *Using the ByRef keyword*

Organizing the Search Algorithm

The search algorithm we will write in this chapter deals with the problem of planning a flight from point A to point B. The first step is to figure out the features we need to implement. Here's a summary:

- A data structure implements the node.

- A node can contain references to other nodes.

- Each node has a description and unique identifier to distinguish it from other nodes.

- All of the nodes have flight information.

- An algorithm will traverse the nodes and keep track of its path.

- The path is returned as a list of nodes.

The data structure is based on the problem of planning a flight between two places, as illustrated in Figure 4-7.

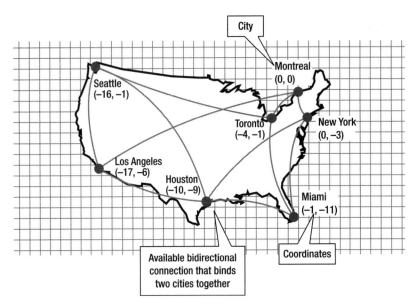

Figure 4-7. *Planning flight routes*

As shown in Figure 4-7, three main attributes describe an individual node in the flight route:

- *City name*: A description that will be used as a key when a user defines a starting and end point.

- *Coordinates:* An illustrative approach used to describe how cities are located in relation to each other.

- *Connections*: A representative connection between two cities. As in real life, not all cities connect to other cities.

For the scope of this chapter, there are only two projects: a class library that contains the depth-first search algorithm and the testing application. The project structure looks like Figure 4-8. As with the examples in the previous chapters, remember to add a reference to the class library (SearchSolution) and to set the test project (TestSearchSolution) as the startup project.

Figure 4-8. *Solution project structure*

Writing the Depth-First Search Code

We will implement the depth-first search algorithm in three main steps. The first step is to define and implement the data structure. The second step is to implement the algorithm and tests. Finally, we'll run the algorithm and see what route has been found.

Defining and Implementing the Data Structure

As I mentioned earlier, for the most part, developers use the Class keyword to define a data structure as a reference type, because of the constraints of using a value type. However, for this example, we will start out by using the Structure keyword to define Node as a value type. The depth-first search algorithm has two distinct implementation details: data structure and algorithm. Because each detail is separate, it seems appropriate to define Node as a value type. So, least let's try it and see what happens.

As per the attributes illustrated in Figure 4-7, the data structure that is added to the SearchSolution project is implemented as shown in Figure 4-9.

Figure 4-9. *The data structure for the depth-first search*

The data structure is declared as a Structure, with the connections represented as an array of Node elements. An array of Node elements is formed when one Node contains a list of references to other Node elements. Think of an array as a collection of sticky notes that say, "Here is a reference to A, B, C, and so on." By having one node reference another node, a sort of never-ending tree is created, because it is possible to travel back and forth between two cities. Thus, the depth-first search algorithm will need to avoid repeating itself.

The Connections data member is an array used to define cities that are the next connection. To reference another city, you can create the reference as an array of Node elements, as in the declaration shown in Figure 4-9. An alternative is to use an array of strings that contain the name of the next city, like this:

```
Public Structure Node
    Public CityName As String
    Public X As Double
    Public Y As Double
    Public Connections As String()
End Structure
```

In this declaration, Connections is an array of strings that references other city names and is what humans would see when they look at a table showing all of the connections for a particular city. The problem with using strings is that it is inefficient from a computing perspective. To traverse a tree of cities, you would first traverse the city names, resolve the city name to a Node object, and then traverse the node. The string array approach requires an extra, unnecessary step. So the more efficient and programmatic approach is to have an array of Node instances.

By using the declaration where Connections is an array of Node instances, you have both the city name and available connections in one cohesive object.

Instantiating and Initializing a Node

In previous code, you have seen how objects can be instantiated using the New keyword. To instantiate a type, you always use the New keyword. After the New keyword is the type that you want to instantiate, followed by a set of parentheses. A node is instantiated using the following code:

```
Dim city As Node = New Node()
```

If you look only at the identifier Node with parentheses, you would get the impression that you are calling a method that has no parameters. The impression is correct, but it is a special type of method call, and that is made apparent by the use of the New keyword. The method that is being called is known as a *constructor*. Every type has a constructor, and it can be used to initialize the state of the object before being returned to the caller.

In the declaration of Node, there is no defined constructor, and thus a default constructor is provided by the CLR. The default constructor does nothing and has no parameters.

After having instantiated a node, we can assign the data members, as in the following code.

```
city.CityName = "Montreal"
city.X = 0.0
city.Y = 0.0
```

Assigning the data members results in setting the city name to Montreal and the coordinates to (0,0).

This is all fine, but shouldn't we need to provide some data members when creating a city node? Does it make sense to instantiate a node without defining the name and coordinates of the city? Technically, a node does not need to be assigned, but logically speaking, an unassigned node is quite useless. And remember that we are working on defining an intelligent data structure, thus a Node instance without city name and coordinates is logically not a valid Node. We also need to have a root for the Node structure, which we will set up as an array.

You can enforce a verifiable correct initial state by defining a constructor with parameters, rather than using the default constructor, as in the following example. When your code provides a constructor, regardless of the declaration, the default constructor is not generated and is not accessible.

```
Public Structure Node
    Public Shared RootNodes As Node()
    Public CityName As String
    Public X As Double
    Public Y As Double
    Public Connections As Node()

    Public Sub New(ByVal city As String, ByVal X As Double, ByVal Y As Double)
        Me.CityName = city
        Me.X = x
        Me.Y = y
        Me.Connections = Nothing
    End Sub
End Structure
```

■Note Nothing is a special value that you can assign to reference variables. It means that the reference variable does not point to a real object. Nothing is a useful value to assign to reference variables in a constructor, if you don't have a meaningful object that they can point to at the outset.

To define a constructor, you define a method of type Sub called New(). And, in most cases, you will use public scope. The parameters of the constructor represent the three pieces of information that are required to instantiate a valid state. Within the constructor, the data members are assigned the values of the parameters.

The defined constructor has parameters, which means that to instantiate Node, you need to provide the three pieces of data. Thus, to instantiate Node, you need to provide enough data to make the node logical. The original instantiation code would not compile, so to compile the code, you need to modify the instantiation to the following:

```
Dim city as Node = New Node("Montreal", 0.0, 0.0)
```

The declaration of the node might reference incorrect data, but that is not the responsibility of the intelligent data structure. An analogy is that a word processor by itself is not responsible for making sure that the text you write makes sense. The role of the word processor is to give you the ability to construct intelligent text.

Examining the Problem of Referencing Using Value Types

As you've learned, a value type is stored on the stack, and its contents are copied, not referenced. When you are trying to build a tree structure with a value type, references that were assigned are not updated with the correct information because values are copied. This effect can be demonstrated by going through a longer example of building a data structure of cities that can be reached from another city. To start off, consider the following declaration of all the cities and their coordinates.

```
Dim montreal As Node = New Node("Montreal", 0, 0)
Dim newyork As Node = New Node("New York", 0, -3)
Dim miami As Node = New Node("Miami", -1, -11)
Dim toronto As Node = New Node("Toronto", -4, -1)
Dim houston As Node = New Node("Houston", -10, -9)
Dim losangeles As Node = New Node("Los Angeles", -17, -6)
Dim seattle As Node = New Node("Seattle", -16, -1)
```

This code creates several Node objects that represent all of the cities from Figure 4-7. The individual objects are cities without connections, and the next step is to connect one city to another. We need to allocate and assign the Connections data member.

Having initialized all of the individual cities, the next step is to cross-reference the destinations of each city. In Visual Basic, the array requires some special understanding. The Connections data member is an empty array without any elements. This is not a problem, as long as you don't attempt to reference or assign any of the elements.

You need to allocate space for the array so that you can store the individual cities. One solution is to reassign the array to another array that contains elements, as follows:

```
montreal.Connections = New Node() {newyork, toronto, losangeles}
```

In this example, the Connections data member is reassigned with the contents of another array that has been allocated to contain the three cities; newyork, toronto, and losangeles. Think of the array as a basket. Using this approach, the original empty basket has been replaced with a basket of three items. These three items can be referenced using three indices (0 = newyork, 1 = toronto, 2 = losangeles). This solution creates a fixed-content basket.

Alternatively, you could create space in the basket and then manually fill the basket, as follows:

```
ReDim montreal.Connections(2)
montreal.Connections(0) = newyork
montreal.Connections(1) = toronto
montreal.Connections(2) = losangeles
```

The ReDim statement takes the array referenced by the data member Connections and reallocates it to a new size. That size could be larger or smaller than the current size. In the example, the size of the array is 2, which does not mean two elements, but rather that it is an array sized from the index 0 to 2.

The ReDim statement actually performs a redimension of an array. The example demonstrates using it on an empty array, but you can also use it with an array that contains data, such as to enlarge an array without losing the old data. To keep the old data in a new array, you use the Preserve keyword, as follows:

```
ReDim Preserve montreal.Connections(2)
montreal.Connections(0) = newyork
montreal.Connections(1) = toronto
montreal.Connections(2) = losangeles
```

However, be aware that if the ReDim statement causes an array to shrink, you can still lose data—whatever elements are located above the array size are discarded. To be safe, before using ReDim, you might want to reference the array's Length property to verify that you are not shrinking the array and losing data.

Using either the fixed-content or ReDim approach, you allocate space for the array and assign the variables representing the cities to the individual elements of the array. Since Connections is an array of value types, the connections within the connections are not set, as shown in Figure 4-10.

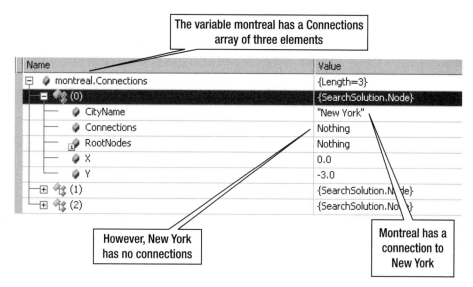

Figure 4-10. *The problem of the missing connections for New York*

The problem is that the Connections array for New York is missing. Of course, you could be logical and say it is missing because the Connections data member for New York has not yet been defined. But, and it is a big but, think about how data is referenced and think about the behavior summarized in Table 4-1.

Node is a value type, and when a value type is assigned, the values within the type are copied. Because the connections for New York have not been assigned, the Montreal Connections array will not contain any connections from New York. And if you modify the original variable for New York and its connections, those changes will not be reflected in the array of connections that Montreal has.

At this point, you might think this is not a problem, but consider the following New York code:

```
ReDim newyork.Connections(2)
newyork.Connections(0) = montreal
newyork.Connections(1) = houston
newyork.Connections(2) = miami
```

In this example, New York has a connection to Montreal, and Montreal has a connection to New York, completing a full circle. Commuters would want this ability to fly back and forth between cities. But because we are using value types, it is not possible to fly back and forth, as illustrated by Figure 4-11.

Figure 4-11 illustrates that recursion with value types does not work. It shows that there are connections from New York to Montreal. But following the connection to Montreal, it would appear that New York has no connections, which is blatantly false, because we can see the connection from New York to Montreal.

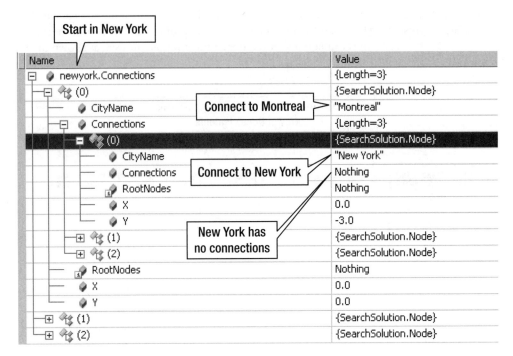

Figure 4-11. *Missing connections for New York*

When value types are assigned, you are copying contents of the value type and thus getting a snapshot of the state of an object at some period in time. In essence, the code illustrates the chicken-and-egg problem of defining the connections for a particular city and then assigning them. For value types, how can you assign the connection of one city to another when the to-be-assigned connection does not exist? The short answer is you can't. The long answer is you can, but it would mean executing an infinite loop, which is of no use to us, because we want to do something with the data once it has been assigned.

Switching to a Class to Define a Node

To fix the chicken-and-egg problem, we need to use reference types instead of value types. This means we need to change the declaration of Node from a Structure to a Class, as follows:

```
Public Class Node
    Public Shared RootNodes As Node()
    Public CityName As String
    Public X As Double
    Public Y As Double
    Public Connections As Node()
```

```
    Public Sub New(ByVal city As String, ByVal X As Double, ByVal Y As Double)
        Me.CityName = city
        Me.X = X
        Me.Y = Y
        Me.Connections = Nothing
    End Sub
End Class
```

The change is a one-liner. After the switch, if we executed the same assignment code as in the previous section when Node was a value type, the data structure shown in Figure 4-12 would be created.

Name	Value
⊟ ◆ newyork.Connections	{Length=3}
├─⊟ ⚸ (0)	{SearchSolution.Node}
│　　◆ CityName	"Montreal"
│　─⊟ ◆ Connections	{Length=3}
│　　─⊟ ⚸ (0)	{SearchSolution.Node}
│　　　　◆ CityName	"New York"
│　　　─⊟ ⚸ Connections	{Length=3}
│　　　　─⊟ ⚸ (0)	{SearchSolution.Node}
│　　　　　　◆ CityName	"Montreal"
│　　　　─⊞ ◆ Connections	{Length=3}
│　　　　　─ RootNodes	Nothing
│　　　　　　◆ X	0.0
│　　　　　　◆ Y	0.0

Figure 4-12. *A valid state for the New York Node instance*

Looking at the node structure in Figure 4-12, you can see that New York points to Montreal and back again. The infinite connection does not mean that you are using infinite resources. Instead, it means one reference is being set to another, as illustrated in Figure 4-13.

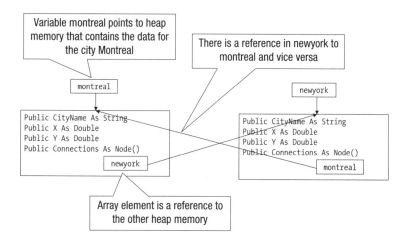

Figure 4-13. *Recursive assignment that seems like infinite resources*

The apparent infinite resources are the cross-reference recursive assignment of two pieces of heap memory. It is fine to do this, and this ability is one of the reasons why people prefer using reference types to value types.

Understanding Static Data Members and Methods

You've seen how a constructor can be used to initialize the state of a particular instance of a type. Now we need to define a constructor for the tree structure shown in Figure 4-2. A tree implies a starting point, but the code for the flight connections does not imply a single starting point. Instead, we have the declaration of a number of variables where the identifier of each variable is a city.

The problem with such a declaration is that, if you want to navigate a tree structure, you need to know the individual names of the variables and navigate the tree structure of each variable. This is not a plausible solution. You want to create a single overall point from where all other cities can be referenced.

The solution lies in using an array like that used for the data member Connections. To address the problem of providing a single access point, we declare a shared data member, as follows:

```
Public Class Node
    Public Shared RootNodes As Node()
    Public CityName As String
    Public X As Double
    Public Y As Double
    Public Connections As Node()

    Public Sub New(string city, double x, double y)
        Me.CityName = city
        Me.X = x
        Me.Y = y
        Me.Connections = Nothing
    End Sub
End Class
```

The bold code shows the declaration of a data member with the modifier Shared to indicate that the data member is shared. So, just what does *shared* mean in this context?

Let's say that your family consists of your significant other and two kids. One day, you wander into the cell phone store and decide to buy four identical cell phones, as the store is having a family deal. When each phone is activated, the state of each cell phone will be unique. Each person will have an individual number, address book, and so on. In the analogy to objects, the cell phone represents a type; each person is an instance of the same type, but with a unique state that represents an instantiation of the type.

Some cell phones have a feature called push-to-talk. Essentially, you convert a cell phone into a walkie-talkie. After buying individual cell phones for the family, the push-to-talk feature is activated for everyone in the family. This means if one person is using the push-to-talk feature, all family members will hear the conversation. The push-to-talk feature does not distinguish between the cell phones, so if multiple people talk at the same time, so be it; you'll hear quite a bit of noise. Push-to-talk is a shared resource, not associated with a particular cell phone. In the same way, Shared refers to a shared resource that is not associated with a particular type instance.

When you associate `Shared` with a data member, as in the code example you just saw, you are saying that, regardless of how many times you instantiate `Node`, there is always a single instance of the data member `RootNodes`. You don't even need to instantiate `Node` to access `RootNodes`. Shared methods are like shared data members, in that they are a shared resource and are not associated with a particular object (as illustrated by the `Main()` method used to start an application).

Figure 4-14 illustrates what you can and cannot do with shared and object instance data members.

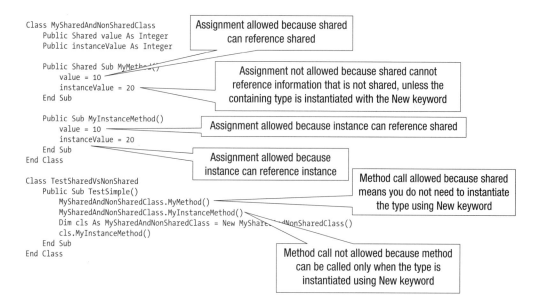

Figure 4-14. *Examples of shared and object instance data members*

The general rule of thumb is that shared data members or methods can be accessed without having to instantiate the type. Also, don't attempt to reference object instance data members or methods in a shared method.

Getting back to the `Node` declaration, the shared data member `RootNodes` is used to define a root for the search tree. As when instantiating a type, there is a constructor for the shared type that is called before the first time it is needed. The shared constructor is like the previously defined constructor, except the `Public` keyword is replaced with `Shared`. For the search tree case, it is used to initialize the tree and state.

We now have a complete definition of the `Node` class, with the following source code. Take a moment to look it over and fit the pieces together.

```
Public Class Node
    Shared Sub New()
        Dim montreal As Node = New Node("Montreal", 0, 0)
        Dim newyork As Node = New Node("New York", 0, -3)
        Dim miami As Node = New Node("Miami", -1, -11)
        Dim toronto As Node = New Node("Toronto", -4, -1)
        Dim houston As Node = New Node("Houston", -10, -9)
        Dim losangeles As Node = New Node("Los Angeles", -17, -6)
```

```
        Dim seattle As Node = New Node("Seattle", -16, -1)
        montreal.Connections = New Node() {newyork, toronto, losangeles}
        newyork.Connections = New Node() {montreal, houston, miami}
        miami.Connections = New Node() {toronto, houston, newyork}
        toronto.Connections = New Node() {miami, seattle, montreal}
        houston.Connections = New Node() {miami, seattle, newyork}
        seattle.Connections = New Node() {toronto, houston, losangeles}
        losangeles.Connections = New Node() {montreal, seattle, houston}
        Node.RootNodes = New Node() {montreal, newyork, miami, toronto, houston, _
                                losangeles, seattle}

    End Sub

    Public Sub New(ByVal city As String, ByVal X As Double, ByVal Y As Double)
        Me.CityName = city
        Me.X = X
        Me.Y = Y
        Me.Connections = Nothing
    End Sub

    Public CityName As String
    Public Connections As Node()
    Public Shared RootNodes As Node()
    Public X As Double
    Public Y As Double
End Class
```

Defining the Algorithm Test

The Node type is a self-contained type, meaning that the algorithm does not need to instantiate the tree structure (the Node constructor does it for you). This is an example of good design, because if you had to add more cities, the only changes required would be to Node itself. Any search algorithm that uses the Node type does not need to be changed.

■**Note** When you have the ability to create code that localizes changes without affecting other pieces of code, it is called *decoupling* code. You want to write code that is decoupled from other code, so that when changes are made in one piece of code, other pieces of code continue functioning. As you will experience when developing code, decoupling of code is a daily struggle.

For illustrative purposes, let's try a first stab at the search algorithm and see where things take us. We could start by defining the search class or start by defining the test that will test the search class. Let's define the test first, because it allows us to figure out what shape the search class should take:

```
Public Sub TestSearch()
  SearchAlgorithm.DepthFirstFindRoute("Montreal", "Seattle")
End Sub
```

In the test, the search algorithm is called directly using
`SearchAlgorithm.DepthFirstFindRoute()`. Here, `SearchAlgorithm` is the name of the class,
and `DepthFirstFindRoute()` is the name of the method. The class name implies that this class
will contain all search algorithm implementations. This is wrong, because most likely, each
search algorithm will require multiple methods, leading to a very large and complicated
`SearchAlgorithm` class. If this is the case, then maintaining the `SearchAlgorithm` class will
become a nightmare.

A better solution would be to identify a single class as being a single implementation of a
search algorithm. Then for each class, we can define a common method identifier that is used
to find the route between two points. Doing this results in the following modified test:

```
Public Sub TestSearch()
  DepthFirstSearch.FindRoute("Montreal", "Seattle")
End Sub
```

Now the test implies that the class `DepthFirstSearch` has a shared method `FindRoute()`.
This is acceptable, and if you were to implement `BreadthFirstSearch`, the naming would be
`BreadthFirstSearch.FindRoute()`. However, there is another problem, which relates to multiple
users being able to use the algorithm during the execution of a program. Going back to the
push-to-talk feature of a cell phone, the method `FindRoute()` is shared and thus a shared
resource. If multiple users do use this algorithm, they will share the resource. This could be
problematic if you are storing temporary data in the data members of the `DepthFirstSearch`
class. Using a shared method could corrupt your found search path.

The more appropriate solution is to define the method `FindRoute()` as a non-shared
method, implying that `DepthFirstSearch` must be instantiated before we can call `FindRoute()`.
We should modify the test again as follows:

```
Public Sub TestSearch()
  Dim cls As DepthFirstSearch = New DepthFirstSearch()
  cls.FindRoute("Montreal", "Seattle")
End Sub
```

To execute the method `FindRoute()`, we need to create a `DepthFirstSearch` object, allowing
multiple users to perform searches without getting state mixed up. At this point, we could pat
ourselves on the back and think that we have written a good test that requires a class
implementation.

The Problem of Magic Data

Our test is not yet complete, because we don't have access to the route found by the algorithm,
but that will be explained in a moment.

In the implementation of `DepthFirstSearch`, a reference to the data structure is necessary.
The search algorithm needs to know which tree to navigate. One way to implement a reference
to the tree is to directly reference the shared data `Node.RootNodes`. An implementation of
`DepthFirstSearch` would be as follows:

```
Public Class DepthFirstSearch
    Public Sub FindRoute(ByVal start As String, ByVal finish As String)
        Dim startNodes As Node() = Node.RootNodes
    End Sub
End Class
```

This example declares a variable called startNodes, which represents the starting point and root of the tree as shown in Figure 4-2. The root of the tree is based on the data member Node.RootNodes, and this assignment is called a *magic type assignment*. A magic type is formed when you call a method, and magically, it happens to know how to reference data, even though you never instructed the type. In the case of DepthFirstSearch, the magic is the ability of FindRoute() to know to reference the correct data member RootNodes.

The assumption is bad because it couples the data member RootNodes to the method FindRoute(). Imagine if the developer of the Node class later decides to add functionality to load the tree from a file on the hard disk. So that FindRoute() is not broken, the developer would need to explicitly copy the hard-disk-loaded tree to the data member RootNodes.

Or what if two different users wanted to create two different flight trees? Node.RootNodes is a shared resource, and thus can process only a single flight tree. The developer of Node might alter RootNodes, and thus FindRoute() would behave erratically.

When you have a case of magic data, whatever data is magic needs to be passed to the type via a constructor or other method. So the test for the flight route would change to the following:

```
Public Sub TestSearch()
  Dim cls As DepthFirstSearch= _
    New DepthFirstSearch(Node.RootNodes)
  cls.FindRoute("Montreal", "Seattle")
End Sub
```

As the root tree node is required, we change the constructor to require that a caller pass in the root tree node. The test code still uses the shared data member RootNodes, but DepthFirstSearch does not need to know where to find the tree. If the Node developer were to alter the behavior of the data member RootNodes, then only the constructor code to DepthFirstSearch would need altering, not the FindRoute() method. Thus, Node and DepthFirstSearch are properly decoupled from each other.

Getting the Found Route

Once you have called the FindRoute() method, you expect an answer. Because the route could involve multiple cities, the found route is stored in an array of Node elements. In programmatic terms, there are two ways of retrieving the array of Nodes. The first is a return value, like this:

```
Public Sub TestSearch()
  Dim cls As DepthFirstSearch = New DepthFirstSearch(Node.RootNodes)
  Dim foundRoute As Node() = cls.FindRoute("Montreal", "Seattle")
End Sub
```

The bold code shows the assignment of the return value to the variable foundRoute.

The second approach is for the FindRoute() method to store the result in an internal data member. The following example assumes that the FindRoute() method stores the result in a data member named FoundRoute:

```
Public Sub TestSearch()
  Dim cls As DepthfirstSearch = New DepthFirstSearch(Node.RootNodes)
  cls.FindRoute("Montreal", "Seattle")
  Dim foundRoute As Node() = cls.FoundRoute
End Sub
```

Each approach seems acceptable, and you are not sure which to use. When you have a choice like this, you need to make a decision. The safest way to make a decision is to write tests and see if there are any problems with either approach.

In the example of calculating a single route, either approach is fine. But let's look at the code when multiple routes are being searched. First, consider the code where the found path is a return parameter value:

```
Public Sub TestSearch()
  Dim cls As DepthFirstSearch = New DepthFirstSearch(Node.RootNodes)
  Dim foundRoute1 As Node() = cls.FindRoute("Montreal", "Seattle")
  Dim foundRoute2 As Node() = cls.FindRoute("New York", "Seattle")
End Sub
```

Now take a look at the code that uses the data member:

```
Public Sub TestSearch()
  Dim cls As DepthFirstSearch = New DepthFirstSearch(Node.RootNodes)
  cls.FindRoute("Montreal", "Seattle")
  Dim foundRoute1 As Node() = cls.FoundRoute
  cls.FindRoute("New York", "Seattle")
  Dim foundRoute2 As Node() = cls.FoundRoute
End Sub
```

Again, it would seem that both choices are adequate. However, there is a difference; the difference is subtle, but distinct enough to matter. In the test implementation where the found route is a return value, the variables foundRoute1 and foundRoute2 represent routes that relate directly to the route being searched. There is no chance that the variables foundRoute1 can represent the route New York–Seattle. With the data member code, it could happen that foundRoute1 points to the route New York–Seattle, as shown in the following code.

```
Public Sub TestSearch()
  Dim cls As DepthFirstSearch = New DepthFirstSearch(Node.RootNodes)
  cls.FindRoute("Montreal", "Seattle")
  cls.FindRoute("New York", "Seattle")
  Dim foundRoute1 As Node() = cls.FoundRoute
  Dim foundRoute2 As Node() = cls.FoundRoute
End Sub
```

By switching the order of the FindRoute() method calls and references to the data member FoundRoute, the variables foundRoute1 and foundRoute2 will reference the same found route, specifically the route New York–Seattle. This is not a good idea. The example shows how data members have no direct relation to methods and can vary independently.

So the choice of returning the found route from a method is the better and more robust approach.

■**Note** Data members are useful when you want to store or retrieve data that spans multiple method calls or is not dependent on the order of how methods are called. When you have data that is dependent on the order of called methods, you should use the Return keyword or ByRef parameters.

The following is the complete test case that includes the verification code that searches for a flight from Montreal to Seattle.

```
Public Sub TestSearch()
    Dim cls As DepthFirstSearch = New DepthFirstSearch(Node.RootNodes)
    Dim foundRoute As Node() = cls.FindRoute("Montreal", "Seattle")
    If foundRoute.Length <> 2 Then
        Console.WriteLine("Incorrect route as route has two legs")
    End If
    If foundRoute(0).CityName.CompareTo("Los Angeles") <> 0 Then
        Console.WriteLine("Incorrect as first leg is Los Angeles")
    End If
End Sub
```

■**Note** We've already used the If construct in earlier chapters. It tests a condition and executes its contained code if that condition is true. The <> means does not equal. We'll examine If in more detail later in this chapter, in the "Using the If Statement" section.

Implementing the Depth-First Search Algorithm

The implementation of the depth-first search algorithm involves creating an algorithm that iterates the tree. Here, we'll implement the algorithm in Visual Basic. In so doing, we'll use decision statements and For loops to iterate the array data. These are incredibly common in Visual Basic programs, and life would be very difficult without them.

We implemented the test code in the previous section, so the next step is to implement a version of DepthFirstSearch that represents a shell, so that all of the code compiles and runs. The shell is structural and is used to hold up the entire application. It is defined as shown in Figure 4-15.

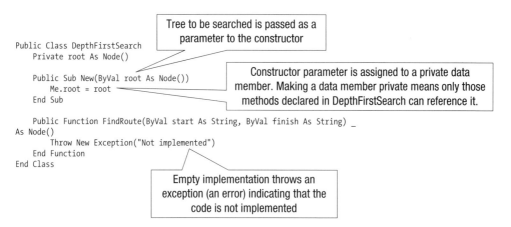

Figure 4-15. *The initial shell of the depth-first algorithm*

With a shell implemented, you could run the application and see if everything works. If you do run the test code, you will get an error, because calling `FindRoute()` generates an exception that indicates `FindRoute()` has not been fully implemented. (Exceptions are discussed in detail in the next chapter.) However, the shell is complete, and we are ready to implement the guts of the algorithm.

Implementing the guts of an algorithm is arguably one of the most difficult steps, as you must go through the logic of what you want to do. Whenever I am confronted with an algorithm that needs implementation and I am not quite sure how to proceed, I just write code, based on an entry point (the method call) and an exit point (the end of a method's execution).

The Keyhole Problem

In the example, the entry and exit point into the algorithm is `FindRoute()`. In turn, the entry of `FindRoute()` is two parameters: `start`, indicating the beginning city, and `finish`, indicating the destination city. The exit of `FindRoute()` is an array of `Node` objects.

The array of `Node` objects needs to be preallocated with space so that all of the found cities can be added. We can make an assumption at this point that we preallocate the number of nodes to the length of the data member `DepthFirstSearch.root` plus one. The assumption is that the longest trip cannot exceed the number of cities available. We know that the root node is an array of all starting point cities, thus the allocation can never be exceeded.

Focusing on the `FindRoute()` method, the updated code looks like this:

```
Public Function FindRoute(ByVal start As String, ByVal finish As String) As Node()
    Dim returnArray(Me.root.Length + 1) As Node
    Return returnArray
End Function
```

The code with the array allocation is a classic keyhole problem (an idea first introduced by Scott Meyers; see `http://www.aristeia.com/TKP/`). The problem of a keyhole is that you implement an algorithm based on assumptions that cause you to write code that works for that specific context, but would fail when executed in another context.

The code allocates an array to the length of the root tree structure, and that is making a grand assumption. Imagine if the Node developers decided to introduce connections that could be reached only via another city that is not included in the root nodes. At that point, you could potentially exceed the available space in the array. Another solution would be to allocate an array of arbitrary length X. But then, if there were $X+1$ unique cities, another array could be violated.

The simplest solution would be to not allocate an array, but instead figure out how many elements you needed after having found a path. However, this would not work, because then you would have no idea which city you had already visited. Another solution (which will be discussed in Chapter 9) would be to use a collection class.

In this case, we are going to wash our hands of the problem and force the Node developers to modify their class. The Node developers are going to add a shared method that tells the search algorithm how big the array needs to be. The following is the modified FindRoute() code.

```
Public Function FindRoute(ByVal start As String, ByVal finish As String) As Node()
    Dim returnArray(Node.GetMaxPossibleDestinationsArraySize()) As Node
    Return returnArray
End Function
```

Now the code doesn't have a keyhole problem from the perspective of DepthFirstSearch, because Node will always indicate the appropriate size for the array. If there is still not enough room, the problem will lie with Node. This is not an ideal solution, but sometimes it's the only option.

Using the For Loop

The root node (root) references a list of cities that are available as a starting point. To start off the search, the first step is to match the starting city with the start parameter by iterating over the list of cities. For that, we need the For loop. Here is the modified source code of FindRoute():

```
Public Function FindRoute(ByVal start As String, ByVal finish As String) As Node()
    Dim returnArray(Node.GetMaxPossibleDestinationsArraySize()) As Node
    For c1 As Integer = 0 To root.Length - 1
        If Me.root(c1).CityName.CompareTo(start) = 0 Then
            returnArray(0) = Me.root(c1)
            FindNextLeg(returnArray, 1, finish, root(c1))
        End If
    Next
    Return returnArray
End Function
```

The For loop starts counting at 0 and goes to the end of the root array using the Me.root. Length property. For each loop iteration, the root(c1).CityName is tested to see if it is the starting city. Then the starting city is assigned as the first city in the array that represents the found travel route (returnArray(0) = Me.root(c1)). Finally, the method FindNextLeg() is used to find a possible route to the destination.

A For loop is used to go through a series based on some logic. For the most part, that series involves incrementing or decrementing numbers, but it can use other kinds of logic.

The For loop has the following form:

```
For [variable] [As type] = [starting condition] To [ending condition] [step size]
      [Operations of doing something]
Next
```

where:

[variable]: Defines the variable that will serve as the counter in the loop.

[As type]: An optional definition used to define the type of the counter in the loop. For the most part, the counter will be a numeric value. However, you can have other types as long as the increment operators are supported.

[starting condition]: Defines the initial state of the counter when the loop is started.

[ending condition]: Defines the ending state that will terminate the looping. An example loop termination is when a counter reaches the maximum length of an array, and thus no more elements can be referenced.

[step size]: The size of the step that the counter should take. By default, the size of a step is 1, indicating an incrementing counter value. If the step size were -1, the counter would decrement. A decrementing counter is OK, but you must remember to assign appropriate starting and ending conditions, where the ending condition has a lesser value than the starting condition.

The main purpose of the For loop is to generate a series of numbers that could be used as indexes to an array. In the case of iterating over the array, it generated a series of numbers (0, 1, 2, 3, and so on), and each number was then used to reference an array element in Me.root.

■Note The rule of thumb for a For loop is that it is employed to generate an index series that is used to reference another piece of information. The index series could be a direct array element reference, or it could be used to perform a calculation, which is then used to generate a reference to a piece of data. The index series does not need to generate incremental or decremental values. The index series does need to generate a logical index series.

Using the If Statement

When the starting point city has been found, the tree will begin to search down the tree. A depth-first search means that the search will travel down the tree as far as it can before backtracking and trying other routes. The recursion of traveling down the tree is managed by the FindNextLeg() method, which is defined as shown in Figure 4-16.

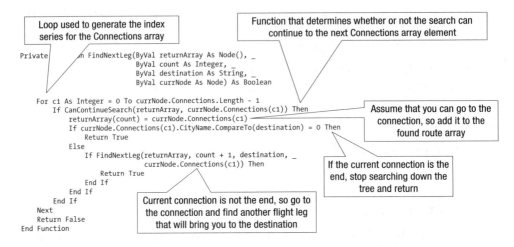

Figure 4-16. *FindNextLeg() looks for the next leg in the journey.*

The big idea here is to create a flight route by traveling the tree of connections in the hope that one of the connections will cause you to end up at your end point. Notice that for each leg, the parameter count is incremented, so as you progress a level deeper in the tree, you assign the city at the level to the found route array.

What makes this function tick is the decision code represented by an If code block. The If code block says, "If this decision test is true, then execute the code within the If block; otherwise, move to the code immediately after the If block."

An If statement has the following form:

```
If [condition] Then
   [Do action]
ElseIf [condition] Then
   [Do action]
Else
   [Do action]
End If
```

The statements If, ElseIf, and Else together represent one piece of logic (for example, if this cannot happen, then test the ElseIf; if that cannot happen, then do the default in the Else). The statements after the first If are optional.

The [condition] must return a True or False value. A True value means to execute the actions within the block, and a False value means to try the next code statement.

The Else statement is a sort of default catchall that is executed if none of the other If statements prove to be true.

Here is an example of logic executed in an If statement:

```
If test1 Then
   ' Code1
ElseIf test2 Then
   ' Code2
```

```
Else
  ' Code3
End If
' Code4
```

The following code steps are executed:

- If test1 is True, then execute Code1. After executing Code1, execute Code4.

- If test1 is False, jump to ElseIf with test2.

- If test2 is True, then execute Code2. After executing Code2, execute Code4.

- If test2 is False, jump to Else.

- Execute Code3. After executing Code3, execute Code4.

Here is another example:

```
If test1 Then
  ' Code1
Else
  ' Code2
End If
' Code3
```

The executed code steps are as follows:

- If test1 is True, then execute Code1. After executing Code1, execute Code3.

- If test1 is False, jump to Else.

- Execute Code2. After executing Code2, execute Code3.

And here is one more example:

```
If test1 Then
  ' Code1
End If
If test2 Then
  ' Code2
Else
  ' Code3
End If
// Code4
```

The executed code steps are as follows:

- If test1 is True, then execute Code1. After executing Code1, jump to If with test2.

- If test1 is False, jump to If with test2.

- If test2 is True, then execute Code2. After executing Code2, execute Code4.

- If test2 is False, jump to Else.

- Execute Code3. After executing Code3, execute Code4.

The following code is illegal:

```
Else
  ' Code2
End If
' Code3
```

And this is also illegal:

```
ElseIf test2 Then
  ' Code2
Else
  ' Code3
End If
```

It is possible to have one If statement embedded within an Else, If, or ElseIf to create a more complex multilevel decision tree.

The condition or test[N] variables are Boolean values that can contain True or False. You have already seen examples of these, like this:

```
If CanContinueSearch(returnArray, currNode.Connections(c1)) Then
```

The If statement says that if the method CanContinueSearch() returns True, then execute the contained code.

Here is another example of a condition:

```
If returnArray(c1) IsNot Nothing  Then
```

This If statement says that if the array element returnArray[(c1) does not have a value of Nothing, then execute the contained code.

In both examples, either the method or comparison must return a Boolean value. If a Boolean value is not returned, the Visual Basic compiler will generate an error indicating that the code does not result in a True or False value.

It is easy to see how a method can generate a True or False value, but the array element not equal to Nothing statement is a bit more complicated. The statement is an example of using operators to perform a comparison. Comparisons test if things are equal to each other or not equal to each other. Table 4-2 shows the comparison operators and what they mean.

Table 4-2. *Comparison Operators*

Expression	Description
a = b	Does a equal b?
a <> b	Does a not equal b?
a > b	Is a greater than b?
a < b	Is a less than b?

Table 4-2. *Comparison Operators*

Expression	Description
a >= b	Is a greater than or equal to b?
a <= b	Is a less than or equal to b?
Not a	A change operator that says if a is True then False, and if a is False then True

Additionally, you can use the following operators in the context of a decision:

- And: If both tests are True, then return True; otherwise, return False.

- Or: If both tests are False, then return False; otherwise, return true.

These operators can be combined, as follows:

```
If a = b And b = c Then
```

This example includes two expressions that test for equality. Then the results are compared using the And operator. If both results are True, then the And operator will return True. In a nutshell, the decision tests if a equals b equals c.

Visual Basic also includes some special short-circuit operators:

- AndAlso: Like an And, but a short-circuit.

- OrElse: Like an Or, but a short-circuit.

Short-circuiting sounds like a funny thing, but it serves a real purpose. Let's look at the compound If statement again.

```
If a = b And b = c Then
```

Suppose that a is 10, b is 20, and c is 20. We have the facts that b equals c, but a does not equal b. As a human, if you mentally went through the If statement, you would test a equals b, and since that is false, you would not test b equals c. That would be pointless, because a does not equal b, and the result of b equals c is irrelevant. However, that irrelevance is not apparent in the Visual Basic language when you use the And operator. The Visual Basic language will go through the steps of verifying both parts of the compound statement, even though it might be pointless. The AndAlso operator used in place of And says if a does not equal b, then stop processing and move to the next piece of code.

The real question is why make the difference between AndAlso and And? I can only postulate, but in the early, early days of Visual Basic, programmers used to write code like this:

```
If a = b And b = code.NextStatement() Then
```

The method NextStatement() not only verifies state, but also modifies state. If a did not equal b, then the state was not modified. And that was a problem, since some programmers relied on the fact that the other piece of code would be called regardless of how it was used. Think about this logically, and you'll see it is not incorrect. After all, what is the difference between the following two pieces of code?

If b = code.NextStatement() and a = b Then

and

If b = code.NextStatement() Then

The answer is nothing, but if And behaved like AndAlso by default, then you would get an inconsistent state.

Preventing Repetition in the Route

The FindNextLeg() method calls the CanContinue() method, which is designed to halt the search. In the case of our depth-first search algorithm, the purpose is to not fly to the same city twice. Contained within the function is code similar to FindNextLeg():

```
Private Function CanContinueSearch(ByVal returnArray As Node(), _
ByVal city As Node) As Boolean
  For c1 As Integer = 0 To  returnArray.Length - 1
    If returnArray(c1) IsNot Nothing Then
      If returnArray(c1).CityName.CompareTo(city.CityName) = 0 Then
        Return False
      End If
    End If
  Next
  Return True
End Function
```

The logic is that CanContinueSearch() will iterate through the returnArray and see if the city being considered (variable city) is already in the found path. If the city is in the path, then we stop searching that part of the tree; otherwise, we continue searching.

Running the Depth-First Search Algorithm

Everything has been implemented, including tests, so we are ready to run the test of finding the flight between Montreal and Seattle. Looking at Figure 4-2, you can see two paths: Montreal to Los Angeles to Seattle, or Montreal to Toronto to Seattle. However, running the algorithm generates the following peculiar result (you have not seen how to display the results, but that is done easily enough with a For loop that iterates over foundRoute):

- Montreal

- New York

- Houston

- Miami

- Toronto

- Seattle

Looking at the result, you are probably thinking that the algorithm does not work, because the proposed flight includes every city except Los Angeles. If a travel agent were to propose such a flight route to you, you would probably have a panic attack.

The algorithm did not fail; rather, the `CanContinueSearch()` function did not include functionality to optimize the flight. Right now, the algorithm says to perform a depth-first search, meaning to go down the tree before backtracking. So let's go through the structure in the `Node` shared constructor again.

We started our route in Montreal, which had the following `Connections` definitions:

```
montreal.Connections = New Node() { newyork, toronto, losangeles }
```

Applying our depth-first algorithm, it means the first array element of the tree is considered a connection, and thus our route takes us to New York. New York has the following flight connections:

```
newyork.Connections = New Node() { montreal, houston, miami }
```

The first connection from New York is Montreal, which is already in the flight route. Thus, the second array element is searched, which is Houston. Houston has the following flight connections:

```
houston.Connections = New Node() { miami, seattle, newyork }
```

Following the flight route from Houston, we travel to Miami, which has the following connections:

```
miami.Connections = New Node() { toronto, houston, newyork }
```

Following the flight route from Miami, we travel to Toronto, which has the following connections:

```
toronto.Connections = New Node() { miami, seattle, montreal }
```

At Toronto, the first connection is Miami, where we have already been. The second connection is Seattle, and that is our end destination.

So from the perspective of the algorithm, everything worked. From the perspective of the traveler, it's not ideal. This demonstrates yet again how important it is to write test routines, as algorithms might be correct, but they will generate responses that you might not have anticipated. Improving the example is one of the exercises at the end of the chapter.

The Important Stuff to Remember

In this chapter, you learned about data structures and algorithms. Here are the key points to keep in mind:

- When developing a program, you need to think of the data structures and algorithms that are involved.

- A single best data structure and a single best algorithm do not exist. Every data structure and algorithm has compromises. You need to choose the data structure and algorithm that best suits your needs with the least number of critical compromises.

- Data structures and algorithms do not need to be the same class. They can be different types and often are.

- Data structures can be implemented using value (Structure) or reference (Class) types.

- Value types when used as data structures have three constraints that you need to be aware of that relate to the fact that data is copied, what happens when you embed reference types in value types, and what happens when you use value types as parameters to methods.

- For the most part, you will use reference types, but you can also use value types. When using value types, you need to be aware of how a value behaves; otherwise, you might get undesirable interactions.

- A constructor is a special type of method that is called when a type is being instantiated. You would assign parameters to a constructor when you want to enforce a verifiably correct state for the object.

- A rule of thumb when trying to decide whether to use value and reference types is to consider the context. Are you creating a simple assign-once structure, or are you creating a complex navigable structure? If your structure is complex, then use a reference type; otherwise, a value type is fine.

- When you instantiate a type, each object has its own set of instances of methods and data members. When a type has methods or data members declared with the Shared keyword, that type has a single instance of the shared method or data member and is not associated with a type instance.

- Writing the test before the type implementation allows a developer to get a feeling of how the type should look and behave, and gives some guidance.

- When you write methods, you don't want to rely too heavily on magic data making everything work. When writing classes, you need to think in terms of IKEA furniture (assembly required), as that will make your code more flexible and a candidate for reuse.

- When you write a For loop, think of the statements in the brackets as being code that generates an index that is used to retrieve the actual information being iterated over.

- Decisions are implemented using a combination of If, ElseIf, and Else statements.

Some Things for You to Do

The following are some exercises to practice what you learned in this chapter.

1. Node was declared to be a reference type. Can you think of where in the declaration of Node it would be more appropriate to use a value type? And if you can think of it, rewrite Node.

2. The shared data member Node.RootNodes is exposed for every class to consume. Is there a way to decouple RootNodes so that the user of Node is not aware of the location of the tree?

3. We discussed a keyhole problem regarding the allocation of an array. Yet there is also a coupling problem between Node and DepthFirstSearch. Explain why there is a coupling problem and outline an alternative algorithm that does not have the coupling problem.

4. Fix the CanContinueSearch() function so that an optimal flight path is found for any two cities. Note that you should extend your test cases to test various scenarios.

5. Implement the breadth-first search algorithm. The breadth-first algorithm will search each connection before going down further in the tree. Hint: modify the behavior of FindNextLeg().

CHAPTER 5

■■■

Learning About Visual Basic Exception Handling

Source code can have thousands, hundreds of thousands, or millions of lines of source code, and no single human could keep track of it all. To keep track of all the source code, you need a team of developers, and that means code written by one developer is going to be used and modified by another developer. Since the two developers can't perform a Vulcan mind meld, they must have a well-understood and useful form of communication. But that's just part of the solution. The code itself must be easy to understand.

The challenge of writing software is not creating a perfect piece of code, but writing code that can be understood by other developers and used by other pieces of software. The goal isn't to be clever and write software that can do everything, but to write simple, robust, and easy-to-understand software. The "keep it simple" approach is the best way forward.

Having understandable code is particularly important when things go wrong. Your code should generate the appropriate errors. For example, suppose your code relies on a file being present. When the file is not present, your code should generate a clear and distinct error, such as "File XYZ is not present and thus I cannot continue." Upon seeing such an error message, another developer would know that he should check whether the file is actually there.

This chapter explains exceptions, as errors in an application are technically known, and how to handle them. We'll begin with an overview of how exceptions fit into the structure of a program.

Understanding Errors, Exceptions, and Exception Handling

An error is when something is not right and could be the result of incorrect data or an incorrect calculation. However, the .NET CLR does not understand errors; it understands only exceptions.

For example, if an error is caused by multiplying two numbers rather than adding them, your program will continue to function, but will produce the wrong results. A similar error occurs when a user enters the wrong data—the answer will be wrong, but the program will still run.

In the case of a serious problem that is beyond the control of the user or that threatens to crash your program, the CLR steps in and treats this as an exception. This interrupts the program and allows your code to deal with the problem, rather than letting the program crash. (Some would argue that an exception will not halt your entire program, but a thread of your program; while this is technically true, it's not an important distinction for this introduction to exceptions.) This is called *exception handling*.

To understand how code organization affects exception handling, think of an application as a large corporation. A corporation has a chief executive officer (CEO), then first-level managers, then mid-level managers. Corporations and management within corporations understand that to get anything done, they must develop a game plan and then carry out the game plan. The CEO or highest level manager will know about the overall game plan. The company is organized so that lower-level managers and workers can carry out discrete tasks as defined in the game plan. In other words, these organizational units carry out the implementation of the plan.

Translating this to software, your code contains two types of methods: methods that organize the functionality and methods that implement the functionality. You create organizational code so that you have the ability to separate each task from the others. The work of one does not affect the other, and thus the code has been modularized.

Note As with corporation reorganization, management code is constantly being reorganized to fix bugs and implement new pieces of functionality. For example, you might reorganize code so that it becomes more streamlined and efficient.

Now we need to put exceptions into the picture. Errors occur when something does not go according to plan. In the management hierarchy, if an error occurs, the CEO is not automatically told. For example, if the company ran out of staples, most likely the CEO would not want to hear about it. If, however, one of the manufacturing plants fell off the side of a cliff, then the CEO would definitely want to know. The information about the error is passed up the chain of command just as far as it needs to go.

Relating this to the different types of methods, in your hierarchical code, the implementation code is responsible for making sure all errors are reported, and the organizational code is responsible for either fixing the error or propagating it to a piece of code that is higher in the hierarchy. The higher piece of code should either fix the problem or delegate it again to a higher piece of code, depending on the seriousness of the error.

For the remainder of this chapter, we'll look at the various ways of dealing with exceptions. The idea is to give you practical solutions that you can use without getting too bogged down in theoretical what-ifs.

When working with exceptions, it is often useful to run the application in Visual Basic's debugger, so let's start there.

Running the Debugger

The Visual Basic debugger runs the application, but adds the ability to monitor what the application is doing. To start the debugger, select Debug ➤ Start Debugging from the menu bar or press F5.

Your application will run as normal, but Visual Basic Express's layout will change slightly. From the perspective of the application, you will not see a difference in its behavior. The application executes in the same way, regardless of whether it is being run or being debugged. To stop debugging, just close your application normally.

■**Tip** You may find it useful to display the Locals and Call Stack panes, which allow you to see what is going on in the application. To do so, start debugging and select Debug ➤ Windows, and then choose the window (Call Stack or Locals).

You can also start the debugger at a certain point in your code by setting a breakpoint, as shown in Figure 5-1. When Visual Basic reaches this breakpoint, it goes into *debug mode*; this mode is different from *application mode*—the state it is in before it reaches the breakpoint and after it leaves the breakpoint. To leave debug mode, you can press the F5 key to switch to application mode and continue executing the application, or press Ctrl+Alt+Break to stop debugging and stop executing the application.

Figure 5-1. *Debugging an application with a breakpoint*

Running an application in the debugger is useful when tracking down exceptions, as you'll see in the next section.

Handling Exceptions

Those who recall the "good old days" of Windows 3.0 and its 16 bits will also remember the dreaded three-finger salute. The three-finger salute refers to pressing Ctrl+Alt+Delete to reboot Windows after a program crashed. You did not have the chance to save your work; you just had to watch everything go down the drain.

If you missed those computing days, count yourself lucky. Nowadays, we have mechanisms to catch unexpected errors and make sure that the program or operating system keeps on processing.

The big deal with modern operating systems and programming environments like the CLR is that they can stop a single task from disrupting the operation of the CPU.

Catching Exceptions

Recall that in Chapter 2, Visual Basic Express interrupted the flow of the program by catching the exception generated by a mathematical overflow situation. This is like your driving teacher realizing you are making a mistake and pressing hard on the brake, so you don't hit a tree, person, or another car. So, in a sense, you can think of the CLR exception-handling mechanism as the teacher stepping on the brake when something devastating is about to happen.

Stepping on the brake stops the devastation, but you, as the driver, will get a shock because of the error that you were about to make. Likewise, when an exception is triggered, the program gets a shock. How you deal with the shock determines the fate of the program. In the example of the overflow error in Chapter 2, the shock was captured by the IDE, and thus a friendly, easy-to-understand user interface was presented.

Consider the source code shown in Figure 5-2, which generates an exception. This is referred to as *throwing* an exception.

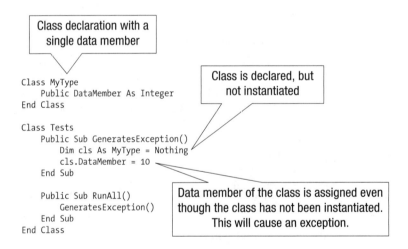

Figure 5-2. *Throwing an exception*

If the RunAll() method were executed, the exception shown in Figure 5-3 would be generated in Visual Basic Express (use F5 to run the debugger).

The exception did not cause the operating system or Visual Basic Express to crash, because Visual Studio's built-in exception handler caught it. Visual Studio hit the brake and made sure that only your program stopped working.

Imagine if Visual Studio were not running. The generated exception would cause the program to stop in its tracks, and a messy error message would appear, referencing objects, line numbers, and the stack. Most users would have no idea what happened, and be left with a program that was not working anymore.

Figure 5-3. *An exception generated by a null reference*

What you want to do is catch the exception as Visual Studio did. For example, if you knew that an exception could occur in RunAll(), you could modify the code as follows:

```
Class MyType
    Public DataMember As Integer
End Class
Class Tests
    Public Sub GeneratesException()
        Dim cls As MyType = Nothing
        cls.DataMember = 10
    End Sub
    Public Sub RunAll()
        Try
            GeneratesException()
        Catch exception1 As Exception
        End Try
    End Sub
End Class
```

The bolded code is an *exception block*, which catches an exception and allows you to respond to it. In this example, nothing happens after catching the exception. If you run this program, Visual Basic will not generate an exception warning, and the program will run without any problems. From the perspective of Visual Basic, everything worked and is running OK.

But if you stop and think about it, is everything really OK? Even though the program continued to execute, was the program logically correct? The answer is no, because what the program did was swallow an exception without doing anything to remedy the problem. You should not do such a thing, because it implies sloppy programming.

■**Note** In practice, there are some cases when you need to swallow errors because you cannot process the data in any other way. This can happen when you are dealing with network connections, database operations, and the like. However, in the majority of cases, you should not swallow the exception.

A real-world example of when you might want to throw an exception is because a parameter is not valid. As you will learn in the "Filtering Exceptions" section later in this chapter, there is an exception type for just this purpose, ArgumentException(). Developers who received that exception would then be able to easily figure out that they must fix a parameter. This saves debugging time and reduces overall development time.

The real work in exception handling is adding all of the possible exceptions that could occur. But what is better: hunting down the cause of the error or adding the code to help you find the error easily? In the long run, adding the code to help track down the error saves time and avoids frustration.

Implementing Exception Handlers

An exception handler is implemented using the Try, Catch, and Finally keywords. When you implement an exception handler, you are saying that for a specific code block, if an exception is generated, you will catch it and process the exception.

An exception handler has the following form:

```
[action 1]
Try
    [action 2]
Catch exception1 As Exception
    [action 3]
End Try
[action 4]
```

The notation of an exception handler is simple. The Try and Catch keywords define the boundaries of a code block that is protected. *Protected* means that any generated exception will need to pass through the exception handler. If an exception is thrown by the protected code, the code in the Catch block will execute and allow you to process the exception. Catch is the keyword defined immediately after the Try block, and the Catch block specifies which exception is caught and defines the steps to take when an exception occurs.

If code within the Try block (action 2 in the example) calls another method, then the code within the called method is protected. This is the case even if the code is not protected from the perspective of the method. Figure 5-4 illustrates how exceptions are caught when multiple methods are involved.

In Figure 5-4, the protected code of action 2 calls a method that has action 2.1, action 2.2, and action 2.4. action 2.2 executes in the context of an exception block, and thus if action 2.2 throws an exception, it will be caught and processed by action 2.3. The Catch block containing action 3 is not aware an exception occurred. From the perspective of the called method, action 2.1 and action 2.4 are not protected, but because the called method is called from action 2, which is protected by the Catch block containing action 3, action 2.1 and action 2.4 are considered protected. If action 2.1 or action 2.4 had thrown an exception, then the Catch block with action 3 would have caught the exception. This example illustrates two things:

- Exceptions can span method calls.

- When an exception is thrown, the handler will catch it closest to the place where the exception occurred.

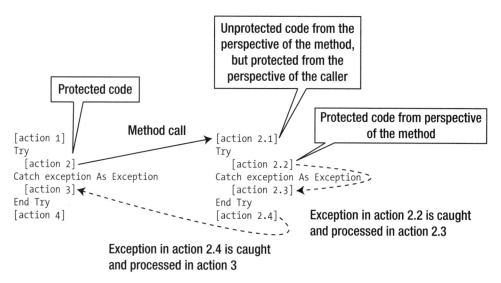

Figure 5-4. *Exceptions and calling methods that generate exceptions*

An example of how exceptions function is our legal court system. Let's say that you want to slap someone with a lawsuit. If the lawsuit is a civil case, it will be heard by the local court. You cannot bring a civil lawsuit directly to the supreme court level until it has been heard by the lower court levels. If the lawsuit is a criminal case, most likely it will be heard at the state/provincial level first. The local municipality will not hear the case because it is not in the jurisdiction of that court.

The same behavior occurs with exceptions and exception handlers. An exception might be caught and processed by one exception handler, without the exception being processed by a higher-level exception handler. This situation is illustrated in Figure 5-3 where an exception was thrown and caught by the IDE. An exception that was thrown several method calls deep was caught at the highest level.

In previous examples, an exception was thrown because the code did something that it was not supposed to do. However, you can throw an exception on purpose by using the following syntax:

```
Throw New Exception()
```

When you throw an exception like this, you instantiate a type that is related to the base type Exception. Associating the Throw keyword with an object creates an exception that can be caught by a Catch block.

In most cases of throwing an exception, you will instantiate the exception type as you throw it. The previous example uses the parameterless Exception() constructor, but other variations are available, as shown in the following code.

```
Try
    Throw New Exception("Exception in action 2.4.")
Catch thrown As Exception
    Throw New Exception("Exception in action 2 has been caught.", thrown)
End Try
```

The first variation, `Exception("Exception in action 2.4.")`, uses the string description constructor parameter that passes text describing what went wrong. The text is meant for human understanding, so don't use text like "Error 168: something went wrong." The second variation, `Exception("Exception in action 2 has been caught.", thrown)`, includes the original exception as an additional constructor parameter in a newly thrown exception. This allows you to pass on even more information.

The generated output of this code looks like this:

```
Unhandled Exception: System.Exception: Exception in action 2 has been caught.
---> System.Exception: Exception in action 2.4.
```

The generated exception tells you clearly where the exception occurred and where it was processed. You have a complete flow of the actions.

■Note An experienced developer may say that the flow is also presented by the stack that is dumped by the program if the exception is not caught. Yes, you could see the program flow based on this stack dump, but deciphering a stack dump where you have a stack of say 10 or 15 is not much fun to figure out or read.

Consider the following amendment to the code, which reduces the amount of information.

```
Try
    Throw New Exception("Exception in action 2.4.")
Catch exception1 As Exception
    Throw New Exception("Exception in action 2 has been caught")
End Try
```

The results are not as enlightening:

```
Unhandled Exception: System.Exception: Exception in action 2 has been caught.
```

If you want to gain access to the error string, you can use the `Message` property of an exception.

```
Try
    Throw New Exception("Exception in action 2.4.")
Catch thrown As Exception
    Console.WriteLine(thrown.Message)
    Throw New Exception("Exception in action 2 has been caught.")
End Try
```

You still have the more specific message, but not as part of the flow of exceptions:

Exception in action 2.4.

Unhandled Exception: System.Exception: Exception in action 2 has been caught.

DON'T REPEAT ERROR MESSAGES

When you throw exceptions, make sure that you don't use the same error message twice. Imagine the situation where you deliver a program into production and the error message "File not found" is generated. If this text is used in multiple places, when the user calls tech support, the support staff will have no idea which file was not found. Instead, in the error message, tell the user which file was not found and why. The more details you deliver, the easier it is for the support desk to help users get around the problem.

If you do need to use the same text in multiple places, add a context identifier. For example, you could generate a load error fault in the context of loading a file using a dialog box. Or you could generate a load error in the context of loading a file based on a command-line argument. Specify each context as an additional piece of information appended or prefixed to the exception text, much like the previous code illustrated when catching an exception in action 2.

Safeguarding Against Stack Unwinding

Exception handling makes it simple for you to stop your program from crashing, but it does not help you from ensuring that the state of your application is still intact. Consider the example shown in Figure 5-5, which illustrates how program state can be corrupted due to an exception that is caught and swallowed.

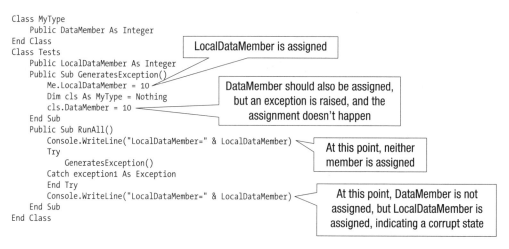

Figure 5-5. *Exceptions can corrupt the state of a program.*

When an exception is caught, the stack is unwound. Consider the example shown in Figure 5-6, where the unwinding of the stack can have the side effect of jumping over a method call.

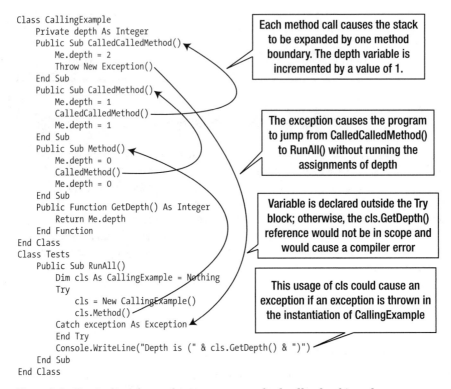

Figure 5-6. *Unwinding the stack can cause a method call to be skipped.*

In the example in Figure 5-6, the methods are called sequentially, starting with RunAll(), and then when a single exception is thrown, the code in the RunAll() method's Catch block is executed immediately. So, depth has a value of 2 instead of a value of 0 (the value you would expect if no exception were thrown) when execution finishes. You can see that the stack has unwound too fast, leaving the program with unpredictable results.

The stack unwinding problem causes corruption and can wreak havoc on your program. A seemingly working program might corrupt itself and slowly fail or generate incorrect data. Fortunately, there are a couple ways to handle stack unwinding correctly.

Using Finally to Process Unfinished Tasks

The simplest solution to the stack unwinding problem is to use the Finally keyword, which indicates that you want to guarantee a piece of code executes, whether or not an exception is thrown. The following shows how you could rewrite the example in Figure 5-6 using Finally. When executed, this code will set the depth data member to the correct value.

```
Class CallingExample
    Dim depth As Integer
    Public Sub CalledCalledMethod()
        Me.depth = 2
        Throw New Exception()
    End Sub
```

```vb
    Public Sub CalledMethod()
        Me.depth = 1
        Try
            CalledCalledMethod()
        Finally
            Me.depth = 1
        End Try
    End Sub
    Public Sub Method()
        Me.depth = 0
        Try
            CalledMethod()
        Finally
            Me.depth = 0
        End Try
    End Sub
    Public Function GetDepth() As Integer
        Return Me.depth
    End Function
End Class

Class Tests
    Sub TestCallingExample()
        Dim cls As CallingExample = Nothing
        Try
            cls = new CallingExample()
            cls.Method()
        Catch  exception1 As Exception
        End Try
        Console.WriteLine("Depth is (" & cls.GetDepth() & ")")
    End Sub
    Public Sub RunAll()
        TestCallingExample()
    End Sub
End Class
```

In this example, each Finally keyword is associated with a Try block. You don't need to associate a Catch block with a Try block if you are using Finally. If the Try block is entered, when the code leaves the Try block, regardless of whether it ran successfully or threw an exception, the code within Finally is executed. Thus, if stack unwinding occurs, it is possible to reset or assign state to a consistent value before the exception is processed elsewhere.

■**Note** When the Finally block is called, you don't know if it is called due to an exception or successful code execution. Thus, you shouldn't assume that Finally is called because an exception was thrown.

Sandboxing Your Code

The sandboxing technique is similar to playing with an Etch A Sketch, in that you attempt to build a state, and if you make a mistake, you can throw the state away. This requires that you separate your code into three distinct steps: declaration, manipulation, and integration. Figure 5-7 illustrates the three steps in sandboxing your code.

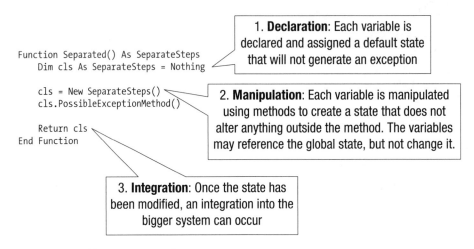

Figure 5-7. *Sandboxing your code*

Figure 5-7 illustrates one way of performing a sandboxing operation, but there are many other possible implementations. In each of the different implementations, the objective is the same: you want to perform the operations that could cause an exception apart from the main code. Then if you do have an exception, it will be localized to the separate code. When the stack unwinds, the other code won't be corrupted.

■**Note** The rule of thumb with sandboxing your code is to keep all of the code manipulations that could generate an exception separate from any existing state that could be corrupted. Once the manipulations have been carried out, you integrate the objects into the global state using method calls that are extremely unlikely to generate exceptions. For those situations when you must manipulate existing state, use a `Finally` handler, so that the previous existing state can be re-created if necessary.

Filtering Exceptions

In all of the examples presented so far in this chapter, the `Catch` statement used the `Exception` type:

```
Catch exception1 As Exception
```

`Exception` will catch every exception.

In Figure 5-3, the IDE caught an exception, referencing `NullReferenceException`, which is a specific type of exception. When you use it in a `Catch` statement, you will catch only null reference exceptions.

By specializing the exception, you have the ability to filter which exception you want to catch. For example, `NotSupportedException` will catch only instances of `NotSupportedException` exceptions. Here is an example:

```
Try
    Throw New NotSupportedException("There is no code")
Catch ex As NotSupportedException
End Try
```

If the code within the `Try` block threw an instance of `Exception`, the `Catch` block would not trigger, because the `Catch` block was looking for a specific exception type.

Exception types can be combined to provide specific filtering capabilities. The specific exception type should be the first exception after the `Try` block, as in this example:

```
Try
    ' . . .
Catch ex1 As NotSupportedException
    '
Catch ex2 As Exception
    '
End Try
```

By combining multiple exception filters, you don't need to figure out which kind of exception is being thrown. For example, without the filtering capabilities of a `Catch` block to catch `NotSupportedException` exception types, you would need to write this code:

```
Try
    Throw New NotSupportedException("There is no code")
Catch ex As Exception
    If ex Is NotSupportedException Then
        ' . . .
    Else
        Throw ex
    End If
End Try
```

Table 5-1 lists common exception types in the `System` namespace that you can throw or can be thrown. There are many more exceptions, and you can even generate your own exceptions by subclassing `Exception`.

Table 5-1. *Common Exception Types*

Exception	Description
Exception	Plain-vanilla exception; a general container for all exceptions. When you get one of these exceptions, look at the Message property for the exact details. If you throw this type of exception, it is important to supply an easy-to-understand string to the exception constructor.
ArgumentException	Thrown if you call a method and one of the arguments is not valid. Typically, in the Message property you can find the problem with the arguments. If this exception is thrown, it is because the contents of the argument are wrong.
ArgumentNullException	Thrown if you call a method where one of the arguments is a Nothing value. This could be because you are passing the Nothing value to the method or one of the arguments has a Nothing value.
ArgumentOutOfRangeException	Thrown if you call a method where one of the arguments is not in the expected range. While this exception sounds similar to ArgumentException, it is more specialized and targets whether an argument is in an acceptable range. Check the documentation of the method or the method implementation on what the acceptable range is. If you throw this exception, note the valid range in the error message.
ArithmeticException	Thrown if a mathematical error is generated.
DivideByZeroException	Thrown if you attempt to divide by zero.
FormatException	Thrown if the format of the parameter is not correct. For example, if a method expects a number to be formatted with a period and you use a comma, an exception is generated.
IndexOutOfRangeException	Thrown if you attempt to reference an index of an array that would be beyond the limits of the array. This exception is thrown if you have not allocated an array and then attempt to reference an element, or if you attempt to reference a negative index of the array.
InsufficientMemoryException	Thrown if not enough memory is available. Although this exception is not generated often, it can be generated if you attempt to allocate an array when you specify something along the lines of 5 trillion elements (due to an improperly assigned array size variable).
InvalidCastException	Thrown if you attempt to cast one type to another type that is not supported. This exception is very common when you use inheritance and attempt a cast.
NotImplementedException	Thrown when using methods or properties without an implementation. Often, you don't have time to implement all of the code at once. For those properties or methods that have not been implemented, don't leave an empty property or method implementation. Instead, throw an exception. Then you will know if you have forgotten to implement something.

Table 5-1. *Common Exception Types*

Exception	Description
NotSupportedException	Thrown when you attempt to use an interface instance and a method that cannot work. For example, if you open a read-write buffer to a read-only CD-ROM, you will get this exception when writing to the CD-ROM. If you attempt to read from the interface instance, an exception will not be thrown.
NullReferenceException	Thrown when you attempt to call a method or property of a variable that has not been assigned with a valid type instance.
OutOfMemoryException	Similar to InsufficientMemoryException.
OverflowException	Thrown when you attempt to perform numeric operations that are not supported, such as adding 2 billion to 2 billion using a 32-bit integer.
SystemException	Thrown by the operating system. Do not attempt to derive from this class.

Writing Exception-Safe Code

Now that you've seen how to implement exception handlers, we'll look at an even better approach to exceptions: not generating them. We'll focus on how you can make your code safer and less likely to generate exceptions.

Writing Defensive Code

All too often, developers get exceptions such as NullReferenceException because they didn't make sure that the state in a piece of code was valid. And if the state is not valid, an exception will occur. In fact, in this chapter, one of the previous examples has just such a situation, which you may have noticed. Here is the code that has a dumb little exception possibility:

```
Sub TestCallingExample()
    Dim cls As CallingExample = Nothing
    Try
        cls = New CallingExample()
        cls.Method()
    Catch  ex As Exception
    End Try
    Console.WriteLine("Depth is (" & cls.GetDepth() & ")")
End Sub
```

The problem is in the bolded line, which assumes that cls will always reference a valid instance of CallingExample. This is an assumption that you cannot afford to make. If an exception occurred while instantiating CallingExample, cls will still be Nothing, and the Catch block will catch the instantiation exception, saving a program crash. However, the use of cls.GetDepth() immediately after that throws your protection out the window, as cls is Nothing and will generate a NullReferenceException. Here's a better way to write this code:

```
Sub TestCallingExample()
    Dim cls As CallingExample = Nothing
    Try
        cls = New CallingExample()
        cls.Method()
    Catch ex As Exception
    End Try
    If cls IsNot Nothing Then
        Console.WriteLine("Depth is (" & cls.GetDepth() & ")")
    End If
End Sub
```

The bolded code illustrates defensive coding that tests if cls is not Nothing, and if so, then allows the referencing of cls.GetDepth(). Now the code is exception-safe. It does not mean exceptions cannot occur, because calling GetDepth() could still generate an exception internally, but with respect to the TestCallingExample() method, you have made everything as safe as possible, and have assumed GetDepth() is a low exception-risk method.

Missing from the TestCallingExample() method is an indication of whether the processing worked. It is assumed from the perspective of the caller of TestCallingExample() that calling TestCallingExample() will always result in something being done. The caller of TestCallingExample() has no way of knowing that something failed, other than if an exception was thrown.

Code that tells you if something went wrong using an exception is both a blessing and a curse. It is a blessing because the code is telling you that something went wrong. But it is a curse because sometimes you know something could go wrong, and that it is OK, but you don't want the exception to travel up the program hierarchy. In these cases, you need to catch the exception, which makes your code more complicated.

For example, say you wanted to parse a number. The .NET parsing routines tend to give a result if everything worked OK, but generate an exception if things are not OK. There is no return value, just an exception. But when parsing a number, you do know that things could go wrong, so you will need to write an exception handler. Following is some source code that parses a number.

```
Function TestGetValue(ByVal buffer As String) As Integer
    Dim retval As Integer = 0
    Try
        retval = Integer.Parse(buffer)
    Catch ex As FormatException
        Console.WriteLine("Exception (" & ex.Message & ")")
    End Try
    Return retval
End Function
```

In the example, the code realizes that if Parse() is called and the string cannot be converted into a number due to incorrect letters or numbers, an exception will be thrown. The exception will be caught, processed (using the exception's Message property to obtain the problem), and then the value of retval will be returned to the caller. But what if an exception does happen? The variable retval is initialized to a default value of 0, which is a valid formatted number and can be interpreted as the result of a successful format processing.

The problem in the code is that a developer is caught in a bind. By capturing the exception, the method `TestGetValue()` is saying, "I will always return to the caller a valid value." Yet there are instances when a valid value is not available. In the case of parsing a number, an exception is thrown. So by capturing an exception, you are doing the completely wrong thing, because you should be letting the exception be caught by a higher-level caller. But things can become sticky here. Do you really want to inform the caller that a parse cannot occur? Perhaps the caller is more interested in whether a valid value is returned. It's like saying to the CEO, "Oops, we just ran out of staples." Sure, staples might be important, and maybe the company will not run as smoothly, but do you really want to inform the CEO about every little problem?

Microsoft developers know about this problem with parsing, and use an approach that you can use as well. As you learned in Chapter 3, there are two variations of parsing a number:

- `Parse()` returns a valid number if the buffer could be parsed, and an exception if a number could not be parsed.

- `TryParse()` returns a `True` or `False` value indicating the result of the parse.

Here's how you could rewrite the `TestGetValue()` method to use `TryParse()`:

```
Function TestGetValue(ByVal buffer As String, ByRef val As Integer) As Boolean
    Dim retval As Boolean = False
    If Integer.TryParse(buffer, val) Then
        retval = True
    End If
    Return retval
End Function
```

In the modified example, `TestGetValue()` returns a `True` or `False` to indicate a success or failure when parsing a number. If a `True` is returned, the parameter `val` will hold a valid number; otherwise, `val` should be not be used.

Some of you might have caught that my use of `Parse()` and `TryParse()` is not very creative. The method `TestGetValue()` could have been reduced to a single line:

```
Function TestGetValue(ByVal buffer As String, ByRef val As Integer) As Boolean
    Return Integer.TryParse(buffer, val)
End Function
```

Using Default State

Default state is a useful technique to guard against exceptions that developers often ignore. When developers are writing their code, they will often return `Nothing` when things don't work out. Using `Nothing` is not a bad idea, but it adds unnecessary baggage. For example, consider the following code:

```
Class DefaultStateWrong
    Private Function Tokenize(ByVal buffer As String) As String()
        Return Nothing
    End Function
```

```vb
        Public Sub IterateBuffers(ByVal buffer As String)
            Dim found As String() = Tokenize(buffer)
            If found IsNot Nothing Then
                For c1 As Integer = 0 To found.Length - 1
                    Console.WriteLine("Found (" & found(c1) & ")")
                Next
            End If
        End Sub
End Class
```

The problem in this example is Tokenize(), which is a method used to convert the parameter buffer into a series of string tokens. Using safe exception coding, if the data could not be parsed, you could throw an exception, or you could return a Nothing value indicating that the buffer could not be parsed.

The caller code knows that there is the possibility of a Nothing value when calling Tokenize(), and thus has an If test to check for the Nothing value. The If test is defensive coding, but it also adds complexity because you need to verify for a Nothing value.

What if Tokenize() were a bit smarter and decided to return an empty array to indicate an empty result set? The logic of this is not incorrect, because the caller expects either a result set with items or a result set with nothing in it. If a dramatically bad parsing error has occurred, the only recourse is to throw an exception. Here is the rewritten code:

```vb
Class DefaultStateRight
    Private Function Tokenize(ByVal buffer As String)  As String()
        Return New String(-1) { }
    End Function

    Public Sub IterateBuffers(ByVal buffer As String)
        Dim found As String() = Tokenize(buffer)
        For c1 As Integer = 0 To found.Length - 1
            Console.WriteLine("Found (" & found(c1) & ")")
        Next
    End Sub
End Class
```

In the rewritten code, Tokenize() returns an empty array that, when iterated using a For loop, will cause zero iterations. This is exception-safe code with improved readability.

But what happens if Tokenize() does throw an exception? With Tokenize() throwing an exception and the lack of a Try/Catch block in IterateBuffers(), it looks like IterateBuffers() is written incorrectly. However, IterateBuffers() is not written incorrectly, because Tokenize() will throw an exception only if something really problematic has occurred. A big problem is beyond the scope of the IterateBuffers() method, and thus needs to be handled at a higher level. Think of it as the situation where you have a criminal case and the local municipal court automatically delegates the case to the provincial or state level, because those courts are equipped to deal with such a case.

Processing Errors That Are Warnings

One of the silliest things that programs do is exit when they could have continued working. It reminds me of when my family lived on the French Rivera, where it does not rain too often. Our two bulldogs were used to the nice weather, and at the slightest hint of moisture in the air, they would refuse to go outside. Our male dog Big Boss (Man) would stand in the doorway, stick his nose out slightly, and take a few deep breaths. If he sensed the slightest bit of moisture, instantly you were dragging an 80-pound concrete block.

The point is that, like our bulldogs, programs sometimes overreact to situations. For fear of having problems or not doing something correctly, they instantly shut down.

Let's say that you have a program that requires a configuration file to run. What happens when the configuration file does not exist? One approach is to panic and exit. The panic approach will work, but what if multiple problems follow from the first one? Then you are painstakingly hitting one error after another. Another approach is to use a default action. In this example, the default action could be to display a dialog box asking the user to select a configuration file, or the program could create a default file, as in this example:

```
Try
    LoadConfiguration()
Catch ex As ConfigurationException
    CreateDefaultConfiguration()
End Try
```

Here, the `LoadConfiguration()` method is in a `Try/Catch` block, but the `Catch` block catches only `ConfigurationException` failures (a built-in Visual Basic exception). If there is a `ConfigurationException` failure, then a default configuration is created. With a default configuration, the program can continue processing. Using the filtering capabilities of exceptions, if another exception is thrown in `LoadConfiguration()`, then some higher-level exception handler will process it.

When processing an error that is a warning, the important steps are to filter for the specific exception and implement an appropriate exception handler that has been properly tested. Don't try to implement a fix-all exception handler, because you will never be able to implement a proper handler and thus will cause more problems. In the handler to fix the problem, make sure that you don't generate an exception. If you do, that exception will be sent to a higher method caller.

The Important Stuff to Remember

In this chapter, you learned about errors and exceptions. Here are the key points to keep in mind:

- Errors and exceptions will always occur in your programs.

- Your code is split into a tree very much like a management hierarchy. The hierarchy contains two types of code: code that organizes and code that implements.

- Exceptions are caught using `Try/Catch` blocks.

- The `Finally` block is used to execute code, regardless of whether an exception is thrown, and to reset state.

- Code that implements has the responsibility of throwing exceptions. Code that implements does not try to fix or swallow the exception. This means code that implements will implement a `Finally` block to reset state, but usually not a `Catch` block.

- Code that organizes has the responsibility of being aware that exceptions might occur. This means code that organizes will implement `Catch` blocks to catch exceptions and process them. Usually, this code will not have a `Finally` implementation, but it may filter exceptions.

- Exceptions can be filtered to determine which exceptions will be captured and which cannot be captured.

- You can help make your code exception-safe by implementing sandboxing functionality.

- Implement default state so that your code is easier to read and maintain.

Some Things for You to Do

To apply what you've learned in this chapter, here's what you can do, summed up in a single step:

1. Rewrite all of the code examples in Chapter 4 to be exception-safe.

CHAPTER 6

■■■

Learning the Basics of Object-Oriented Programming

At this point, you should be comfortable with writing basic Visual Basic code, but your coding style would solve problems directly without considering reusability or other more advanced concepts. You could code yourself out of a wet paper bag, but once you were out of the bag, you would have no idea what to do next. (In case you're interested, the phrase, "You couldn't do [fill in topic] out of a wet paper bag" implies that your skills in a certain area are so weak that a wet paper bag is more overpowering. The reference to wet paper bag comes from the fact that wet paper bags have no holding power and will tear at the slightest nudging.)

This chapter focuses on reusing base functionality, where two classes share methods and properties in common to solve a particular problem. To demonstrate the concepts, we will create a simple currency exchange application. This application will use object-oriented programming, a powerful set of techniques common in modern programming languages such as Visual Basic.

In this chapter, you'll learn about the following topics:

Object-oriented programming: Object-oriented, often abbreviated as OO, refers to a way of building applications using instantiated types. First, you define the type and its behavior. Then, when instantiated, the type has a state. When you are developing, you don't know the state of the object, so you can only guess at it.

Data member scopes: Types have methods, and methods can be called by other types. But do you want to let all types call all of a type's methods? Think of it as follows. When you are at a party, do you want to allow everyone to grab into your pockets? No, you want to control access to your pockets, just as you want to control access to your type's methods.

Properties: There are methods, and there are properties. Methods are supposed to do things to a type. Properties are external state representations of a type.

Base classes: The term *base class* denotes common functionality. We use the word *base*, because in object-oriented programming, hierarchy is defined from the base upwards. We use the word *class*, because class is the basic type that contains functionality.

Let's begin with some background on how currency exchange works, which applies to the currency converter application we'll develop in this chapter to demonstrate object-oriented programming concepts.

Understanding Currency Spreads

This chapter's sample application deals with exchanging different currencies. Did you know that when you exchange one currency for another, you never need to pay a processing fee? Whether you are exchanging currencies at some airport or on an exchange, you should not be charged any processing fees. It makes you wonder how people earn money by accepting one currency and then giving out another currency. The answer lies in how currency exchange works.

When dealing with currencies, you are always dealing with currency pairs. This is different from something like buying a stock, when you are dealing with only that stock. A currency by itself is actually quite useless. Suppose you have a $100 in your hand. What will it be worth one year from now? The answer is simple: $100. Yes, you can argue that the $100 will not buy as much next year, but that would be complicating the issue with concerns not related to this discussion. The fact is that if you have 100 dollars, 100 yen, 100 euros, and so on into infinite time, you will always have 100 currency units.

Currency exchange involves comparing one currency to another currency. The value of a currency is what one person would give in comparison to another currency.

Foreign exchange (forex) market traders make their money by dealing in *spreads*. Spreads are tricky because, as the exchange rate moves up or down, so does the spread. For example, hotels always give you horrible rates, and you may wonder why they are ripping you off. But hotels are not ripping you off; they are hedging themselves on the safe side.

Consider the following example of a spread:

EUR.USD   1.4686   1.4687

The EUR.USD term means you are converting one euro (EUR) into a number of US dollars (USD). The first number is the bid, which means that a trader is willing to give 1.4686 US dollars for every euro. The second number is saying a trader wants 1.4687 US dollars for every euro. Essentially, the buyer and seller are 0.0001 US dollars apart. The exchange spread is normal, and it moves around because some might be willing to sell at a lower conversion rate, and others might be willing to buy at a higher conversion rate.

Let's say one day you enter a hotel in Austria on a skiing holiday. In your hand, you have 1,000 US dollars, but Austria belongs to the European Union (EU). To buy anything in the EU zone, you need euros. Being clever, you decide to go on the Internet and check out the going spread. It turns out to be the one you've just seen.

Standing in the hotel foyer, you have US dollars in your pocket and you need to buy euros. Thus, you will need to go in the direction USD.EUR. The way to do that is to divide one by the posted spread values. This calculation gives the following conversion rates:

USD.EUR   0.6809   0.6808

The numbers are a bit wrong, because the buyer is willing to give a higher value than the seller. Granted, this happens at times on the forex markets, but here, it's because we used a raw conversion of EUR.USD. The market might be a bit higher and lower, but generally speaking, you have a feeling of what to expect.

You advance to the hotel desk, and you kindly ask what the going rate is for US dollars to euros. The concierge gives the following exchange rate:

USD.EUR   0.65120

EUR.USD   1.5010

Doing your calculations, this rate doesn't seem right. The hotel is giving you 651.20 euros for your 1,000 US dollars, but the forex market clearly says the traders would be willing to give you 680.91 euros. The hotel appears to be ripping you off by approximately 29 euros. But the hotel is not ripping you off; rather, it is hedging its risks. The spot conversion rates will go up and down during the day, and the hotel is not in the business of exchanging money. The hotel is in the business of giving you room and board. The hotel managers need to make sure that when they go to the bank to exchange your dollars for euros, they don't lose money in the process. They ensure this by giving you less money.

Whenever you exchange monies, you should always look at the spreads. Sometimes the spreads are good; sometimes they are horrible. I have found the best spreads are at the banks. It is a bit more work to get money from your home bank, but usually worth the effort. Another option is to pull the money from your credit card; however, sometimes credit cards charge interest on the money you withdrew.

Now that you have an idea of what's involved in currency exchange, let's see what our sample application will do.

Organizing the Currency Exchange Application

The currency application takes a number of currency units and converts it to a number of other currency units. The application will implement the following features:

- Accept and store a currency exchange rate

- Store the currency unit identifiers

- Convert to a currency and back to the original currency

- Distinguish between active currency traders and hotel currency traders

- Implement a spread for hotel currency traders

As in the examples in the previous chapters, the project structure of the currency applica-tion will consist of two projects: a console testing application, named TestCurrencyTrader, and a library component, named CurrencyTrader, which contains the functionality of the hotel trader and the active trader.

Writing Tests for the Currency Exchange Application

Since we don't know exactly how the implementation will appear, let's start by writing some tests that will use our implementation. We want to build the application incrementally, so we'll write some tests, write some code, test the code, and continue. The overall big picture is to be able to convert from one currency to another.

Getting Started with Structural Code

At the heart of the application are an exchange rate, currency units, and a calculation that combines the exchange rate with the currency units. Thus, a logical first step would be to write test code that combines these elements, something like this:

```
Dim cls As CurrencyTrader = New CurrencyTrader()
cls.ExchangeRate = 1.46
Dim haveUSD As Double = 100.0
Dim getEUR As Double = cls.Convert(haveUSD)
Console.WriteLine("Converted " & haveUSD & " USD to " & getEUR)
```

This code is unique in that the test code has all of the responsibility of making sure the correct data is assigned to the structure. To clarify this, here is the same code with random variable names used instead of the identifiers for the currency variables:

```
Dim cls As CurrencyTrader = New CurrencyTrader()
cls.ExchangeRate = 1.46
Dim ukfkisd As Double = 100.0
Dim didkfdbnfd As Double = cls.Convert(ukfkisd)
Console.WriteLine("Converted " & ukfkisd & " USD to " & didkfdbnfd)
```

This code is structural, rather than architectural. *Structural* code is code that requires an intelligent programmer—a programmer who knows what the individual items mean. In this case, the programmer must know that the Convert() method converts from USD to EUR and therefore needs to supply the correct values at the correct time.

Architectural code, on the other hand, is more idiot-proof and requires less knowledge, because many parts are encapsulated. The user needs to understand only how to use the classes.

Put another way, structural code is knowing how to add two numbers. Architectural code is knowing how to punch in the two numbers and hit the plus sign on a calculator. You can argue that by not knowing how to add and relying on the calculator, you have no idea if the calculator is doing its job properly. That is a valid point, and that is why tests are important to ensure that the calculator is doing its job properly.

Understanding Base Classes

The first test code, which is structural, is not wrong. Structural code forms the basis of what is called a *base class*. A base class is a class that provides certain functionality that will be reused by other classes. In this case, converting the currency units is functionality that we will need in both the active trader and hotel trader. You define base classes so that you get consistent behavior when performing identical operations. In lieu of base classes, you would need to copy and paste the functionality to reuse it.

Base classes have some very important characteristics:

- Only developers who understand what the base class code is trying to do should use the base class code. In other words, only those with expert domain knowledge should touch the internals of the base class. To control access, we will use scope.

- Base classes describe properties and methods that are common across multiple applications.

- Base classes need extensive testing because their functionality will be used throughout your code. If the base classes have bugs, most likely a large chunk of your code will have bugs.

■**Note** Base classes are a general concept that only developers understand fully. A general concept is called a *design pattern*. Design patterns create a developer lingo where words like *factory*, *state*, and *visitor* refer to specific coding concepts that developers understand without needing to explain the coding concept. I suggest that you learn more about design patterns. The Data & Object Factory web site (`http://www.dofactory.com/Patterns/Patterns.aspx`) has some excellent coding examples of essential patterns used by developers.

In the current example, the `CurrencyTrader` class needs to be converted into a base class that can be used only by knowledgeable developers (those who know about currency trading). You want to prevent your source code from being used in the wrong context.

One way to stop usage in the wrong context is to declare the `CurrencyTrader` class as `MustInherit`. The `MustInherit` keyword says that the class in question cannot be instantiated. You can reference the class, but you cannot instantiate the class. Consider the following code, which declares `CurrencyTrader` as `MustInherit`.

```
MustInherit Class CurrencyTrader
End Class
```

Using `MustInherit` implies that someone needs to create a class that can be instantiated, using a mechanism called *inheritance*. Note that any class can be extended in this way, but `MustInherit` marks a class that is specifically designed to be extended. From a developer perspective, the idea behind `MustInherit` is to embed reusable logic used by some other class. Using `MustInherit` implies inheritance.

Understanding Inheritance

Inheritance is similar to a genealogy tree, in that you have a tree structure where there is a parent, and the descendants of the parent are children. And like the genealogy tree, the structure can have multiple levels. However, inheritance is not quite like genealogy, because genealogy requires a pair of humans to create a tree.

A class uses inheritance to gain functionality from the base class and becomes a subclass of that base class. Inheritance, and in particular .NET, has a tree structure where there is only a single root parent. When you use inheritance, you can gain functionality, but you can also *override* functionality, as illustrated in Figure 6-1.

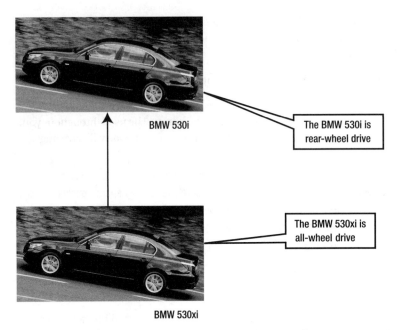

Figure 6-1. *Simple two-level inheritance example using the awesome BMW 530i and 530xi*

The pictures in Figure 6-1 seem to illustrate the same car, but in fact, they are two different models with a major difference in their power trains. From an inheritance perspective, the BMW 530i could be considered the parent of the BMW 530xi.

■**Note** The order of which is the parent and which is the child is my logic; some might disagree. This disagreement is healthy and part of the object-oriented design process.

The first model that you would design would probably be the rear-wheel-drive model, since it is simpler to design, cheaper, and more popular. You would consider all-wheel drive as a feature. The all-wheel-drive model is not a completely new car. Both the 530i and 530xi would share the same tires, motor, steering wheel, body trim, and so on. What would be different is that the 530xi replaces the power train, thus changing the behavior of the car.

Let's say that you are a driver sitting in the seat driving your BMW, and it's a snowy night in Canada. Whether you are driving the 530i or the 530xi, you would use the same steering wheel, blinkers, gas pedal, brake, and so on. But the behavior of the 530i and 530xi would be different—the rear-wheel-drive car might slide around a bit more than the all-wheel-drive car. The power train overrides behavior, which means the consumer of the hierarchy sees the same interface (for example, methods and properties), but gets different behavior.

Another way to use inheritance is not to replace functionality, but to enhance functionality, as illustrated in Figure 6-2. This is called *overloading* behavior.

Figure 6-2. *A more extensive inheritance tree illustrating how functionality can be enhanced*

In Figure 6-2, all of the cars are related in that they are the 530 line. The new model is the BMW 530xi Sports Wagon, which, from an inheritance perspective, is based on the functionality of the BMW 530xi. But here is the twist: the functionality of the 530xi Sports Wagon requires you to get accustomed to the Sports Wagon. For example, even though you press a single button to open the trunk, the Sports Wagon's trunk is slightly different from the trunk in the 530xi and 530i, and thus exposes the driver to a slightly different user interface and behavior.

When you use inheritance to overload functionality, you are adding functionality that is called in the same way, but is used and behaves differently. With this form of inheritance, you don't just change behavior, you also change the user interaction.

In our example, we will use inheritance to extend functionality, and not override or overload.

Using Visual Basic Properties

So far, the test code would call a data member reference, as in this line:

```
cls.ExchangeRate = 123.45
```

The data member could be implemented as follows:

```
Public MustInherit Class CurrencyTrader
    Public ExchangeRate As Double
End Class
```

Exposing the data member using a public scope worked in previous chapters, but we don't really want to do this because we are exposing the internal state of the object. In object-oriented programming, exposing the internal state is a bad idea (as explained in more detail shortly).

Rather than expose the data member publicly, we will change the test code to use properties. Properties also expose the internal state of an object, but they provide a layer of abstraction. As you will learn, some properties expose both internal state and external state. This is the case with the ExchangeRate property that we will use to access and modify the exchange rate. If we did not use the ExchangeRate property, we would need to create a method that assigns the exchange rate and a method that retrieves the exchange rate. The methods would behave like the property, but they would not be as convenient to use.

Rewriting the Test Code to Use Properties

The interesting thing about Visual Basic properties is that they look and behave like data members. This means with Visual Basic properties, the test code does not need to be rewritten, as the test code still assumes a direct access to the variable. Consider the rewritten CurrencyTrader that exposes ExchangeRate as a Visual Basic property, shown in Figure 6-3.

Figure 6-3. *Exposing ExchangeRate as a Visual Basic property*

To completely fool the test, the name of the property must be identical to the name of the previously declared data member. So that there is no identifier collision, the data member ExchangeRate is renamed to _exchangeRate, and the scope changes from public to private.

Properties look like methods without parameters, but have a return value. Also, each property must have at least a Get code block or a Set block (it can have both), which are called *getters* and *setters*. If a property has only a Get code block, you have created a read-only property. If a property has only a Set code block, you have created a write-only property. Within the context of a property, you can have only the Get or Set keyword. You cannot add any other code.

The following code will execute the code defined in the Get code block and retrieve the state from the object to the variable.

```
value = cls.ExchangeRate
```

And the following code will execute the code in the Set code block and assign the state from the variable to the object.

```
cls.ExchangeRate = value
```

Each code block has special features. The Get code block must always return data to the caller and thus requires the use of the Return keyword. The Set code block has no requirements to do anything. However, if you want to know what data is being passed to the property, you can use the value parameter.

Understanding the Problems with Properties

Many programmers feel that properties promote bad programming practices. Properties expose the internal state of an object. Looking at the previous source code, you will see that the data member _exchangeRate has a one-to-one relationship to the property ExchangeRate. If the caller assigns the property ExchangeRate, then the private data member _exchangeRate is immediately assigned. This exposes the internal state, even though the exposure is indirect.

As an example, say that you want to preheat an oven to a certain temperature to bake something. The simplest way to preheat the oven is to monitor the temperature and create a property Temperature, like this:

```
Class Oven
    Private _temperature As Integer

    Public Property Temperature() As Integer
        Get
            Return _temperature
        End Get
        Set(ByVal Value As Integer)
            _temperature = Value
        End Set
    End Property
End Class
```

The class Oven exposes its temperature as a property, which is a direct reference to the variable _temperature. The caller of Oven would periodically ask the oven for its temperature and decide when the oven has been preheated.

So, is Oven in its current implementation actually a structural class? The user of Oven has quite a bit of responsibility in that it must periodically query the temperature and decide if the oven is preheated. A better implementation is to define a class that takes care of itself. The caller would then just need to ask, "Are you ready?" Here's how that code would look:

```
Class Oven
    Private _temperature As Integer

    Public Sub SetTemperature(ByVal temperature As Integer)
        _temperature = temperature
    End Sub
    Public Function AreYouPreheated() As Boolean
        ' Check if oven temperature matches prescribed temperature
        Return False
    End Function
End Class
```

In the modified implementation of Oven, the data member _temperature is not externally exposed. And in this situation, the role of the data member _temperature is not to represent the temperature of the oven, but to act as an upper limit to which the oven should be heated. The upper limit is assigned using the SetTemperature() method. To check the temperature of the oven, you don't retrieve the temperature of the oven, but call the AreYouPreheated() method. The caller receives either a True or False value to indicate whether or not the oven is ready.

The caller of Oven has the responsibility only of setting the upper temperature and asking if the oven is preheated. From this example, it would seem that you don't need properties. However, you still need properties because Oven in its current form represents an easy-to-use class that can be integrated at the architectural business-logic level.

The challenge of the developer is to bridge the gap between a raw structural class and the exposure of an architectural business-logic-level class. That challenge will be met when the hotel currency trader and active currency trader are implemented.

Even with these arguments and the distinction between base class and architectural business-logic-level classes, some still naysay properties. The reason has to do with controlling access.

Suppose you are in a grocery store, waiting at the cash register. The cashier tallies up the items, arrives at a total, and asks you to pay. Do you open your purse or wallet and let the cashier get the credit card or cash? Along the same lines, why can't you just place the cash into the cash register? The answer to these questions is one of trust. As trustworthy as the cashier and shopper might be, we feel better when we know we have the control.

Let's go back to an example I mentioned at the beginning of the chapter: allowing people to grab into your pockets. The previously defined Temperature property is allowing someone to grab into your pockets. You wouldn't generally allow it, but what if that person were your spouse or your mom? Would you still disallow it? The answer is very different, because you probably trust your mom or spouse. In the same way, often state and its exposure are a matter of trust and using the right scope.

▪Note In this discussion of properties and object-oriented design, my goal is to explain that there is a place and time for both, and you should not feel biased toward one approach or the other. When you design a type that does not reveal its state, you are designing a type that fulfills an abstract intention. When you design a type that reveals its state (to some extent) through properties, you are designing a type that is used at the lower technical level. Also keep in mind that sometimes internal state is external state, such as the exchange rate example. You cannot abstract away the exchange rate state because it is a number used in a calculation.

Understanding Inheritance and Scope Modifiers

At this point, the ExchangeRate property is a mechanical property that will be used by any class that subclasses CurrencyTrader. So now we need to decide whether access to the property should be restricted. The answer is that it should be restricted to only those developers who truly understand how to convert currencies. Access should be restricted to those classes that will subclass CurrencyTrader. Following is the rewritten version of CurrencyTrader.

```
Public MustInherit Class CurrencyTrader
    Private _exchangeRate As Double

    Protected Property ExchangeRate() As Double
        Get
            Return _exchangeRate
        End Get
        Set (ByVal value As Double)
            _exchangeRate = value
        End Set
    End Property
End Class
```

The bolded code highlights three examples of scope access:

Public: The type, method, data member, or property can be accessed and referenced by any other type. In the context of a crowd of people, it means anyone can reach into your pocket and inspect your wallet.

Private: The method, data member, or property can be accessed and referenced only by the type declaring the method, data member, or property. In the context of a crowd of people, it means only you can reach into your pocket and inspect your wallet.

Protected: The method, data member, or property can be accessed and referenced by the type declaring the method, data member, or property or by types that subclass the declaring type. In the context of a crowd of people, it means only you and people who you have allowed can reach into your pocket and inspect your wallet.

If you happen to declare a type, method, or property without a scope modifier, the default is assumed, which means public is implied. Data members are private by default. The Private and Protected modifiers cannot be assigned to a type. You'll learn more about other modifiers and details about type scope declarations in the next chapter.

Using Visual Basic Inheritance to Subclass Another Type

The rewritten version of CurrencyTrader will cause the test code to break, because it uses the MustInherit keyword, and thus cannot be instantiated directly. Here is the broken code:

```
Dim cls As CurrencyTrader = New CurrencyTrader()
cls.ExchangeRate = 123.44
```

The code will not work for two reasons:

- CurrencyTrader uses the MustInherit keyword and thus cannot be instantiated.

- ExchangeRate is protected and cannot be referenced externally.

This broken code puts us in a bind. Up to this point, whenever we tested code, we assumed all of the pieces that were to be tested could be referenced. One solution would be to change the scope declarations and remove the MustInherit and Protected keywords. Yes, that solves the problem, but it is a cop-out. The better approach is to test CurrencyTrader as it was intended to be used: as a class that is derived from. So, the solution is to use inheritance and create a test class that derives from CurrencyTrader, as follows:

```
Public Class TestCurrencyTrader
    Inherits CurrencyTrader
    Public Sub InitializeExchangeRate()
        ExchangeRate = 100.0
    End Sub
End Class
```

TestCurrencyTrader is a test class that is added to the test source code. To inherit from a class, you define a class, and in the following line, use the keyword Inherits. This line says that the class TestCurrencyTrader is subclassing CurrencyTrader.

To expose a method outside the class declaration, you use the Public modifier.

Inheritance means identifiers that are scoped Protected or Public can be referenced in the subclassed type. For example, notice how ExchangeRate seems to be all on its own, without any object reference. The lonely reference to ExchangeRate is fine, because the base class CurrencyTrader has an identifier with that name. The property ExchangeRate can be referenced locally because of its protected scope The identifier ExchangeRate has an implied Me reference (Me.ExchangeRate), so it is not necessary to add that, unless you have multiple identifiers with the same name or you want to explicitly reference a certain identifier.

And now the tests will not test CurrencyTrader, but will test TestCurrencyTrader, which should contain some verification code to make sure everything works correctly.

Understanding Private, Protected, and Public Scope

Let's dig a bit deeper into how the three types of scope work. To start, consider the CurrencyTrader implementation:

```
Public MustInherit Class CurrencyTrader
    Private _exchangeRate As Double

    Protected Property ExchangeRate() As Double
        Get
            Return _exchangeRate
        End Get
        Set (ByVal Value As Double)
            _exchangeRate = value
        End Set
    End Property
    Protected Function ConvertValue(ByVal input As Double) As Double
        Return _exchangeRate * input
    End Function
    Protected Function ConvertValueInverse(ByVal input As Double) As Double
        Return input / _exchangeRate
    End Function
End Class
```

The new class ActiveCurrencyTrader subclasses CurrencyTrader and is written as follows:

```
Public Class ActiveCurrencyTrader
    Inherits CurrencyTrader
End Class
```

The data member CurrencyTrader._exchangeRate is declared as Private, and thus can be referenced only in CurrencyTrader. If _exchangeRate had no scope declaration, private scope would be implied. For example, the following code would not compile.

```
Public Class ActiveCurrencyTrader
    Inherits CurrencyTrader
    Public Sub Method()
       _exchangeRate = 100.0
    End Sub
End Class
```

The ActiveCurrencyTrader class is not part of CurrencyTrader, and thus _exchangeRate cannot be referenced.

Considering the ActiveCurrencyTrader class, ExchangeRate, which has been declared as Protected, could be referenced as follows:

```
Public Class ActiveCurrencyTrader
    Inherits CurrencyTrader
    Public Sub Method()
        ExchangeRate = 100.0
    End Sub
End Class
```

Protected scope means only those classes that derive from a class (and the class itself) can view the methods, properties, or data members. How many times and levels a class subclasses another class is not important.

Public scope is the loosest and simplest of all scopes. You use Public whenever you want to expose functionality that other classes or derived classes want to reference.

Here are some guidelines for using each scope:

Private scope: You will use Private for most data member declarations because data member declarations imply the state of an object. Sometimes, when developing algorithms, you will break apart the logic into several methods. The broken-apart methods are used to solve a problem, and thus should be used only in the context of the class, implying the methods need to be declared using Private.

Protected scope: You will use Protected whenever you want to enforce an inheritance architecture. Very often, Protected and MustInherit go hand in hand, as both are intended for inheritance. The main objective behind Protected is to offer a derived class access to the private state of a parent class, or to offer reusable functionality that should be used only by knowledgeable developers who are creating the subclasses.

Public scope. As a rule, think carefully before using `Public`. You will use public scope for the most part, but it is also the scope that can cause the most problems. For example, once you declare something as `Public`, trying to later change the scope could wreak havoc in the code that uses the class. It might be harder to develop using the other scopes, but you will have code that will have fewer maintenance issues. It all comes down to which methods and properties you want to expose to the outside world.

Handling Verification

To run the test class `TestCurrencyTrader`, the following code is used.

```
Dim cls As TestCurrencyTrader = New TestCurrencyTrader()
cls.InitializeExchangeRate()
```

The modified test code entails instantiating `TestCurrencyTrader` and then calling the method `InitializeExchangeRate()`. But is this a test? After all, the `InitializeExchangeRate()` method doesn't have a parameter or return value. Think of it as sending a letter via mail. You don't know if the letter will arrive, but it probably will. Tests that are probably passed are a really bad idea.

We need to move the verification code from the test routine to the `TestCurrencyTrader` class, like this:

```
Class TestCurrencyTrader
    Inherits CurrencyTrader
    Public Sub InitializeExchangeRate()
        ExchangeRate = 100.0
        If ExchangeRate <> 100.0 Then
            Throw New Exception("100.0 verification failed")
        End If
    End Sub
End Class
```

The bolded code illustrates the verification code used to ensure that the value assigned to `ExchangeRate` is the same one that is retrieved.

■**Note** The tests we're using are becoming more complicated, and you may wonder, "Why do it that way?" For this book, we are writing tests and creating our own testing framework. Normally you would not do that. You would use a testing framework such as NUnit (`http://www.nunit.org`) or the Microsoft Visual Studio Professional tools to help create the tests. But here I want to demonstrate how to use Visual Basic, not a testing tool. By learning how to write the tests from the ground up, you will understand what to expect from testing frameworks.

Using Conditional Statements

Having verification code within a class is acceptable in the context of the test class `TestCurrencyTrader`. However, the problem of testability is still present in those classes that do not expose their state.

To understand the problem, let's return to the code for preheating the oven that you saw earlier in the section about the problems with properties. Imagine rewriting Oven to include a verification test, like this:

```
Class Oven
    Private _temperature As Integer

    Public Sub SetTemperature(ByVal temperature As Integer)
        _temperature = temperature
        If _temperature <> 100.0 Then
            Throw New Exception("100.0 verification failed")
        End If
    End Sub
    Public Function AreYouPreHeated() As Boolean
        ' Check if oven temperature matches prescribed temperature
        Return False
    End Function
End Class
```

The bolded code illustrates a verification much like that used in CurrencyTrader, which verifies the parameter temperature for a specific value. While the verification is useful for a particular test, it is not useful in the big picture. As the code is written, the only valid value of temperature is 100.0; anything else will generate an exception. It is definitely not a solution.

To get around this problem, you could use Visual Basic conditional statements. Conditional statements are special keywords that allow a developer to define whether a piece of source code is compiled. Following is an example of source code that includes conditional statements.

```
Class TestCurrencyTrader
    Inherits CurrencyTrader
    Public Sub InitializeExchangeRate()
        ExchangeRate = 100.0
#If INTEGRATE_TESTS Then
        if ExchangeRate <> 100.0 Then
            Throw New Exception("100.0 verification failed")
        End If
#End If
    End Sub
End Class
```

The conditional statement always starts with a hash character (#), immediately followed by a keyword—If in this example. Between the #If and #End If is code that is conditionally compiled. This is known as a *preprocessor directive*. In this example, the condition means to compile the code contained within the #If and #End If block if the value INTEGRATE_TESTS is true.

You can define a compilation identifier like INTEGRATE_TESTS in the source code or in your IDE. In Visual Basic Express, you can assign INTEGRATE_TESTS as follows:

1. Right-click your project and select Properties.

2. Select the Compile tab.

3. Click the Advanced Compile Options button.

4. Add the INTEGRATE_TESTS value to the Custom Constants text box.

Using Partial Classes for Verification

Conditional compilation is useful when you want to include or remove code depending on a configuration. However, some programmers will frown upon having conditional compilation code within a function, as that would be a maintenance nightmare. Another solution is to use the Partial class keyword in conjunction with conditional compilation statements.

Thus far in all of the examples, whenever we defined a class, all of the methods and code were declared between the Class/End Class pair. By using *partial* classes, it is possible to declare a class in multiple places. When the Visual Basic compiler compiles the source code, the individual class pieces will be assembled into a single class definition. For our test code, we can create an implementation partial class and a conditionally compiled test partial class implementation. The following is the modified TestCurrencyTrader class that could be used to test the state without exposing the state.

```
Partial Class TestCurrencyTrader
    Inherits CurrencyTrader
    Public Sub InitializeExchangeRate()
        ExchangeRate = 100.0
    End Sub
End Class


#if INTEGRATE_TESTS Then
Partial Class TestCurrencyTrader
    Inherits CurrencyTrader
    Public Sub VerifyExchangeRate(ByVal value As Double)
        If ExchangeRate <> value Then
            Throw New Exception("ExchangeRate verification failed")
        End If
    End Sub
End Class
#End If
```

The keyword Partial prefixes the Class keyword. The first implementation of TestCurrencyTrader is an example of not exposing state. The second implementation of TestCurrencyTrader, which is declared in the context of a conditional compilation statement, contains the method VerifyExchangeRate(). This is a verification method that tests the ExchangeRate property for a particular value.

■**Note** You can use partial classes only in the context of a single assembly, as the `Partial` keyword cannot be used across assembly boundaries. When I say "single assembly," I am referring to the compiled pieces of .NET source code illustrated in Chapter 1. In other words, if you define a partial class in a library, then all pieces of the partial class need to be defined in the library.

Partial classes make it simple to separate functionality into various source code files. This example demonstrates using partial classes to manipulate internal state of a class without violating the do-not-expose-internal-state rule. Another use of partial classes is in the context of code generators, where one source code file contains the custom code, and the other source code file contains the generator code.

■**Note** Only one part of a partial class needs to be explicitly qualified as `Partial`. The compiler is smart enough to realize that if it sees one part as `Partial`, then all the other parts must also be partial (even if they aren't explicitly qualified with the `Partial` keyword).

Finishing the Base Class

The `ExchangeRate` property is one of the pieces of shared functionality. Another piece of shared functionality we want to implement is the calculation of the exchange rate. We'll do this with `ConvertValue()` and `ConvertValueInverse()` methods, which convert a currency from one value to another using multiplication or division. The following shows the methods in the completed base class implementation of `CurrencyTrader`.

```
Public MustInherit Class CurrencyTrader
    Private _exchangeRate As Double

    Protected Property ExchangeRate() As Double
        Get
            Return _exchangeRate
        End Get
        Set (ByVal Value As Double)
            _exchangeRate = Value
        End Set
    End Property
    Protected Function ConvertValue(ByVal input As Double) As Double
        Return _exchangeRate * input
    End Function
    Protected Function ConvertValueInverse(ByVal input As Double) As Double
        Return input / _exchangeRate
    End Function
End Class
```

The bolded code highlights the methods that convert the currency from one unit to another. Notice that there is no declaration of specific currency units, because the base class is a utility class used to help us realize an active trader or hotel trader implementation.

■**Note** Base class functionality, even when appearing trivial, is defined to ensure consistency in implementation. Without consistency, you encounter the problem where one implementation does one thing and another implementation does something completely different.

This completes our test code. Now we will implement the active trader and hotel trader components of the currency exchange application.

Writing the Active Trader and Hotel Trader Currency Converters

With the TestCurrencyTrader test solution completed, it's time to turn our attention to the CurrencyTrader solution. As mentioned earlier, this consists of the active trader and hotel trader currency converter components. Here, you'll see more clearly what it means to use inheritance.

Implementing ActiveCurrencyTrader

The ActiveCurrencyTrader class implements the logic of the active currency trader. To begin, we'll add its constructor.

Adding a Constructor to ActiveCurrencyTrader

To give ActiveCurrencyTrader some default state, we use a constructor. However, the constructor will serve another purpose, in that any class that instantiates ActiveCurrencyTrader will consider the instance as immutable. *Immutable* means that once data has been assigned to the instance, it cannot be altered. In other words, it is unchangeable.

■**Note** The String type is immutable because once a string variable has been assigned, it cannot be changed. Take a look at the methods associated with String, and you will see nothing that allows you to modify the contents. An immutable type is good because it allows you to implement a set-it-and-forget-it object, and it prevents other classes from accidentally changing the contents. Overall, an immutable type is robust and predictable (though they are the exception, not the rule; most types allow you to modify state).

The following shows the constructor code added to ActiveCurrencyTrader.

```
Public Class ActiveCurrencyTrader
    Inherits CurrencyTrader
    Private _fromCurrency As String
    Private _toCurrency As String

    Public Sub New(ByVal currExchange As Double, ByVal fromCurrency As String,
        ByVal toCurrency As String)
        ExchangeRate = currExchange
        _fromCurrency = fromCurrency
        _toCurrency = toCurrency
    End Sub
End Class
```

The constructor has three parameters: currExchange represents the current exchange rate, fromCurrency indicates the source currency (for example, USD), and toCurrency indicates the destination currency (for example, EUR). These three parameters are assigned to data members, whereby only the current exchange rate is assigned to the base class CurrencyTrader.ExchangeRate.

Defining Informational Read-Only Properties

The characters that represent the from currency and to currency are stored as strings, and are purely for informational purposes. For example, let's say that you have instantiated a bunch of currency pairs so that the trader can comprehend the currency pair in which the values of _fromCurrency and _toCurrency will be presented. This means that the currency strings are read-only properties and are coded as follows:

```
Public Class ActiveCurrencyTrader
    Inherits CurrencyTrader
    Private _fromCurrency As String
    Private _toCurrency As String

    Public Sub New (ByVal currExchange As Double,
        ByVal fromCurrency As String, ByVal toCurrency As String)
        ExchangeRate = currExchange
        _fromCurrency = fromCurrency
        _toCurrency = toCurrency
    End Sub
    Public ReadOnly Property FromCurrency() As String
        Get
            Return _fromCurrency
        End Get
    End Property
    Public ReadOnly Property ToCurrency() As String
        Get
            Return _toCurrency
        End Get
    End Property
End Class
```

The naming of the properties (FromCurrency and ToCurrency) corresponds closely to the naming of the data members (_fromCurrency and _toCurrency). I do this throughout my code so that I know what each piece of code means. My convention is to use a leading underscore to name private data members, but you can use a different notation if you prefer.

Adding the Conversion Methods

The last step to make the ActiveCurrencyTrader class complete is to add the functionality to convert a value from or to a currency pair. The ActiveCurrencyTrader class will use the exact currency exchange rate. The ConvertValue(), and ConvertValueInverse() methods have protected scope, and thus are not exposed outside the inheritance hierarchy. ActiveCurrencyTrader needs to define a pair of publicly scoped methods that will call the protected scope methods. The following is the complete ActiveCurrencyTrader implementation.

```
Public Class ActiveCurrencyTrader
    Inherits CurrencyTrader
    Private _fromCurrency As String
    Private _toCurrency As String

    Public Sub New (ByVal currExchange As Double,
        ByVal fromCurrency As String, ByVal toCurrency As String)
        ExchangeRate = currExchange
        _fromCurrency = fromCurrency
        _toCurrency = toCurrency
    End Sub
    Public ReadOnly Property FromCurrency() As String
        Get
            Return _fromCurrency
        End Get
    End Property
    Public ReadOnly Property ToCurrency() As String
        Get
            Return _toCurrency
        End Get
    End Property
    Public Function ConvertTo(ByVal value As Double) As Double
        Return ConvertValue(value)
    End Function
    Public Function ConvertFrom(ByVal value As Double) As Double
        Return ConvertValueInverse(value)
    End Function
End Class
```

The ConvertTo() and ConvertFrom() methods are wrappers to the ConvertValue() and ConvertValueInverse() methods, and provide no added value. But remember the problem of the cashier and credit card. Just because it seems like there is no added value, the reality is that you are writing code that is acting as a gatekeeper and giving yourself flexibility.

For example, suppose that `CurrencyTrader.ConvertValue()`, and `CurrencyTrader.ConvertValueInverse()` were declared using `Public` rather than `Protected`. Then any user of `ActiveCurrencyTrader` could use the functionality exposed by `CurrencyTrader`. Suppose someone decided to change the functionality of `ConvertValue()` and `ConvertValueInverse()`. At that point, you would have problems, because the changes to `CurrencyTrader` automatically imply changes in `ActiveCurrencyTrader`. By defining your own methods, you are controlling and making sure that if things change in the future, you can accommodate them without needing to change the callers of `ActiveCurrencyTrader`.

We have now completed the functionality of `ActiveCurrencyTrader`, so let's implement `HotelCurrencyTrader`.

Implementing HotelCurrencyTrader

The difference in features between `HotelCurrencyTrader` and `ActiveCurrencyTrader` is the existence of a sizable spread.

Adding a Constructor to HotelCurrencyTrader

Again, we'll begin by adding a constructor. The `HotelCurrencyTrader` constructor needs an additional parameter value referencing a spread. Following is the code for the `HotelCurrencyTrader` class, including its constructor.

```
Public Class HotelCurrencyTrader
    Inherits CurrencyTrader
    Private _fromCurrency As String
    Private _toCurrency As String
    Private _spread As Double

    Public Sub New (ByVal currExchange As Double, ByVal spread As Double,
        ByVal fromCurrency As String, ByVal toCurrency As String)
        ExchangeRate = currExchange
        _fromCurrency = fromCurrency
        _toCurrency = toCurrency
        _spread = spread
    End Sub

    Public ReadOnly Property FromCurrency() As String
        Get
            Return _fromCurrency
        End Get
    End Property
    Public ReadOnly Property ToCurrency() As String
        Get
            Return _toCurrency
        End Get
    End Property
End Class
```

In the constructor of HotelCurrencyTrader, you can see the additional parameter spread. The spread parameter is assigned to the data member _spread and represents a calculation that modifies the exchange rate.

Adding the Conversion Methods to HotelCurrencyTrader

Remember in the previous section how the methods ConvertTo() and ConvertFrom() seemed to add no extra value. For HotelCurrencyTrader, they will add value and illustrate why it is useful to create indirect exposure. Calculating what people will receive for their currency depends on the exchange rate, and in the case of the hotel, the exchange rate has a spread. As explained earlier in this chapter, this means you will never get as much as you hoped and will always pay more than you expected.

The following is the source code for the HotelCurrencyTrader implementations of ConvertTo() and ConvertFrom().

```
Public Class HotelCurrencyTrader
    Inherits CurrencyTrader
    Private _fromCurrency As String
    Private _toCurrency As String
    Private _spread As Double

    Public Sub New (ByVal currExchange As Double, ByVal spread As Double,
        ByVal fromCurrency As String, ByVal toCurrency As String)
        ExchangeRate = currExchange
        _fromCurrency = fromCurrency
        _toCurrency = toCurrency
        _spread = spread
    End Sub

        Public ReadOnly Property FromCurrency() As String
        Get
            Return _fromCurrency
        End Get
    End Property
    Public ReadOnly Property ToCurrency() As String
        Get
            Return _toCurrency
        End Get
    End Property

    Public Function ConvertTo(ByVal value As Double) As Double
        Dim realExchange As Double = ExchangeRate
        ExchangeRate = realExchange - _spread
        Dim retval As Double = ConvertValue(value)
        ExchangeRate = realExchange
        Return retval
    End Function
```

```
    Public Function ConvertFrom(ByVal value As Double) As Double
        Dim realExchange As Double = ExchangeRate
        ExchangeRate = realExchange + _spread
        Dim retval As Double = ConvertValueInverse(value)
        ExchangeRate = realExchange
        Return retval
    End Function
End Class
```

The ConvertTo() and ConvertFrom() methods have the added logic in that the spread will be added or subtracted from the exchange rate. The methods read the current exchange rate, assign it to a temporary variable, define a new exchange rate taking into account the spread, calculate the currency, and then reassign the exchange rate.

The ConvertTo() and ConvertFrom() methods swap values to achieve the desired calculations. There is absolutely nothing wrong with doing this, and you will often swap values in your own code. What is important is to restrict access on what classes can do this. Because ExchangeRate is a property with protected access, it means only those classes that subclass can assign and change the value of ExchangeRate. And this implies that the class doing the subclassing knows what it is doing to the data. It is a valid assumption and one that you can use to your benefit. The caller is not aware of this swapping, because HotelCurrencyTrader is taking advantage of the object-oriented technique to not expose the state of the type.

That's it—we're finished with the currency exchange application. For the remainder of this chapter, I will fill in some extra details that are important.

Learning More About Preprocessor Directives, Properties, and the MustOverride Keyword

Some details about preprocessor directives, properties, and the MustOverride keyword that did not come up in this chapter's example are worth mentioning. These are things you should know about when writing your own code.

More Preprocessor Directive Details

Earlier in the chapter, you saw how you can use the hash character (#) and conditional statements to conditionally include code during compilation. The technical term for this jargon is called *preprocessing* the code, and the statements are called *preprocessor directives*. Table 6-1 shows the preprocessor directives you can use.

Table 6-1. *Available Preprocessor Directives*

Hash Code	Description
#Const	Used to define the compilation identifier, such as the INTEGRATE_TESTS identifier used in this chapter's example. You would define this at the top of a source code file to activate conditional preprocessor statements used throughout the source code file. Using a #Const directive does not span multiple source code files.
#If and #End If	Used to conditionally include or not include a piece of source code. You would use a conditional directive whenever you wanted to define source code configurations, such as for debug or production builds.

Table 6-1. *Available Preprocessor Directives (Continued)*

Hash Code	Description
#ElseIf	Instead of a single #If block, you could have multiple tests for code inclusion. You would use #ElseIf when you have more than a single preprocessor directive, such as for debug, production, and performance builds.
#Else	A default code block that is included if the other #If statements did not trigger.
#Region and #EndRegion	These have absolutely nothing to do with the compilation of the source code. They are used by Visual Studio to create regions of source code that can be "folded." Folding means to collapse a block code out of sight temporarily. Source code files can be become long, and constantly paging up and down becomes tedious. By folding the code, you are reducing the amount of times that you need to page up and down, even though the code still exists.

The following example demonstrates how to use the preprocessor directives.

```
#Const ACTIVATE_1 = True

Namespace TestDefine
    Class Example
#If ACTIVATE_1 Then
        Private _dataMember As Integer
#ElseIf Not NO_ACTIVATE_10 Then
        Private _dataMember3 As Integer
#Else
        Private _defaultValue As Integer
#End If
    End Class
End Namespace
```

In general, you will use preprocessor directives when you are building debug mode or release mode code. *Debug mode* means that the code is compiled such that it can be debugged and analyzed using pretty symbols. *Release mode* means when the code is compiled, the code can still be debugged, but the pretty symbols are missing.

■**Note** Visual Basic Express does not give you the flexibility to choose debug mode or release mode for development. To get this feature, you need the full version of Visual Studio.

Think of the pretty symbols as milestones on the road. Every time your code executes in debug mode, the code is saying, "You are now calling this method in this source code file," or "Oops, that property code in the source code file is not working properly." In release mode, the pretty symbols are more like road signs saying, "Place X y Miles/Kilometers." The signs help guide you, but the information you get from them is very limited; that is, you don't know which towns you're passing.

More Property Scope Details

In this chapter's examples, the Get and Set parts of the properties always had the same scope. However, properties can have mixed scope; that is, the Get and Set parts can have different scopes. Scope splitting works only if you specify both the Get and Set parts of the property. The idea behind splitting the scope is to enable the implementation of the logic where classes in the inheritance chain are allowed to assign a property, and classes external to the inheritance chain are allowed only to read the property. The following is an example where a property is declared as Public and the assignment of the property is Protected.

```
Class PropertyScopeExample
    Private _value As Integer

    Public Property Value() As Integer
        Protected Set(ByVal value As Integer)
            _value = value
        End Set
        Get
            Return _value
        End Get
    End Property
End Class
```

The MustOverride Keyword

In this chapter's example, the keyword MustInherit was used to declare a class that could be referenced, but not instantiated. It is also possible to define methods that need to be implemented. In Visual Basic, to require a derived class to implement the method, you use MustOverride. The idea behind declaring methods that need to be overridden is that it allows a developer to define an intention in a base class that can then be implemented in the subclass.

In the implementation of HotelCurrencyTrader and ActiveCurrencyTrader, two methods were defined: ConvertTo() and ConvertFrom(). A developer could come to the conclusion that the methods are common to both classes, and thus they could be defined in the base class CurrencyTrader. That is not a bad idea. Let's revisit the CurrencyTrader class and see how these two methods could be added to CurrencyTrader as MustOverride methods.

```
Public MustInherit Class CurrencyTrader
    Private _exchangeRate As Double

    Protected Property ExchangeRate() As Double
        Get
            Return _exchangeRate
        End Get
        Set (ByVal Value As Double)
            _exchangeRate = Value
        End Set
```

```
    End Property
    Protected Function ConvertValue(ByVal input As Double) As Double
        Return _exchangeRate * input
    End Function
    Protected Function ConvertValueInverse(ByVal input As Double) As Double
        Return input / _exchangeRate
    End Function
    Public MustOverride Function ConvertTo(ByVal value As Double) As Double
    Public MustOverride Function ConvertFrom(ByVal value As Double) As Double
End Class
```

A MustOverride method is declared without an implementation. Any class that subclasses CurrencyTrader is required to implement ConvertTo() and ConvertFrom(). In the case of HotelCurrencyTrader and ActiveCurrencyTrader, this is not a problem, because the methods are already implemented. However, the methods need to be changed slightly, as follows:

```
    Public Overrides Function ConvertTo(ByVal value As Double) As Double
        ' . . .
    End Function
    Public Overrides Function ConvertFrom(ByVal value As Double) As Double
        ' . . .
    End Function
```

The slight change is the addition of the keyword Overrides to indicate that the ConvertTo() and ConvertFrom() methods in HotelCurrencyTrader and ActiveCurrencyTrader override the functionality in CurrencyTrader.

While you have seen all of the technical aspects, the bigger question is why you would do this in the first place. Let's go back to the implementation of ActiveCurrencyTrader, which has no MustOverride method implementations. To use the class and the method ConvertTo(), you would write the following code.

```
Dim cls As ActiveCurrencyTrader = New ActiveCurrencyTrader(1.46, "USD", "EUR")
Dim converted As Double = cls.ConvertTo(100.0)
```

Imagine the situation where the values to convert to and from are text. To keep things general, you would write the following code (which takes the value from a text box in a Windows form).

```
Public Function ConvertToTextField(ByVal cls As ActiveCurrencyTrader) As Double
    Return cls.ConvertTo(Double.Parse(text1.Text))
End Function
```

The implementation of ConvertToTextField() makes one major mistake in that it assumes that you will always be converting a currency using the ActiveCurrencyTrader implementation. If you wanted to use the class HotelCurrencyTrader, you would need to implement another method with a parameter of type HotelCurrencyTrader.

This problem is a classical *polymorphism* issue and is solved by using MustOverride methods (as you'll see in Chapter 7, the Overridable keyword also allows polymorphism). Consider the following rewritten ConvertToTextField() method.

```
Public Function ConvertToTextField(ByVal cls As CurrencyTrader) As Double
    Return cls.ConvertTo(Double.Parse(text1.Text))
End Function
```

This implementation of `ConvertToTextField()` uses the `CurrencyTrader` base class, and since `ConvertTo()` and `ConvertFrom()` are declared, they can be referenced.

How you call `ConvertToTextField()` and how you instantiate `HotelCurrencyTrader` or `ActiveCurrencyTrader` will not be covered in this chapter, because polymorphism is the subject of the next chapter. Just keep what you've learned about the `MustInherit` and `MustOverride` keywords in mind as you read that chapter, which covers concepts such as interfaces, because you can do the same types of things with them.

The Important Stuff to Remember

In this chapter, you learned some of the basics of object-oriented programming. Here are the key points to remember:

- Your code will be composed of structural (or base class functionality) and architectural business-related functionality.

- Base class functionality is focused on a particular problem. Base class functionality requires specific knowledge of the field. Think of it as implementing a calculator where your main concern is ensuring that the calculations are correct.

- Architectural business-related functionality is higher-level functionality where general business knowledge is needed. The idea is to take the base classes and use them to solve a business problem. Think of it as using a calculator and your main concern is getting the results of the calculations.

- Properties should be used instead of exposing data members publicly.

- Many developers dislike properties because they promote bad programming practices. You need to get beyond those comments and think in terms of the credit card and the cashier. Properties have their time and place.

- Classes should, in general, not expose their state. To get around exposing state, create methods that implement the general intent of the purpose of the class.

- Inheritance is a fundamental part of Visual Basic and you will need to know how to use it.

- Overriding is when you keep the interface the same and change behavior.

- Overloading is when you derive a class and define an identifier that happens to be the same as some base class identifier. Your overloaded identifier may change behavior and usage.

- Conditional compilation statements can be effective when you want to include code in certain configurations.

- Partial classes are very useful when you want to separate functionality that serves a specific purpose. In this chapter's example, it meant having the ability to add test code without violating the rule of exposing state.

Some Things for You to Do

To apply what you've learned in this chapter, you can do the following exercises.

1. The code for HotelCurrencyTrader.ConvertTo() and HotelCurrencyTrader. ConvertFrom() contains a potentially big bug. Identify the bug and fix it.

2. In the examples, the exchange rate is assigned by the caller of the HotelCurrencyTrader and ActiveCurrencyTrader. Implement functionality such that the exchange rate can be retrieved dynamically.

3. The currency ExchangeRate property is a Double. Implement ExchangeRate using the Decimal type.

4. Write test code for ActiveCurrencyTrader and HotelCurrencyTrader.

■■■

Learning About Components and Class Hierarchies

The previous chapter covered the basics of object-oriented programming. You learned how one class can subclass another class, thus building a hierarchy. Using a class hierarchy, classes can share functionality.

This chapter will focus on the details of class hierarchies, including how to extend them so that derived classes can specialize shared functionality. To demonstrate these concepts, we will build a tax application. This type of application is a good example of using class hierarchies, because the general idea of paying taxes is identical, regardless of the country, but the details are different.

From a technical perspective, we'll cover the following topics:

- Interfaces, which are the basis of software components

- Details of overloading and overriding methods

- How and when to use factories

We'll begin with some basic tax concepts that relate to our sample application.

Understanding Some Basic Tax Concepts

Taxes and death are two sure things in life. Regardless of where you live, the government has managed to create a system where you pay taxes (for the good of the people, of course). As a result, people hate paying taxes, and many figure out creative ways to not pay taxes. Honest people who would normally not break the law find clever ways of bending the rules in their favor. In some countries, they even expect that you will cheat, and will calculate your "true" tax figure.

Taxes seem like a complex topic, but they are rather simple. The volumes of rules associated with taxes are what make them complicated. Taxes boil down to the fact that if you buy or do *X*, then you can deduct or charge *Y*. Sometimes, the taxes make sense; sometimes they don't. Overall though, the tax rules are similar in logic, and that means a hierarchy of classes can be designed.

Taxable income is the sum of monies that you earned for which a tax rate is applied. The taxable income may or may not be equal to the sum of money that you earned during a year.

Taxable income can be less due to deductions and income deferment. And in some cases, taxable income can be more due to deferment.

Deductions are items that can be charged against taxable income. People mistakenly believe that deductions can be charged directly against the tax payable amount. Or they mistakenly believe a tax deduction is always an advantage. For example, let's say you have $1,000 of tax deductions. If your income is $2,000,000, then the deduction is not worth much, since your taxable income is still $1,999,000.

Partial taxation is when a partial amount of earned monies is added to the total taxable income. Often, partial taxation is applied to capital gains. *Capital gains* refer to when you have bought something like a property and then sold it at a higher price than you paid for it. The difference between the two prices is subject to capital gains tax.

A variation of partial taxation is *income splitting*, so that a lower tax rate is achieved. Let's say that you have a household of two people. One of the two earns the income, and the other stays at home. In such a case, the household would be taxed at the same level as a single-person household. Yet the two-person household has more expenses. Thus, some countries allow a household to declare a single tax, where in effect, a single earner in a two-person household is taxed at half the rate.

When calculating the total tax, some countries linearly increase the taxation rate. Typically, the linear tax rate is less for lower incomes and more for higher incomes. Another approach is to divide income in chunks with different tax rates for each. This means that those monies earned up to a certain amount are taxed at a certain rate. Monies above that amount and below another higher amount are taxed at a higher rate. This chunking of the amounts and rates keeps on being calculated until a highest tax rate is reached, where any amounts over that upper limit are taxed at the highest rate.

Organizing the Tax Application

As a general rule, in each country, you must pay an income tax, which is calculated against your total income. From your income, you can deduct certain expenses, thus lowering your taxable income. The aspects that differ from country to country are what you can deduct and the individual tax rate. These will be addressed by the tax application we will build in this chapter.

For the tax application, the following features will be implemented:

- Define a taxable income.

- Define a series of deductions.

- Implement a tax-calculation engine that has the ability to account for families or single earners.

As in previous examples, the project structure of the taxation application will consist of two projects: a console testing application and a library component that contains the functionality. The library component will be in a project called LibTax, and the testing application will be in a project called TestTax.

Before we start coding, however, you need to understand the concepts of interfaces and components.

Programming Using Ideas

At this moment, we don't have a clue where to start building the tax application, because the problem is in the details of the implementation. Unlike previous examples, where it was possible to gauge what tests were needed, in this example, we simply do not know. We could start by implementing the general tax rules and then applying them to a specific system. But what if our general tax rule implementations didn't actually work out? We would have wasted time writing code that we would end up throwing out.

Consider the following situation: you write a series of base classes that represent a generic taxation kernel based on the information in the "Understanding Some Basic Tax Concepts" section. The base classes need a task, and thus wait for a client. A little while later, an individual from the United Kingdom desires a tax program based on the base classes. The developers, eager to show off the usefulness of their base classes, implement the tax program. The idea is that you save time by using the base classes to implement something specific. Without the base classes, you would, in theory, have a longer development time.

Experience has shown that unless the base classes are developed from highly experienced business analyses, the odds of the base classes helping you are rather slim. What most likely will happen is your base class code will need to be warped, twisted, and fitted to make the program work. The result is that if another client from another country asks for a tax program, the base classes will yet again need to be warped, twisted, and fitted to make the program work. The managers, seeing this brute-force technique, start to realize that the monies invested in the base classes were not such a good idea.

Who is at fault? Is it the fault of the developers who created the base classes? Is it the fault of the complexity of implementing a tax program? The answer is that it is the fault of the idea of the base classes. The original developers wanted to create base classes based on a problem that does not exist. It is like trying to build the foundation of the bridge across the water before you have an idea of how many people will use the bridge and what kind of people will use the bridge. Logically, engineers don't start building a bridge before they figure out the details of the bridge. Yet, in the software industry, time and time again, we see projects focusing on developing a general framework without having a concrete problem to solve.

I am not saying that base classes themselves are a bad idea, nor is the idea of developing a general framework. What I am saying is that to be able to develop useful base classes, you need to understand the domain of the base classes. If you don't, then you should not be writing base classes.

But how do you gain experience in the domain to write well-designed base classes? You can start by writing down some ideas as Visual Basic constructs and then implementing the ideas. Coming up with ideas and then implementing them is part of the development process called *test-driven architecture*.

To start test-driven architecting, you think of the requirements and then come up with a general solution. In the case of our example, the requirement is to create a tax engine to calculate income tax. Generally speaking, it means figuring out what the total taxable income is, subtracting the total deductions, and applying a tax rate to the remaining sum to calculate the total tax.

In programming terms, the general ideas are converted into source using Visual Basic *interfaces*.

Representing Ideas Using Visual Basic Interfaces

Think of Visual Basic interfaces as programmatic constructs you can use to jot down ideas. When you jot down ideas to solve a problem, you usually implement a bread-crumb trail approach— you start with one idea, and then follow it to another idea, which leads to another idea, until you have jotted down all of your ideas.

Your first idea is the central idea. In our tax application, the central idea is the tax engine itself. The tax engine is used to perform a tax calculation and to pull together all of the other pieces. The other pieces are some nebulous things that you need to complete the tax engine. I like to call these other pieces *dependencies*. The dependencies are ideas that you need to finish the previous idea, hence the metaphor of following bread crumbs to your solution.

Ideas by themselves are designs that solve a particular problem or give an inkling of how to solve the particular problem. When an idea is converted into source code, it becomes a blueprint that forces the implementation to take a certain shape. Ideas when coded are Visual Basic interfaces, which cannot be executed by themselves. From a programmatic point of view, an interface is like a MustInherit base class in that you can reference an interface, but you cannot instantiate an interface. To get a working idea, you write an implementation, or implement an interface.

The following is an example of a Visual Basic interface.

```
Interface IExample
End Interface
```

The keyword Interface is associated with an identifier IExample, and from a syntax perspective is used like the Class keyword. You can associate the public scope with an interface. The interface contains methods and properties that determine the behavior of the classes that implement the interface. Consider the following source code, which defines an interface with a single method and single property.

```
Interface IExample
    Sub Method()
    Property ExampleProperty As Integer
End Interface
```

When you define an interface, the included methods and properties do not have an implementation because you are defining a signature. A class that implements an interface will play a game called "match the properties and method signatures."

■**Note** Generally speaking, the naming convention used to define a type is verbose and self-explanatory. When I define interfaces, I use identifiers prefixed with a capital I, like IExample. The capital I is a common convention used to identify interfaces. You should use this notation to be consistent with other .NET code.

The following code is a rudimentary implementation of the defined interface.

```
Class ExampleImplementation
    Implements IExample

    Public Sub Method() Implements IExample.Method
    End Sub

    Public Property ExampleProperty() As Integer Implements IExample.ExampleProperty
        Get
            Return 0
        End Get
        Set(ByVal value As Integer)
        End Set
    End Property
End Class
```

ExampleImplementation implements the interface IExample using an explicit cross-reference of the method or property signature. The cross-reference of interface to implementation in the sample method is prefixed with the keyword Implements, and the appropriate interface and method. The method name doesn't need to be the same as the interface's method name. All that matters is the signature of the method, or property.

■**Note** Visual Basic and the CLR are single-inheritance models in that a class can subclass only a single class. But a Visual Basic class can implement as many interfaces as necessary. If a class subclasses another class, it uses Inherits; if it implements interfaces, it uses Implements. The class is the first identifier after the colon.

When implementing an interface, all of the methods and properties of the interface must be implemented in the class. If they are not, then when the source code is compiled, the compiler will complain about missing methods or properties and consider the implementation as incomplete.

As inheritance is used, you can think of IExample as a base class that has no implementation. The following code illustrates how to instantiate the implementation and assign the instance to a variable that has the interface as its type.

```
Dim cls As IExample = New ExampleImplementation()
cls.Method()
```

In the example, the class ExampleImplementation is instantiated and assigned to a variable cls of type IExample. Think of it as saying, "I am instantiating ExampleImplementation and assigning the instance to the type IExample that is in my inheritance hierarchy." When the method cls.Method() is called, the caller is really calling ExampleImplementation.Method(), although the caller would not know that, as it is using the base type IExample.

The mechanics of defining an interface and its associated implementation are straightforward, but why would you do it? To explain, I'll use a real-life analogy.

Let's say that you are going to a restaurant for an evening of fine dining. When you are sitting at the table, you expect a waiter to take your order, serve your food, remove the used dishes, and give you the bill. All of these actions are ideas used to run a restaurant that serves a clientele. You make use of the idea, as do millions of other clients. The idea is applied across all restaurants.

Think about this a bit. The idea is a waiter, but the implementation is a human. When you sit down, your waiter may introduce himself by his name, but do you ever use the name? Most people don't, because they think of the waiter as a human that takes their order, serves their food, and so on. The point is that the human is the implementation, but you really only care about a waiter fulfilling the scope of the task. For example, while you might be sympathetic that your waiter is having a bad day, you want him to be chipper and happy, and to do his job of taking your order, serving your food, and so on. Bluntly put, you probably would not care if the waiter's puppy had been run over by a truck.

This is exactly what interfaces and implementations are about. The interface defines a role of tasks that an implementation is supposed to implement. You don't care if the implementation is capable of doing more, or if the implementation is "having a bad day." All you care about is that the implementation does what the interface says it should do.

What you have is a decoupling of the idea from the interface, just like at the restaurant, where you don't care if Tom, Dick, Mary, or Jane is your server. In fact, would you care if the human waiter were replaced by a robot? Probably not, because what you really care about is eating the food. This is an important aspect of interfaces and implementations, in that implementations are replaceable, and you want to be able to swap one implementation for another.

When you use interfaces and types that implement interfaces, you are writing component-oriented software. Components and inheritance are two different object-oriented techniques. You use inheritance to implement interfaces, but components serve the purpose of making ideas happen.

Understanding How Inheritance and Components Work

Inheritance is the act of defining base classes with functionality that may or may not be overridden or overloaded, as explained in the previous chapter. Components define subsystems that are put together like pieces of a puzzle. The idea behind components is to be able to associate two interface instances and make them work with each other without knowing what the other does.

To get a feeling of the difference between inheritance using classes and components that use interfaces and classes, we will look at a classic example of inheritance and how that example translates to components.

Illustrating Inheritance Using a Shape, Rectangle, and Square

One of the most popular examples of using inheritance involves shapes and how to calculate the area of a shape. The starting point of this inheritance is a MustInherit base class that has a single property and method to indicate a single dimension and its associated area. For example, the following would be an appropriate base class definition.

```
MustInherit Class Shape
    Public MustOverride Function CalculateArea() As Double
End Class
```

The method CalculateArea() is used to calculate the area of the shape. It is declared as MustOverride and must be implemented by a derived class.

For starters, let's define Square, which represents the square shape.

```
Class Square
    Inherits Shape

    Private _width As Double
    Public Property Width() As Double
        Get
            Return _width
        End Get
        Set(ByVal value As Double)
            _width = value
        End Set
    End Property

    Public Overrides Function CalculateArea() As Double
        Return Width * Width
    End Function
End Class
```

A square has only one dimension, Width, which represents the width of a particular shape. In the case of a square, width means one of the four sides. We've implemented the CalculateArea() method, which calculates the surface area of the square by multiplying the Width property by itself.

A rectangle is a form of square, and therefore Rectangle derives from Square:

```
Class Rectangle
    Inherits Square

    Private _length As Double
    Public Property Length() As Double
        Get
            Return _length
        End Get
        Set(ByVal value As Double)
            _length = value
        End Set
    End Property

    Public Overloads Function CalculateArea() As Double
        Return Width * Length
    End Function
End Class
```

Rectangle cannot be described using a single dimension, thus we need to add the property Length. In the implementation of the Rectangle.CalculateArea() method to calculate the area, the length is multiplied by the width.

Take a good look at how CalculateArea() is declared. In the case of Rectangle.CalculateArea(), the Overloads keyword is used, not Overrides. This is because you want to enforce calculation consistency. Calculation consistency is when you perform a specific calculation on a type and get the answer expected of that type, and not some other type.

So, say you instantiate Rectangle, and then cast it to Square. When you call CalculateArea(), you want it to calculate as if the rectangle were a square, not a rectangle. Thus, by adding the Overloads keyword in the Rectangle.CalculateArea() method, a square is calculated as a square, and a rectangle is calculated as a rectangle.

But there is a consequence. Let's say Rectangle is cast to Shape. As the inheritance is declared when calling CalculateArea(), the area of a square is calculated, which is not correct. Thus it would seem that using New is incorrect, and Overrides should be used instead. So using Overrides solves the Shape.CalculateArea() problem, but when a rectangle is converted into a square, the area represents a rectangle and not square.

To illustrate the differences, assuming the use of Overloads, look at the following source code, which calculates the area of a Rectangle.

```
Dim cls As Rectangle = New Rectangle()
cls.Width = 20
cls.Length = 30
Dim area As Double = cls.CalculateArea()
```

In the example, Rectangle is instantiated, and the properties Width and Length are assigned values of 20 and 30, respectively. When the CalculateArea() method is called, the found area is assigned to the variable area.

The source code does what we expect. It instantiates a rectangle, assigns the rectangle dimensions, and calculates the area of the rectangle. But a Rectangle object can also be assigned to a square variable. Consider the following modified source code:

```
Dim rectangle As Rectangle = New Rectangle()
rectangle.Width = 20
rectangle.Length = 30
Dim square As Square = rectangle
Dim area As Double = square.CalculateArea()
Console.WriteLine("Square Area is " & square.CalculateArea() & _
    " Rectangle Area is " & rectangle.CalculateArea())
```

In the example, the variable rectangle is of type Rectangle. The dimensions of the rectangle are assigned, and then the rectangle is converted into a square and assigned to the variable square. Using the keyword Overloads, the area is 400, which is correct because when we ask for the dimensions of the square, we get a width of 20.

The various techniques used in this example are explained in the remainder of this chapter.

Note The example illustrates that by using inheritance, you can cast a type and get the appropriate behavior. But this works only if you design your inheritance hierarchy properly. You need to understand that behavior depends on the type that you have from the inheritance tree. And if you are not careful, you can get some very odd side effects. Visual Basic allows you to explicitly define what each method does, and you should think very hard about what each method should do.

Illustrating Components Using a Shape, Rectangle, and Square

Another way to implement a shape is to use components. Using components means to define an idea, and then define an implementation of the idea. Designing and implementing components is not similar to designing and implementing inheritance trees. With inheritance, you need to consider type casting, base class functionality, and how to override or overload methods or properties. (*Type casting* is when you cast to a specific type with or without an explicit cast operator.) With components, you need to think in terms of ideas and how they would be implemented as interfaces.

Having looked at the Shape, Rectangle, and Square implementation, you might define an interface (named IShape) as follows:

```
Interface IShape
    Function CalculateArea() As Double
    Property Width() As Double
End Interface
```

For the IShape declaration, you might even add a Length property, but the overall idea of the IShape interface is wrong. When you think of a shape, do you think in terms of length and width? Probably not. Rather, you think in terms of area, perimeter, and other features that are common to all shapes. Length and width are not common to all shapes. A circle has a radius or diameter; a triangle has base width, height, and triangle peak offset. The point is that the idea of a shape is not the idea of a rectangle or a square.

The correct way to define the ideas as interfaces would be as follows:

```
Interface IShape
    Function CalculateArea() As Double
End Interface

Interface ISquare
    Inherits IShape
    Property Width() As Double
End Interface

Interface IRectangle
    Inherits IShape
    Property Width() As Double
    Property Length() As Double
End Interface
```

This code contains three interfaces: IShape, which defines a shape; IRectangle, which describes a rectangle; and ISquare, which describes a square. The IRectangle and ISquare interfaces subclass the IShape interface, indicating that an IRectangle is also an IShape. The ISquare interface is separate from the IRectangle interface, because the idea of a square (four equal sides) is not the same as the idea of a rectangle (only the parallel sides of the four sides must be equal), even though the shapes might appear similar (in real life, a square is a rectangle, but a rectangle is not necessarily a square).

This separation of the square and rectangle interface illustrates that when designing interfaces, you need to focus on the specific behavior of the interface. You don't want to focus on the general behavior. The general behavior is managed when you design the classes. The modeling of your real-life experiences is defined in the implementations, as illustrated by the following example.

```
Class SquareImpl
    Implements ISquare, IRectangle
End Class

Class RectangleImpl
    Implements IRectangle
End Class
```

The SquareImpl class implements the behavior of ISquare and IRectangle, and models real life, where a square is also a rectangle. And RectangleImpl implements only the behavior IRectangle, illustrating that a rectangle can only be a rectangle and not a square. Now you cannot write code where the implementation produces inconsistent results.

■**Note** When defining ideas, the resulting interfaces could be considered as behavior characteristics that an implementation can have. It is entirely possible for an implementation to have multiple behavior character- istics. For example, this could mean that an implementation could be both a square and rectangle at the same time. In terms of the restaurant, waiters are humans with hobbies, feelings, and desires, although you don't know these other aspects, as you see only the waiters.

An optimization could have been the following interface inheritance.

```
Interface ISquare
    Inherits IShape
    Property Width() As Double
End Interface

Interface IRectangle
    Inherits ISquare
    Property Length() As Double
End Interface
```

or

```
Interface ISquare
    Inherits IRectangle
End Interface

Interface IRectangle
    Inherits IShape
    Property Width() As Double
    Property Length() As Double
End Interface
```

However, this isn't a good idea, because at the interface level, you are implying that a square and rectangle are related. They might be at the implementation level, but they also might not be. For example, imagine you are creating a super shape that has the characteristics of a rectangle and a triangle. When creating a relationship between interfaces, you are implying that the super shape depending on the interface inheritance used must have the characteristics of a square, even though it might not. Thus, when using inheritance with interfaces, IShape as a base interface of IRectangle and ISquare is acceptable, but a relation between IRectangle and ISquare is not.

Now that you have an idea of the differences between inheritance and components, we can get started with our tax application. As we work through the example, you'll learn the details of implementing interfaces.

Implementing a Tax Engine

So far, we've discussed some basic tax concepts; the features of the tax application; and the theory of inheritance, interfaces, and components. We're ready to implement the tax engine. The preferred approach is to design the core idea and then create the other pieces, or dependencies.

Defining the Interfaces

Putting everything together and starting with the tax engine, we can create the following interface structure.

```
Public Interface ITaxIncome
    ReadOnly Property RealAmount() As Double
    ReadOnly Property TaxableAmount() As Double
End Interface

Public Interface ITaxDeduction
    ReadOnly Property Amount() As Double
End Interface

Public Interface ITaxAccount
    Sub AddDeduction(ByVal deduction As ITaxDeduction)
    Sub AddIncome(ByVal income As ITaxIncome)
    Function GetTaxRate(ByVal income As Double) As Double
    ReadOnly Property Deductions() As ITaxDeduction()
    ReadOnly Property Income() As ITaxIncome()
End Interface

Public Interface ITaxEngine
    Function CalculateTaxToPay(ByVal account As ITaxAccount) As Double
    Function CreateDeduction(ByVal amount As Double) As ITaxDeduction
    Function CreateIncome(ByVal amount As Double) As ITaxIncome
    Function CreateTaxAccount() As ITaxAccount
End Interface
```

We have four interfaces here: ITaxIncome, ITaxDeduction, ITaxAccount, and ITaxEngine. ITaxIncome and ITaxDeduction are pure behavioral interfaces. *Pure behavioral* means the interface does one thing, but it might be implemented in conjunction with other interfaces. ITaxEngine and ITaxAccount are behavioral functional interfaces. *Behavioral functional* means that the interfaces are typically implemented by themselves, and usually not with another interface.

For example, you might implement a Swiss tax system where there are two classes, defined as follows:

```
Class SwissTaxEngine
    Implements ITaxEngine
End Class

Class SwissTaxAccount
    Implements ITaxAccount
End Class
```

And if you wish to implement an American tax system, the two classes would be defined as follows:

```
Class AmericanTaxEngine
    Implements ITaxEngine
End Class

Class AmericanTaxAccount
    Implements ITaxAccount
End Class
```

The user of either the American or Swiss tax system will not know the specific details of those tax systems. Initially, users would need to determine which tax system they wished to use. This decision is made using something called a factory, as explained in the upcoming "Abstracting Instantiations with Factories" section.

Implementing a Base Class Tax Engine

Whenever you define interfaces, you will need to implement them. In most cases, you will create a MustInherit base class that provides a certain amount of default functionality. The MustInherit base class serves the same purpose as outlined in the previous chapter: to provide a certain amount of basic functionality.

In the case of the tax engine, we need to implement the ITaxEngine interface and provide default implementations for some methods. The following is the complete base class implementation.

```
Public MustInherit Class BaseTaxEngine
    Implements ITaxEngine

    Protected _calculatedTaxable As Double

    Public Overridable Function CalculateTaxToPay(ByVal account As ITaxAccount) _
        As Double Implements ITaxEngine.CalculateTaxToPay
```

```
        _calculatedTaxable = 0.0

        For Each income As ITaxIncome In account.Income
            If income IsNot Nothing Then
                _calculatedTaxable = _calculatedTaxable + income.TaxableAmount
            End If
        Next

        For Each deduction As ITaxDeduction In account.Deductions
            If  deduction IsNot Nothing
                _calculatedTaxable = _calculatedTaxable - deduction.Amount
            End If
        Next

        Return account.GetTaxRate(_calculatedTaxable) * _calculatedTaxable
    End Function

    Public Overridable Function CreateDeduction(ByVal amount As Double) _
        As ITaxDeduction Implements ITaxEngine.CreateDeduction
        Return New TaxDeduction(amount)
    End Function

    Public Overridable Function CreateIncome(ByVal amount As Double) As ITaxIncome _
        Implements ITaxEngine.CreateIncome
        ' Second argument is the tax rate
        Return New TaxIncome(amount, 1.0)
    End Function
    Public MustOverride Function CreateTaxAccount() As ITaxAccount _
        Implements ITaxEngine.CreateTaxAccount
End Class
```

The base class must implement all interface methods, regardless of whether or not the method has an implementation. The CalculateTaxToPay(), CreateDeduction(), and CreateIncome() methods have implementations. The CreateTaxAccount() method does not have an implementation and is declared as MustOverride. The methods with implementations have an Overridable keyword associated with them, indicating any class derived from BaseTaxEngine can override the functionality if they don't like the default functionality.

In the implementation of CalculateTaxToPay(), the income (account.Income) is added together and deductions (account.Deductions) are subtracted from the income. The resulting total is used as a query amount (account.GetTaxRate()) to retrieve the actual tax rate used to calculate against the payable tax.

■**Note** The implementation of CalculateTaxToPay() is a shared functionality, which implies that there cannot be any code specific to a derived type. All of the calculations and data manipulations are executed against an interface, making it possible to generalize operations. Whenever you implement base class methods or shared pieces of code, you should try to keep the source code derived class-agnostic.

Overriding for Specialized Functionality

In the base class implementation, the data member _calculatedTaxable is declared as Protected. As you learned in the previous chapter, this means that _calculatedTaxable can be manipulated in a derived class. However, if you look at how the data member is used, you will see that only CalculateTaxToPay() assigns the data member. The purpose of the data member is to provide information about the operation CalculateTaxToPay() without giving the exact details of the operation.

The idea behind _calculatedTaxable and the declaration of CalculateTaxToPay() is to provide a mechanism where the derived class does not need to calculate things again. Consider the example of a country where, if your taxable income is above 400 currency units, a surtax of 10 currency units is calculated. You don't know what your taxable income is until the function CalculateTaxToPay() is executed, and that function returns only the total payable taxes. So how do you know if you should apply the surtax in this situation? One solution is to reverse-calculate the payable taxes, but that would involve quite a few additional steps. An easier solution is to write some code in the base class method of CalculateTaxToPay() that stores the taxable income so the subclass has access to it.

The original implementation of CalculateTaxToPay() does not consider a surtax, so the derived class must contain that functionality. Since CalculateTaxToPay() can be overridden without the data member _calculatedTaxable, the derived class would need to implement the functionality in the base class to calculate whether or not the surtax applies. Following is an sample derived class implementation of the tax engine for such a situation, stored in a namespace called Surtax, to distinguish it from the base functionality.

```
Namespace Surtax
    Friend Class TaxEngine
        Inherits BaseTaxEngine

        Public Overrides Function CalculateTaxToPay(ByVal account As ITaxAccount) _
            As Double
            Dim taxToPay As Double = MyBase.CalculateTaxToPay(account)
            If _calculatedTaxable > 400 Then
                taxToPay = taxToPay + 10
            End If
            Return taxToPay
        End Function

        Public Overrides Function CreateTaxAccount() As ITaxAccount
            Throw New Exception("The method or operation is not implemented.")
        End Function
    End Class
End Namespace
```

In the implementation of CalculateTaxToPay(), we replace the Overridable keyword with Overrides, implying that the functionality of TaxEngine replaces the functionality of BaseTaxEngine. Since our fictional country calculates the basic tax similarly to most countries, the functionality of BaseTaxEngine.CalculateTaxToPay() can be used. Thus, the first line of TaxEngine. CalculateTaxToPay() is MyBase.CalculateTaxToPay(), meaning the base class (BaseTaxEngine) method CalculateTaxToPay() is called.

Calling the base class results in calculating a basic tax to pay amount. We need to figure out if a surtax applies, and that is where the protected data member _calculatedTaxable comes into play. Having called `BaseTaxEngine.CalculateTaxToPay()`, the data member _calculatedTaxable is assigned and contains the amount that is being taxed. Thus, `TaxEngine.CalculateTaxToPay()` can make a decision if more than 400 currency units have been earned. And if so, then the variable taxToPay is incremented with another 10 currency units. Had _calculatedTaxable not existed, `TaxEngine.CalculateTaxToPay()` would have needed to call the base class functionality to get the basic tax rate, and then recalculate the taxable monies to figure out if the surtax applied.

■Note When you use Overrides with methods, you are saying that you need something special. This does not imply that the base class functionality will be called. It implies that you might call the base class functionality and perform some additional operations. Thus, when designing base class functionality, it is important to track calculations or operations using protected data members. The data members avoid having derived classes perform the same operations multiple times, slowing down the application and avoiding potential errors.

USING NAMESPACES

Namespaces are used to define classes, interfaces, and structures that belong together. In this chapter's example, there is an American tax engine, a Swiss tax engine, and so on. For organizational purposes, each should have its own namespace. Sometimes you might even create a custom assembly for each set of interface implementations, but you would still need to create a namespace. Creating a namespace is independent of the fact of whether or not you create a separate assembly.

In the examples, I use namespaces like Surtax and Canada. Whenever you create a class or a module, or some other type, you can embed the type within the namespace. Then to use the newly defined namespaces in code pieces that are not part of the namespace, use the Imports keyword.

Abstracting Instantiations with Factories

Take a good look at the scope declaration of the tax engine shown earlier and compare it with the scope declaration for the ITaxEngine interface. What you will notice is that ITaxEngine is declared as Public scope, as is BaseTaxEngine, and TaxEngine is declared as Friend. Going back to our project structure, this scope declaration implies that any reference to LibTax will see the interface ITaxEngine and BaseTaxEngine, but not TaxEngine. For example, the following test code will not work.

```
Dim taxengine As ITaxEngine = New Surtax.TaxEngine()
```

The reason the test code will not work is that any type that is not declared with Public scope is private to the solution containing the declaration. You may be thinking, "That's great—you declare a type that you cannot instantiate. So, how can I use that type?"

The scope declarations are not a mistake and illustrate a design pattern called a *factory*. A factory is a way of abstracting the instantiation away from the caller so that the interface can vary from its implementation. In our restaurant analogy, it means when you want a waiter, you don't want to need to know his name. You would rather have a generic mechanism where the restaurant presents to you the waiter. Otherwise, to eat at a restaurant, you would need to know the name of your waiter before being able to order something. That would be inefficient.

The correct way of defining a factory is as follows:

```
Public Module EngineCreator
    Public Function CreateSurtaxTaxEngine() As ITaxEngine
        Return New Surtax.TaxEngine()
    End Function

    ' Required for country-specific tax calculations
    Public Function CreateCanadianTaxEngine() As ITaxEngine
        Return New Canada.TaxEngine()
    End Function
End Module
```

The factory is typically declared in a module because a module is not instantiated. Generally speaking, you don't want to add a factory to an object that can be instantiated because it could result in context-specific instantiation. In other words, you usually want a fresh object created from scratch each time, so it's not affected by the current state of the application. In the implementation of CreateSurtaxTaxEngine(), the type Surtax.TaxEngine is instantiated, and the instance is cast to the interface type ITaxEngine.

The EngineCreator module is declared with public scope, implying any code that references the assembly can see the module. Thus, the test code can be rewritten as follows (we need to import the LibTax project, of course):

```
Dim taxengine As ITaxEngine = EngineCreator.CreateSurtaxTaxEngine()
```

After calling EngineCreator.CreateSurtaxTaxEngine(), the test code has a valid instance of ITaxEngine. It's very important to note that the test code has no idea what type implemented the interface. This allows the assembly to change which type is referenced in the implementation of CreateSurtaxTaxEngine() without having to inform the caller of the method.

Putting this into the context of the restaurant, it means waiters can be replaced. So if you repeatedly visit a restaurant and get a waiter called John, but one day John gets sick and is not working, you can still order and receive your food from the waitress called Mary. It would be a bad idea for a restaurant to depend on a particular server for a particular guest.

Using Default Implementations

In some cases, base classes are not necessary. Sometimes you can create a default implementation that could span multiple subsystems. In the case of the tax engine, an income is an income in Canada, an income in the United States, and an income in Germany. What varies is how the income is treated in each country when calculating taxes. Another consistency across countries is that if income is a capital gain, not all of the income is taxable.

In the case of income, you can create an implementation that would be identical across different tax engines, as follows:

```
NotInheritable Class TaxIncome
    Implements ITaxIncome

    Private _amount As Double
    Private _taxableRate As Double

    Public Sub New(ByVal amount As Double, ByVal taxableRate As Double)
        _amount = amount
        _taxableRate = taxableRate
    End Sub

    Public ReadOnly Property RealAmount() As Double _
        Implements ITaxIncome.RealAmount
        Get
            Return _amount
        End Get
    End Property

    Public ReadOnly Property TaxableAmount() As Double _
        Implements ITaxIncome.TaxableAmount
        Get
            Return _amount * _taxableRate
        End Get
    End Property
End Class
```

The ITaxIncome interface has two properties that are implemented in TaxIncome: RealAmount and TaxableAmount. The values for the two properties are considered read-only and are defined by the constructor of TaxIncome. The purpose of the constructor is to assign two values and then consider the object as immutable. If you wanted to change the values of the ITaxIncome interface, you would need to instantiate a new instance of TaxIncome. While it sounds like a pain to need to instantiate a new instance whenever you want to change the value of the RealAmount and TaxableAmount properties, this approach has some advantages in terms of performance and resource management.

In the sample code, the TaxableAmount property is the result of multiplying the data members _amount and _taxableRate. For example, when calculating the taxable income of a capital gain in Canada, you multiply the total amount by 50%. Thus, the _taxableRate data member would have a value of 0.50.

Another item to note is that the declaration of TaxIncome is lacking a Public scope, but has a NotInheritable keyword prefixed to the identifier. When a class is prefixed with NotInheritable, it means that the class cannot be subclassed. From a design perspective, the code is saying TaxIncome is a shared class that should not be subclassed lest it affect the shared behavior.

The NotInheritable keyword can also be applied to a method, which means that the method cannot be overloaded or overridden. You would use NotOverridable on a method when you do not want a derived class to change the behavior of the method. Though to be able to use the NotOverridable keyword, you first need to define a method that overrides another method.

The implementation of ITaxDeduction is similar to ITaxIncome:

```
NotInheritable Class TaxDeduction
    Implements ITaxDeduction

    Private _amount As Double

    Public Sub New(ByVal amount As Double)
        _amount = amount
    End Sub

    Public ReadOnly Property Amount() As Double _
        Implements ITaxDeduction.Amount
        Get
            Return _amount
        End Get
    End Property
End Class
```

TaxIncome and TaxDeduction are sealed classes because the functionality will be shared among implementations. But is it wise to expose the interfaces and not the classes themselves? Interfaces are used to separate implementation from ideas. Interfaces change very little, whereas implementations can and will change more often. But if an implementation behaves like an interface in terms of changing interface signature, why not just expose the class itself? The answer is that sometimes you will expose the class, and sometimes you will expose the interface. For the tax engine, exposing the sealed classes TaxIncome and TaxDeduction would probably have been fine. The rule of thumb is that you expose classes only when you are sure that the interface signatures of methods and properties will not change very often.

Implementing a Base Tax Account

The ITaxAccount interface is also a candidate for base class functionality. The implementation of this interface looks like this:

```
MustInherit Class BaseTaxAccount
    Implements ITaxAccount

    Private _deductions(100) As ITaxDeduction
    Private _incomes(100) As ITaxIncome

    Public Sub AddDeduction(ByVal deduction As ITaxDeduction) _
        Implements ITaxAccount.AddDeduction
        For c1 As Integer = 0 To 100
            If _deductions(c1) Is Nothing Then
                _deductions(c1) = deduction
                Exit For
            End If
        Next
    End Sub
```

```
    Public Sub AddIncome(ByVal income As ITaxIncome) _
        Implements ITaxAccount.AddIncome
        For c1 As Integer = 0 to 100
            If _incomes(c1) Is Nothing Then
                _incomes(c1) = income
                Exit For
            End If
        Next
    End Sub

    Public ReadOnly Property Deductions() As ITaxDeduction() _
        Implements ITaxAccount.Deductions
        Get
            Return _deductions
        End Get
    End Property

    Public ReadOnly Property Income() As ITaxIncome() _
        Implements ITaxAccount.Income
        Get
            Return _incomes
        End Get
    End Property

    Public MustOverride Function GetTaxRate(ByVal income As Double) As Double _
        Implements ITaxAccount.GetTaxRate
End Class
```

Let's take stock of what has been accomplished and decide if the tax engine is complete from a base functionality perspective.

- Ideas have been defined for a complete tax engine.

- Some interfaces have been implemented in the form of base classes.

- Some interfaces have been implemented as sealed default implementations.

The tax engine can be considered complete because all of the interfaces have been defined and accounted for from a base functionality perspective as either base classes or default implementations. It is does not mean that interfaces will always be implemented. Sometimes some interfaces will not have a base functionality or base classes.

The important aspect to remember when defining the base functionality is to account for all interfaces to serve a purpose. Do not define an interface as a placeholder for potential future functionality. When seeing an interface, a user expects it to serve some type of purpose.

Note The rule of thumb for interfaces is that once defined and put into production, they are not changed. This rule of thumb is almost written in concrete. You never change interfaces once they are in production because doing so would wreak havoc—all the code that uses the interface would need to be updated. In general, if you feel the need to change an interface, create a new one.

With base functionality complete, we are ready to implement a tax system for a particular country.

Using the Base Functionality of the Tax Engine to Calculate Taxes

We will use the base functionality of the tax engine to calculate Canadian taxes. I chose the Canadian tax system because that is the system that I happen to know and understand, and there is plenty of online documentation on how to calculate the tax rate.

SOME BACKGROUND ON CANADIAN TAXES

The first thing I would like to say about Canadian taxes is that Canadians pay too much—way too much. The second comment is that Canadian taxes are simple, in that they don't let you write off many deductions (for example, interest payments on your house), which brings us back to the first point that Canadians pay way too much. Of course, people in other countries would probably say the exact same thing.

Canadian taxes are based on calculating the tax rate at the federal level and at the provincial level. Thus, to calculate your taxes, you need to know in which province and in which year you are paying your taxes. Canadian taxes change quite a bit depending on the year. From an implementation perspective, it means the tax engine must know about provincial taxes, federal taxes, and which year.

Capital gains in Canada are calculated on a 50% basis. This means if I made a capital gain of 200 Canadian dollars, then only 100 Canadian dollars are declared as taxable monies.

Implementing a Tax Engine and Tax Account

Implementing a Canadian tax engine means deriving a class from `BaseTaxEngine`, and that means implementing the `CreateTaxAccount()` method. The implementation of the Canadian tax engine will be in a new namespace, and a good name would be `Canada` (as this is in the `LibTax` project, it will have a root namespace of `LibTax`, so `LibTax.Canada` is the full namespace). The code will not show the namespace details, as they are implied.

The implementation is as follows:

```
Friend Class TaxEngine
    Inherits BaseTaxEngine
    Public Overrides Function CreateTaxAccount() As ITaxAccount
        Return New TaxAccount()
    End Function
```

```
End Class
```

In the implementation of the CreateTaxAccount() method, the TaxAccount class is instantiated. TaxAccount is a class that derives from BaseTaxAccount and thus implements the ITaxAccount interface. The implementation of TaxAccount is as follows:

```
Friend Class TaxAccount
    Inherits BaseTaxAccount

    Private _province As Province
    Private _year As Integer

    Public Overrides Function GetTaxRate(ByVal income As Double) As Double
        If _year = 2008 Then
            If _province = Province.Ontario Then
                Return OntarioTax2008.TaxRate(income)
            End If
        End If
        Throw New NotSupportedException("Year " & _year & " Province " & _
            _province & " not supported")
    End Function
End Class
```

The purpose of the GetTaxRate() method is to return the applicable tax rate for the given amount. In Canada, the tax rate is determined by which province you live in and the year. The calculation in GetTaxRate() has the ability to calculate the taxes for the year 2008 in the Ontario province. Here's the skeleton of the OntarioTax2008 class:

```
Public Class OntarioTax2008
    Public Shared Function TaxRate(ByVal income As Double) As Double
        ' Return the appropriate rate
    End Function
End Class
```

Yet there is a problem, and it involves the data members _province and _year. The data members are used in the calculation GetTaxRate(), but they are not assigned. This is a problem.

Assigning State When the Interface Cannot

The problem of the Canadian tax account is a common one that you will encounter in many situations. The essence of the problem is the need to assign state that is specific to an implementation without violating the intention of the general interface.

To illustrate the problem, let's say that the method GetTaxRate() will include a reference to the province and year. The rewritten ITaxAccount interface would be as follows:

```
Public Interface ITaxAccount
    Sub AddDeduction(ByVal deduction As ITaxDeduction)
    Sub AddIncome(ByVal income As ITaxIncome)
    Function GetTaxRate(ByVal income As Double, ByVal province As Province, _
    ByVal year As Integer) As Double
```

```
    ReadOnly Property Deductions() As ITaxDeduction()
    ReadOnly Property Income() As ITaxIncome()
End Interface
```

The bolded code illustrates the added parameters that are used to calculate Canadian taxes. But is this a good solution? No, it's a particularly bad solution. The parameters are specific to an implementation, and particularly to a Canadian implementation.

The parameter year could be justified because most countries do have specific tax rates and implementations that are dependent on a year. Yet the parameter province has no justification. Imagine trying to implement a British tax system and needing to specify a province, when Britain does not collect income tax at a local level.

A solution might be to redefine the interface as follows:

```
Public Class Specifics
    Public CanadianProvince As Province
    Public AmericanState As State
End Class

Public Interface ITaxAccount
    Sub AddDeduction(ByVal deduction As ITaxDeduction)
    Sub AddIncome(ByVal income As ITaxIncome)
    Function GetTaxRate(ByVal income As Double, ByVal year As Integer, _
    ByVal specifics As Specifics) As Double
    ReadOnly Property Deductions() As ITaxDeduction()
    ReadOnly Property Income() As ITaxIncome()
End Interface
```

This new implementation has a specifics parameter, which is of type Specifics. The purpose of Specifics is to define a class that is a hodgepodge of information that is needed to determine the correct tax rate. However, the Specifics approach is wrong, for the following reasons:

- It requires knowing the implementation, which in the case of the interface is a bad idea. It is like going to a restaurant and saying you would like a waitress with blond hair.

- Even if the type Specifics were acceptable, you would be adding and removing data members depending on how many tax systems you have implemented. That is a bad idea and introduces maintenance issues.

The proposed solutions are not acceptable. Additionally, there is still the problem of having to figure out which tax rate to use.

Implementing Ideas with Specifics

To implement a solution, let's first start by fixing the TaxAccount class. The modified version will have some type of functionality that has data members that reference the year and province. Here is the modified and correct implementation of TaxAccount:

```
Friend Class TaxAccount
    Inherits BaseTaxAccount

    Private _province As Province
    Private _year  As Integer

    Public Sub New (ByVal province As Province, ByVal year As Integer)
        _province = province
        _year = year
    End Sub

    Public Overrides Function GetTaxRate(ByVal income As Double)  As Double
        If _year = 2008 Then
            If _province = Province.Ontario Then
                Return OntarioTax2008.TaxRate(income)
            End If
        End If
        Throw New NotSupportedException("Year " & _year & " Province " & _
            _province & " not supported")
    End Function
End Class
```

The fix is to add a constructor that has province and year as parameters. This sort of fix is quite common, in that you don't change the interfaces, rather you change how the implementations are instantiated. Remember that when you instantiate a specific implementation, you know what functionality you want, and thus can give the additional parameters. Once you are at the interface level, you should need to use only general ideas.

Now the TaxEngine class needs to be fixed. TaxEngine is responsible for instantiating TaxAccount, and thus to instantiate a Canadian TaxAccount, TaxEngine needs additional parameters, as follows:

```
Friend Class TaxEngine
    Inherits BaseTaxEngine
    Public Overrides Function CreateTaxAccount() As ITaxAccount
        Return New TaxAccount(Province.Ontario, 2008)
    End Function
End Class
```

In the implementation of CreateTaxAccount(), the province Ontario and year 2008 are assumed. Thus, whenever TaxEngine is instantiated, you need to make sure that the person is in Ontario and paying taxes for the year 2008. The implementation solves nothing and skirts the issue of having to figure out how to deal with someone paying their taxes in British Columbia and the year 2009.

If you look at the implementation of TaxEngine, you will notice it is short. One obvious solution would be to create a TaxEngine type for each province and each year. Here are two examples:

```
Friend Class Ontario2008TaxEngine
    Inherits BaseTaxEngine

    Public Overrides Function CreateTaxAccount() As ITaxAccount
        Return New TaxAccount(Province.Ontario, 2008)
    End Function
End Class

Friend Class BritishColumbia2009TaxEngine
    Inherits BaseTaxEngine

    Public Overrides Function CreateTaxAccount() As ITaxAccount
        Return New TaxAccount(Province.BritishColumbia, 2009)
    End Function
End Class
```

This solution is not that bad, because to be able to instantiate the correct tax engine, you just need to define a factory that knows which class to instantiate. But for the problem at hand, this solution is extremely tedious, as you could end up with hundreds, if not thousands, of TaxEngine definitions. You would use the specific implementation approach when you have fewer than a dozen variations.

The better approach is to add an interface specific to the Canadian tax system. Think of it as follows. When you are instantiating the tax engine, you will need to know which tax system to use. The factory protects you from needing to know which type to instantiate, but there is nothing wrong with giving some extra information that could be used by a factory.

Thus, the solution is to define a new interface called ICanadaTaxEngine. The purpose of ICanadaTaxEngine is to add factory methods that are used to instantiate types with parameters specific to the implementation. Following is the definition of the ICanadaTaxEngine.

```
Public Enum Province
    Alberta
    BritishColumbia
    Manitoba
    NewBrunswick
    NewfoundlandLabrador
    NovaScotia
    Nunavut
    Ontario
    PrinceEdwardIsland
    Quebec
    Saskatchewan
    Yukon
End Enum

Public Interface ICanadaTaxEngine
    Function CreateTaxAccount(ByVal province As Province, _
        ByVal year As Integer) As ITaxAccount
    Function CreateCapitalGain(ByVal amount As Double) As ITaxIncome
End Interface
```

The definition of ICanadaTaxEngine contains two additional methods:

- CreateTaxAccount() is used to instantiate a tax account specific to a province and year.

- CreateCapitalGain() is used to instantiate an income using the Canadian capital gains calculation.

Thus, the implementation of TaxEngine becomes the following.

```
Friend Class TaxEngine
    Inherits BaseTaxEngine
    Implements ICanadaTaxEngine

    Public Overrides Function CreateTaxAccount() As ITaxAccount
        Return New TaxAccount(Province.Ontario, 2008)
    End Function

    Public Overloads Function CreateTaxAccount(ByVal province As Province, _
                                               ByVal year As Integer) _
    As ITaxAccount _
        Implements ICanadaTaxEngine.CreateTaxAccount
        Return New TaxAccount(province, year)
    End Function

    Public Function CreateCapitalGain(ByVal amount As Double) As ITaxIncome _
        Implements ICanadaTaxEngine.CreateCapitalGain
        Return New TaxIncome(amount, 0.50)
    End Function
End Class
```

In the modified implementation of TaxEngine, the class still derives from BaseTaxEngine, fulfilling the requirement of being a general tax engine. However, for the additional requirements of the Canadian tax system, we implement the ICanadaTaxEngine interface.

Defining a specific interface that implies a certain implementation is fine, because the specific interface is not bound to a certain implementation. The better way to understand this implementation technique is to consider the specific interface as a characteristic that an implementation is capable of supporting. This goes back to the shape example, where a square can support both the ISquare and IRectangle interfaces.

Using the Tax Engine

The last step is to use the tax engine to calculate some taxes. The following is an example of calculating the taxes for Ontario in 2008.

```
Dim engine As ITaxEngine = EngineCreator.CreateCanadianTaxEngine()
Dim canadaEngine As ICanadaTaxEngine = TryCast(engine, ICanadaTaxEngine)
Dim account As ITaxAccount = canadaEngine.CreateTaxAccount(Province.Ontario, 2008)

Dim income As ITaxIncome = engine.CreateIncome(100)
Dim capitalGain As ITaxIncome = canadaEngine.CreateCapitalGain(100)
```

```
account.AddIncome(income)
account.AddIncome(capitalGain)

Dim deduction As ITaxDeduction = engine.CreateDeduction(20)
account.AddDeduction(deduction)
Dim taxToPay As Double = engine.CalculateTaxToPay(account)
Console.WriteLine("Tax to pay (" & taxToPay & ")")
```

Notice the definition of the variables engine and canadaEngine. This is fine, because what we are doing with the interfaces is choosing a characteristic that can be dynamically queried.

Learning More About Inheritance and Type Casting

This chapter introduced interfaces and components, and delved deeper into inheritance. Here, I'll provide more details about inheritance and type casting.

More Inheritance Details

In this section, I am going to clearly lay out how inheritance works in Visual Basic. I will present examples of usage for six scenarios. Each example is followed by a list explaining the key points to understand. My goal is to illustrate all of the possible scenarios so that you have a reference to how inheritance works.

Note All of the examples demonstrate using methods, but it is possible to apply the same inheritance techniques using properties.

Scenario 1: Overloading Base Class Functionality

```
Class Base
    Public Sub Method()
        Console.WriteLine("Base.Method")
    End Sub
End Class

Class Derived
    Inherits Base
    Public Overloads Sub Method()
        Console.WriteLine("Derived.Method")
    End Sub
End Class
```

```
Module Test
    Public Sub Run()
        Dim derivedCls As Derived = New Derived()
        Dim baseCls As Base = derivedCls

        ' Calls Derived.Method
        derivedCls.Method()
        ' Calls Base.Method
        baseCls.Method()
    End Sub
End Module
```

- Keywords used: Overloads in the derived class to indicate the method is being overloaded.

- Overloading a method means to change the functionality of the method in the derived class.

- Which method is called in the inheritance depends on the type of the variable on which the method is called. Thus, if the variable is of type Base, Base.Method() is called; if the variable is of type Derived, Derived.Method() is called.

Scenario 2: Overriding Base Class Functionality

```
Class Base
    Public Overridable Sub Method()
        Console.WriteLine("Base.Method")
    End Sub
End Class

Class Derived
    Inherits Base
    Public Overrides Sub Method()
        Console.WriteLine("Derived.Method")
    End Sub
End Class

Module Test
    Public Sub Run()
        Dim derivedCls As Derived = New Derived()
        Dim baseCls As Base = derivedCls

        ' Calls Derived.Method
        derivedCls.Method()
        ' Calls Derived.Method
        baseCls.Method()
    End Sub
End Module
```

- Keywords used: Overridable in the base class to indicate the method behavior can be changed in the derived class. Overrides is used in the derived classes to indicate a method with the new behavior. Multiple levels of inheritance require multiple usages of Overrides.

- Overriding a method means to change the behavior of the method in the base class to that of the derived class. If there are multiple levels of inheritance, then the functionality used is the instantiated type.

- You can also define a Overridable base class method using the MustOverride keyword. The difference between Overridable and MustOverride is that Overridable has a method or property implementation in the base class, whereas MustOverride has no implementation in the base class.

Scenario 3: Implementing an Interface

```
Interface IInterface
    Sub Method()
End Interface

Class Implementation
    Implements IInterface
    Public Sub Method() Implements IInterface.Method
        Console.WriteLine("Implementation.Method")
    End Sub
End Class

Module Test
    Public Sub Run()
        Dim implementation As Implementation = New Implementation()
        Dim inst As IInterface = implementation

        ' Calls Implementation.Method
        implementation.Method()
        ' Calls Implementation.Method
        inst.Method()
    End Sub
End Module
```

- Keywords used: none.

- The class that implements the interface has a behavior, like when a class subclasses and implements a MustOverride method.

- Whether the variable is an interface type or an implementation type, the method Implementation.Method() is called.

Scenario 4: Implementing Two Interfaces with Same Method/Property Name

```
Interface IInterface1
    Sub Method()
End Interface

Interface IInterface2
    Sub Method()
End Interface

Class Implementation
    Implements IInterface1, IInterface2
    Public Sub Method1() Implements IInterface1.Method
        Console.WriteLine("Implementation.IInterface1.Method")
    End Sub

    Private Sub Method2() Implements IInterface2.Method
        Console.WriteLine("Implementation.IInterface2.Method")
    End Sub
End Class

Module Test
    Public Sub Run()
        Dim implementation As Implementation = New Implementation()
        Dim inst1 As IInterface1 = implementation
        Dim inst2  As IInterface2 = implementation

        ' Calls Implementation.Method1
        inst1.Method()
        ' Calls Implementation.Method2
        inst2.Method()
    End Sub
End Module
```

- Keywords used: special notation for the implementation of a particular interface method (for example, Implements IInterface1.Method and Implements IInterface2.Method).

- The methods that are converted to implement a particular interface can still be called. In the example, Method1() is declared as Public, and thus if you have a reference to Implementation, then you can call Method1().

Scenario 5: Implementing an Interface That Allows Overriding

```
Interface IInterface
    Sub Method()
End Interface
```

```vbnet
Class Implementation
    Implements IInterface

    Public Overridable Sub Method() Implements IInterface.Method
        Console.WriteLine("Implementation.Method")
    End Sub
End Class

Class ImplementationDerived
    Inherits Implementation

    Public Overrides Sub Method()
        Console.WriteLine("ImplementationDerived.Method")
    End Sub
End Class

Module Test
    Public Sub Run()
        Dim implementation As ImplementationDerived = _
          New ImplementationDerived()
        Dim inst As IInterface = implementation

        ' Calls ImplementationDerived.Method
        implementation.Method()
        ' Calls ImplementationDerived.Method
        inst.Method()
    End Sub
End Module
```

- Keywords used: Overridable and Overrides.

- By default, when you implement an interface without using the Overridable keyword, you are saying that the derived class can overload only the method. In many cases, this is appropriate, as you will want to override the method and thus will need to use the Overridable and Overrides keywords.

- This is a common problem, and most beginning Visual Basic programmers are puzzled by the overloading behavior.

Scenario 6: An Inheritance Tree That Overrides and Overloads

```vbnet
Class Base
    Public Overridable Sub Method()
        Console.WriteLine("Base.Method")
    End Sub
End Class
```

```
Class Derived1
    Inherits Base

    Public Overrides Sub Method()
        Console.WriteLine("Derived1.Method")
    End Sub
End Class

Class Derived2
    Inherits Derived1

    Public Overloads Overridable Sub Method()
        Console.WriteLine("Derived2.Method")
    End Sub
End Class

Class Derived3
    Inherits Derived2

    Public Overrides Sub Method()
        Console.WriteLine("Derived3.Method")
    End Sub
End Class

Module Test
    Public Sub Run()
        Dim derivedCls As Derived3 = new Derived3()
        Dim baseCls As Base = derivedCls
        Dim derived2cls As Derived2 = derivedCls

        ' Calls Derived3.Method
        derivedCls.Method()
        ' Calls Derived1.Method
        baseCls.Method()
        ' Calls Derived3.Method
        derived2cls.Method()
    End Sub
End Module
```

- Keywords used: Overridable, Overrides, and Overloads.

- The inheritance hierarchy is saying that Derived1.Method() overrides the behavior of Base.Method(). Derived2.Method() overloads the behavior of Derived1.Method(), while establishing a new overriding base method. Derived3.Method() overrides the behavior Derived2.Method(), and not Base.Method() (very important).

- When confronted with a complex inheritance hierarchy as illustrated by scenario 6, it is important that you start at the base class and work up the inheritance hierarchy.

More Type-Casting Details

This chapter illustrated some type-casting examples. In Visual Basic, you have two ways to type cast:

- A forced type cast, which can also be used on value types

- A type cast that queries if a type cast is possible

Consider this hierarchy:

```
Class Base
    Public Sub Method()
        Console.WriteLine("Base.Method")
    End Sub
End Class

Class Derived
    Inherits Base

    Public Overloads Sub Method()
        Console.WriteLine("Derived.Method")
    End Sub
End Class
```

The next step is to instantiate the type `Derived` and cast the instance to the base type:

```
Dim derivedCls As Derived = New Derived()
Dim baseCls As Base = derivedCls
```

When casting from a derived type to a base class type, a type cast is not necessary and you can assume it is implied.

A type cast is necessary when you want to cast a base class instance to a derived class instance. Following is the source code for a forced type cast, assuming the inheritance hierarchy from the previous cast.

```
Dim backToDerived As Derived = DirectCast(baseCls, Derived)
```

The forced cast is the use of the method `DirectCase`. The cast is forced because a conversion to the desired type will occur, regardless if it is possible or not. If the cast is not possible, a cast exception is thrown.

Another way to perform a type cast is to use a query cast, as illustrated by the following code, again assuming the inheritance hierarchy of this section.

```
Dim backToDerived As Derived = TryCast(baseCls, Derived)
```

In the code, the cast involves using the `TryCast` method. This cast is a query because a cast will be attempted. If the cast is successful, then an instance of the type is assigned to the variable `backToDerived`. If the cast is not possible, then `backToDerived` is assigned a `Nothing` value. No exception is thrown. This casting technique is possible only for reference types.

The Important Stuff to Remember

In this chapter, you learned about interfaces and implementations. Here are the key points to remember:

- Using interfaces is not like using inheritance. They are two separate designs, even though interfaces will use inheritance.

- Interfaces at an abstract level imply ideas of how you would like your application to work.

- Ideas when implemented as interfaces should be general and applicable to multiple application implementations for the domain.

- Ideas are represented using Visual Basic interfaces. And interfaces are implemented using classes or structures. But note that interfaces are reference types.

- Factories are used to instantiate implementations and return an instance that implements an interface. Using a factory means that the user of an interface does not need to know which type of implementation object is instantiated.

- Interfaces can be considered as facets that might be targeting a specific characteristic of an implementation. However, as illustrated in the previous chapter, interfaces do not expose Friend state or the Friend workings of the implementations.

- Components are a fundamental way of developing code and should be your primary way of writing code. For the remainder of this book, interfaces will be used whenever possible. Take notice and try to understand what the idea behind the interface is.

Some Things for You to Do

The following are a couple things for you to do to apply what you've learned in this chapter.

1. Implement your own tax system using the predefined base classes.

■**Note** Because of the number of possible tax systems, I do not provide an answer for exercise 1. If you want me to review your answer, please send it to me at christianhgross@gmail.com.

---

2. Add functionality to the tax engine's base classes that implement the behavior of a minimum tax-free amount. This means if your income is not above the minimum tax-free amount, you do not pay taxes.

CHAPTER 8

■■■

Learning About Component-Oriented Architecture

So far, you have learned the essentials of Visual Basic. With the essentials, you can write a functional application that uses classes, objects, interfaces, and inheritance. In this chapter, you'll learn about a Visual Basic programming technique that some developers define as *structural*. A structural programming technique is when the code does not directly serve to solve a business problem, but solves a problem relating to building the application.

Another purpose of this chapter is to give you more experience with developing component-oriented code. In particular, you'll learn how to develop a kernel. Developing a kernel demonstrates the power and flexibility of the component-oriented development approach. You can build a working system even though you might not know what all of the implementations are ahead of time. This type of development makes it possible to modularize development, in that individual teams are responsible for certain interfaces. Then once the pieces have been implemented, they are fitted together like a jigsaw puzzle. Of course, interfaces and components do not guarantee success, but they do ensure one team does not need to wait for another team to finish its code.

To demonstrate all of these concepts, we'll build an application that controls lighting in buildings, using the kernel programming approach.

Understanding Kernels

Imagine you are the owner of a house or commercial building, and you want to reduce your electricity bill. One way of doing that is to automate the lighting system of your building so that lights are on when they need to be. What is unique about this system is that you have a controller and the devices that are controlled.

The controller controls devices that it does not know about ahead of time, but fulfills a contract. The lighting system is a controller, programmatically called a *kernel*, because the rooms that it controls are not known initially. The rooms are known when the controller is used to manage the lighting system. The kernel programming approach is one where a core of functionality is developed. The core functionality by itself does not work, because it relies on other pieces to perform certain tasks. In programming terms, this is called developing components that use interfaces and implementations.

Components are implemented at the technical level using interfaces and classes that subclass the interfaces. The interface represents an idea, and the classes represent the implementation of an idea. A class could implement multiple interfaces, where each interface represents a unique characteristic of the class implementation. Ideas and interfaces also represent contracts or standards. The kernel defines a standard, and the component has the responsibility of implementing that standard.

Implementing a kernel is like being a coach. A coach thinks of where to place players in the field and develops strategies that the players need to implement. But on game day, the players will do what they think is best, and the coach is powerless. A coach can teach the players, but whether they apply that knowledge is up to the individual players.

In programming terms, the kernel is the coach, and the external implementations to manipulate are the players. When designing interfaces that other pieces of functionality will implement, you cannot watch over the shoulders of the programmers and make sure they do things correctly. You need to trust, but you also need to implement a mode of programming where you assume the programmers are going to do things incorrectly. This has nothing to do with the personal abilities of the other programmers. It has to do with the ability to make sure your kernel continues functioning, even when someone makes a mistake.

Remember that when implementing a kernel, you are implementing a controller, and you are devising the strategy of the application. You are just not doing all of the implementations.

When you write production code, and you have been put in charge of writing a kernel, count yourself lucky. But remember with the job of building a kernel comes great responsibility. If your kernel is buggy or badly designed, then the external implementations will also be buggy and potentially badly designed. The kernel is the rock and foundation of the application.

Organizing the Lighting Application

For the moment, imagine we are not developing software, but actually building a house. And in this house, we are going to add a central lighting system. The make of light bulbs, lamps, and lighting controller are not identical. This is interesting in that multiple companies make products that work with each other's device, because all companies adhere to a particular standard.

The process of standardization is all around us, and is as simple as the electricity that comes out of our electrical outlets. However, what is a standard in one country is not necessarily the standard in another country. Different countries will have different standard voltages. In terms of software, the kernel represents a standard that allows the integration of components.

The lighting application will include these features:

- A room where the light can be controlled using either a simple on/off switch or a gradual light-intensity mechanism.

- The controller represents a building, and the rooms within the building can be grouped, making it simpler to perform group operations.

- Rooms are associated with identifiers that allow each room to be isolated individually.

- Rooms can be associated with a set of attributes that indicate the behavior they do and do not support.

The source code will implement the controller as a library project named LibLightingSystem. This library project will also define the interfaces that the components will implement. To demonstrate building a complete working application, two other projects implement the interfaces and represent components: Museum and Home. The key characteristics of a museum are that some rooms are made dark at night and are completely managed by the controller, while other rooms are controlled individually in the room itself and also can be managed by the controller. The key characteristics of a home are that all of the rooms are individually controlled, but they have sensors that allow automatic control. Some of the lighting associated with the house depends on certain prerequisites being fulfilled. For example, night-lights might turn on depending on the time of year, or room lights might be turned on and off automatically when no one is home. As usual, we will use a testing console application, named TestLightingSystem, to test the three assemblies (it is the startup project). Figure 8-1 shows the project structure.

Figure 8-1. *Lighting system application project structure*

Building the Kernel

The lighting system is a two-part implementation. The first part is that we must write code that works properly. The second part is to integrate code that someone else has written and make sure that if that code does not work properly for some reason, those problems will not affect the code that we wrote.

This application is complicated by the fact that we are dealing with the unknown. In the previous examples, we had control of every class, interface, and definition. This time, we are not in control, and thus we need to use a defensive style of programming. This means we need to write many tests and keep certain information private.

Defining the Interfaces

The core of the lighting controller is to control the lighting in a room that is part of the building. We can define and organize the rooms by using interfaces. We need four interfaces:

- IRoom: A placeholder interface for the idea of a room

- INoRemoteControlRoom: An interface for rooms that should not be controlled by the lighting controller

- IRemoteControlRoom: An interface for rooms that should be completely controlled by the lighting controller

- ISensorRoom: An interface for rooms whose control is based on state (whether or not a person is in the room)

The interfaces for the rooms where lighting may be controlled, IRemoteControlRoom and ISensorRoom, will depend on certain pieces of logic. The interfaces will need to provide input data and accept output data. The logic might also seek input from other sources, such as time of day or amount of sunlight outdoors. It boils down to defining some type of logic that the kernel implements. This is key, and it relates to the children-and-parent issue. While you accept your children as being intelligent beings that can make decisions, at the end of the day, it is usually the parent who makes the final decisions. Likewise, while your kernel might accept input and potential decisions, the kernel makes the final decisions.

Defining IRoom, a Placeholder Interface

For design purposes, the simplest and base idea is the room itself, which can be defined as follows (in the controller library LibLightingSystem):

```
Public Interface IRoom
End Interface
```

The interface does not have any methods or properties. It is called a *placeholder* interface. A placeholder type serves no other purpose than identifying that the implementation is of a certain type. Placeholder interfaces make it simpler to group objects that have certain capabilities.

Imagine defining objects without a placeholder interface, something like this:

```
Class Type1
End Class
Class Type2
End Class
```

Looking at Type1 and Type2, you cannot see any correlation between the two types; there is no way to say that Type1 and Type2 have anything in common. (Well, technically there is a correlation in that both types are derived from Object, but that type of correlation is like saying that all people are humans.) Using a placeholder interface, Type1 and Type2 can be correlated, as follows:

```
Class Type1
    Implements IRoom
End Class
Class Type2
    Implements IRoom
End Class
. . .
Dim rooms As IRoom() = New IRoom() {New Type1(), New Type2()}
```

Having Type1 and Type2 implement the IRoom interface, which means do nothing other than subclass IRoom, establishes a correlation between Type1 and Type2. The correlation is that both Type1 and Type2 are rooms. We have no idea what kind of rooms, and we have no idea if the rooms are in the same building. We only know that they are rooms.

The use of placeholder interfaces is very important in kernel design. Placeholders establish that a type wants to be part of a grouping. The kernel can use that grouping to define a list of elements that are all similar. It is like knowing the age of people to determine whether they are eligible to drive. The age does not indicate the sex or intelligence, nor if they are good or bad drivers. The age is a placeholder that says, "Yes you are part of a grouping that is allowed to take a driving test to give you the right to drive."

In the case of our lighting control, defining the IRoom placeholder interface is saying that whatever instance is associated with IRoom is indicating its interest in being part of the lighting controller kernel. When you have identified a type using a placeholder interface, you are saying your type can be used in a certain context. The context is determined by the placeholder interface.

Defining the INoRemoteControlRoom Interface

Although the purpose of the lighting system is to control the lighting, some rooms should not be controlled by the system. Perhaps the room is private, or controlling its lighting would cause problems.

For example, should a bedroom in a house be controlled by the lighting controller? If the lighting controller controls the lighting in the bedroom, it might turn off the lights while a person is reading. Or maybe it will turn on the lights when the person has decided to sleep in. Of course, the person could just switch the light on or off manually, but that is disruptive. The inconvenience of the controller getting it wrong outweighs the benefit of the controller getting it right, so the controller should not deal with this room.

The definition of an interface that indicates that the controller should do nothing is as follows (in the controller library LibLightingSystem):

```
Public Interface INoRemoteControlRoom
    Inherits IRoom
End Interface
```

As you can see, INoRemoteControlRoom lacks methods and properties, like our placeholder interface IRoom. However, in this case, there are no methods or properties because the kernel system does not require them. The idea behind the INoRemoteControlRoom interface is to indicate that the type implementing the interface is a room, but a room that should not be managed by the controller. Using the bedroom as an example, the implementation is as follows (defined in the Home project):

```
    Imports LibLightingSystem
    Public Class Bedroom
        Implements INoRemoteControlRoom
    End Class
```

The definition of the bedroom allows the kernel to use an instance of a room, as follows:

```
Dim rooms As IRoom()= New IRoom(10) { }
rooms(0) = New Bedroom()
. . .


If TypeOf(rooms(0)) Is INoRemoteControlRoom Then
    ' Take appropriate action
End If
```

This code creates an array of rooms and assigns the index 0 to an instance of Bedroom. The If statement asks if the IRoom instance in index 0 is of type INoRemoteControlRoom.

■**Note** Using placeholder interfaces and inheritance sets up a very powerful architecture that allows you to create groupings. You can then filter individual instances based on refinements of the grouping. All of this is possible in the Visual Basic language using `TryCast()` and `Is`, which allow queries of subclassed types of an instance. The queries are noninvasive and do not cause exceptions to be thrown. The queries give you the ability to make decisions based on whether an instance would like to be associated with a particular grouping based on an interface.

Defining the IRemoteControlRoom Interface

Another type of room is one where the lighting is completely managed by the controller. The controller does not seek the input of the room and manages the lighting based on the logic that seems appropriate to it.

For example, a public-viewing area in a museum does not require light at certain times of day. When the museum is closed and the cleaners are finished, the lights can be turned off. When the museum is open, the lights are turned on. This is a simple logic and can be completely managed by the controller.

The interface for the controlled room is defined as follows (in `LibLightingSystem`):

```
Public Interface IRemoteControlRoom
    Inherits IRoom
    ReadOnly Property LightLevel() As Double
    Sub LightSwitch(ByVal lightState As Boolean)
    Sub DimLight(ByVal level As Double)
End Interface
```

The only input that `IRemoteControlRoom` provides is information about whether the light is on, off, or at a certain level. This is through the `LightLevel` property. The `LightLevel` property is read-only, because the controller and the light level might become out of sync.

For example, suppose it's time for the museum to close, and the lights are switched off in the public-viewing area. But today, the cleaners took a little while longer than usual. They turn the lights back on so that they can see what they are doing. The local device can do one of two things: allow the light to be turned on without the approval of the controller, or not allow the light to be turned on, requiring a controller intervention. The best approach is to allow a local override and let the cleaners turn on the light. The `LightLevel` property is necessary so that the controller can verify if the state of the light is what the controller expects it to be.

■**Note** When you are defining a kernel, sometimes it is necessary to add functionality into an interface that verifies the state of the implementation. Because the kernel is not in control of the implementation, the kernel should not assume the state, as the state could change for some reason. In the case of the lighting system, the change could be due to a cleaner turning on the light after it was turned off.

The IRemoteControlRoom methods LightSwitch() and DimLight() turn the light on or off and set the light to a certain level, respectively. These methods are used to control the state of the implementation.

Defining the ISensorRoom Interface

Another type of room is one that can be controlled under certain circumstances. Let's go back to the cleaner example where the cleaner turned on the light. If the controller notices that the light is on, even though it was turned off, should the controller turn off the light? You might say sure, the controller should turn off the light. However, that is not completely correct. Imagine the situation where the cleaner turns on the light and the controller turns it off. The cleaner would immediately turn the light back on, and the controller would turn it off. The cleaner would tape the light switch down so that a constant battle of the light going on and off ensues (because this battle is in milliseconds, the light remains on). A smarter approach would be to allow a timing of the light. But how much time—a quarter of an hour, a half hour, an hour?

Another approach is not to use a time interval, but to enhance the interface and allow the controller to figure out the state. This enhanced interface, called ISensorRoom, is defined as follows (in LibLightingSystem):

```
Public Interface ISensorRoom
    Inherits IRemoteControlRoom
    ReadOnly Property IsPersonInRoom() As Boolean
End Interface
```

The ISensorRoom interface has a single property IsPersonInRoom, which is a Boolean property. If the property has a value of True, then a person is in the room; otherwise, no person is in the room. How the implementation determines whether or not a person is in the room is not the problem of the kernel. The kernel assumes the implementation knows how to figure this out.

■Note As a general rule of thumb, the kernel can communicate with the implementation only via the interface. The kernel should never assume a certain implementation of an interface. The kernel should take the approach that what it sees is what it gets. Thus, if the kernel needs additional information, the interface should be extended during design, or another interface should be implemented. Of course, this does not mean for every piece of state the interface should be extended. Sometimes, you will need to define a specific interface, such as in the tax application example in the previous chapter (ICanadianTaxEngine).

Now that we've created the interfaces, we're ready to implement the kernel.

Implementing the Kernel

In this example, the kernel will be a single class that contains all of the functionality of the controller. This definition means that the individual implementations, testing, and applications will interact with a single class.

Here is an example of implementing the light-dimming method using the LightingController class (in LibLightingSystem):

```
Public Class LightingController
    Public Sub DimLights(ByVal grouping As Object, ByVal level As Double)
    End Sub
 End Class
```

The user of LightingController would dim a light using this code:

```
Dim controller As LightingController = New LightingController()
Dim grouping As Object = Nothing
controller.DimLights(grouping, 0.50)
```

The user code instantiates the type LightingController directly and uses the method DimLights() directly. Using classes directly has the cost that the controller code cannot change without affecting the users, as there is a tight coupling between the user code and the kernel. And this is why I have been writing at length about using interfaces, ideas, and implementations. Yet, the controller appears to throw all of that out of the window.

The reason for using a class goes back to the previous chapter's example and the interfaces ITaxDeduction and ITaxIncome. That example had only a single implementation of each interface, and those implementations were not going to change. As I explained in the previous chapter, the interfaces could have been represented as classes. The same logic applies with respect to the controller. The controller is not going to change much from a method and property signature perspective, and there is going to be only a single implementation of the controller. Therefore, an interface is not necessary. Using a class is completely acceptable, and it's the approach we're using in this chapter. However, I'll talk about when you might want to implement the kernel as an interface a little later in the chapter, in the "Defining the Kernel As an Interface Instead of a Class" section.

The controller represents a building that has the ability to organize rooms into groupings. Based on the groupings, the controller can perform operations such as turning the lights on or off, or setting lights to a specific dimness. When each of these operations is executed, the controller must respect the intentions of the individual rooms, by querying for a particular interface as defined by the previous section.

The controller has two main responsibilities: calling the appropriate interface methods and organizing the interface instances. The organization of the instances involves using collections, arrays, or a linked list. We'll use a linked list in this example.

Storing a Collection Using a Linked List

In the examples in previous chapters, we created a collection of objects using an array, like this:

```
Dim array As MyType() = New MyType(9) { }
array(0) = New MyType()
array(2) = New MyType()
```

This creates an array that can contain 10 elements at most (MyType(9)). If you needed to store 20 elements, you would need to use the ReDim keyword with Preserve (as explained in Chapter 4). Another feature of an array is that you don't need to assign the elements in a sequential manner. The example assigns the first and third positions, with the second position being Nothing.

Thus, some code that iterates the array will need to verify that the array element is not Nothing. The sample code generates the structure illustrated in Figure 8-2.

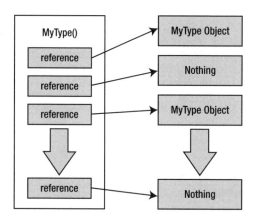

Figure 8-2. *Array structure of referenced elements*

Figure 8-2 reveals a very important aspect of reference types: an array holds a reference to the object and not the value of the object. If the array were value types, then the entire value would be stored in the array.

The array could just as easily have been some object with a number of variables, like this:

```
Class MyTypeArray
    Public Element1 As MyType
    Public Element2 As MyType
. . .
End Class
```

Since array elements are a bunch of references stored in a type, you could make use of this knowledge to create a type that serves no other purpose than referencing a list of elements, more commonly called a *linked list*.

In a linked list, the individual objects are linked together and reference another element nearby. A doubly linked list will only ever hold references to two other objects: the next one and the previous one. (Another type is a singly linked list, which holds a reference to only one other object: the next one.)

In a doubly linked list, the type will have data members named NextItem and PrevItem. Each of these data members is used to reference another element in the list, as illustrated in Figure 8-3. To iterate a list, you start from either the left or right side and then go to the NextItem or PrevItem data members, respectively. Here is an example:

```
Dim curr As MyType = GetHeadOfList()
Do While (curr IsNot Nothing)
    ' Do something with curr
    curr = curr.NextItem
Loop
```

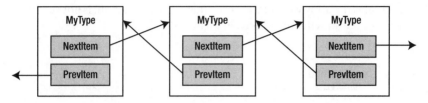

Figure 8-3. *Structure of doubly linked list*

As you can see, you can easily add elements to linked lists. The drawback is that it is expensive to find a particular object, as that requires iterating through the list.

■**Note** For the most part, you will be using the standard .NET List class, but there is also a LinkedList class. If you're interested, you can find information about the .NET version of System.Collection. Generics.LinkedList in the MSDN documentation. We'll make our own linked list to demonstrate Visual Basic programming techniques, but you should use the standard collection classes in almost every case.

For our application's kernel, we'll use a doubly linked list to link together a number of rooms into a set of groupings.

Creating a Linked List

The initial structure of the BaseLinkedListItem class is as follows (defined in LibLightingSystem):

```vb
Public MustInherit Class BaseLinkedListItem
    Private _next As BaseLinkedListItem
    Private _prev As BaseLinkedListItem

    Public ReadOnly Property NextItem() As BaseLinkedListItem
        Get
            Return _next
        End Get
    End Property
    Public ReadOnly Property PrevItem() As BaseLinkedListItem
        Get
            Return _prev
        End Get
    End Property
End Class
```

BaseLinkedListItem is declared as MustInherit to indicate that using this class implies that you must derive a class. PrevItem and NextItem are Visual Basic properties that can only read the values of the private data members of _prev and _next.

Inserting and Removing Linked List Items

Inserting an object into a linked list or removing an object from a linked list requires some careful coding. You need to make sure that the actions will not corrupt the list. This is not a task that you want to delegate to the users of the linked list, as they could unintentionally corrupt the list. The following is the code to insert and remove an object from a linked list, and is part of the `BaseLinkedListItem` class.

```
Public Sub Insert(ByVal item As BaseLinkedListItem)
    item._next = _next
    item._prev = Me

    If _next IsNot Nothing Then
        _next._prev = item
    End If
    _next = item
End Sub

Public Sub Remove()
    If _next IsNot Nothing Then
        _next._prev = _prev
    End If
    If _prev IsNot Nothing
        _prev._next = _next
    End If
    _next = Nothing
    _prev = Nothing
End Sub
```

The `Insert()` method assumes that you want to insert an object into the head of a list, which has at least one element. The `Insert()` method assumes the following code at a minimum.

```
Dim singleElement As BaseLinkedListItem = GetHeadOfList()
Dim anotherElement as BaseLinkedListItem = CreateListElement()
singleElement.Insert(anotherElement)
```

The first step is to assign the data members (`_next`, `_prev`) of the object (`item`) that is going to be added to the list.

■**Note** Notice how in the `Insert()` method, it is possible to assign the private data members of another object instance. You learned that private scope means that only the declared type can read private properties and methods. This rule has not been violated, because the rule implies types can read the private data members and private methods of other instances of that type.

Once the data members of the item have been assigned, the item is integrated into the list, by redirecting the _prev property of the next object (if it is not Nothing), and then assigning the local _next property to the object to be inserted.

The Remove() method does the same as Insert(), but in reverse. The first step is to redirect the _next and _prev properties of the previous and next objects, assuming that they are not Nothing. And then the object to be removed has its _next and _prev properties assigned to Nothing.

■**Note** The declaration of PrevItem and NextItem is a common architecture where data members can be read, but to assign them, you need to use methods. Using read-only properties is one way to make sure that the internal state cannot be corrupted, if you must expose the internal state.

Testing the Linked List

BaseLinkedListItem is a core class and serves a utility purpose. This makes the class eligible to be declared in the kernel or a definitions assembly. As the class is a core class, it means you need a more exhaustive testing framework to ensure that there will be no problems. In this section, we will go through one test that demonstrates what you should be testing for and how you should be testing a core class.

BaseLinkedListItem is declared as MustInherit and needs an implementation. The purpose of the implementation is to give us enough information on the state and context of the object. In this case, we want to define an object that tests every part of the class BaseLinkedListItem. If you have ever seen pictures of a test car tire hooked up to dozens of wires, then you will understand what the test class needs to do. Following is a sample implementation, placed in the TestLightingSystem project. Remember to include a reference to LibLightingSystem (right-click References in TestLightingSystem and select Add Reference and then Projects ➤ LibLightingSystem).

```
. . .
Imports LibLightingSystem

Class LinkedItem
    Inherits BaseLinkedListItem

    Private _identifier As String

    Public Sub New(ByVal identifier As String)
        _identifier = identifier
    End Sub

    Public ReadOnly Property Identifier As String
        Get
            Return _identifier
        End Get
    End Property
```

```vb
    Public Overrides Function ToString() As String
        Dim buffer As String
        buffer = "Me(" & _identifier & ")"
        If NextItem IsNot Nothing Then
            buffer = buffer & " next(" & _
                    DirectCast(MyBase.NextItem, LinkedItem).Identifier & ")"
        Else
            buffer = buffer & " next(Nothing)"
        End If
        If PrevItem IsNot Nothing Then
            buffer = buffer & " prev(" & _
                    DirectCast(MyBase.PrevItem, LinkedItem).Identifier & ")"
        Else
            buffer = buffer & " prev(Nothing)"
        End If
        Return buffer
    End Function
End Class
```

The LinkedItem class has a single data member declaration, _identifier, which is used
to identify the instance. The test code will call the Insert() and Remove() methods, and then
generate a visual representation of the linked list. The visual representation is used to understand what the problem might be if anything goes wrong. You will not write tests against the
visual representation because that would overcomplicate the testing.

To generate a visual representation of the object, the ToString() method is overridden. By
default, all objects have a ToString() implementation, which does absolutely nothing other
than spit out the identifier of the object reference. To make ToString() do something useful,
you need to override it. In the example, ToString() will generate a buffer that contains the
LinkedItem identifier and the next and previous object identifiers. These three pieces of information tell you the structure of the linked list.

The next step is to write a test in TestLightingSystem's Module1.vb that verifies that the
Insert() method works properly, and it is implemented as follows:

```vb
    Module Module1
        Sub Main()
            TestInsert()
        End Sub

        Public Sub TestInsert()
            Console.WriteLine("**************")
            Console.WriteLine("TestInsert: Start")
            Dim item1 As LinkedItem = New LinkedItem("item1")
            Dim item2 As LinkedItem = New LinkedItem("item2")
            Dim item3 As LinkedItem = New LinkedItem("item3")

            Dim toString As String = item1.ToString()
            Console.WriteLine(toString)
            If (item1.NextItem IsNot Nothing) OrElse _
```

```vbnet
                    (item1.PrevItem IsNot Nothing) Then
                        Throw New Exception( _
                            "TestInsert: Empty structure is incorrect")
                End If

                item1.Insert(item2)
                toString = item1.ToString()
                Console.WriteLine(toString)
                If (item1.NextItem IsNot item2) OrElse _
                    (item1.PrevItem IsNot Nothing) Then
                        Throw New Exception( _
                            "TestInsert: Item 1->Item2 structure is incorrect")
                End If
                toString = item2.ToString()
                Console.WriteLine(toString)
                If (item2.NextItem IsNot Nothing) OrElse _
                    (item2.PrevItem IsNot item1) Then
                        Throw New Exception( _
                            "TestInsert: Item 2->Item1 structure is incorrect")
                End If
                item2.Insert(item3)
                toString = item2.ToString()
                Console.WriteLine(toString)
                If (item2.PrevItem IsNot item1) OrElse _
                    (item2.NextItem IsNot item3) Then
                        Throw New Exception( _
                            "TestInsert: Item2->Item1, Item3 structure is incorrect")
                End If
                toString = item3.ToString()
                Console.WriteLine(toString)
                 If (item3.PrevItem IsNot item2) OrElse _
                    (item3.NextItem IsNot Nothing) Then
                        Throw New Exception( _
                            "TestInsert: Item3->Item2, structure is incorrect")
                End If

                toString = item1.ToString()
                Console.WriteLine(toString)
                toString = item2.ToString()
                Console.WriteLine(toString)
                toString = item3.ToString()
                Console.WriteLine(toString)
                Console.WriteLine("TestInsert: End")
        End Sub
    End Module
```

This test generates pretty output like this:

```
**************
TestInsert: Start
Me (item1) next(Nothing) prev(Nothing)
Me (item1) next(item2) prev(Nothing)
Me (item2) next(Nothing) prev(item1)
Me (item2) next(item3) prev(item1)
Me (item3) next(Nothing) prev(item2)
Me (item1) next(item2) prev(Nothing)
Me (item2) next(item3) prev(item1)
Me (item3) next(Nothing) prev(item2)
TestInsert: End
```

The pretty output is not a verification of what went right. Rather, the extensive output makes it simpler to perform postmortem debugging to understand why something failed.

In the TestInsert() method, a situation is created where three LinkedItem instances are instantiated: item1, item2, and item3. Initially, the three items are not linked, but we use the Insert() method to link them into a structure, as shown in Figure 8-4.

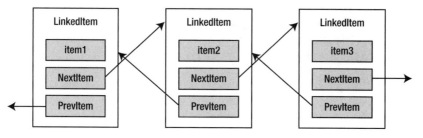

Figure 8-4. *Testable doubly linked list structure*

But to get to the structure in Figure 8-4, some intermediate steps are required, and in the implementation of the method TestInsert(), those intermediate steps are tested. The NextItem and PrevItem properties for each and every item are tested for the proper values at each step. If some of the values don't match, an exception is thrown to indicate an improper structure. If an exception is thrown, the generation of the visual structure becomes important. As an aside, while developing the Insert() and Remove() algorithms, the visual structures and test code helped me figure out a bug.

The TestInsert() method is an example of an exhaustive test of a context. The downloadable source code contains several other examples of exhaustive tests.

DEBUGGING AND TESTING TOOLS

Some of you might be thinking that to figure out why a test failed, you should use a debugger. However, with proper tests that are part of an extensive testing framework and that generate extensive output, the need for a debugger is reduced. Among the people who believe in a test-driven development (TDD) environment (including me), there is a question on the merits of a debugger. According to Wikipedia's Test-Driven Development entry (http://en.wikipedia.org/wiki/Test-driven_development), "Programmers using pure TDD on new ('greenfield') projects report they only rarely feel the need to invoke a debugger. Used in conjunction with a Version control system, when tests fail unexpectedly, reverting the code to the last version that passed all tests may often be more productive than debugging."

A debugger is good for finding problems, but bad for understanding the nature of the problem. Good tests verify scenarios. The more scenarios, the more tests, and the more tested your code is. If a particular scenario fails, you know that you have a problem. And if everything was OK until you made a slight change that caused the tests to fail, you know you have a problem. Test scripts are signposts that tell you what is working and what might not be working. By using a debugger, you are often testing large chunks of code where you need to labor to find the bug. A debugger has its uses, but when writing good tests in many scenarios, you will rarely need to use it.

And speaking of writing tests, as I noted in Chapter 6, in this book, I could introduce a testing framework like NUnit (http://www.nunit.org) or Microsoft Visual Studio Team System (http://msdn2.microsoft.com/en-us/vstudio/default.aspx). When you are writing production code, you will probably use such a testing framework. Testing frameworks do not help you to write your tests, but rather help you by providing support code to generate errors, log problems, and indicate progress of the tests. Do not get misled by tools that say they can write the tests for you. No tool can write your tests, because that would imply the tool understands the context of your code. And since such a tool does not yet exist, you will need to write your own tests.

Implementing Room Groupings

Room groupings are collections of rooms that fall into a specific organization. The idea behind a grouping is to perform group operations without having to explicitly examine a room before performing an operation. For example, in the case of the museum, we don't need to figure out whether a room is public or private each time a global operation is being performed.

The organization of the collection is that there can be multiple room groupings that are linked together, and within a grouping, there are multiple rooms that can be grouped together. The linked list structure has two levels and is coded as follows (in LibLightingSystem):

```
Class RoomGrouping
    Inherits BaseLinkedListItem
    Public Rooms As Room
    Public Description As String
End Class

Class Room
    Inherits BaseLinkedListItem
    Public ObjRoom As IRoom
End Class
```

The class declaration Room represents an individual room. But notice how it derives from BaseLinkedListItem, which seems to imply that Room is actually many rooms. This is part of the linked list implementation; it is like a chain, where the chain is created by individual links.

The RoomGrouping class has two data members: Rooms, which represents the list of rooms in the grouping, and Description, which represents an easy-to-understand description of the grouping. The single data member for Room is a reference to an IRoom interface instance.

The room groupings are managed by the LightingController class. An initial implementation of LightingController is as follows:

```
Public Class LightingController
    Private _roomGroupings As BaseLinkedListItem = New RoomGrouping()
End Class
```

When dealing with linked lists, you have a problem: which is the first element of a list? When you use arrays, an empty list of arrays is an array with no references. But there is an explicit array object. Using the linked list, an empty linked list is a list that does not exist. Thus, when you want to create a list, you need a room. In LightingController, the first element is an instance of RoomGrouping, which is not a room grouping, but serves as a placeholder. To insert a room grouping, you could simply use this code:

```
_roomGroupings.Insert(NewRoomGroup())
```

Without the placeholder, you would need to write the following code whenever you wanted to add an element into the list.

```
If _roomGroupings Is Nothing Then
    _roomGroupings = NewRoomGroup()
Else
    _roomGroupings.Insert(NewRoomGroup())
End If
```

The code that uses the placeholder is shorter and simpler; however, it also requires a dangling instance of RoomGrouping that has no real value. I chose the dangling approach because I am making the decision that a room grouping with no identifier is the default room grouping.

Adding a Room Grouping

The following code adds a room grouping (added to the class LightingController).

```
Public Function AddRoomGrouping(ByVal description As String) As Object
    Dim grouping As RoomGrouping = New RoomGrouping() _
    With { _
        .Description = description, _
        .Rooms = Nothing
        }
    _roomGroupings.Insert(grouping)
    Return grouping
End Function
```

To add a new room grouping, you instantiate RoomGrouping, assign the data members, and then call the method _roomGroupings.Insert() to insert the new room grouping into the linked list.

Let's look at the technique for assigning data members, called *object initialization*. In previous examples, when an object was instantiated and we wanted to assign default values, we would create a constructor with the appropriate parameters. However, another way is to instantiate the object and define a block that assigns the appropriate data members or properties. In the case of RoomGrouping, there are two publicly defined data members: Description and Rooms:

```
.Description = description, _
.Rooms = Nothing
```

The Description and Rooms data members have assign access, which is important as this technique only works with properties that are not read-only. To assign a data member or property, after the object instantiation, add the With keyword, and then within curly brackets, assign each individual data member using a key/value pair, in this form:

```
With { .Key1 = value1, .Key2 = value2 }
```

The key represents the data member property to assign, and the value is the data that is assigned to the data member or property. In the form example, the properties Key1 and Key2 are set.

Another technique of interest in the code to add a room grouping is the definition of a data handle when passing information:

```
Return grouping
```

In the implementation of AddRoomGrouping(), the variable grouping is assigned an instance of RoomGrouping. The declaration of the RoomGrouping class limits its scope to the LibLightingSystem assembly only, while the declaration of LightingController is public. If the method AddRoomGrouping() had attempted to return an instance of RoomGrouping, the compiler would have marked this as an error, because the scope is inconsistent. Assuming for the moment that you did want to return an instance of RoomGrouping, your only solution would be to declare RoomGrouping as public. The declaration change is the wrong solution, because RoomGrouping is a class without declared methods (other than the base class methods) and has public data members. It is a class for a specific purpose and should not be shared.

Declaring RoomGrouping as public is the wrong approach, so another solution is needed. You could add a counter data member to the RoomGrouping declaration and return an Integer value indicating the RoomGrouping instance you are referring to in the list. However, that would mean having access to the list somewhere, and then needing to iterate to find the appropriate RoomGrouping instance.

The solution is to declare the method as returning a type Object. When you use Object, you are defining that your method is giving you an object instance. The caller may or may not know what the instance type is, and in the case of AddRoomGrouping(), it doesn't. But that is fine, because you, as the user, will consider the instance as a key that is managed by the class LightingController. In technical jargon, the object instance is a *handle* that you hold and pass to some other component that knows what to do with it. In the example, it means giving the handle to LightingController because it knows that the handle is an instance of RoomGrouping.

> ■**Note** Handles were very popular in the C programming days and were consider pointers to memory. The caller did not know what the pointer pointed to, but kept using it when interacting with an API. These days, handles have lost significance as we have objects, .NET generics, and other programming constructs. However, at times, handles are very useful. They can help you to avoid the problem of having to expose the internal state of your API, while not having to maintain an object hierarchy to watch which objects are being referenced.

Finding a Room Grouping

When a number of room groupings have been added, you will want to find a room grouping with a particular description. As room groupings are a doubly linked list, it means needing to iterate the list, as follows (added to `LightingController`):

```
Public Function FindRoomGrouping(ByVal description As String) As Object
    Dim curr As RoomGrouping = _roomGroupings.NextItem
    Do While curr IsNot Nothing
        If curr.Description.CompareTo(description) = 0 Then
            Return curr
        End If
        curr = TryCast(curr.NextItem, RoomGrouping)
    Loop
    Return Nothing
End Function
```

In the iteration code, the iteration is similar to the code illustrated earlier in the "Storing a Collection Using a Linked List" section. The one difference is that the `curr` variable is of type `RoomGrouping`, and because `NextItem` is of type `BaseLinkedListItem`, a type cast is necessary. Then an iteration using a `While` loop is carried out; during each iteration, a test comparing `curr.Description` to the parameter `description` is made. If an object is found, the handle to the `RoomGrouping` is returned, and if nothing is found, `Nothing` is returned, indicating that the `RoomGrouping` could not be found.

This method would be used as follows:

```
Dim foundHandle As Object = controller.FindRoomGrouping("description")
```

Visual Basic has constructs that make it possible to convert the `LightingController` class into a class that has array functionality. The following method in `LightingController` declares array-like functionality, which is called a *default property*

```
Default Public ReadOnly Property Item(ByVal description As String) As Object
    Get
        Return FindRoomGrouping(description)
    End Get
End Property
```

A Visual Basic default property is defined like a property, except that the property is prefixed with a `Default` keyword. The default property is named `Item` by convention, and this name is used by all .NET collection classes for consistency. The implementation of a property is just like other properties. However, the default property is unique in that you use it like an array reference. You could use the default property as follows:

```
Dim foundHandle As Object = controller("description")
```

In the example, the array index is a string and behaves more like a property bag. However, if description were of type Integer, then the default property would behave like an index.

■**Note** Default properties are utility-based and best added to classes that manage collections. In the case of the LightingController, which manages a collection of room groupings, use of a default property is appropriate.

To find a particular room grouping, you would use the methods or default property of LightingController. However, sometimes a user would like to work with all of the room groupings that are available and iterate over them.

The previous indexer example and the FindRoomGrouping() method returned an object. When you iterate the room groupings, you don't want an object, because you don't know what the object represents. If you call the FindRoomGrouping() method and you search based on a description, the object that is returned is cross-referenced with the description. However, if you iterate using a numeric default property, the returned object means nothing to you other than being associated with a specific index. What you really want to know is the description of each object.

You could define a default property with a numeric value, as in the following code, and iterate the individual elements to obtain descriptions.

```
Default Public ReadOnly Property Item(ByVal index As Integer) As String
    Get
        . . .
    End Get
End Property
```

■**Note** A type can have multiple default property definitions, but each default property definition must have different array parameters.

Suppose we implemented a numeric default property. To iterate the individual room groupings, we would need to use the following code.

```
For c1 As Integer = 0 To controller.Length - 1
    Dim description As String = controller(c1)
Next
```

This iteration code is acceptable and something that we could use, but it involves adding the property Length to the LightingController class. Another approach is to use For Each, as follows:

```
For Each rg As RoomGrouping In controller.RoomGroupingIterator()
    ' Do something with the rg
    Console.WriteLine(rg.Description)
Next
```

The For Each syntax is simpler. It doesn't matter that we've lost the information about which offset is which description, because that information is useless. Remember we are dealing with a linked list that can change its order however it pleases. Thus, having a numeric identifier is completely meaningless. The only reliable way to find a room grouping is to know its description or hold a specific index for the collection.

Note Unless you are absolutely sure that the collection you are manipulating does not move elements around, holding an index as a unique description of the object can be dangerous, and potentially could corrupt the state of an application. In this chapter, I have illustrated two other techniques that can be used to reference a particular object: a handle and a default property.

We'll come to the RoomGroupingIterator() method in a bit, but first we need to see the enumerable that it returns.

The LightingController class has no For Each functionality built in. To give it this functionality, you need to create a class that can be enumerated and a class that can be an enumerator, which is a class that can perform the iteration. The complete implementation of a class that can be enumerated for BaseLinkedListItem is as follows (it is also the enumerator class, as you'll see).

```
Public Class LinkedListEnumerable
    Implements IEnumerable, IEnumerator
    Private _currNode As BaseLinkedListItem
    Private _firstNode As BaseLinkedListItem

    Public Sub New(ByVal linkedList As BaseLinkedListItem)
        _currNode = linkedList
        _firstNode = linkedList
    End Sub

    Public Function GetEnumerator() As IEnumerator _
    Implements IEnumerable.GetEnumerator
        Return Me
    End Function
```

```
Public ReadOnly Property Current() As Object _
Implements IEnumerator.Current
    Get
        Return _currNode
    End Get
End Property

Public Function MoveNext() As Boolean _
Implements IEnumerator.MoveNext
    If _currNode Is Nothing Then
        Return False
    End If
    _currNode = _currNode.NextItem
    If _currNode Is Nothing Then
        Return False
    Else
        Return True
    End If
End Function

Public Sub Reset() _
Implements IEnumerator.Reset
    _currNode = _firstNode
End Sub
End Class
```

A class that can be enumerated must fulfill two objectives: implement the IEnumerable interface and implement the IEnumerator interface. The IEnumerable class has a single method, GetEnumerator(), which is used to retrieve a class instance that implements the IEnumerator interface. The two interfaces are split because retrieving the iteration functionality and iterating the collection are two separate steps. However, in the case of LinkedListEnumerable, these steps are combined into one class, and that is often the case.

The best way to explain how LinkedListEnumerable works is to go through the code and explain what methods and properties are called.

1. The code in the client application starts a For Each loop, and sets up a context where a collection of elements is being iterated.

2. The code calls the collection iterator. In the example, this means calling the method RoomGroupingIterator().

3. RoomGroupingIterator() returns an instance of LinkedListEnumerable, which is assigned the linked list that will be iterated.

   ```
   Public Function RoomGroupingIterator() As IEnumerable
       Return New LinkedListEnumerable(_roomGroupings)
   End Function
   ```

4. The method LinkedListEnumerable.GetEnumerator() is called, and an instance of IEnumerator is returned.

5. The code calls the method LinkedListEnumerable.MoveNext().

6. The implementation of MoveNext() returns True to indicate that it was possible to move to the next element. If False is returned, it means that the end of the collection—or in this case, the linked list—is reached.

7. If MoveNext() returns True, then the property LinkedListEnumerable.Current() is called to retrieve the current linked list element.

8. The retrieved linked list element is assigned to the variable of the For Each loop, which is rg in this example.

9. Control is returned to the For Each loop, and the user code does something with the linked list element.

10. When the For Each loop attempts another iteration, steps 5 through 9 are repeated until MoveNext() returns False.

11. When MoveNext() returns False, the iterator exits, causing an exit of the For Each loop.

Adding Rooms to Groupings

The data handle that we defined when adding the grouping is used when we add a room to a grouping. The idea of the handle is to provide a reference that the kernel can use. Since the handle is an instance of a RoomGrouping type, whenever a room is added to a grouping based on a handle, it is not necessary to find the room grouping. The handle is the room grouping, and all that is necessary is a type cast. The following demonstrates how to add a room to a room grouping (in LightingController).

```
Public Sub AddRoomToGrouping(ByVal grouping As Object, ByVal room As IRoom)
    Dim roomGrouping As RoomGrouping = TryCast(grouping, RoomGrouping)
    If roomGrouping Is Nothing Then
        Throw New Exception( _
            "Handle grouping is not a valid room grouping instance")
    End If
    Dim oldRooms As Room = TryCast(roomGrouping.Rooms, Room)
    If  oldRooms Is Nothing Then
        roomGrouping.Rooms = New Room() With {.ObjRoom = room}
    Else
        roomGrouping.Rooms.Insert(New Room() With {.ObjRoom = room})
    End If
End Sub
```

In the implementation of AddRoomToGrouping(), the first step is to cast the handle grouping to an instance of RoomGrouping. The cast used is the TryCast() function, so that if the cast fails, it is only necessary to test if roomGrouping is not Nothing. Executing the Nothing test is absolutely vital; otherwise, you might perform operations that will cause an exception to be thrown.

Once the handle has been cast to a RoomGrouping instance, adding a room to the linked list is trivial. Adding a room involves only assigning the head of the list if there are no rooms in the list, or calling the method Insert() if there are rooms.

Performing Operations on a Group

With a grouping defined, you can perform global operations that affect all rooms of a grouping. One example is turning off the lights in all the rooms in a grouping, which is based on the IRoom interface instance. Here is the code to turn off all of the lights in a grouping:

```
Public Sub TurnOffLights(ByVal grouping As Object)
    Dim enumerableGrouping As LinkedListEnumerable = _
      New LinkedListEnumerable(TryCast(grouping, BaseLinkedListItem))
    For Each room As IRoom In enumerableGrouping
    Dim remote As IRemoteControlRoom = TryCast(room, IRemoteControlRoom)
    Dim sensorRoom As ISensorRoom = TryCast(room, ISensorRoom)
    If sensorRoom IsNot Nothing Then
        If Not sensorRoom.IsPersonInRoom Then
            Continue For
        End If
    ElseIf remote IsNot Nothing Then
        remote.LightSwitch(False)
    End If
    Next
End Sub
```

Notice that the handle is not converted into a RoomGrouping instance. The handle is type cast to BaseLinkedListItem, and then passed to the LinkedListEnumerable constructor. For each iteration of the For Each loop, the IRoom instance room is cast into the types IRemoteControlRoom and ISensorRoom. A cast to both of these types is necessary because, depending on the room type, certain algorithms need to be executed. For example, if the room is of type ISensorRoom and the property IsPersonInRoom is True, then the lights should be left as is. If the lights are to be left as is, that means performing the next iteration using the Continue For keywords.

If the processing continues, we check if the room can be remotely controlled, which means it implements the interface IRemoteControlRoom. If remote is not Nothing, then we can call the LightSwitch() method with a parameter of False to turn off the lights. The iteration continues for all rooms in the grouping.

This completes the kernel, but before you how it fits with a lighting application, I would like to discuss an alternative approach to implementing the kernel.

Defining the Kernel As an Interface Instead of a Class

As I noted earlier, rather than defining the kernel as a class, another approach would be to define the kernel as an interface that is implemented. If a company were to distribute multiple implementations of a controller, an interface would be appropriate, but only if the multiple implementations of the interface used the same set of methods.

Do not confuse multiple implementations with multiple implementations that offer a completely different feature set. For example, controller version 1 and controller version super-duper 1000 might control the same room types, but the inputs, outputs, logic, and algorithms contained in each might be completely different. In that case, using an interface gains no advantage. You might use a version 1 interface on a version super-duper 1000 for legacy integration, since the old interface has older ideas.

You would use an interface for the controller when multiple controllers implement the same interface. You would use an interface if you want the flexibility to later implement multiple implementations using the same interface. On the other hand, if there will only ever be a single implementation for a single interface declaration, it's much easier to use a class declared as `Public`.

If you do decide to declare the controller using an interface and implementation, you need to structure the project differently than the organization used for this chapter's example. The reason is that you cannot declare the interfaces and implementations in the same project. Imagine trying to offer multiple kernel implementations, but for the users to be able to use the interfaces, they must reference a project that contains a particular kernel implementation.

You will need to modularize the structure and have an organization similar to that shown in Figure 8-5.

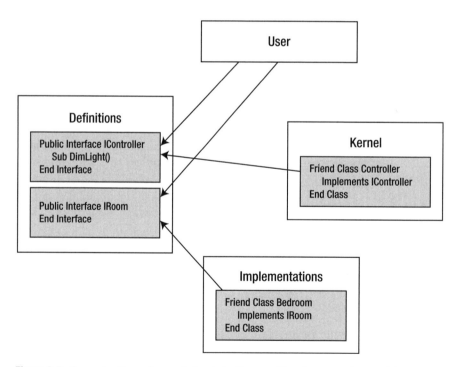

Figure 8-5. *Organization of a modular interface and implementation architecture*

In Figure 8-5, the individual boxes represent a single .NET assembly. Each assembly serves a unique purpose:

- Definitions: An assembly that contains all interfaces used by all of the other assemblies. This represents a single assembly that changes very rarely and is a cornerstone of the application. Along with interfaces, you would add general utility classes that all assemblies would reference.

- User: The main application that interacts with the interfaces of objects that are implemented in either the Kernel or Implementations assemblies. The User assembly is responsible for wiring together all of the types.

- Kernel: An assembly that defines the main functionality of the application and manipulates instances that implement interfaces from the Definitions assembly. The kernel does not know where the interfaces are implemented, and it expects some other piece of code to know where the implementations are.

- Implementations: An assembly that contains the implementations of the interfaces that the kernel manipulates. The programmer may create a single implementation assembly or multiple assemblies. The implementations are only aware of the Definitions assembly; they are unaware of the Kernel assembly.

Building a Complete Application

All of the code illustrated thus far is related to the kernel, and it would seem that our application is complete. In reality, the kernel has done nothing other than organize and manipulate the rooms. The kernel has not defined any implementations for a particular room. Now let's see how to define some rooms and use the rooms in the context of the kernel.

The idea is to enable a developer to add functionality to the kernel without affecting the code of the kernel. The example that we will go through defines a couple of rooms in a museum (the Museum project).

■**Note** The implementation of the Home project is not discussed here, but it is available in this book's downloadable source code.

Defining Some Rooms

The rooms are defined in a separate assembly called Museum and are not part of the kernel. The following is an example of a room implementation. Again, remember to include a reference to LibLightingSystem (right-click References in Museum and select Add Reference then Projects ➤ LibLightingSystem).

```
. . .
Imports LibLightingSystem

    Friend Class PrivateRoom : Implements INoRemoteControlRoom
    End Class

    Friend Class PublicRoom : Implements ISensorRoom
        Public ReadOnly Property IsPersonInRoom() As Boolean _
            Implements ISensorRoom.IsPersonInRoom
            Get
                Return False
            End Get
        End Property

        Private _lightLevel As Double

        Public ReadOnly Property LightLevel() As Double _
            Implements ISensorRoom.LightLevel
            Get
                Return _lightLevel
            End Get
        End Property

        Public Sub LightSwitch(ByVal lightState As Boolean) _
            Implements IRemoteControlRoom.LightSwitch
            If lightState Then
                _lightLevel = 1
            Else
                _lightLevel = 0
            End If
        End Sub

        Public Sub DimLight(ByVal level As Double) _
            Implements IRemoteControlRoom.DimLight
            _lightLevel = level
        End Sub
    End Class
```

The two room declarations, PrivateRoom and PublicRoom, are both internal to the assembly. Each room implements the interface that it deems appropriate. PrivateRoom implements the interface INoRemoteControlRoom, indicating that LightingController should leave the room alone.

PublicRoom implements ISensorRoom, indicating that it will tell the controller when a person is in the room and allow itself to be controlled. The implementation of PublicRoom is trivial and frankly not that useful, but it illustrates the bare minimum of what needs to be implemented. In a production environment, PublicRoom would have access to external devices such as a heat sensor and lights. The objective of PublicRoom would be to give and take signals from the LightingController and take action. It is not up to PublicRoom to ask whether or not a decision is correct. For example, if LightingController indicated to turn the light off even though a person is in the room, then PublicRoom would not ask why the light is being turned off.

■**Note** When you are designing a kernel-like architecture, the implementations are realizations of ideas and should never question the controller. The implementations might not be aware of a bigger picture and thus might prevent an algorithm from functioning properly. Of course, the exception to this rule is if the decision would cause physical damage or cause the program to crash. In that case, the implementation should throw an exception, indicating that the decision is faulty.

Instantiating PublicRoom and PrivateRoom

As described in the previous chapter, when you are developing components, you want to separate the interfaces from the implementations. This gives you the flexibility to change the implementation in an assembly without requiring the users of the assembly to recompile their code.

To instantiate the implementations, you need a factory, and the museum with its PrivateRoom and PublicRoom implementations is no different. However, a builder method that assembles a building of potential PrivateRoom and PublicRoom combinations will be offered with the museum. The builder method is useful because it predefines a canned building that has all the room groupings and rooms properly added.

■**Note** Think of a builder method as a way of creating a predefined structure, thus saving users from having to do that themselves. A builder method is only a starting point, and you should be able to manipulate the structure afterward for fine-tuning purposes.

The following is the implementation of the museum factory, which is added to the project Museum.

```
Public Module FactoryRooms
    Public Function CreateBuilding() As LightingController
        Dim controller As New LightingController()
        Dim publicAreas As Object = _
          controller.AddRoomGrouping("public viewing areas")
        Dim privateAreas As Object = _
          controller.AddRoomGrouping("private viewing areas")
        controller.AddRoomToGrouping(publicAreas, New PublicRoom())
        controller.AddRoomToGrouping(privateAreas, New PrivateRoom())
        Return controller
    End Function
End Module
```

```
    Public Function CreatePrivateRoom() As IRoom
        Return New PrivateRoom()
    End Function

    Public Function CreatePublicRoom() As IRoom
        Return New PublicRoom()
    End Function
End Module
```

The implementation has three methods: CreateBuilding(), CreatePrivateRoom(), and CreatePublicRoom(),. The fact that CreatePrivateRoom() and PrivateRoom() have similar naming is purely coincidental. The method could just as well have been called CreateNonControlledRoom(). The CreatePrivateRoom() and CreatePublicRoom() methods are intended to define method identifiers that users can understand. What is instantiated in the method must return an IRoom instance.

The CreateBuilding() method is a builder method, and it returns a LightingController instance. It is fine to return a LightingController instance, because it is a globally defined type and can serve as a basis for the builder method. In the implementation of the builder method, the room groupings and rooms are instantiated and added to the LightingController instance. This is the work that the builder should save the end user. Additionally, by providing a builder method, you avoid creating museum structures that have glaring errors in their structures.

■Note Factory types serve to instantiate types and define builder methods, but can also be used to perform generic structural operations. Let's say that in your museum there is a wing, which contains three public rooms and a private room. You could define a builder method that creates a wing, and the wing is added to an already created building. The general idea behind the factory type is to avoid errors and centralize repeated instantiations.

Learning More About Private Classes and Object Initialization

In this chapter, you learned how to apply interfaces, implementations, and components in a kernel-type situation. This is very much the type of programming that you will encounter as you continue using Visual Basic. Here, I will provide a few more details about using private classes and initializing objects with nested data types.

Private Classes

The RoomGrouping and Room classes are defined in the LibLightingController project and are private to the library. This is because RoomGrouping and Room are classes only LightingController needs to support its functionality. The declaration of each class is internal to the assembly, which is good, but it still means that some developers could use the classes within the kernel assembly for their own purposes. Sometimes that is a desirable feature; sometimes it is not.

In the case of LightingController, another approach is to declare the classes in the context of LightingController, as follows:

```
Public Class LightingController
    Private Class RoomGrouping
    End Class
    Private Class Room
    End Class
End Class
```

The Room and RoomGrouping classes are declared within the class, and their declarations are Private. This means that only LightingController can instantiate and use the classes, and there can never be the situation where another class will instantiate the types. In the case of LightingController, this would have been a better solution.

Private classes are also used in the factory context. For example, imagine the situation where you don't ever want anyone but the factory to instantiate a room. A possible IRoom declaration and factory could be as follows:

```
Public Module Factory
    Private Class MyRoom : Implements IRoom
    End Class
    Public Function CreateMyRoom() As IRoom
        Return New MyRoom()
    End Function
End Module
```

In this implementation of MyRoom, you can be sure that only Factory can ever instantiate MyRoom, and you can always be sure that the only way to manipulate MyRoom is through the IRoom interface. All too often, developers become lazy and instantiate types within the assembly, and switch to the implementation type whenever the interface does not have the methods or properties that they want.

Object Initialization with Nested Data Types

In this chapter, you saw how to use object initialization to assign data members in lieu of a constructor. Object initialization also works using nested data types. Consider the situation where a type references another type. Using object initialization, you can instantiate and assign multiple levels of objects.

Suppose you had this source code:

```
Class MyType
    Private _dataMember As Integer

    Public Property DataMember() As Integer
        Get
            Return _dataMember
        End Get
```

```
                Set (ByVal value as Integer)
                    _dataMember = value
                End Set
            End Property
    End Class

    Class EmbeddedMyType
        Private _embedded As MyType

        Public Property MyTypeProperty() As MyType
            Get
                Return _embedded
            End Get
            Set (ByVal value As MyType)
                _embedded = value
            End Get
        End Property
    End Class
```

The type EmbeddedMyType has a property that references MyType. If you were to instantiate EmbeddedMyType, you would probably also want to instantiate and assign the property MyType. You can do that with object initialization, like this:

```
        Dim cls As EmbeddedMyType = _
            New EmbeddedMyType() With { _
                .MyTypeProperty = _
                    New MyType() With {.DataMember = 10}}
```

The Important Stuff to Remember

In this chapter, you learned about writing a kernel, using Visual Basic default properties, and the implementing enumeration functionality. The main items to remember are as follows:

- A kernel is a component-oriented architecture where you are not in control of certain implementations. Components make it possible to modularize a development process so that separate teams have their own tasks.

- Interfaces are contracts between modules, and you test against the interface, not the implementation.

- Placeholder interfaces are used to make it simpler to group object instances.

- Default properties are structural, and thus they serve as a tool to help you accomplish a task quicker.

- Default properties make it possible for your type to behave like an array.

- To iterate something that does not support iteration, you add enumeration functionality, which implies implementing the IEnumerable and IEnumerator interfaces.

Some Things for You to Do

The following are some exercises that will help you apply the concepts you learned in this chapter.

1. The LightingController.AddRoomGrouping() method has a mistake. Write some tests to find the error, and then fix the code and rerun your tests to verify that the error has been fixed.

2. The TestInsert() test method is one example of an insertion test, but not all variations have been tested. Write another test method that implements the remaining variation(s) that need to be tested.

3. The declarations of RoomGrouping and Room are not optimal. Fix the declarations.

4. Implement a general collection class based on the experience of using the class in the class LightingController. Hint: look at how the linked list for Room is declared and figure out a way to abstract that into some general collection class.

5. When the method LightingController.AddRoom() is called, the method is tested internally to see if the handle is of type RoomGrouping. Can you think of a more defensive programming technique to make sure that the code someone else passes to the kernel will not cause the kernel to fail? Hint: think about the methods to turn on or off the lights and think of what could go wrong.

■ ■ ■

CHAPTER 9

Learning About Lists, Delegates, and Lambda Expressions

One of the most common pieces of code that you will write is code that manages many object instances. In the previous examples, many object instances were managed using an array. In Chapter 8, you learned that a linked list used in conjunction with a default property could make a plain-vanilla object look like a collection. This chapter introduces the .NET collection classes, which provide an easy way to manage a set of object instances. Think of a collection object as an infinite sack where things can be added, iterated through, and retrieved.

The chapter begins with a discussion of how to manage collections. Then we will look at different ways of iterating the data using a delegate. Finally, we will look at lambda expressions and closures to illustrate another way of processing data.

The project structure used in this chapter is a single console application. As we will not be building an overall application, but rather a set of sample code snippets, no tests or libraries are involved.

Managing Collections

When you have a collection, what you actually have is an object that happens to point to many other objects.

Visual Basic provides collection classes for managing collections. Visual Basic 2005 introduced a different approach to collections, which solved many of the problems that came up in earlier Visual Basic versions. Here, we'll look at managing collections both before and after Visual Basic 2005, which will help you to understand how collections are used.

Managing a Collection Before Visual Basic 2005

Before Visual Basic 2005, the main collection classes were stored in the namespace `System.Collections` (and, of course, these classes are still available for you to use). The following are some of the classes and interfaces in that namespace:

- ArrayList: A general collection that manages all of the referenced objects using an internal array. This class manages the problem of increasing the size of an array.

- Hashtable: A collection class where the individual objects are stored using key/value pairs. In the previous chapter, the indexer was used to retrieve a room grouping based on its identifier. You could use a Hashtable to accomplish the same thing.

- ICollection: An interface implement by ArrayList that provides basic functionality that copies the references to another array.

- IDictionary: An interface implemented by Hashtable that allows a programmer to associate a key with a value.

- IList: An interface implemented by ArrayList that provides a general-access mechanism for manipulating a collection of items.

- Queue: A collection that implements the first in, first out (FIFO) mechanism. You could use a queue when you are processing a set of instructions. The first instruction to process would be the first instruction added to the collection.

- Stack: A collection that implements the last in, first out (LIFO) mechanism. Think of it as a stack of papers. When one piece of paper is laid on top of another, the first piece of paper that is processed is the last piece of paper added to the stack of papers.

All of the collection types—ArrayList, Hashtable, Queue, and Stack—implement a way to store a set of types. The difference in the collection types lies in how the individual objects are stored and retrieved from the collection. For examples of using these collection types, see the "Learning More About Collection Types" section later in this chapter.

Let's walk through an example of using these collection classes. Begin by creating a console application and call it OneToManySamples. Then add a new class (right-click your console application project and select Add ➤ Class). Call it Example.vb and add all of the following code to it:

```
Class Example
    Public Property Value() As Integer
        Get
            Return _value
        End Get
        Set(ByVal value As Integer)
            _value = value
        End Set
    End Property

    Private _value As Integer
End Class

Friend Module Tests
    Private Sub PlainVanillaObjects()
            Dim objects As IList = New ArrayList()
```

```
            objects.Add(New Example With {.Value = 10})
            objects.Add(New Example With {.Value = 20})
            For Each obj As Example In objects
                Console.WriteLine("Object value (" & obj.Value & ")")
            Next
        End Sub
        Public Sub RunAll()
            PlainVanillaObjects()
        End Sub
    End Module
```

This is the type of code written before Visual Basic 2005, and it follows a standard set of steps:

1. You define a custom type (Example in this example).

2. You instantiate the custom type and add the instances to a collection. In the example, two instances of Example are added to the collection type ArrayList.

3. The collection is manipulated to allow you to access and manipulate the instances of the custom types. In the example, the collection ArrayList is an interface instance of IList.

The bolded code in the example is where the action takes place. Instantiating the type ArrayList is the instantiation of a collection manager. The ArrayList instance is then assigned to the variable objects, which is of type IList. IList is an interface making it possible to use the collection in the context of a component-oriented development environment. To add two objects to the collection, we call the Add() method twice. To iterate the elements in the collection, we use the For Each statement.

Note The fact that the collection classes can be used in the context of a component-oriented application is no coincidence. When Microsoft created its .NET library, components were an essential part of the library.

To run the tests, open Module1.vb in your console application and edit it as follows:

```
Module Module1
    Sub Main()
        BeforeVisualBasic8.Tests.RunAll()
        Console.ReadKey()
    End Sub
End Module
```

Press Ctrl+F5 to run the application and see the results.

Note We did not need to import the System.Collections namespace because it is imported by default in Visual Basic 2008.

The Problem of Mixed Types

What is unique about the sample code is that the For Each statement works and happens to know that the objects in the collection are of type Example. However, the following code adds a different object to the collection, which will cause the iteration to fail.

```
Class Another
End Class

Dim objects As IList = New ArrayList()

objects.Add(New Example With {.Value = 10})
objects.Add(New Example With {.Value = 20})
objects.Add(New Another())
For Each obj As Example In objects
      Console.WriteLine("Object value (" & obj.Value & ")")
Next
```

The bolded code illustrates how the collection object contains two instances of Example and one instance of Another. The code will compile, which misleads you into believing everything is fine. If you try to run the application (either normally or in debug mode), you will see something similar to the following:

```
Unable to cast object of type 'OneToManySamples.Another' to type
'OneToManySamples.Example'.
```

So, should a collection contain multiple types? There are arguments for and against the idea, but the problem is not the ability to mix types. The problem is that you can mix types, even if you don't really intend to do that.

Using the For Each statement with mixed types will result in an exception, because for each iteration, the object in the collection is cast to a type Example. As the last item in the collection is of type Another, the cast will fail, and an exception will be generated. Collections before .NET 2.0 could not enforce type consistency, and that was a problem.

Had you desired to mix types, the proper For Each loop would have been as follows:

```
Dim objects As IList = new ArrayList()

objects.Add(New Example With {.Value = 10})
objects.Add(New Example With {.Value = 20})
objects.Add(New Another())
For Each obj As Object In objects
    If TypeOf (obj) Is Example Then
        Dim example As Example = CType(obj, Example)
        Console.WriteLine("Object value (" & example.Value & ")")
    ElseIf TypeOf (obj) Is Another Then
        Console.WriteLine("This is another object")
    End If
Next
```

The Problem of Value Types

Another issue with pre-Visual Basic 2005 collections is that they have performance problems. Consider the following code that manipulates value types.

```
Dim objects As IList = New ArrayList()
objects.Add(1)
objects.Add(2)
For Each val as Integer in objects
    Console.WriteLine("Value (" & val & ")")
Next
```

In the example, an `ArrayList` is again instantiated, but this time, the numbers 1 and 2 are added to the collection. Then, in the `For Each` statement, the integers are iterated. The code works, but there is a hidden performance hit. The items added to the collection are value types, which means you are manipulating stack-based memory.

However, the definition of `IList` uses objects:

```
Public Interface IIList
    Inherits ICollection, IEnumerable

    ' Methods
    Function Add(ByVal value As Object) As Integer
    Sub Clear()
    Function Contains(ByVal value As Object) As Boolean
    Function IndexOf(ByVal value As Object) As Integer
    Sub Insert(ByVal index As Integer, ByVal value As Object)
    Sub Remove(ByVal value As Object)
    Sub RemoveAt(ByVal index As Integer)

    ' Properties
    ReadOnly Property IsFixedSize() As Boolean
    ReadOnly Property IsReadOnly() As Boolean
    Property Item(ByVal index As Integer) As Object

End Interface
```

How `IList` is defined and how a value type is defined should raise alarms. An object is a reference type, and thus you have a conflict: `IList` stores reference types, but `Integer` is a value type.

What's happening is that the .NET environment knows that there is a conflict and adds a fix. Don't think of the fix as a hack, but as a way of solving a problem that all virtual machine environments like .NET need to address. The .NET environment uses the terms *boxing* and *unboxing* to denote converting a value type into a reference type and then back again, respectively.

To understand boxing and unboxing, let's consider the context. You are creating a list that references value types. The array is a reference type that is stored on the heap, but value types are stored on the stack. If you get the array to reference data on the stack, you will have a consistency issue, since the stack changes. Thus, you will need to move the memory from the stack to the heap, but that would violate the principle behind value types. The solution is the compromise of boxing and unboxing.

To illustrate what boxing does, I have written some code that is similar to the boxing of a value type. The difference is that my code is explicit and boxing is done automatically.

```
Class ReferenceHeap
    Public Value As Integer
End Class
. . .
Public Sub Method()
    Dim onStack As Integer = 1
    Dim onHeap As ReferenceHeap = New ReferenceHeap() With { .Value = onStack }
End Sub
```

In the example, Method() declares a value-type variable named onStack, which is allocated in the context of a method and is thus on the stack. The type ReferenceHeap is a class, and thus a reference type, and automatically all of its data is stored on the heap. When the variable onHeap is allocated and initialized, the value from onStack is copied to the heap and assigned to the instance onHeap. This is what boxing does, except Visual Basic does it automatically and transparently.

■**Note** It is important to remember that when you box and unbox, you are copying values back and forth between the stack and the heap. Thus, if the variable onStack is changed, the value of onHeap does not change.

Unboxing refers to copying the value from the heap to the stack, which in the case of the example, means transferring the value from the variable onHeap to onStack.

Boxing/unboxing happens automatically, but it has a performance penalty, since memory is allocated and assigned.

Managing a Collection After Visual Basic 2005

The two problems of storing mixed object types and the performance penalty of boxing/unboxing required Microsoft to carefully consider a solution. After much debate and thinking, Microsoft introduced *.NET generics*. In a nutshell, .NET generics solve both collection problems by enforcing a type. (.NET generics solve broader problems as well.)

Collections are an ideal application of .NET generics because collections are utilitarian. You don't use collections to solve the problem of calculating taxes. You use collections to solve the problem of how to create a collection of incomes and a collection of deductions.

Here is an example of how to use .NET generics-based collections (they are in the System.Collections.Generic namespace, which we also do not need to import):

```
Dim lst As IList(Of Example) = New List(Of Example)()
lst.Add(New Example() With { .Value = 10 })
lst.Add(New Example() With { .Value = 20 })
For Each item As Example In lst
    Console.WriteLine("item (" & item.Value & ")")
Next
```

The bolded line represents the .NET generics-based code. The code used to add an object and the `For Each` loop are identical to that used in the pre–Visual Basic 2005 example.

Between the brackets in the type declaration and after the `Of` keyword is an identifier that is the specialization of the general approach. Whatever is inside the brackets when you declare an `IList` or `List` is saying, "I want my collection to contain instances of the type defined inside the brackets." You cannot add any objects that are not related to the type defined in `IList` or `List`, so the following code would not compile.

```
lst.Add(New Another())
```

This is because the .NET generics collection is type-safe and does not allow mixed types. It allows only objects of type `Example`.

When you declare a list like this:

```
Dim lst As IList(Of Example)
```

you are saying that the list has a method declared like this:

```
Sub Add(ByVal item As Example)
```

If you are programming with Visual Basic 2008, you should use Visual Basic 2005 and later collection classes. The non-.NET generics collection classes are, to a large degree, legacy code. Whenever possible, use .NET generics-based collection classes.

Now that you know how to manage a collection of objects, the next section will present a common collection-related problem and then solve the problem.

Adding Numbers and Finding Maximum Values

Let's start out with a common problem: addition of all elements in a collection. Consider the following code.

```
Dim elements As IList(Of Integer) = New List(Of Integer)()

elements.Add(1)
elements.Add(2)
elements.Add(3)

Dim runningTotal = 0
For Each value As Integer In elements
    runningTotal = runningTotal + value
Next
```

This code has three parts: initialization of `elements`, adding of numbers to `elements`, and iteration of all values in `elements` that are added to the variable `runningTotal`. The code seems acceptable. But let's say that you need to write another piece of code where, instead of calculating the running total, you want to find the maximum value, like this:

```vb
Dim elements As IList(Of Integer) = New List(Of Integer)()

elements.Add(1)
elements.Add(2)
elements.Add(3)

Dim maxValue As Integer = Integer.MinValue
For Each value As Integer In elements
    If value > maxValue Then
        maxValue = value
    End If
Next
```

The difference between the two code pieces is the bolded code. The inner loop is different, which is a potential problem. In separate code files, the repetition is not apparent, but what if you wanted to combine the code bases? The following code adds all elements and finds the maximum value.

```vb
Dim elements As IList(Of Integer) = New List(Of Integer)()
elements.Add(1)
elements.Add(2)
elements.Add(3)
Dim runningTotal As Integer = 0
For Each value As Integer In elements
    runningTotal = runningTotal + value
Next
Console.WriteLine("RunningTotal (" & runningTotal & ")")

Dim maxValue As Integer = Integer.MinValue
For Each value As Integer In elements
    If value > maxValue Then
        maxValue = value
    End If
Next
Console.WriteLine("Maximum value is (" &  maxValue & ")")
```

Another variation is as follows:

```vb
Dim elements As IList(Of Integer) = New List(Of Integer)()
elements.Add(1)
elements.Add(2)
elements.Add(3)
Dim runningTotal As Integer = 0
Dim maxValue As Integer = Integer.MinValue
For Each value As Integer In elements
    If value > maxValue Then
        maxValue = value
    End If
    runningTotal = runningTotal + value
Next
```

For one or two instances, writing the For Each loop is not that problematic, but it would be if you needed to use the iterator code in a dozen places. This type of code is harder to maintain and extend. One way of being more efficient is to delegate the code to an abstract base class that is implemented to calculate the running total or maximum value. The following is the complete code (you can place the three classes in separate files called IteratorBaseClass.vb, RunningTotal.vb, and MaximumValue.vb if you want to test this).

```vb
MustInherit Class IteratorBaseClass
    Protected Sub New(ByVal collection As IList(Of Integer))
        _collection = collection
    End Sub

    Public Function Iterate() As IteratorBaseClass
        Dim element As Integer
        For Each element In Me._collection
            ProcessElement(element)
        Next
        Return Me
    End Function

    Protected MustOverride Sub ProcessElement(ByVal value As Integer)

    Private _collection As IList(Of Integer)
End Class

Class RunningTotal
    Inherits IteratorBaseClass
    Public Sub New(ByVal collection As IList(Of Integer))
        MyBase.New(collection)
        Total = 0
    End Sub

    Protected Overrides Sub ProcessElement(ByVal value As Integer)
        Total = Total + value
    End Sub

    Public Total As Integer
End Class

Class MaximumValue
    Inherits IteratorBaseClass
    Public Sub New(ByVal collection As IList(Of Integer))
        MyBase.New(collection)
        MaxValue = Integer.MinValue
    End Sub
```

```
        Protected Overrides Sub ProcessElement(ByVal value As Integer)
            If (value > MaxValue) Then
                MaxValue = value
            End If
        End Sub

        Public MaxValue As Integer
    End Class

Module Module1
    Sub Main()
        Dim elements As IList(Of Integer) = New List(Of Integer)()
        elements.Add(1)
        elements.Add(2)
        elements.Add(3)

        Dim runningTotal As Integer = _
          TryCast(New RunningTotal(elements).Iterate(), RunningTotal).Total

        Dim maximumValue As Integer = _
          TryCast(New MaximumValue(elements).Iterate(), MaximumValue).MaxValue

        Console.WriteLine("RunningTotal (" & runningTotal & ")")
        Console.WriteLine("Maximum Value (" & maximumValue & ")")
    End Sub
End Module
```

The rewritten code is much longer, even though the bolded code, which represents the user code, is much shorter. However, this code still isn't right. The code is ill fitting because the problem that it addresses can be solved using another, simpler technique. So, in a nutshell, you can say the problem is that you want to solve a single particular technical problem using an elegant piece of code that does not include repeated sections that have been copied and pasted. A better solution is consider the code as two code blocks, and in the following section, you'll see how delegates can solve the problem of adding and keeping a running total.

WEIGHING THE ADVANTAGES OF REUSING CODE

Very often, when you write code, the code that performs the task directly is shorter and to the point. When you abstract the code and develop general classes, the code will begin to bloat and expand, but the advantage is that the code can be reused. So, when is abstracting code worth the effort?

Consider the analogy of building a house. You are constructing the trusses for the house. You have a blueprint that indicates that you need to build 50 trusses. You could build each of the 50 trusses individually, or you could build a jig to speed up building the trusses. And herein lies the problem. If the trusses can be built without a jig in 10 hours, and with the jig in 2 hours, you would think building the jig was a good idea. But not so fast. What if building the jig takes 20 hours? Then the time that you saved by using the jig you lost by building the jig.

Software is no different. Sometimes, even though the code is more complicated and bloated, if the code is reused often enough, abstracting it saves time, as the end-user code is simplified. Experience will tell you when to code specifically or when to write general code that can be reused. A rule of thumb is to start out by solving the problem, and if it looks like the code can be reused, then abstract the specific code.

Using Delegates

Since the beginning of Visual Basic, there has been a concept called a *delegate*. A delegate is a type that represents a method signature. For example, consider the following interface definition.

```
Interface IExample
    Sub Method()
End Interface
```

The equivalent delegate would look like this:

```
Delegate Sub Method()
```

A delegate and interface can share the same role, in that they are two different ways to represent the signature for a method that you implement elsewhere. An interface can have multiple methods and properties. A delegate is a method signature and can define only the parameters and return types for that method signature. The purpose of delegates is to be able to define a generic method-calling mechanism without needing to add the baggage of implementing an interface.

The approach used in the delegate solution to the problem presented in the previous section is to define a chunk of functionality that performs the iteration, called an *iterator*. And then to do something with the iteration, another chunk of functionality is integrated via a delegate.

Following is the complete rewritten For Each code that uses delegates. The entire solution is shown for a big picture purposes, and then will be split into smaller chunks for explanation purposes.

```
Imports System.Runtime.CompilerServices

Namespace DelegateImplementation
    Delegate Sub ProcessValue(ByVal value As Integer)

    Module Iterator
        ' Methods
        Public Sub Iterate(ByVal collection As ICollection(Of Integer), _
                        ByVal cb As ProcessValue)
            Dim element As Integer
            For Each element In collection
                cb(element)
            Next
        End Sub

    End Module
```

```
Module Tests
    ' Fields
    Private _maxValue As Integer
    Private _runningTotal As Integer

    Private Sub ProcessMaximumValue(ByVal value As Integer)
        If (value > Tests._maxValue) Then
            _maxValue = value
        End If
    End Sub

    Private Sub ProcessRunningTotal(ByVal value As Integer)
        _runningTotal = _runningTotal + value
    End Sub

    Public Sub RunAll()
        Dim lst As New List(Of Integer)()
        lst.Add(1)
        lst.Add(2)
        lst.Add(3)
        lst.Add(4)
        _runningTotal = 0

        Iterator.Iterate(lst, New ProcessValue(AddressOf ProcessRunningTotal))
        Console.WriteLine(("Running total is (" & _runningTotal & ")"))
        _maxValue = Integer.MinValue
        Iterator.Iterate(lst, New ProcessValue(AddressOf ProcessMaximumValue))
        Console.WriteLine(("Maximum value is (" & _maxValue & ")"))
    End Sub
End Module
End Namespace
```

Declaring the Delegate

The beginning of the code is the single line that contains the Delegate keyword. Any delegate implementations must match this signature (in our case, ProcessMaximumValue() and ProcessRunningTotal() match the delegate signature):

```
Delegate Sub ProcessValue(ByVal value As Integer)
```

The declaration of the delegate is outside the scope of a class or interface, but the usage of a delegate must be in the context of a class (as it is in our case).

The type of the delegate is the name of the method, which is ProcessValue in our case. The delegate will be used in the code example to provide a general callback mechanism in the iterator. The iterator is declared as follows:

```
Module Extensions
    Public Sub Iterate(ByVal collection As ICollection(Of Integer), _
                    ByVal cb As ProcessValue)
        Dim element As Integer
        For Each element In collection
            cb(element)
        Next
    End Sub
End Module
```

A module method can be called as follows:

```
Iterator.Iterate(lst, delegate)
```

The first parameter of the Iterate() method is the list to iterate, and the second parameter is a delegate instance that matches the method signature of the ProcessValue delegate.

In the implementation of Iterate(), each element of the collection is iterated using For Each, and then in the loop, the variable cb is called as if it were a method. The calling of cb is what separates the iterator from the processing of the iteration. Imagine having implemented a method that calculates the running total or maximum. To iterate all of the elements, you would instantiate the delegate with the method and call Iterate(), as follows:

```
Iterator.Iterate(lst, New ProcessValue(ProcessRunningTotal))
. . .
Iterator.Iterate(lst, New ProcessValue(ProcessMaximumValue))
```

The code that wants to automatically iterate code must provide only a delegate implementation.

Implementing Methods That Match the Delegate

Implementing methods that match a delegate is straightforward in that you need to declare only a method in a class that has the same method signature. This can be implemented using a shared method or an instance method; it does not matter. The following code demonstrates methods that match the ProcessValue delegate's signature using both types of methods.

```
Class DelegateImplementations


    Private Sub InstanceProcess(ByVal value As Integer)
    End Sub

    Private Shared Sub SharedProcess(ByVal value As Integer)
    End Sub
End Class
```

In the example, the InstanceProcess() and SharedProcess() methods match the signature of the delegate ProcessValue. If you have two delegates with identical parameter and return type signatures, then a method with the same signature can be used for either delegate definition.

The following shows how to have the methods be recognized as a delegate.

```
Dim instanceMethod As New ProcessValue(AddressOf InstanceProcess)
Dim sharedMethod As New ProcessValue(AddressOf SharedProcess)
```

These two lines instantiate the delegate using the New keyword, and each instantiation has a single constructor parameter, which is the method to associate with the delegate instance.

Now let's look at the running total and maximum value example and see the methods that will be wrapped up by delegates.

```
Module Tests
    Private _maxValue As Integer
    Private _runningTotal As Integer

    Private Sub ProcessMaximumValue(ByVal value As Integer)
        If (value > Tests._maxValue) Then
            _maxValue = value
        End If
    End Sub

    Private Sub ProcessRunningTotal(ByVal value As Integer)
        _runningTotal = _runningTotal + value
    End Sub
End Module
```

The ProcessMaximumValue() and ProcessRunningTotal() methods both have the same signatures as ProcessValue, and therefore are delegate candidates. In each delegate implementation, the running total is calculated or the maximum value is found. The following code uses the delegates.

```
Public Sub RunAll()
    Dim lst As New List(Of Integer)()
    lst.Add(1)
    lst.Add(2)
    lst.Add(3)
    lst.Add(4)
    _runningTotal = 0

    Iterator.Iterate(lst, New ProcessValue(AddressOf ProcessRunningTotal))
    Console.WriteLine(("Running total is (" & _runningTotal & ")"))
    _maxValue = Integer.MinValue
    Iterator.Iterate(lst, New ProcessValue(AddressOf ProcessMaximumValue))
    Console.WriteLine(("Maximum value is (" & _maxValue & ")"))
End Sub
```

In the example, the RunAll() method instantiates and assigns lst. Then to iterate the individual elements, the Iterator.Iterate() method is called with lst and the ProcessRunningTotal() method. After having calculated and presented the running total, the maximum value is calculated and displayed.

The delegate solution is more compact than the previous abstract base class solution. The big advantage is the ability to solve a problem using a smaller, piecemeal approach. It is not hard to implement a delegate, and it is not hard to use a delegate.

Understanding Lambda Expressions

Lambda expressions are an extension of delegates, but solve a specific problem. Let's take the example of calculating sales tax. Sales tax in general is a simple calculation in that you take the total amount, multiply it by the sales tax, and add the result to the amount. This gives you the total a customer must pay. Calculating a sales tax is not difficult, but it is something that would be nice to encapsulate into a small piece of functionality. Thus, calculating sales tax is an excellent use of lambda expressions.

A lambda expression is declared as a Function that has a single expression as a body. Following is the declaration of a lambda expression.

```
Dim calculate = Function(tax As Double, amount As Double) (tax * amount) + amount
```

The lambda expression is declared as a function without a return type. The code after the brackets is a single expression that uses the parameters to perform some action. In the example, that single expression is the calculation of the sales tax that is added to the amount to generate a new total.

The lambda expression could be used as follows:

```
Console.WriteLine("Tax (" & calculate(0.1, 100) & ")")
```

The calculate lambda expression is called with two numbers that are of type Double, which generates an expression similar to this:

```
Function $sdfsdfsdf(tax As Double, amount As Double) As Double
    Return (tax * amount) + amount
End Function
```

Notice a return type of Double is declared in the generated code. The compiler did this by inferring from the code.

Single-expression lambda expressions have some use, but their real value is in the ability to create a closure that establishes a context. A closure holds the evaluated lambda expression with its bound variables for other functions to use, which is how the context is established.

Let's say that we are going to calculate the sales tax for a particular place like Quebec, Canada. The sales tax there is 15%, and thus when using the lambda expression, we abstract and create code similar to the following.

```
Console.WriteLine("Tax (" & calculate(SalesTax.Quebec, 100.0) & ")")
```

The value for the sales tax is held in the property SalesTax.Quebec, and whenever we use the lambda expression, we need to specify the property.

With lambda expressions and closure, you have the ability to save a context. For starters, let's redefine the lambda expression to have only a single parameter:

```
Function(amount As Double) (tax * amount) + amount
```

Notice that the lambda expression still uses the tax rate in its calculation. This is where context comes in. We can save the context of a certain tax rate and then use the lambda expression in that context. To do so, we need a lambda expression that returns our new one-parameter lambda expression:

```
Function(tax As Double) Function(amount As Double) (tax * amount) + amount
```

We can set the tax rate with the first lambda expression, and then call the second to calculate the tax:

```
Dim prepareTax =
  Function(tax As Double) Function(amount As Double) (tax * amount) + amount

Dim doQuebec = prepareTax(0.1)
Console.WriteLine(doQuebec(100))
```

The call to prepareTax defines doQuebec as prepareTax(0.1) and sets the tax variable in the context of doQuebec. Now when we call doQuebec, we can calculate the total amount without ever needing to specify the tax rate again.

Lambda expressions allow only a single expression. If you want to implement a lambda expression that should make a decision, you have a problem. To solve this problem, you can use an If statement variation that is like a function. Imagine a country where the applicable sales tax depends on the amount you purchased. This logic could be implemented using a closure and ternary If statement, as follows:

```
Dim setMinimumSalesTax = Function(minimumSalesTax As Double)
                Function(amount As Double)
                    If(amount > minimumSalesTax,
                        (0.15 * amount) + amount,_
                        (0.1 * amount) + amount)

Dim calculateTotal = setMinimumSalesTax(100)

Console.WriteLine(calculateTotal(80))
Console.WriteLine(calculateTotal(500))
```

The ternary If is a function that has three parameters. The first parameter is the expression you want to test. Typically, whatever you would write in a regular If block, you would write as the first parameter. In the example, it is a test of whether or not the bought amount is greater than a minimum amount. The second parameter is an expression that is executed whenever the first parameter results in a True value. The third parameter executes if the first parameter results in a False value.

Another variation of the If function is a two-parameter version that can be used to test whether or not an object has a value of Nothing, as follows:

```
Dim cleanUpList = Function(defaultObject As Object)_
                Function(objToTest As Object) If(objToTest, defaultObject)
```

The implementation of the lambda expression has an If with two parameters. The first parameter is the object to test for Nothing, and the second parameter represents the expression to execute if the object is Nothing.

Learning More About Collection Types

In the beginning of this chapter, I talked about the different collection types, but not how to use them. This section presents examples of using the types.

Using a Plain-Vanilla List

A plain-vanilla list is a list of specific types such as Integer, Double, or some other object type. Instantiate the list as follows:

```
Dim lst As List(Of MyType) = New List(Of MyType)()
```

The default type List is used for most of your coding situations, but if you are adding and removing elements frequently, the following code is better.

```
Dim lst As IList(Of MyType) = New LinkedList(Of MyType)()
```

The type LinkedList implements the logic that was presented in the previous chapter, whereas List manipulates a fixed-length array. LinkedList has a downside in that it does not support the IList interface, and the sample code will not compile. Thus, to make the code work, you would need to use ICollection:

```
Dim lst As ICollection(Of MyType) = New LinkedList(Of MyType)()
```

Add an element to IList as follows:

```
lst.Add(New MyType())
```

To add elements to your list according to an order, use the following form (note that ICollection doesn't have this method).

```
lst.Insert(0, New MyType())
```

This adds an element to the front of the list. If you are adding elements at the beginning of the list or somewhere in the list, it is better to use the LinkedList type, as it is more efficient. Using the class List incurs an array copy resource penalty.

You can also add one list to another:

```
Dim lst As List(Of MyType) = New List(Of MyType)()
Dim lstToBeAdded As List(Of MyType)
lst.AddRange(lstToBeAdded)
lst.InsertRange(0, lstToBeAdded)
```

The AddRange() method is used to append the list lstToBeAdded to lst. The InsertRange() method inserts all of the elements in lstToBeAdded to the front of the list lst.

Delete an element from the list like this:

```
lst.Remove(existingMyType)
```

The `Remove()` method expects an instance of a type to remove from the list. To delete a particular element at a particular index, use the following form.

```
lst.RemoveAt(0)
```

This code would remove the element at the front of the list.

Using a Key/Value Pair List

A key/value pair list is a list that has a cross-reference. It is like a dictionary where you have a word and associated meaning. In computing terms, the word is a type and its definition is another type. The word is a key and the definition is a value. A key/value pair definition would be as follows, using the `IDictionary` interface and `Dictionary` class.

```
Dim dictionary As IDictionary(Of String, Object) = _
    New Dictionary(Of String, Object)()
```

You could also use `SortedDictionary`, but that implies the elements within the list are sorted. To add values to the dictionary, use the `Add()` method:

```
dictionary.Add("List", lst)
dictionary.Add("List To Be Added", lstToBeAdded)
```

When working with `IDictionary` objects, you might want to know whether or not a key is available. The following code is used to verify if a key exists.

```
If dictionary.ContainsKey("List") Then
    . . .
End If
```

If you want to iterate the keys, use this form:

```
For Each key As String In dictionary.Keys
Next
```

Iterate the values as follows:

```
For Each value As Object In dictionary.Values
Next
```

Using a Stack

A `Stack` is a special list that behaves like a stack of paper on a table. When you add three items on the `Stack`, the last one added to the `Stack` is the first one off the `Stack`. Here is an example of using a `Stack`:

```
Dim stack As Stack(Of String) = New Stack(Of String)()

stack.Push("first")
stack.Push("second")
stack.Push("third")

Dim popped As String = stack.Pop()

If popped.CompareTo("third") = 0 Then
    ' This is what we expect
End If
```

The code demonstrates using the Push() method to push items on the stack and the Pop() method to remove items from the stack. Remember that Push() is an explicit addition, and Pop() an explicit removal (though a call to Pop() returns the object removed from the stack so you can do something with it, as shown in the code).

If you want to know what is on the top of the stack, use Peek(), which acts like Pop(), except it does not remove the item from the list.

Using a Queue

A Queue is another special type of list that behaves like a queue that you would encounter at ticket counter. As people start queuing, the first person to be served is the one at the front of the line. Here is an example of using a Queue:

```
Dim queue As Queue(Of String) = New Queue(Of String)()

queue.Enqueue("first")
queue.Enqueue("second")
queue.Enqueue("third")

Dim dequeued As String = queue.Dequeue()

If dequeued = "first" Then
    ' This is what we expect
End If
```

The Important Stuff to Remember

In this chapter, you learned about using delegates, lambda expressions, extension methods, and lists. The main items to remember are as follows:

- You are using Visual Basic 2008, and thus you should use the .NET generics-based collection classes.

- There are many different types of lists. The main types are the simple object collection, key/value collection, stack, and queue.

- .NET generics-based classes are type-safe and have better performance than old-style collections.

- Delegates help you define a generic method-calling mechanism without needing to implement an interface.

- Delegates can be shared methods, instance methods, or module methods. The only important aspect to the method is to make sure the method signature matches the delegate declaration.

- Lambda expressions are a specialized form of delegate method that enable you to write deferred execution code. The advantage of deferred execution is that the code can contain a state whenever it is executed.

Some Things for You to Do

The following are some things for you to do to start applying your budding knowledge of software engineering to improving the code base.

1. Collection classes before Visual Basic 2005 allowed you to mix types. With Visual Basic 2005 and later, the .NET generics classes do not allow you to mix types. Provide a solution where you could mix types with Visual Basic 2005 and later collections.

2. Create a list that contains the numbers 1 to 20. Remove the numbers, 15, 10, and 3 to 7.

3. Create a list with an object that is defined as follows:

```
Class MyType
    Public Value as String
End Class
```

4. Add ten elements to the list, and then sort the list alphabetically from *A* to *Z*. Hint: look at the method Sort() and implement a custom IComparer(Of). As part of this exercise, you need to investigate and figure out how to use IComparer(Of). My suggestion is to search the MSDN and Code Project web sites.

■ ■ ■

CHAPTER 10

Learning About Persistence

Your programs will probably need to read and/or write data to some type of storage device. That storage device might be a hard disk, USB drive, or even the network. The key concept is that you are taking information from memory and transferring it to some other location. Later, you will retrieve that information and use it to execute some task.

Taking data from memory and transferring it to another place is referred to as *persistence*. Most examples of persistence involve creating an object, and then saving that object via a file to the hard disk. However, reading and writing an object is not just saving data to the hard disk, even though that is often the result. Reading and writing data to the hard disk is about reading and writing to *data streams*. This chapter focuses on the process of reading and writing data to streams.

This chapter's example is a set of applications for a lottery-prediction system. You'll see how streams are generic concepts that can apply to files, the console, or even the network.

Throughout this book, the examples use console applications to test some code, and this chapter's example also includes console applications. Although Visual Basic is typically used as a GUI development tool, the point of using the console is to help you understand the Visual Basic programming language. One of the biggest criticisms of Visual Basic developers has been that they can't develop like real developers. This book is intended for real developers who happen to use Visual Basic.

Organizing the Lottery-Prediction System

Let's say we want to predict the next set of lottery numbers. We have a program that saves the numbers drawn, and each week, we run a program that retrieves the drawn numbers and predicts the next set of numbers. Many will argue that lottery numbers are random and thus cannot be predicted. But that doesn't mean that we can't write a program to generate the probabilities, and that usually entails knowing which numbers have been drawn previously.

The lottery-prediction example involves three applications: TextProcessor, which is used to read a messed-up lottery number file that will be cleaned up; Binary2Text, which converts a binary stream into text; and Text2Binary, which converts a text stream into binary. Five projects are defined for these applications:

- Binary2Text: A console program that is used to convert a binary lottery ticket stream into a text stream.

- LottoLibrary: A class library that contains the definition of the Ticket type that represents a lottery ticket in memory.

- `ReaderWriter`: A class library that contains the infrastructure code for processing streams and command-line arguments.

- `Text2Binary`: A console program that is used to convert a text lottery ticket stream into a binary stream.

- `TextProcessor`: A console application that will read and write a text file. This application will become a prototype example of how to write a console-based application. It contains a reference to the `ReaderWriter` class library.

Piping Data Using a Console

Console applications are not very interactive; for the most part, they are keyboard-based applications. The main advantage of console applications is their ability to dynamically string data-stream manipulations together, a process called *piping*.

For the lottery-prediction example, `TextProcessor` is a console application that will be fed data by a pipe and generate data using a pipe, as illustrated Figure 10-1. A file feeds a pipe, which feeds the console application that manipulates the data, which then feeds an outgoing pipe that could be used to feed another console application.

Figure 10-1. *Pipeline approach to processing*

`TextProcessor` will read a file of lottery numbers, clean them up (for example, by removing empty lines of text), and remove any duplicates. The console program will not worry about how the data is used. The main focus of `TextProcessor` is to read data, clean it up, and write out semantically correct data.

Reading Data from the Console

Reading data from the console can happen in two ways:

- Supply the path of the file to be read to the application as a console argument.

- Pipe the data from another application to the console application.

Our example will be able to accept data streams in both ways.

Reading from a File

Reading from a file is programmatically the simplest way of obtaining the data. In our case, we'll use a command-line argument to get the file's name. For example, to simply load a file named `lotto.txt` into the `TextProcessor` program, the command line is as follows:

```
TextProcessor.exe lotto.txt
```

A single command-line parameter, `lotto.txt`, is passed as a string to `TextProcessor.exe`. Command-line arguments are separated from each other using spaces. In the context of Windows, this is a problem, because paths can contain spaces. For example, the following command line would be passed as two command-line arguments.

```
TextProcessor.exe c:\My Documents\user\lotto.txt
```

The space between `My` and `Documents` tells the console that there are two arguments. To fix that problem, you need to enclose the path in quotation marks:

```
TextProcessor.exe "c:\My Documents\user\lotto.txt"
```

The command line may also include additional parameters, as in this example:

```
TextProcessor.exe -count 10 lotto.txt
```

The parameter `-count` expects a value, which is 10 in this example. Traditionally, options are specified using key/value pairs, because console applications allow the options to be placed in any order. The exception is the last argument, which is usually the data on which to operate.

■**Note** For more information about the permutations and combinations of command lines, and what a console can do, see `http://en.wikipedia.org/wiki/Command_line_interface`.

Piping Data

Another solution is to use a command that reads the file and pipes the contents of the file to a stream. The console application reads the stream and processes the data. The following is an example of a command line that pipes data. The pipe operation is indicated by the pipe character (`|`).

```
type lotto.txt | TextProcessor.exe
```

In the example, the command `type`, which ordinarily reads a file and displays it on the console, reads in the `lotto.txt` file and pipes it to the console. Then `TextProcessor.exe` reads from the console, processes the data, and pipes it back to the console.

For the scope of the TextProcessor application, the command lines listed in Table 10-1 are valid.

Table 10-1. *TextProcessor Command Lines*

Command	Description
TextProcessor.exe	Without any arguments, the data will be read from the console pipe and written back to the console pipe.
TextProcessor.exe [filename]	Using one argument, the data will be read from the specified file and written to the console pipe.
TextProcessor.exe -out [filename] [filename]	Using the -out parameter with two arguments, the first file specified is where the data will be written, and the last file specified is the file to read.
TextProcessor.exe -out [filename]	Using the -out parameter with one argument, the data is read from the console pipe and written to a file. Notice that the output file name is explicitly defined; otherwise, if a single identifier is given, the console application would not know whether you are reading or writing to a file.
TextProcessor.exe -help	Outputs to the console how to use TextProcessor. The help is also generated when the parameters are specified incorrectly.

Building a Shell

Implementing TextProcessor from an architectural perspective involves writing two pieces of code: a module to read/write to a stream and a module to process the stream. By separating the two modules, the processor is not dependent on where the data originated. This also allows the developer to define an interface that is implemented to process the data.

Assembling the Pieces Using an Echo Program

The lottery-prediction program is a case where I know something about the topic, but not all the details. Developing code is a constant challenge of figuring out which APIs to use. In this type of situation, so that I don't get bogged down in API hunting, I first assemble all of the pieces I need for the application. I develop what I call an *echo program*. An echo program has all of its pieces in place, and when called will seem like it functions. The echo part comes in when the end piece of functionality is called and it returns the data that was sent to it. In essence, the end piece is acting like an echo. The cleverness behind the echo is that it requires no implementation, yet it demonstrates the complete flow of data and whether that data flow is workable.

The echo program is not a final program. The echo program is a temporary solution for an intermediate goal. When building an application with intermediate goals, you are using an iterative development technique. The iterations are not visible to your other team members and are completely private. However, the iterations will keep you focused on solving a problem, rather than trying to implement a large piece of code that you will not be able to fully test for a while.

Test-driven development, for the most part, is a bottom-up development approach. You develop a core piece of functionality, test it, and then write code that uses the tested piece of functionality. But sometimes you need to develop in a top-down fashion. I typically develop code top-down when I am trying to nail down an overall architecture. The problem with developing top-down is that you don't yet have the bottom code. In other words, you are writing code with no working code. So that your code does have some meaning, you develop an echo. The echo solves the problem of working code and allows you to focus on getting the individual pieces to fit together. Once the pieces are working, and the echo was successful, you can start filling in the implementations. Some developers call the echo a *mock* implementation.

Here, I'll explain developing the sample application by assembling individual pieces in a top-down manner, focusing on getting a single echo implemented. Then once the overall flow is complete, the individual pieces will be implemented completely. Figure 10-2 illustrates a complete architecture for the lottery-prediction program, including the pipeline for the TextProcessor console application.

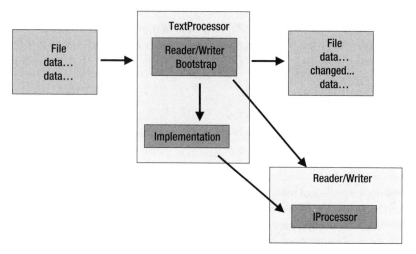

Figure 10-2. *Architecture of a reader/writer application using a general assembly*

Reading and Writing to a Stream

For developing the lottery-prediction application, we'll use a piece of bootstrap code to initiate the reading and writing library, which then calls the specific implementation. *Bootstrap code* is code that does not actually perform the processing, but is responsible for setting up and initiating another piece of source code that will do the processing.

This is the same sort of architecture as we set up in Chapter 8's example, for the application to control the lights of a building. In that case, the controller was a generic piece of software that called an interface, but did not know about the individual implementations. The focus there was on developing the room implementations, and the lighting controller was left as a nebulous to-do task. Here, we'll go through the creation of a complete working application, including the controller and implementation. Note this chapter is light on testing routines, both for brevity and because one of the exercises at the end of the chapter is for you to come up with a testing plan.

We want to be able to process the following command line.

```
type lotto.txt | TextProcessor.exe
```

If TextProcessor.exe cannot read the data from the pipe, an exception will be thrown at the console level, indicating that the piped data was not read.

■**Note** For the application to work, the lotto.txt and TextProcessor.exe files must be in the same directory. By default, TextProcessor.exe is in the [*Visual Studio project*]\bin\debug directory. Copy TextProcessor.exe into the lotto.txt directory, or vice versa, or you could even copy them both into another directory.

In the architecture of TextProcessor, the bootstrap code is in the ReaderWriter project. The TextProcessor console application must call the bootstrap code and instantiate a local type that has implemented the IProcessor interface. The Main() method of TextProcessor is implemented as follows (this is the best time to add a reference to the ReaderWriter project by right-clicking TextProcessor and choosing Add Reference ➤ Projects ➤ ReaderWriter):

```
Imports ReaderWriter

Public Module Module1
    Sub Main(ByVal args As String())
        Bootstrap.Start(args, New LottoTicketProcessor())
    End Sub
End Module
```

TextProcessor.Main() passes all of the given arguments (contained in the args array) to the actual processing routine (Bootstrap.Start()). The LottoTicketProcessor class implements the IProcessor interface and will serve for the temporary purpose of echoing data. The IProcessor interface is defined in the ReaderWriter project as follows:

```
Public Interface IProcessor
    Function Process(ByVal input As String) As String
End Interface
```

The IProcessor interface has a single method Process(), which accepts a string to be processed, and the return value is the processed string.

The implementation of LottoLibrary.LottoTicketProcessor is as follows (remember to add a reference to ReaderWriter):

```
Imports ReaderWriter

' TODO: Finish implementing the class
Public Class LottoTicketProcessor : Implements IProcessor
    Public Function Process(ByVal input As String) As String _
    Implements IProcessor.Process
        Return input
    End Function
End Class
```

The implementation of the Process() method takes the input parameter and returns it as the answer. There is no processing at the moment, just a redirection of the data.

Now let's look at implementing the ReaderWriter project. For this first phase, the reader/writer will also be minimal, so that we can see that all of the pieces are in place and working. The first phase will assume that the data is received on the console and will be sent on the console. Here is the implementation of ReaderWriter.Bootstrap module:

```
Imports System.IO

    Public Module Bootstrap
        Public Sub Start(ByVal args() As String, ByVal processor As IProcessor)
            Dim reader As TextReader = Console.In
            Dim writer As TextWriter = Console.Out

            writer.Write(processor.Process(reader.ReadToEnd()))
        End Sub
    End Module
```

The implementation performs two main steps: assign the streams and manipulate the streams. In the computing world, streams are wonderful things, because they are a generic concept like string buffers. A stream could be a text file, console input, or even a network connection. A stream can be text-based or binary-based, with or without a formatted protocol. Thus, when processing a stream, you don't work specifically with the console or a file, but use interfaces like System.IO.TextReader and System.IO.TextWriter.

Assigning the console streams involves assigning the properties In and Out to TextReader and TextWriter, respectively. The code that calls the processor.Process() method sends a stream to the processor and awaits a response that is sent as another stream.

Knowing that TextReader and TextWriter are general interfaces, or technically abstract base classes, you could be tempted to redesign the IProcessor interface as follows:

```
Public Interface IProcessor
    Function Process(ByVal input As TextReader, ByVal output As TextWriter)
End Interface
```

There is nothing wrong with this declaration of IProcessor, but I would not be tempted to use it because it relies on the interfaces TextReader and TextWriter. In the case of our example, that is acceptable, and you might find that it is good enough for your application. But I like to keep things general and then be more specific when necessary. Later in this chapter, when we work with binary data streams, we will need to be specific and will use an interface declaration similar to the one shown here.

■**Note** As a general rule of thumb, it is always easy to write specific code because you have easy access to the methods and properties you need. It is harder from a design perspective to keep things general. The advantage of keeping things general is your code is more flexible and can be used in multiple contexts. However, you shouldn't make it a hard rule that all code will be general. The rule of thumb is to try to stay as general as possible using interfaces and have the implementation define the specifics.

Having implemented all of the pieces, you could compile the source code and run the command to read piped data. The only thing missing is the file that contains the data, lotto.txt. For the example, create a file called lotto.txt and add text such as the following, where each line represents the date of the lottery draw, then the six lottery numbers, and then the bonus number (you could also use the lotto.txt file included with this book's downloadable code).

```
1970.01.10 7 8 12 17 32 40 24
1970.01.17 7 12 22 24 29 40 36
1970.01.24 16 22 25 27 30 35 24
1970.01.31 3 11 21 22 24 39 8
1970.02.07 2 5 11 16 18 38 37
```

Now run the following piping command (open a command prompt and navigate to TextProcessor\TextProcessor\bin\Release from the Visual Basic Express base directory):

```
type lotto.txt | TextProcessor.exe
```

You should see the contents of lotto.txt. If that is what you get, you have a successful round-trip and have created all of the puzzle pieces.

REMEMBERING TO IMPLEMENT ALL THE PIECES

Some readers may argue that having an echo implemented in LottoTicketProcessor is the wrong approach because there might be a communication failure among team members, leading to buggy code. Also, you might miss implementing some code, creating bugs when there should not have been any. Although those risks are involved, this approach has important benefits, and there are ways to mitigate the risks.

One of the challenges for Visual Basic developers is knowing not only the language, but also the .NET API. This book will not talk about the API because you could die of old age before you read everything there is to know about the .NET API.

The .NET API is vast, but you will not need to use all of the API all the time. What you need to be aware of are the general classes of the API. What part of the API is used to read and write streams? What part of the API is used to create GUI elements? This means you are not ever going to be an expert on all parts of the API, although you might be an expert Visual Basic programmer and understand the general concepts.

When I understand a domain quite well, I develop using a bottom-up approach. This works because I know which interface and implementation need to talk to which other interface and implementation. When I don't understand a domain fully, I develop using a top-down approach. Using a top-down approach, I can figure out what the pieces are in a simplified manner. I create my echo program, which gives a complete round-trip without getting bogged down in the details of the API.

Think of a bunch of guys putting together a barbecue grill. They might look at the instructions, but more likely, they will look at the parts and try to mentally fit the pieces together. They might even put a couple of pieces together to get an idea of what each piece does and how the overall grill should appear. Once they become confident of their prototype, they build the real thing, which hopefully resembles a barbecue grill.

When you use this approach, what you are doing is building a *mockup, proof of concept,* or *prototype.* Maybe two or three team members might help develop this prototype, but the fact that your code needs to be declared as a prototype is extremely important.

Visual Basic Express and the Visual Studio products help you in that they allow you to embed task markers. Go back to the source code example where LottoTicketProcessor was illustrated and look at the comment:

```
' TODO: Finish implementing the class
```

Notice TODO is in all capital letters. That type of comment is special. It is called a *task* and is tracked by Visual Basic Express in the Task List window. To open comments in the Task List window, select View ➤ Other Windows ➤ Task List, and then select Comments from the drop-down list at the top of the window.

This allows a team of developers to add markers throughout the entire code base, indicating what is done and not done. That way, you will not forget to do certain tasks.

Some other identifiers that you can use are HACK to identify some code that is not correct, but hacked in so that it works, and UNDONE. If you happen to be using a Visual Studio edition other than Express, you can define your own comment identifiers. For more information, see the MSDN article "Visual Studio How to: Create Custom Comment Tokens" (http://msdn2.microsoft.com/en-US/library/ekwz6akh(VS.80).aspx).

Implementing Stream Reading and Writing

Finishing the stream reading and writing means looking at the possible arguments that can be given, and then implementing the code to process the arguments. Here is the complete source code for ReaderWriter.Bootstrap:

```
#Const DEBUG_OUTPUT = True
Imports System.IO

Public Module Bootstrap
    Public Sub DisplayHelp()
        Console.WriteLine("You need help? Right now?")
    End Sub

    Public Sub Start(ByVal args As String(), ByVal processor As IProcessor)
        #If DEBUG_OUTPUT Then
            Console.WriteLine("Argument count(" & args.Length & ")")
            For Each argument As String In args
                Console.WriteLine("Argument (" & argument & ")")
            Next
        #End If

        Dim reader As TextReader = Nothing
        Dim writer As TextWriter = Nothing
        If args.Length = 0 Then
            reader = Console.In
            writer = Console.Out
        ElseIf args.Length = 1 Then
            If args(0) = "-help" Then
                Bootstrap.DisplayHelp()
                Return
            End If
```

```vbnet
        reader = File.OpenText(args(0))
        writer = Console.Out
    ElseIf args.Length = 2 Then
        If args(0) <> "-out" Then
            Bootstrap.DisplayHelp()
            Return
        End If
        reader = Console.In
        writer = File.CreateText(args(1))
    ElseIf args.Length = 3 Then
        If args(0) <> "-out" Then
            Bootstrap.DisplayHelp()
            Return
        End If
        reader = File.OpenText(args(2))
        writer = File.CreateText(args(1))
    Else
        Bootstrap.DisplayHelp()
        Return
    End If
    writer.Write(processor.Process(reader.ReadToEnd))

    End Sub
End Module
```

In the code, before the first If block, the variables reader and writer are assigned to the value Nothing, indicating that there is a reader and there is writer, but we don't know whether they will reference streams or files. Then the If blocks go through the different combinations and variations of the command-line arguments (see Table 10-1).

The code follows a truth table approach, which could be considered following a set of conditions and then acting on the conditions. For example, a state could be defined as If A = X, and B != Y then do C. To process the command-line arguments, we define all of the possible states and then all of the possible resulting actions.

■**Note** By going through each and every variation of the command-line arguments in a sequential manner, I am ensuring that I am testing for each situation. When running various tests and then acting on the tests, you need to be explicit and redundant, because the code is easier to follow. All too often, programmers take shortcuts and miss a particular test, causing a bug that is extremely hard to track down.

The first If block tests if the argument count is zero, then the second tests if there is a single argument, and so on. Let's look at the first test:

```
If args.Length = 0 Then
    reader = Console.In
    writer = Console.Out
    ...
End If
```

Here, the source and destination of the lottery number data stream are the console input and output streams. The code assigns the reader and writer variables.

If the command line had no arguments or if one of the command-line argument tests has been verified, the IProcessor implementation is called:

```
writer.Write(processor.Process(reader.ReadToEnd()))
```

The code directly executes writer.Write(), processor.Process(), and reader.ReadToEnd(). There is no verification of whether writer, processor, or reader point to actual object instances. There could be a case for adding code that verifies if processor references an actual object instance, but there is absolutely no point to adding code to verify if writer and reader reference actual object instances. Doing so would imply that your truth test block is incomplete and you have not thought through all the permutations that assign writer and reader.

Let's look at the next truth test, which indicates that there is one command-line argument. When there is one command-line argument, you need to verify which of the two command-line variations it is:

TestProcessor.exe -help

or:

TextProcessor.exe lotto.txt

The first variation has an explicit command-line parameter -help. The second variation is the identifier of a file that contains the input data. Thus, the second If block contains another If block to test another aspect of the truth test:

```
ElseIf args.Length = 1 Then
    If args(0) = "-help" Then
        Bootstrap.DisplayHelp()
        Return
    End If
    reader = File.OpenText(args(0))
    writer = Console.Out
```

When testing for the -help argument, immediately after calling DisplayHelp(), you must use the Return keyword. This is extremely important because, when the console application calls DisplayHelp(), it is saying, "I don't care where the input or output data is coming from since I am doing something else and thus must stop processing." If you were to continue processing, the writer and reader could reference invalid states and cause an exception to be generated.

If all tests have been tried and failed, then the final Else calls the method DisplayHelp() to indicate that the command line is incorrect, and the help shows the correct command line.

Doing a complete test and debug of the console application is difficult because of the streaming facilities. When you stream data from one process to another, a process is started and stopped without an easy way for the debugger to jump in between. Thus, to be able to debug and verify if everything works, another strategy is needed. The solution is to use preprocessor directives (discussed in Chapter 6), like the following.

```
#If DEBUG_OUTPUT Then
    Console.WriteLine("Argument count(" & args.Length & ")")
    For Each argument as String in args
        Console.WriteLine("Argument (" & argument & ")")
    Next
#End If
```

The directive code is executed if `DEBUG_OUTPUT` is defined. In the example, the argument count and arguments are output to the console. To activate the directive, the item `DEBUG_OUTPUT` is defined at the project level or near the top of the source code file.

The shell is complete, and all that remains is the implementation of the text processor.

Implementing the TextProcessor Application

In implementing the text processor, the problem that confronts us is how to fix a data stream so that it is consistent. The main reasons for data inconsistencies are human error and carelessness.

Figure 10-3 shows what is displayed when you load the lottery number text file in Notepad. It seems very obvious that something is not right with this file.

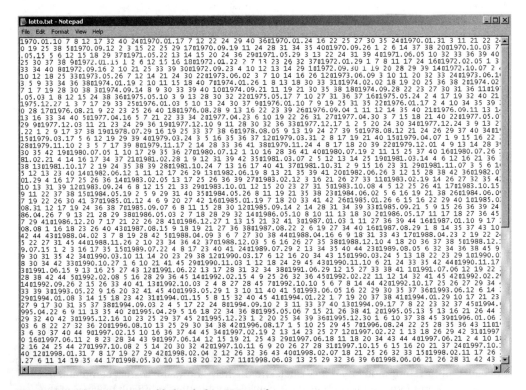

Figure 10-3. *The lottery text file loaded in Notepad*

However, what appears wrong in the Notepad display is not the real problem. When the text file is loaded using another text editor, such as Vim, the text is displayed as shown in Figure 10-4. As you can see, Vim has loaded the text file without any formatting errors.

■**Note** Vim is available from `http://www.vim.org`. It is a vi-derived clone that can be used on Windows systems.

Figure 10-4. *Vim loads the text file in a nicely formatted display.*

The real pressing problem lies in the structure of the data, which is illustrated in Figure 10-5. Here, the data has new formatting, with extra columns, and the first column is not always in the proper data format. And to make matters worse, the badly formatted data has repeating information.

The challenge of the application is to read the stream and fix all of the problems. This requires a thorough understanding of string processing and the different ways that text can be stored, as discussed in Chapter 3. When you are processing data streams, you need to be aware of the format of the data stream. In this example, we are processing ASCII text, and thus will be manipulating bits according to the rules of the ASCII lookup table.

Whitespace characters are special characters in the text lookup table. They are associated with numbers, but their representation is in the form of an action that the user can see. For example, the character between single quotation marks (' ') is a space, the character \t is a tab, and the character \n is a newline. The reason Notepad does not format the lottery text file nicely (Figure 10-3) is because of the whitespace characters used to indicate a newline. In Figure 10-6, the highlighted buffer entry 0A is the hexadecimal character that indicates a linefeed, or newline, in the lottery text file.

Figure 10-5. *Structural problems of this data stream*

Figure 10-6. *Newline character used in lotto.txt*

Figure 10-7 is a file created by Notepad. Notepad expects not a single whitespace character, but two whitespace characters to indicate a newline: 0D and 0A.

Figure 10-7. *Newline characters used by Notepad*

Deciphering the Format

The echo has served its purpose of providing a way to develop an application in a top-down manner. The next step is to remove the echo code and start writing the code that will fix the data stream.

Fixing the data stream is not a trivial undertaking, because you are yet again faced with a state problem. You don't want to fix one part of the stream, only to end up with a problem in another part of the stream. Thus, you need to incrementally fix the stream and make sure at each step that there are no ramifications.

The first step is to break the data stream into individual fields (each value in a column is a field in this case). In Figure 10-5, the data stream had two parts, where the upper part seemed to have a single space between the numbers and the lower part had the amount of space necessary to align the numbers. The difference between the upper and lower parts is the whitespace characters used. So, the first step will be to clean up the whitespace.

The following is the code that reads the buffer, splits it up, and reassembles the content into a new buffer. The code is intermediate code that adds special bracket markers to indicate what the text contains.

```
Imports System.IO
Imports System.Text

' TODO: Fix up this class
Public Class LottoTicketProcessor : Implements IProcessor
    Public Function Process(ByVal input As String) As String
    Implements IProcessor.Process
        Dim reader As TextReader = New StringReader(input)
        Dim retval As New StringBuilder()
```

```
            Do While reader.Peek() <> -1
                Dim splitUpText As String() = _
                  reader.ReadLine.Split(New Char() {" "c, ControlChars.Tab})
                Dim c1 As Integer
                For c1 = 0 To splitUpText.Length - 1
                    retval.Append(("(" & splitUpText(c1) & ")"))
                Next
                retval.Append(ControlChars.NewLine)
            Loop
            Return retval.ToString()
        End Function
    End Class
```

In the implementation of Process(), the text will be parsed line by line. Then each line is split into the individual fields. You could write the parsing routines yourself, but to parse a buffer line by line, it is more efficient to use StringReader. StringReader accepts the string to parse and is then assigned to a TextReader interface instance.

As each line of text is parsed, the most efficient approach to building a buffer is to use StringBuilder. You could keep appending data to the string, but if you do that too often the application's performance will suffer.

The String type is an immutable type, which means once an object is initialized, you cannot change the state of the object. The advantage of immutable types is that they increase the speed of your application, because code can assume once an object has been assigned, it will never change. The downside is that once an object is assigned, to modify the object state even slightly, you must instantiate a new object, which would be the case if we used the = and ± operators. The StringBuilder type is like String, except the referenced text can be modified.

In the Process() implementation, the Do While loop calls the method Peek(), which reads, but does not remove, a character value from the stream. If there is nothing more to read, a -1 value is returned. Otherwise, data is available, and the method ReadLine() can be called. ReadLine() will read a buffer of characters until a newline or return character is encountered. Having read a line of text, it is split into the individual fields using the Split() method. The split characters are the space and tab character (ControlChars.Tab).

When the Split() method returns, the individual fields are assigned to the array splitUpText. Those array elements are iterated and appended to the StringBuilder variable retval, but each element is surrounded by a set of brackets. The brackets provide a set of boundaries that you can inspect to see what data has been found. I include the brackets purely for debugging purposes. Because I am trying to reformat the stream, I append a newline character (ControlChars.NewLine) to the variable retval.

When all of the lines of text and fields within the lines of text are iterated, a string representation of the StringBuilder instance is returned using the ToString() method. Running the code shows how many fields each line of text has and how you should format the text file. This gives you an understanding of how the file is structured.

The following is sample output from the lotto.txt file.

```
(2000.01.15)(6)(10)(25)(26)(38)(42)(20)
(2000.01.19)(2)(16)(18)(23)(32)(43)(26)
(2000.01.22)(4)(5)(6)(24)(34)(38)(9)
(2000.01.26)(3)(20)(22)(24)(34)(39)(9)
(2000.01.29)(7)(12)(13)(34)(38)(39)(28)
(2000.02.02)(1)(18)(22)(28)(35)(43)(32)
(2000.02.05)(4)(13)(15)(31)(32)(45)(37)
(2000.02.09)(1)(29)(31)(34)(39)(41)(25)
...
(2006-12-27)(11)(13)(17)(21)(24)(26)(38)(578199)(735993)()()
(2006-12-30)(3)(13)(22)(30)(35)(41)(34)(142968)(472679)()
()
()
()
(2007-01-03)(5)(24)(37)(39)(41)(44)(9)(049802)(133875)()()
(2007-01-06)(3)(7)(23)(27)(30)(32)(38)(687442)(874814)()()
(2007-01-10)(7)(9)(13)(23)(35)(37)(25)(039498)(648301)()()
(2007-01-13)(3)(17)(22)(37)(39)(43)(34)(968842)(162860)()()
(2007-01-17)(12)(16)(27)(33)(37)(41)(24)(663824)(765917)()()
```

The sample output shows that we have the following items to fix:

- There are empty lines of text where no data has been defined.

- Some lines of text have empty fields at the end.

- Some fields have an incorrect date format.

- Some dates have duplicates, which need to be removed.

- Some lines of text have too many fields. We need to figure out which fields we want to keep and which we can discard.

■**Note** When processing streams and cleaning them up, it is important to take the stream apart first and see what you are up against. Do not make assumptions until you have looked at the individual pieces of data. Then you will be able to determine the steps you need to undertake to fix the stream.

Fixing the Stream

The final solution uses the same code used to parse the lines of text and individual fields, as follows (note, however, that we need the individual lines if the date format is correct, so we store each one in the lineOfText variable):

```
Public Class LottoTicketProcessor : Implements IProcessor
    Private _dates As IList(Of String) = New List(Of String)()
    . . .
    Public Function Process(ByVal input As String) As String
    Implements IProcessor.Process
        Dim reader As TextReader = New StringReader(input)
        Dim retval As StringBuilder = New StringBuilder()
        Do While reader.Peek() <> -1
            Dim lineOfText As String = reader.ReadLine()
            Dim splitUpText As String() =
              lineOfText.Split(New Char() {" "c, ControlChars.Tab})
            If _dates.Contains(splitUpText(0)) Then
                Continue Do
            End If
            If splitUpText(0).Length = 0 Then
                Continue Do
            End If
            If splitUpText(0).Contains("-") Then
                Dim dateSplit As String() = splitUpText(0).Split(New Char() {"-"c})
                Dim newDate As String =
                    dateSplit(0) & "." & dateSplit(1) & "." & dateSplit(2)
                If _dates.Contains(newDate) Then
                    Continue Do
                End If
                _dates.Add(newDate)
                retval.Append(newDate)
                For c1 As Integer = 0 To 7
                    retval.Append(" " & splitUpText(c1))
                Next
            Else
                _dates.Add(splitUpText(0))
                retval.Append(lineOfText)
            End If
            retval.Append(ControlChars.NewLine)
        Loop
        Return retval.ToString()
    End Function
    . . .
End Class
```

■**Note** In the downloadable source code, the individual steps taken to clean up the data stream are demonstrated. For reference, the intermediate development steps in the source code are called Process01() through Process05().

Let's review how this code fixes the five problems we discovered.

Empty Lines of Text

The following code removes the empty lines of text.

```
If splitUpText(0).Length = 0 Then
    Continue Do
End If
```

When lotto.txt was processed, the output data stream generated a single field array for an empty line. So, we know that if the first field element has a length of zero, the line of text should be ignored.

Empty Fields and Too Many Fields

The next problem in our list is that some lines have empty text fields at the end. Solving this problem would probably entail a solution similar to the previous one, but you should think of the big picture and understand that solving one problem might also solve another problem. In this case, solving the problem of the empty fields also helps solve the problem of having too many fields.

Both of these problems are solved by knowing the data that is being manipulated. As you've seen, the data stream assumes the following format: date, then lottery numbers 1 to 6, and then the bonus number. The parts of the data stream that are not correct have the same format, with some extra information like replay number and empty fields. Thus, the fix is to copy the date and append the remaining fields, as follows:

```
retval.Append(newDate)
For c1 As Integer = 0 To 7
    retval.Append(" " & splitUpText(c1))
Next
```

The first line of code appends the date to the StringBuilder buffer (retval). Then in the For loop that follows, a space and the fields 0 to 7 are copied to the StringBuilder buffer.

Incorrect Data Format

In some of the fields, the date has a period separator; in others, it has a hyphen. The correct format is a period, and the code that fixes the date format is as follows:

```
If splitUpText(0).Contains("-") Then
    Dim dateSplit As String() = splitUpText(0).Split(New Char() {"-"c})
    Dim newDate As String =
        dateSplit(0) & "." & dateSplit(1) & "." & dateSplit(2)
```

A fix is needed if the first field contains a hyphen. The If statement tests for this using the Contains() method. If a fix is needed, the first field is separated again into three subfields, where each subfield represents a part of the date (year, month, day). Then those three subfields are recombined and separated using the period and assigned to the variable newDate.

Duplicate Dates

The last problem that needs to be solved is having duplicate dates in the data stream. The following code fixes this problem (the duplicate date code is bolded).

```
        If _dates.Contains(splitUpText(0)) Then
            Continue Do
        End If
        If splitUpText(0).Length = 0 Then
            Continue Do
        End If
        If splitUpText(0).Contains("-") Then
            Dim dateSplit As String() = splitUpText(0).Split(New Char() {"-"c})
            Dim newDate As String = _
                dateSplit(0) & "." & dateSplit(1) & "." & dateSplit(2)
            If _dates.Contains(newDate) Then
                Continue Do
            End If
            _dates.Add(newDate)
            retval.Append(newDate)
            For c1 As Integer = 0 To 7
                retval.Append(" " & splitUpText(c1))
            Next
        Else
            _dates.Add(splitUpText(0))
            retval.Append(lineOfText)
        End If
```

Of all the problems we needed to solve, this is the trickiest, because it required multiple pieces of code in multiple places. The code processes the data stream and keeps a list of dates. A date is added to the list only if the date does not exist in the list, which is checked using the Contains() method. The .NET lists expose this method to verify if the object being passed to it equals one of the list members. The way that most lists implement the method is to iterate each method and call the Equals() method. The catch is that if you declare a custom type, the Equals() method defaults to verifying if one reference value equals another. You would need to implement a custom Equals() method.

■**Note** When you encounter situations where you need to write multiple pieces of code in multiple places, that is a sign that you are about to create code that is hard to maintain. You should take a close look at the code, and if possible, rewrite it. Of course, this depends on a lot of factors. So sometimes, you will need to just write the code, test it, and hope that it works.

With the final solution, the console application TextProcessor is complete. You could process lotto.txt and get a correctly formatted data stream.

Piping Binary Data

When working with the console, for the most part, you will be transferring text data from one process to another or from one file to another file. However, when developing in .NET, working with text is not always the best choice. A more efficient approach might be to store the data in a binary format.

The easiest way to understand the difference between text data and binary data is to open a binary file using a text editor, as shown in Figure 10-8.

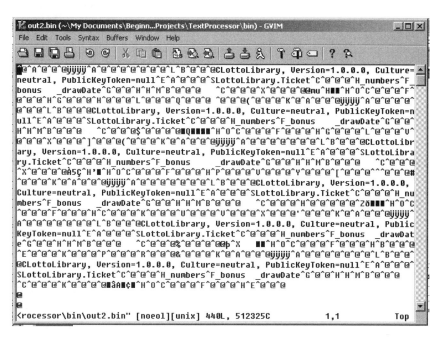

Figure 10-8. *A binary file in a text editor*

In Figure 10-8, you see just a bunch of funny characters with some text scattered throughout. A binary file is different from a text file in that the format of a binary file is whatever the program that reads and writes the binary data decides. The advantage of using a binary file is that you can create complex structures. The disadvantage is that only the developer of the reader/writer program knows what the file contains.

Binary files are not always smaller, but they are more efficient because you do not need to parse and process the data. For example, in the text-based lottery data stream reader, we needed to parse every single line and then split the line of text into individual fields, which were then parsed as integers and assigned to a variable. Using a binary file, you only need to create a binary type, and read or write that type.

In this section, we will continue with the example of the lottery-prediction application, but this time, create it as a console application that converts a text data stream into a binary data stream and then back to a text stream. You'll see how you can pipe the data from one stream to another by sending it from one application to another application. When we are finished building this application, the following command line will be valid.

```
type lotto.txt | TextProcessor.exe | Text2Binary.exe | Binary2Text.exe
```

The command line starts with generating a text data stream using the `type` command. The command `TextProcessor.exe` generates a clean data stream that is then piped into

Text2Binary.exe, which generates a binary data stream. Finally, the binary data stream is converted back into a text stream using Binary2Text.exe, which displays the data on the console.

The architecture of TextProcessor with its implementation of the IProcessor interface and a general architecture of grabbing a file or console input/output stream worked. However, IProcessor is not usable for binary streams, so we need to implement a new interface and architecture.

■**Note** The examples that follow illustrate a very common situation where an architecture worked and the ideas of the architecture could be applied in the new context. What does not work is the actual implementation of the original architecture. You may be tempted to modify the working architecture so that it will work with the new context. As much as you would like to do that, don't. Often, the abstractions you create will complicate the architecture and make the resulting code more complex. Your challenge is to know when to generalize an architecture and when to keep the ideas of an architecture but create a new implementation, and you'll learn this with experience.

Defining the Interfaces and Implementing the Shell

In .NET, the data streams are split into two types of streams: binary and text. The TextWriter and TextReader types are used to read text-based data streams. As was demonstrated with the StringReader type, when dealing with text-based streams, certain assumptions can be made, such as being able to find new lines in the stream. With binary data streams, no such assumptions can be made. Binary streams have their own format, which is known by only the program doing the reading or writing.

The binary stream-based types can be used to process text data streams, but doing so would require knowing the details of the data stream. Remember that .NET gives you a text-handling system that understands the different Unicode code pages. A Unicode code page is a specific translation map. If you decide to manipulate the text streams using binary stream types, you are telling .NET that you will manage the details of the Unicode code pages. Of course, you don't want to do that, and thus should never mix data streams. So, for our sample application, we need to design two different interfaces: one to stream from text to binary and one to stream from binary to text.

■**Note** For more information about Unicode and other text-related issues, see the MSDN "International Text Display" section (http://msdn2.microsoft.com/en-us/library/ms776131.aspx).

The following is the binary-to-text data stream interface, Binary2Text.IBinary2TextProcessor.

```
Imports System.IO

Public Interface IBinary2TextProcessor
    Sub Process(ByVal input As Stream, ByVal output As TextWriter)
End Interface
```

The IBinary2TextProcessor interface has a single method, Process(), which has two parameters: the binary stream and the text stream. The implementation of IBinary2TextProcessor would be responsible for reading the data from the binary stream and saving data to the text stream.

The text-to-binary interface, IText2BinaryProcessor, follows a similar interface design, except that the input and output stream types are reversed.

```
Imports System.IO

Public Interface IText2BinaryProcessor
    Sub Process(ByVal input As TextReader, ByVal output As Stream)
End Interface
```

The idea of both interface declarations is to focus on transferring data from one stream to another.

The shell for both data stream interfaces is very similar to the shell of the text-processing stream, except that binary and text streams are involved. The TextProcessor shell was responsible for knowing if the data stream was from the console or from a file. When manipulating binary streams, the source still needs to be ascertained, but instead of creating text streams, binary streams are created. If you understand the mechanics of using a text stream, you will understand the mechanics of using a binary stream.

The following is the complete implementation of the text-to-binary bootstrap class.

```
Imports System.IO

Public Module Text2BinaryBootstrap
    Public Sub DisplayHelp()
        Console.WriteLine("You need help? Right now?")
    End Sub

    Public Sub Start(ByVal args As String(), _
                     ByVal processor As IText2BinaryProcessor)
        #If DEBUG_OUTPUT Then
            Console.WriteLine("Argument count(" & args.Length & ")")
            For Each argument As String In args
                Console.WriteLine("Argument (" & argument & ")")
            Next
        #End If

        Dim reader As TextReader = Nothing
        Dim writer As Stream = Nothing
        If args.Length = 0 Then
            reader = Console.In
            writer = Console.OpenStandardOutput()
        ElseIf args.Length = 1 Then
            If args(0) = "-help" Then
                Text2BinaryBootstrap.DisplayHelp()
                Return
            End If
```

```
            reader = File.OpenText(args(0))
            writer = Console.OpenStandardOutput()
        ElseIf args.Length = 2 Then
            If args(0) <> "-out" Then
                Text2BinaryBootstrap.DisplayHelp()
                Return
            End If
            reader = Console.In
            writer = File.Open(args(1), FileMode.Create)
        ElseIf args.Length = 3 Then
            If args(0) <> "-out" Then
                Text2BinaryBootstrap.DisplayHelp()
                Return
            End If
            reader = File.OpenText(args(2))
            writer = File.Open(args(1), FileMode.Create)
        Else
            Text2BinaryBootstrap.DisplayHelp()
            Return
        End If
        processor.Process(reader, writer)
        writer.Close()

    End Sub
End Module
```

The implementation is nearly identical to the Bootstrap class; the differences are bolded. Notice that instead of using the predefined Console.Out data member, the OpenStandardOutput() method is called, and instead of File.CreateText(), the File.Open() method is called.

The implementation of the binary-to-text stream shell is nearly identical to the one for the text-to-binary stream shell. You can find it in this book's downloadable source code.

Defining the Type

The central piece when converting from a text stream to a binary stream or vice versa is the definition of a type. The type might be a class or a struct, and it is identified as being a type that can be read and written. Identifying a type to be read and written is necessary so that when .NET reads or writes the type, the underlying infrastructure knows what to do. Remember that a binary data stream is a data stream where only the program knows what it means. To help .NET read and write those types, you add identifiers that tell .NET what to do. Fortunately, you don't need to know the inner details of binary serialization, but just give .NET an indication of how to manage it.

For the lottery-prediction example, we will define a type that represents a lottery ticket. The lottery ticket will contain the draw date, numbers, and bonus number. Following is the complete declaration (in the LottoLibrary project).

```vb
<Serializable()> _
Public Class Ticket

    Public Sub New()
    End Sub

    Public Sub New(ByVal drawDate As DateTime, ByVal numbers As Integer(), _
                ByVal bonus As Integer)
        _drawDate = drawDate
        _numbers = numbers
        _bonus = bonus
    End Sub

    Public Property Bonus() As Integer
        Get
            Return _bonus
        End Get
        Set(ByVal value As Integer)
            _bonus = value
        End Set
    End Property

    Public Property DrawDate() As DateTime
        Get
            Return _drawDate
        End Get
        Set(ByVal value As DateTime)
            _drawDate = value
        End Set
    End Property

    Public Property Numbers() As Integer()
        Get
            Return _numbers
        End Get
        Set(ByVal value As Integer())
            _numbers = value
        End Set
    End Property

    Private _bonus As Integer
    Private _drawDate As DateTime
    Private _numbers As Integer()
End Class
```

Ticket is plain-vanilla data class. However, the bolded parts deserve an explanation. The first bolded part is a set of angled brackets surrounding the identifier Serializable, which represents a .NET *attribute*. In .NET, you have the ability to describe types, methods, and so on.

Attributes are descriptions that are used in a particular context. As opposed to the identifiers `Public` and `MustInherit`, which are descriptions that fundamentally describe how a type will behave, the `Serializable` attribute describes the behavior of a type in a specific context—when the object is to be converted from memory to a data stream and vice versa. Fundamental descriptions are important to the .NET runtime, whereas .NET attributes are generally not important to the runtime, but important to libraries that the runtime will execute.

■**Note** *Serialization* is the process of turning an object into a format that can be saved or sent over the network. *Deserialization* is the process of retrieving the serialized object.

The `Serializable` attribute describes the ability to serialize the type as it is declared. When `Ticket` is converted into a binary stream, the programmer does not need to do anything other than pass an instance to the data stream. The data stream libraries handle all of the other details.

In the declaration of `Ticket`, the parameterless constructor has been bolded to emphasize that this type of constructor is necessary when converting a data stream into an object instance. When binary streams restore types, they instantiate an empty object and then assign the data members. Thus, when an object is created, a parameterless constructor is needed.

Converting a Text Stream into a Binary Stream

To convert the stream from text to binary involves breaking apart the text stream, instantiating a `Ticket` instance, assigning the data members, and saving the instance to the binary stream. All of these steps are performed in the following source code (you'll need a reference to `LottoLibrary` in `Text2Binary`).

```
Imports System.IO
Imports System.Runtime.Serialization.Formatters.Binary
Imports System.Text

Public Class LottoTicketProcessor : Implements IText2BinaryProcessor

    Public Sub Process(ByVal reader As TextReader, ByVal writer As Stream) _
        Implements IText2BinaryProcessor.Process
        Dim retval As StringBuilder = New StringBuilder()
        Do While reader.Peek() <> -1
            Dim lineOfText As String = reader.ReadLine()
            Dim splitUpText As String()= lineOfText.Split(New Char() {" "c})
            Dim dateSplit As String() = splitUpText(0).Split(New Char() {"."c})

            Dim ticket As LottoLibrary.Ticket = _
                New LottoLibrary.Ticket( _
                    New DateTime( _
                        Integer.Parse(dateSplit(0)), _
                        Integer.Parse(dateSplit(1)), _
                        Integer.Parse(dateSplit(2))), _
```

```
                    New Integer() { _
                            Integer.Parse(splitUpText(1)), _
                            Integer.Parse(splitUpText(2)), _
                            Integer.Parse(splitUpText(3)), _
                            Integer.Parse(splitUpText(4)), _
                            Integer.Parse(splitUpText(5)), _
                            Integer.Parse(splitUpText(6)) }, _
                            Integer.Parse(splitUpText(7)))

            Dim formatter As BinaryFormatter = New BinaryFormatter()

            formatter.Serialize(writer, ticket)
        Loop
    End Sub
End Class
```

The code splits the text stream by reading a line of text and then splitting apart the fields. The split-apart fields are then converted into numbers by using the `Integer.Parse()` method. This process of splitting and conversion is called *marshaling* data. *Marshaling* is a technical term that means to convert a type from one medium to another.

We manage the text marshaling, but .NET manages the binary marshaling, which is still there behind the scenes. The `System.Runtime.Serialization.Formatters.Binary.BinaryFormatter` type manages marshaling of the `Ticket` instance to the binary stream. The `Serializable` attribute is used by the `BinaryFormatter` as an indicator that the `Ticket` type is allowed to be serialized and deserialized. In essence, converting from a text stream to a binary stream means to marshal a text-defined ticket into a .NET-defined ticket, and that is then marshaled into a binary-defined ticket.

Converting a Binary Stream into a Text Stream

Converting a binary stream into a text stream involves using the .NET-provided formatter to create a `Ticket` instance that is then converted into text. The following is the complete source code (you'll need a reference to `LottoLibrary` in `Binary2Text`).

```
Imports System.IO
Imports System.Runtime.Serialization.Formatters.Binary

Public Class LottoTicketProcessor : Implements IBinary2TextProcessor
    Public Sub Process(ByVal input As Stream, ByVal output As TextWriter) _
        Implements IBinary2TextProcessor.Process
        Dim builder As StringBuilder = New StringBuilder()
        Try
            Do While True
                Dim formatter As BinaryFormatter = New BinaryFormatter()

                Dim ticket As LottoLibrary.Ticket = _
                    DirectCast(formatter.Deserialize(input),
                            LottoLibrary.Ticket)
```

```
                builder.AppendFormat( _
                    "{0}.{1}.{2} {3} {4} {5} {6} {7} {8} {9} {10}",
                    ticket.DrawDate.Year,
                    ticket.DrawDate.Month,
                    ticket.DrawDate.Day,
                    ticket.Numbers(0),
                    ticket.Numbers(1),
                    ticket.Numbers(2),
                    ticket.Numbers(3),
                    ticket.Numbers(4),
                    ticket.Numbers(5),
                    ticket.Bonus,
                    ControlChars.NewLine)
            Loop
        Catch e As Exception
        End Try
        output.Write(builder.ToString())
    End Sub
End Class
```

In the code, a binary stream is read using the `BinaryFormatter` class, which reads the data for an object from the data stream. Notice how the method `Deserialize()` does not ask which type to read. This is because all of that information is saved in the stream. `Deserialize()` will read data from the stream, associate the data with a type, instantiate it, and populate the data members.

The bolded code in the preceding listing points out where deserialization becomes tricky, which centers around when to read what type. A binary stream when processed by the `BinaryFormatter` will read and write objects. `BinaryFormatter` will instantiate whatever it encounters and assumes that the caller of `BinaryFormatter` knows which type is being manipulated. If the caller does not know this, an exception will occur because the type cast to the specific type will fail.

The exception block is necessary because you don't know how many `Ticket` objects have been saved, as the count has not been saved to the stream. .NET provides the `Position` and `Length` properties to determine if any instances are left to be read, but those properties work only with files. If the binary stream being read is a console data stream, there is no length or position. Thus, the only real solution is to keep reading until you can't do so anymore and assume processing is complete.

INTENTION AND IMPLEMENTATION

The fact that `Position` and `Length` have different behaviors depending on the implementation might seem to break the contract of being able to separate intention from implementation. It seems to break the component software paradigm because, as a developer, you do need to know about the stream implementation. The rule has not been broken, but been put on hold, because sometimes you are left with no other option. A file stream and console stream share many characteristics, but knowing the length is not one of them. A programmer could force the console stream to give back some value, but that would be incorrect. The smarter approach, and the one chosen by the .NET implementers, is to generate an exception.

The binary stream formatter can become even pickier. Look at Figure 10-8 again and notice how the type information with version identifiers is stored in the stream. Imagine the situation where you create an assembly that saves some objects. Then *x* years and *n* versions of the program later, you try to load the file. You can't, because the version of the type does not exist. It is smart for the binary formatter to not instantiate a version of a type that does not exist, because otherwise there could be serialization failures.

Tweaking Serialization

When dealing with serialization, you may come across a particular text or binary format that will require some extra work. Also, you may have some objects that you want to exclude from serialization.

Performing Custom Serialization

Sometimes I think there are as many file formats as there are grains of sand on a beach. As just two examples, specializations of text formats are XML and JSON (for JavaScript Object Notation, used in JavaScript for your web browser). In most cases, the default serializations will work. However, you may need to tweak a particular serialization.

Many serialization techniques allow custom serializations of a particular object. The default serialization implies a certain marshaling. For example, it might mean an integer will be marshaled as an integer in another representation (in SQL Server, for example). Sometimes, however, you might want different representations in different streams. In that case, you need to implement the marshaling of the data member yourself. With most serialization platforms, it means implementing a particular interface.

Following is an example that performs a custom serialization for a .NET binary stream.

```
Imports System.Runtime.Serialization

<Serializable()> _
Class MyObject
    Implements ISerializable
    Private value As Integer

    Public Sub New()
    End Sub

    Public Sub New(ByVal info As SerializationInfo,
                ByVal context As StreamingContext)
        value = Integer.Parse(CStr(info.GetValue("value", GetType(String))))
    End Sub

    Public Sub GetObjectData(ByVal info As SerializationInfo,
                        ByVal context As StreamingContext)
    Implements ISerializable.GetObjectData
        info.AddValue("value", value.ToString())
    End Sub
End Class
```

In the example, the interface System.Runtime.Serialization.ISerializable is implemented. This means when BinaryFormatter serializes or deserializes MyObject, BinaryFormatter will not manipulate the binary stream, but delegate the manipulation to MyObject. With many serialization platforms, there is an explicit method, property, or flag to indicate whether MyObject is being written to the stream or read from the stream. In the case of binary serialization, when an object is written to the stream, the GetObjectData() method is called, and when the object is being read from the stream, the constructor is called.

Serialization involves two directions, and a developer must implement both, in the same way. In the example, the AddValue() method is called, indicating that the data member is written as a string, and when reading, the value data member must be read as a string.

▓**Note** One of the biggest challenges with serialization is that each and every serialization platform seems to have its own way of doing things. Sometimes there will be common methods and attributes, but other times they will not exist. A universal approach to serialization won't work. You should avoid performing custom serialization whenever possible. Most serialization platforms are smart enough to know what to do with each data member. So the best approach is to let the platform figure things out.

Declaring a Data Member As Nonserializable

In the example of the Ticket type, all of the data members were serialized. However, sometimes that is not desired. Suppose an object that you want to serialize has a network connection or some other data value that will not make any sense if the object is serialized and then deserialized some time later. When the object is serialized, the network connection will also be serialized, which is not appropriate. It is not appropriate to serialize a network connection because that object is transient and applies only to the context of the object instance.

To mark a data member as nonserializable, attributes are often used, as in the following example.

```
<Serializable()>
Class MyObject2
    <NonSerialized()>
    Private _networkIdentifier As Integer
End Class
```

In the example, _networkIdentifier will not be written or read from the data stream.

Separating Data Objects from Action Objects

Another approach is to develop a number of data objects whose only role is to be used in serialization and data referencing. Such an approach is useful when using binary serialization, because you are then able to more effectively manage the version problem. The following is an example of how such an architecture would be realized.

```
<Serializable()>
Class MyObject2
End Class

Class Doer
    Private _object As MyObject2
    Private _networkIdentifier As Integer
End Class
```

The class Doer has no serialization attribute and will not be serialized, but it references MyObject2. The network identifier data member has been moved from MyObject2 to Doer. The result is that MyObject2 contains nothing that is transient.

Completing Custom Types

When writing custom types, two methods are often implemented, especially where objects are to be compared a lot: Equals() and GetHashCode(). These two methods are used by the .NET library API when comparing and manipulating instances in a list or a collection. It just happened in this chapter's example that a list of string types did the right thing. If TextProcessor had used the Ticket type, then the Equals() method of the list used to find date duplicates would not have worked. The default implementations of Equals() and GetHashCode() are not implemented properly. This is not the .NET API's fault. Rather, it is a recognition that Microsoft cannot know the structure of an object and what is considered as making a type unique.

Implementing GetHashCode()

The MSDN documentation for Object.GetHashCode defines the GetHashCode() method as follows (http://msdn2.microsoft.com/en-us/library/system.object.gethashcode(VS.90).aspx):

> *The GetHashCode method can be overridden by a derived type. Value types must override this method to provide a hash function that is appropriate for that type and to provide a useful distribution in a hash table. For best results, the hash code must be based on the value of an instance field or property instead of a static field or property.*

> *Objects used as a key in a Hashtable object must also override the GetHashCode method because those objects must generate their own hash code. If an object used as a key does not provide a useful implementation of GetHashCode, you can specify a hash code provider when the Hashtable object is constructed.*

But what does this actually mean? The purpose of GetHashCode() is to identify the object in a collection of other objects using a hash code. Imagine creating a table of same-type instances. The situation occurs when you create a collection and store a bunch of instances in the collection. With the GetHashCode() method, you can generally separate each instance from each other. I say "generally" because GetHashCode() is an approximation. To verify if one object instance equals another, the Equals() method needs to be implemented.

Implementing a hash code is best delegated to a helper class that does the heavy lifting. The book *Effective Java Programming Language Guide* by Joshua Bloch (Prentice-Hall, 2001) outlines a robust technique. Basically, you store some constant nonzero value, such as 17, in a variable. Then, for each data member of the type, perform a mathematical operation that results in Integer values that are successively multiplied and added, where the operation is specific to the type and defined as follows:

- *Boolean*: If true return 0; otherwise return 1.

- *Byte, Char, Short, or Integer*: Return the value of the type.

- *Long*: Return CInt(value Xor (value >> &H20)). &H20 is the hexadecimal for 32.

- *Single*: Return Convert.ToInt32 of the value.

- *Object*: Return the value generated by calling Object.GetHashCode().

- *Array*: Iterate and treat each element individually.

The rules are implemented in a class called HashCodeAutomater. The following source code is an implementation in an abbreviated form:

```
Public Class HashCodeAutomater
    Private Readonly _constant As Integer
    Private _runningTotal As Integer

    Public Sub New()
        _constant = &H25
        _runningTotal = &H11
    End Sub

    Public Function AppendSuper(ByVal superHashCode As Integer) As HashCodeAutomater
        _runningTotal = ((_runningTotal * _constant) + superHashCode)
        Return Me
    End Function

    Public Function Append(ByVal obj As Object) As HashCodeAutomater
        If (obj Is Nothing) Then
            Me._runningTotal = (Me._runningTotal * Me._constant)
        ElseIf Not obj.GetType.IsArray Then
            Me._runningTotal = ((Me._runningTotal * Me._constant) + obj.GetHashCode)
        ElseIf TypeOf obj Is Long() Then
            Me.Append(DirectCast(obj, Long()))
        ElseIf TypeOf obj Is Integer() Then
            Me.Append(DirectCast(obj, Integer()))
        ElseIf TypeOf obj Is Short() Then
            Me.Append(DirectCast(obj, Short()))
        ElseIf TypeOf obj Is Char() Then
            Me.Append(DirectCast(obj, Char()))
```

```
        ElseIf TypeOf obj Is Byte() Then
            Me.Append(DirectCast(obj, Byte()))
        ElseIf TypeOf obj Is Double() Then
            Me.Append(DirectCast(obj, Double()))
        ElseIf TypeOf obj Is Single() Then
            Me.Append(DirectCast(obj, Single()))
        ElseIf TypeOf obj Is Boolean() Then
            Me.Append(DirectCast(obj, Boolean()))
        Else
            Me.Append(DirectCast(obj, Object()))
        End If
        Return Me
    End Function


    Public Function Append(ByVal array As Long()) As HashCodeAutomater
        If (array Is Nothing) Then
            Me._runningTotal = (Me._runningTotal * Me._constant)
        Else
            Dim i As Integer
            For i = 0 To array.Length - 1
                Me.Append(array(i))
            Next i
        End If
        Return Me
    End Function


    Public Function Append(ByVal value As Long) As HashCodeAutomater
        Me._runningTotal = _
            ((Me._runningTotal * Me._constant) + CInt((value Xor (value >> &H20))))
        Return Me
    End Function


    Public Function ToHashCode() As Integer
        Return _runningTotal
    End Function
End Class
```

The different implementations of the Append() method belong to a single grouping for a single data type, Long. For example, there is an Append() method that accepts a Long and a Long array. The full implementation of HashCodeAutomater would have an Append() method for Short and Short array, and all the other data types. There is no specific group implementation for the String type, because it is treated like an object that has its own hash-code calculation implementation.

Notice in the implementations of the Append() methods how a calculation is performed and then added to the data member _runningTotal. The return value is a Me reference, so that the methods can be chained together. This allows a client to use the HashCodeAutomater class, as the following GetHashCode() implementation demonstrates:

```
Class HashcodeExample
    Public value As Integer
    Public buffer As String

    Public Sub New (ByVal val As Integer, ByVal buf As String)
        value = val
        buffer = buf
    End Sub
    Public Overrides Function GetHashCode() As Integer
        Return New HashCodeAutomater()
            .Append(value)
            .Append(buffer).toHashCode()
    End Function
End Class
```

The implementation of HashcodeExample has two data members: value and buffer. The two data members make up the class's state. Not all data members are used when calculating a class instance's hash-code value. For example, if HashcodeExample had a data member that referenced a database connection, it should not be used when calculating the hash code, because the database connection is the type used to get the state and does not influence the state—it is a means to an end.

Implementing Equals()

Once the GetHashCode() method has been implemented, the Equals() method can be implemented:

```
Public Overrides Function Equals(ByVal obj As Object) As Boolean
    If TypeOf(obj) Is HashCodeExample Then
        If obj.GetHashCode() = Me.GetHashCode() Then
            Return True
        End If
    End If
    Return False
End Function
```

Because the rule for GetHashCode() is that two object instances with identical hash-code values must return the same value, it makes sense to implement Equals() using GetHashCode(). However, what started out as a good idea turns out to be a bad idea, as the following illustrates:

```
Dim s1 As String = "Hello"
Dim s2 As String = "World"
Dim x1 As Integer = 17 * 17 + s1.GetHashCode()
Dim x2 As Integer = 17 * 17 + s2.GetHashCode()

Dim h1 As HashCodeExample = New HashCodeExample (x2 * 37, s1)
Dim h2 As HashCodeExample = New HashCodeExample (x1  * 37, s2)
```

```
Dim ht As Hashtable = New Hashtable()
ht.Add(h1, Nothing)
ht.Add(h2, Nothing)
```

This shows that having two objects with completely different states results in the same hash-code value and generates an exception because Equals() has been implemented incorrectly. In the implementation of Hashtable, when an added object collides with another already existing object, an equality test is made. If the equality test returns True, then the exception is generated because Hashtable does not allow you to add an object with the same state as another object.

The solution is not to fix the GetHashCode() method, but rather to modify the Equals() method:

```
Public Overrides Function Equals(ByVal obj As Object) As Boolean
    If TypeOf (obj) Is HashcodeExample Then
        If obj.GetHashCode() <> Me.GetHashCode() Then
            Return False
        End If

        Dim toTest As HashcodeExample =
          DirectCast(obj, HashcodeExample)
        If toTest.value = Me.value Then
            If toTest.buffer = Me.buffer Then
                Return True
            End If
        End If
    End If
    Return False
End Function
```

The logic of the modified Equals() method is to first test if both types are identical. If not, then False is returned. Next, test if GetHashCode() returns unequal values. GetHashCode() will always return different values for objects that have different data members. If the hash-code values are equal, then comes the hard work of individually testing each data member for equality. The hard work is delegated as the last step, because any object that reaches that point will probably be identical, but you need to be 100% certain.

The Important Stuff to Remember

In this chapter, you learned how to process a stream of data using the console. Here are the main items to remember:

- When data is moved from one medium to another, it is streamed.

- There are two major types of streams: text and binary.

- Text streams are universal and can be read by all computers.

- Binary streams are specific to the program and sometimes to the processor. Imagine the situation of having to decipher a C++ data stream generated by a PowerPC chip. Most likely, the numbers that you read will be wrong because of the way that Intel or AMD chips store their numbers. Generally speaking, with binary streams, you will be conversing with two .NET implementations. If not, use text streams.

- When streaming data, it is best to customize as little as possible. Doing so will complicate your program, and potentially introduce errors where none should exist.

- It is important that you understand the concept of marshaling and the fact that each medium will have a different representation of the type. A large part of your programming day will involve moving data from one stream to another.

Some Things for You to Do

The following are some exercises to apply what you learned in this chapter.

1. In the implementation of TextProcessor, the display help routine was not very helpful. Fix the implementation.

2. There were no testing routines for TextProcessor. Devise some realistic tests. By realistic tests, I mean tests that don't just focus on the class library and consider the application tested. Focus on complete application tests.

3. Having implemented the display help routine, think about whether or not the implementation is correct. The class Bootstrap is a general class that uses an IProcessor instance, which means that different console applications will process different data. Thus, writing a general help output might work, but it will not help in resolving problems. Fix the console application TextProcessor and ReaderWriter project so that the help message is both specific and general.

4. In the Bootstrap class, when the output was redirected to a file (as indicated by the -out argument), there was no check on whether or not the file exists. Extend the Bootstrap class to include an additional command-line argument that verifies if it is fine to overwrite the output file if it exists. If an output file does exist and there is no explicit overwriting, generate an error and stop processing.

5. The code in the final solution for IProcessor.Process() has been identified as being hard to maintain because the code to check for duplicate dates is scattered throughout the method. Rewrite the method implementation so that the code is logical and maintainable.

CHAPTER 11

■■■

Learning About .NET Generics

Chapter 9 explained how to use lists, delegates, and lambda expressions. In that chapter, you also saw an example of .NET generics when using lists to manage a collection of object instances.

The main focus of this chapter is .NET generics and how to use them in a black box context (the code doesn't know the specifics of the .NET generics parameter types). The secondary focus is an implementation of lambda expressions using a spreadsheet. The idea is to get you well versed in .NET generics and lambda expressions, which you will likely use in your own production code, so that that there will be no surprises in your projects.

Why Use .NET Generics?

Here's a surprise for you: there is no imperative need for .NET generics, so you could skip this chapter and read the next one, right? Wrong. I could just as easily have said there is no need for Visual Basic properties, nor any other Visual Basic construct that enriches your programming abilities. The reasons we have Visual Basic properties and .NET generics are programming elegance and expressiveness.

To understand what I am trying to get at, consider this sentence:

Ducks walk flat feet quack loud

Reading the sentence, you get an idea of what is being said, but you are not completely sure. Visual Basic without .NET generics is like this sentence, in that you express your ideas in code, but some things are not as clear as you would like.

Visual Basic with .NET generics is like this sentence:

Ducks walk in a funny manner due to their flat feet, and when they quack, it is very loud.

The sentence is clearer and uses more words to describe the same thing. The reason we talk using a more sophisticated language is that we want to explain concepts and be understood. If you accept that, then you can accept why there is a need and context for .NET generics. And if not, feel free to skip this chapter and read the next one.

An example that illustrates how using .NET generics makes your code clearer, as well as more concise, than code that does not use .NET generics is a container. A *container* is a type that is used to manage other types; lists and collections are examples of containers. To keep things simple, let's look at a container that manages a single reference. The following is the less concise version that uses the Object type.

```
Public Class Container
    Private _managed As Object

    Public Sub New(ByVal toManage As Object)
        _managed = toManage
    End Sub

    Public ReadOnly Property Managed() As Object
        Get
            Return _managed
        End Get
    End Property

End Class
```

In the code, the class Container has a constructor with a parameter and a single property, Managed, which references the variable _managed. The idea behind this class is to assign an object in the constructor that can be referenced using the property. The class Container does not know what the variable _managed does or its capabilities. Container does not care, because Container is acting like a basket that holds an instance of whatever is given to it.

The Container class could be used as follows:

```
Dim container As Container = New Container(New MyType())

TryCast(container.Managed, MyType).Method()
```

When Container is instantiated, the _managed data member is assigned an instance of MyType. MyType is a type that is used for illustrative purposes and has a single method, Method(). To retrieve and use the managed type, the property Managed is referenced. However, the method Method() cannot be called directly because the property Managed is of type Object, and thus you need to cast the property to type MyType so that the call to Method() is legal.

The cast using TryCast will result in a valid instance of MyType or a Nothing value, resulting in a null object reference exception. Here's a safe way of using the Managed property:

```
Dim container As Container = New Container(New MyType())

If TypeOf container.Managed Is MyType Then
    TryCast(container.Managed, MyType).Method()
End If
```

The bolded code is the addition of the If block to test whether the container references the type MyType. Not shown is what the code should do if the property Managed is not MyType. The fact that you need to verify that the container references the correct type, and you also need to think of an alternative plan if the type is incorrect, adds quite a bit of code. It's like that sentence about the duck—sure, you get the general idea of what is being said, but are you 100% sure of the meaning?

Now look at the following code, which implements a container using .NET generics.

```
Public Class GenericsContainer(Of ManagedType)
    Private _managed As ManagedType

    Public Sub New(ByVal toManage As ManagedType)
        _managed = toManage
    End Sub

    Public ReadOnly Property Managed() As ManagedType
        Get
            Return _managed
        End Get
    End Property
End Class
```

You can write code that uses .NET generics and code that provides types based on .NET generics. The definition of GenericsContainer demonstrates code that provides types based on .NET generics. You'll see the code that uses .NET generics next.

.NET generics parameters are associated with types, such as classes and interfaces, or with methods. In the case of GenericsContainer, the .NET generics parameter ManagedType is a placeholder for an actual type.

■**Note** Commonly, developers use the notation of a single letter when defining a .NET generics parameter. I am not a fan of that notation, because it tells me nothing, especially when there are multiple parameters. I recommend using an identifier that describes what the parameter does, appended with the word Type, to indicate a .NET generics parameter is being defined.

With GenericsContainer, ManagedType is used as an identifier in the place of the identifier object in the type Container. This is a rule of thumb. Whenever you find yourself using an object generically to define a type, you probably could use .NET generics. Think of .NET generics types as general things.

The following code demonstrates how to use GenericsContainer with MyType.

```
Dim container As GenericsContainer(Of MyType) = _
    New GenericsContainer(Of MyType)(New MyType())
container.Managed.Method()
```

When instantiating GenericsContainer, notice how the identifier ManagedType must be replaced with an identifier that represents an already existing type. This identifier replacement results in a new and unique type (also called a *concrete type*). The advantage of .NET generics is that when you provide a concrete type, you don't need to check to make sure that everything is correct.

The .NET runtime will generate a type that has an intent similar to the following code.

```
Public Class GenericsContainerMyType
    Dim _managed As MyType

    Public Sub New(ByVal toManage As MyType)
        _managed = toManage
    End Sub

    Public ReadOnly Property Managed() As MyType
        Get
            Return _managed
        End Get
    End Property
End Class
```

Visual Basic compiles a .NET generics type as an incomplete type. When the incomplete type is concretized, .NET creates a brand-new type, and does this without requiring the developer to do anything in particular. This means that if you use GenericsContainer with 15 different types, .NET will generate 15 definitions of GenericsContainer while the program is executing.

ABSTRACTION AND .NET GENERICS

With .NET generics, you can verify and ensure that everything is being said properly, with the cost being complexity. Consider the sentence that clearly described the duck. To produce it, you need to have learned additional rules regarding grammar. When using .NET generics, you need to master creating abstractions.

.NET generics are an abstraction. Just as interfaces are an abstraction of classes, .NET generics are an abstraction above interfaces. Interfaces define an intention, and .NET generics define an abstract implementation of an intention.

What is challenging with .NET generics is getting your thoughts together into an abstract intention implementation. It is like writing a document—you write it once, read it over, rewrite it, read it over, and rewrite it again. With .NET generics, you are gathering thoughts together into a general plan of action. This is why some people are completely confused and don't understand .NET generics. Writing your own .NET generics code requires some forethought.

The Theory of a Server-Side Spreadsheet

The example in this chapter is a spreadsheet for security traders. When you trade securities—whether they are equities, bonds, options, or futures—you will be confronted with information overload. You might have seen pictures of traders with desks full of desktop monitors. A trader might have seven to eight monitors displaying various bits of information. A trader is a very specialized type of domain that requires its own ways of processing information. One aspect that makes writing applications for traders difficult is that the nature of the data constantly changes, and types get more in the way than they help. As a result, traders adore spreadsheets.

Spreadsheets are useful because they can process large amounts of information in a relatively ad hoc manner. However, one downside to spreadsheets is that the processing time can dramatically increase due to the constant pushing and pulling of the data to and from the spreadsheet. To speed up processing, we will define and implement a spreadsheet that has the advantages of a traditional client-side spreadsheet.

Note The theory and solution presented here are specific to the domain of trading, where the cost of hardware is well worth the ability to trade properly. Therefore, specific design aspects assume that you have the latest and greatest hardware.

An initial attempt at a spreadsheet would be the following code that uses .NET generics:

```
Class Spreadsheet
    Public Cells As Func(Of Object)(,)
    Public State As Object(,)

    Public Sub New()
        Cells = New Func(Of Object)(10, 10) {}
        State = New Object(10, 10) {}
    End Sub

    Public Sub Execute()
        For col As Integer = 0 To Cells.GetLength(1) - 1
            For row As Integer = 0 To Cells.GetLength(0) - 1
                Console.WriteLine(col & " " & " " & row)
                If Cells(row, col) IsNot Nothing Then
                    State(row, col) = Cells(row, col)()
                End If
            Next
        Next

    End Sub
End Class
```

The sample spreadsheet is defined using the data members Cells and State. Both data members are arrays with two dimensions. The first dimension represents the rows, and the second dimension represents the columns. You could define as many dimensions as you wish, but for the scope of the server spreadsheet, we take a two-dimensional approach.

The Execute() method goes through the individual rows and columns of the Cells data member, calculates the state of the cell, and assigns the state to the State data member. The data member Cells represents a function that is executed to generate the result of a particular cell that is assigned to the data member State. Both data members store and manipulate Objects, which makes the spreadsheet flexible. However, a gain in one aspect means a reduction in another aspect; in this case, the loss is in performance. But performance is what algorithmic trading software cannot sacrifice, and native types would be best.

To make the spreadsheet perform as fast as it can, we need to use fixed-dimension arrays. However, with fixed-dimension arrays, we are moving away from a traditional object-oriented approach. You could argue that spreadsheets are not object-oriented at all and are a problem with respect to programmability. I would agree with that comment, but spreadsheets solve one class of problems very elegantly. In the case of financial trading software, they solve the problem of managing very large amounts of data efficiently.

■**Note** Object-oriented code is maintainable and extendable. However, object-oriented code can be slow. I have done tests where I found fixed-dimension arrays perform two to three times faster than the equivalent object-oriented application. But performance is not always the primary consideration. Also, fixed-dimension arrays will not always give you the desired performance boost, because other parts of your code might be much slower. Therefore, generally, you should not use fixed-dimension arrays.

The Cells data member is a delegate, or lambda expression, that is defined using code similar to the following. When we want to fill a cell, we call the appropriate function on CellFactories, which in turn returns the lambda expression that represents the new value stored in the cell:

```
Module CellFactories
    Public Function DoAdd(ByVal cell1 As Func(Of Object), _
                          ByVal cell2 As Func(Of Object)) As Func(Of Object)
        Return Function() CType(cell1(), Double) + CType(cell2(), Double)
    End Function

    Public Function DoMultiply(ByVal cell1 As Func(Of Object), _
                              ByVal cell2 As Func(Of Object)) As Func(Of Object)
        Return Function() CType(cell1(), Double) * CType(cell2(), Double)
    End Function

    Public Function FixedValue(ByVal value As Object) As Func(Of Object)
        Return Function() value
    End Function
End Module
```

The lambda expressions can be used to add two cells together, multiply two cells together, or store a fixed value. With the lambda expressions and the spreadsheet, you have two pieces of source code that, when combined, have the ability to solve complicated problems. The key idea that you need to take away is that the Spreadsheet class and the lambda expressions defined in CellFactories do not know about each other. The lambda expressions could be used in a context other than a spreadsheet. The only requirement is that the function types and signatures match.

The sample spreadsheet that would be used to add and multiply some cells together would be as follows:

```
Dim spreadsheet As Spreadsheet = New Spreadsheet()

spreadsheet.Cells(1, 0) = CellFactories.FixedValue(10.0)
spreadsheet.Cells(0, 1) = CellFactories.FixedValue(10.0)
```

```
spreadsheet.Cells(1, 2) =  _
   CellFactories.DoAdd(spreadsheet.Cells(1, 0), spreadsheet.Cells(0, 1))
spreadsheet.Cells(2, 2) = CellFactories.DoMultiply(spreadsheet.Cells(1, 2), _
   CellFactories.FixedValue(2.0))
spreadsheet.Execute()

Console.WriteLine("Contents of (1, 2): " & spreadsheet.State(1, 2).ToString())
Console.WriteLine("Contents of (2, 2): " & spreadsheet.State(2, 2).ToString())
```

The sample code illustrates a rudimentary example of a spreadsheet and how lambda expressions can be used. In this chapter, the focus will be on how to create a spreadsheet implementation that is effective, mostly object-oriented, and maintainable.

Architecting a Server-Side Spreadsheet

To architect a server spreadsheet, the following requirements must be met:

- *Performance*: Wherever possible, the design should not sacrifice performance.

- *Usability*: The server-side spreadsheet must be easy to program from a Visual Basic perspective. If the server-side spreadsheet is too complex or difficult to understand, it will not be used properly, potentially incurring errors.

- *Maintainability*: The server-side spreadsheet implementation should be somewhat maintainable. Otherwise, bugs could creep into the code, impeding the spreadsheet's effective use.

Not listed is the requirement for extensibility. A spreadsheet by itself is not extensible because it implements a certain paradigm, which is a two-dimensional document of numbers and calculations.

And if you are wondering where the spreadsheet code comes from, it is a subset of the actual code that I use in my own security trading system.

■**Note** To code the spreadsheet to do more than it is originally designed for might be an interesting goal, but not one that is worth pursuing. Sometimes it is best to solve a problem, and leave paradigm thinking for another time. I have seen developers think about paradigms, not finish their code, and then have the code made obsolete by a paradigm that they did not consider.

Three projects are defined for this example:

- `Devspace.Trader.Common`: A class library that is a distilled form of my trading library. I decided to include such a library to give you a taste of how a production class library looks and feels.

- `ServerSideSpreadsheet`: A class library that represents the implementation of a server-side spreadsheet.

- `TestServerSideSpreadsheet`: A console application that tests the `ServerSideSpreadsheet` project.

Designing the Architecture

The original implementation of the spreadsheet code provides a great starting point. Using lambda expressions to calculate the state of a cell makes it easy to create a worksheet of numbers. What is not so great is the fact that the class SpreadSheet is a single worksheet. Most spreadsheets applications (like Microsoft Excel) offer the ability to create multiple worksheets.

The server-side spreadsheet that we will create will consist of two concepts: workbook and worksheet, as illustrated in Figure 11-1.

Figure 11-1. *Spreadsheet design based on workbook and worksheet types*

The workbook is a type that acts like a collection class of the worksheet type. The worksheet type is an individual spreadsheet of fixed dimension that is responsible for storing the state, and the cell calculations reference the individual lambda expressions.

The workbook and worksheet could be defined as interfaces or as classes. Which would be better? Let's assume that workbook will be defined as an interface and then implemented by a class. The approach is a commitment to a component architecture, allowing you to implement multiple types of workbooks. However, the likelihood of implementing multiple workbook types is rather remote, so why use interfaces? Because interfaces fit better into a bigger context.

Let's say that you have completed your super-duper server-side application and want to programmatically share the code with multiple machines. Having one computer call .NET functionality on another machine is almost trivial, but to attain the best performance and resource usage, you should use interfaces.

Defining the Server Spreadsheet Interfaces

Defining the interfaces for the server spreadsheets is actually rather complicated because of the requirements. The requirements state performance and usability are important, which, in this case, is asking quite a bit, as you will see as we work through the example. Let's start with a bottom-up development approach and outline the interfaces.

Defining the Debug Interface

Because the spreadsheet is from a production coding example, included in the discussion will be pieces of code that demonstrate good programming practices. The following is the base interface for all of my interfaces, which is defined in the Devspace.Trader.Common project.

```
Public Interface IDebug
    Property Debug() As Boolean
End Interface
```

The IDebug interface has a single Boolean property called Debug, which can be assigned and retrieved. The idea behind the IDebug interface is to enable a component to generate debug output. One of the major headaches with debugging applications that process large amounts of data is finding where the problem is. Imagine processing several million records, and the bug happens in record 900,001. You don't want to debug 900,000 records before hitting the bug. Thus, the challenge is figuring out what went wrong without using the debugger. This is where IDebug comes into play. It provides a mechanism to let the implementation say what is going on, so if a bug needs to be deciphered, you do so by looking at the output.

The following example demonstrates how to use the Debug flag. The class that contains this code implements the IDebug interface and sets the Debug flag at the beginning of its execution.

```
Dim baseType As String() = _
  typeToInstantiate.Split(New String() { "[[", "]]" }, StringSplitOptions.None)
If baseType.Length = 0 Then
    Throw New Exception("There is no base type, which is an error")
End If
If Debug Then
    For Each str As String In baseType
        GenerateOutput.Write("Workbook.Load", "baseType(" & str & ")")
    Next
End If
```

The first line of code is used to split up a buffer into individual pieces, where double square brackets delimit the buffers. The Debug property is used to output the split-up buffer using the command GenerateOutput.Write().

■**Tip** Although I have defined my own debugging infrastructure, there is another infrastructure that you can use, called log4net (http://logging.apache.org/log4net/). This is a comprehensive infrastructure that you may want to investigate.

A Debug flag was used to output some text; otherwise, that information is not usually visible. Without a Debug flag, the only way to get that information is by setting a breakpoint after the Split() statement, and then individually investigating the resulting buffers. If you had to do that for 900,000 records, you would become bored very quickly, and let's not even talk about how much time you would waste.

The Debug flag serves two purposes. The first is to generate output to allow you to do a post-mortem analysis when trying to figure out a bug. The second is to generate output when a bug occurs in a production context. By giving the user the ability to define a Debug flag, you are no longer reliant on having the user explain to you step by step how to reproduce the bug. All you need to do is tell the user to activate the Debug flag (your program would probably have a menu item for this), run the program until the bug occurs, and then send you the debug log file output for analysis.

Defining the IWorksheetBase and IWorksheet Interfaces

The worksheet is implemented using worksheet and workbook interfaces. Remember that one of the requirements is to have a spreadsheet implementation that is very fast. This would mean if a spreadsheet contained numbers, the best implementation would be a spreadsheet of Double types. However, if the spreadsheet contained string buffers, the best implementation would be a spreadsheet of String types. Figure 11-2 shows a spreadsheet of Double and String types.

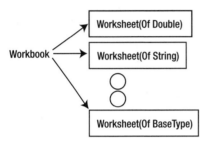

Figure 11-2. *Spreadsheet of strings and doubles*

In Figure 11-2, the workbook references a worksheet of type Worksheet(Of Double) and Worksheet(Of String), and in the general case, Worksheet(Of BaseType). You can see how an interface using .NET generics for a worksheet could be potentially defined: define a general worksheet and define the actual type using .NET generics. The problem with this solution is that a workbook would define a collection of mixed types.

You might be tempted to believe that Worksheet(Of Double) and Worksheet(Of String) are of the type Worksheet(Of BaseType), and thus are all a single type. This is not the case, because with .NET generics, a type that hasn't been concretized is not a type at all. Think of it as being an almost type, and to make the program work, you need to concretize everything. Figure 11-2 shows two concrete types: Worksheet(Of Double) and Worksheet(Of String). These are two different types. The two different types make it complicated for the workbook, because the workbook wants to maintain a single collection of worksheets. If we assume for the moment that the worksheet interface is defined as follows:

```
Interface IWorksheet(Of BaseType)
End Interface
```

the workbook could reference the worksheet as this collection:

```
Dim _worksheets As List(Of IWorksheet(Of BaseType))
```

However, that reference is incomplete, and the compiler would want to know what BaseType references. To keep your options open, one solution is to not complete the BaseType, but let the user of workbook figure things out, thus defining workbook as follows:

```
Class Workbook(Of BaseType)
    Dim _worksheets As List(Of IWorksheet(Of BaseType))
End Class
```

This solution seems to be a good one, but, in fact, it's passing the buck. The solution does not address the problem of Figure 11-2 and forces the end user to solve it. The core problem is that Figure 11-2 uses .NET generics to define worksheets of specific types, which means mixed types that need to be addressed by the workbook. In other words, a workbook can contain only spreadsheets of a certain type, as in this example:

```
Workbook(Of String) workbook1
Workbook(Of Double) workbook2
```

It would seem that .NET generics make everything more complicated. However, there's more to this than first appears.

.NET generics have not made things more complicated, but rather have required us to be more explicit about what we actually want to do. We want to be able to define specific worksheet types, which means we have a mixed list of types that the workbook must manage. As explained in Chapter 9, non-.NET generics list types cannot control whether or not a list contains mixed types.

To solve the worksheet problem, we need to put on our object-oriented thinking caps. First, what is a worksheet? It's a spreadsheet that fulfills the role of a two-dimensional thing, and it applies to all worksheets regardless of types. Therefore, the first interface to define is a base worksheet, as follows (do this in the ServerSideSpreadsheet project, as well as adding a reference to the Devspace.Trader.Common project):

```
Imports Devspace.Trader.Common

Public Interface IWorksheetBase
    Inherits IDebug
    Sub Dimension(ByVal rows As Integer, ByVal cols As Integer)
    ReadOnly Property MaxCols() As Integer
    ReadOnly Property MaxRows() As Integer
End Interface
```

The interface definition of IWorksheetBase has one method and two properties. The method Dimension() is used to assign the maximum rows and columns of the individual spreadsheet. The properties MaxRows and MaxCols return the maximum rows and columns. The properties and method have nothing to do with the specific type managed by the worksheet, but the interface manages to uniquely identify the instance as being a type of spreadsheet.

In the workbook code, the list of worksheets would be defined as follows:

```
Private _worksheets As IDictionary(Of String, IWorksheetBase) = _
    New Dictionary(Of String, IWorksheetBase)
```

Now the workbook knows it has a series of worksheets, but the workbook does not know or care about the types of the worksheets. When users of the workbook want to manipulate an individual worksheet, they can retrieve the worksheet from the workbook, but the users need to know the worksheet's type.

The spreadsheet is typically addressed using rows and columns, but to simplify declarations, there is also the ability to define something called the SheetCoordinate, which is a type that has a row and column. The SheetCoordinate is defined in ServerSideSpreadsheet as follows:

```
Public Structure SheetCoordinate
    Public Row As Integer
    Public Column As Integer
    Public Sub New(ByVal row As Integer, ByVal column As Integer)
        If (row < 0) Then
            Throw New ArgumentOutOfRangeException("Row is below zero")
        End If
        If (column < 0) Then
            Throw New ArgumentOutOfRangeException("Column is below zero")
        End If
        Me.Row = row
        Me.Column = column
    End Sub

    Public ReadOnly Property OneUp() As SheetCoordinate
        Get
            Return New SheetCoordinate((Me.Row - 1), Me.Column)
        End Get
    End Property

    Public ReadOnly Property OneDown() As SheetCoordinate
        Get
            Return New SheetCoordinate((Me.Row + 1), Me.Column)
        End Get
    End Property

    Public ReadOnly Property OneLeft() As SheetCoordinate
        Get
            Return New SheetCoordinate(Me.Row, (Me.Column - 1))
        End Get
    End Property

    Public ReadOnly Property OneRight() As SheetCoordinate
        Get
            Return New SheetCoordinate(Me.Row, (Me.Column + 1))
        End Get
    End Property

End Structure
```

In the declaration of SheetCoordinate, notice that Structure is used rather than Class. We could have used a class, but SheetCoordinate serves the purpose of being a piece of data. SheetCoordinate is a type where you store information that is used by another type. A data type might do some processing, but only to make it easier to manipulate the data. For example, notice how SheetCoordinate has properties to generate a new instance of SheetCoordinate that might be one row higher or lower, or a column to the right or left.

The next step is to extend the worksheet definition and use .NET generics to define the type of worksheet. The following is the complete definition of the IWorksheet. These methods are used to calculate the values of cells in the worksheet and work with the contents of individual cells (the state of those cells). We can also assign the function that carries out the calculation of a cell's contents, using either a SheetCoordinate type or the row and column coordinates.

```
Public Interface IWorksheet(Of BaseType)
    Inherits IWorksheetBase

    Sub AssignCellCalculation(ByVal coords As SheetCoordinate, _
        ByVal cb As Func(Of IWorksheet(Of BaseType), Integer, Integer, BaseType))

    Sub AssignCellCalculation(ByVal row As Integer, ByVal col As Integer, _
        ByVal cb As Func(Of IWorksheet(Of BaseType), Integer, Integer, BaseType))

    Sub AssignColCalculation(ByVal col As Integer, _
                        ByVal cb As Func(Of IWorksheet(Of BaseType), _
                        Integer, Integer, BaseType))
    Sub Calculate()

    Function Calculate(ByVal coords As SheetCoordinate) As BaseType

    Function Calculate(ByVal row As Integer, ByVal col As Integer) As BaseType

    Sub CalculateCol(ByVal col As Integer)

    Sub CalculateRow(ByVal row As Integer)

    Function GetCellState(ByVal coords As SheetCoordinate) As BaseType

    Function GetCellState(ByVal row As Integer, ByVal col As Integer) As BaseType

    Sub SetCellState(ByVal coords As SheetCoordinate, ByVal val As BaseType)

    Sub SetCellState(ByVal row As Integer, ByVal col As Integer, _
                    ByVal val As BaseType)

    ReadOnly Property Data() As BaseType (,)
End Interface
```

The declaration of IWorksheet is as a .NET generics type, where BaseType is a .NET generics parameter that represents the type of the spreadsheet. Since IWorksheet is a type of spreadsheet, it subclasses the IWorksheetBase interface, allowing IWorksheet to be part of a mixed collection of IWorksheet instances. The IWorksheet interface is fairly complex and contains many methods. However, here we are focusing on the interface concept, rather than the individual methods.

Look at the bolded parts and notice how the interface is specific about the operations, but vague about the type used in the operations. This is what you want to achieve when using .NET generics. You want to take a high-level approach and indicate which operations are available, but leave out the types being manipulated in the operations. The types will be specified later by another programmer.

■**Note** The technique of having a .NET generics type (such as IWorksheet) subclass a non-.NET generics type (such as IWorksheetBase) allows you to identify the general type that you are trying to describe with some specialization in the .NET generics type declaration.

Defining the IWorkbook Interface

Now that we've completed the IWorksheet(Of BaseType) and IWorksheetBase interfaces, we can define the workbook interface. The workbook interface will not be a .NET generics type, since a workbook will contain multiple worksheet types. However, as you will see, we can optimize this interface to make it easier to use the workbook.

For the moment, let's consider the plain-vanilla IWorkbook interface with no .NET generics types, which is defined as follows in the ServerSideSpreadsheet:

```
Imports System.Reflection
Imports Devspace.Trader.Common

<DefaultMember("Item")> _
Public Interface IWorkbook
    Inherits IDebug

    ReadOnly Property Identifier() As String
    Default Property Item(ByVal identifier As String) As IWorksheetBase
End Interface
```

The IWorkbook interface defines an Identifier property and a default property Item. Notice how the attribute DefaultMember is defined to indicate the default property identifier (it is from the System.Reflection namespace). Any class that implements IWorkbook is expected to contain multiple references to IWorksheet(Of BaseType) instances. How those references are managed is not the responsibility of the IWorkbook interface, but of the IWorkbook interface implementation.

■**Note** The IWorkbook interface does not provide a Clear() method to reset the workbook and delete all of the referenced worksheets. It would seem logical to have a Clear() method, but in a garbage-collected environment, that's completely unnecessary. If you don't want to use a workbook anymore, just don't reference it, and the garbage collector will take care of the rest. Think of it as having the option of serving dinner to your guests on real plates or paper plates. Real plates might seem better, but they break and you need to wash them. Paper plates are used once and thrown away. Of course, with paper plates you have recycling issues that you don't have in .NET, because the memory is recycled for you.

The property Identifier identifies the workbook represented by the current IWorkbook object. The identifier might be a path or file name and is completely dependent on the implementation of IWorkbook.

The default property, `Item`, is the primary way of getting and retrieving worksheets, where each worksheet is referenced using a string identifier. The identifier does not need to be a string—it could have been a custom type, enumeration, or interface that is implemented. Using a string keeps things simple, but there are maintenance issues.

Let's say all workbooks have a configuration worksheet. So for most of the code, the string identifier "`configuration`" is used. However, a new programmer decides to use "`Configuration`" (with a capital C). This slight change will cause problems because "`configuration`" is meant to have a lowercase c. Here's the example:

```
Dim workbook As IWorkbook
Dim worksheet1 As IWorksheetBase = workbook("configuration")
Dim worksheet2 As IWorksheetBase = workbook("Configuration")
```

This approach uses a buffer that is typed in by hand and is considered hard-coded. The preferred alternative is to hard-code a structure that is then referenced throughout the source code, like this:

```
Public Module WorksheetIdentifiers
    Public Const Configuration As String = "configuration"
End Module


Dim workbook As IWorkbook
Dim worksheet1 As IWorksheetBase = workbook(WorksheetIdentifiers.Configuration)
Dim worksheet2 As IWorksheetBase = workbook(WorksheetIdentifiers.Configuration)
```

The module `WorksheetIdentifiers` still contains a hard-coded string buffer, but this buffer has been centralized to a single location. The workbook default property references the identifier within the class `WorksheetIdentifiers`. Thus, if you change the class `WorksheetIdentifiers`, you also change the identifiers used by the default property. That way, the chances of having a typo break an application are reduced.

Let's get back to the `IWorkbook` interface and, in particular, the default property. The default property is of the type `IWorksheetBase`, which is a bit tedious because the `IWorksheetBase` interface is a rudimentary interface and most likely not the interface that you will use, because we have `IWorksheet(Of BaseType)`, and therein lies the problem. To get an `IWorksheet` instance, you would need a cast, as follows:

```
Dim workbook As IWorkbook
Dim worksheet As IWorksheet(Of String) = _
    TryCast(workbook(WorksheetIdentifiers.Configuration), IWorksheet(Of String))
```

The bolded code is the cast you need each and every time you want to reference an `IWorksheet` instance. The cast is not a big deal, but it is tedious. I personally would prefer being able to call a property, method, or default property that returns the type I want.

Therein lies the problem, because the way I want to use a default property, property, or method is as a mixed type, and you can't define a default property with mixed types. You can define a default property that is a fixed type. To understand this problem, look at the following declaration of a workbook, which does compile.

```
Imports System.Reflection
Imports Devspace.Trader.Common

<DefaultMember("Item")> _
Public Interface IWorkbook(Of BaseType)
    Inherits IDebug
    Default Property Item(ByVal identifier As String) As IWorksheet(Of BaseType)
    ReadOnly Property Identifier() As String
End Interface
```

In this declaration of IWorkbook, a .NET generics type is used, but then the problem is that the default property can return only IWorksheet instances of a single type, such as Double or String. Remember that there are multiple worksheet types (as illustrated in Figure 11-2).

What we want to do is use method-level .NET generics declarations, like this:

```
<DefaultMember("Item")> _
Public Interface IMixedType
    Default Property Item(Of BaseType)(ByVal identifier As String) _
      As IWorksheet(Of BaseType)
End Interface
```

The problem with the method-level declaration is that it does not compile. There are two ways to declare a .NET generics parameter. The first is what you have seen the most often, and that is at the type level:

```
Class MyType(Of GenericType)
End Class
```

Declaring at the type level means that whenever you use the type and specify a type for the .NET generics parameter, MyType becomes fixed to a certain type. So say you declared MyType as follows:

```
Dim cls As MyType = New MyType(Of Integer) ()
```

Now any references to GenericType within MyType will become Integer. This form of .NET generics solves many problems, as illustrated in Chapter 9.

But in the case of the IWorkbook, we don't want a fixed type. We want the ability to have a collection type contain mixed types of IWorksheet. The way to achieve that is to use .NET generics methods, like this:

```
Function Method(Of GenericType)() As MyType(Of GenericType)

End Function
```

Now the .NET generics parameter is associated with the method, rather than the type. And that means MyType can mix types. So we could have different IWorksheet types in a single workbook. And wouldn't it be great if there were a default property with mixed types? But you can't have .NET generics default properties and properties that are not declared at the type level. Thus, the use of a .NET generics parameter with a default property or property will not work. In my opinion, that is a real design flaw in Visual Basic, because it means we need to write code like this:

```
Imports Devspace.Trader.Common
Imports System.Reflection

<DefaultMember("Item")> _
Public Interface IWorkbook
    Inherits IDebug

    Function GetSheet(Of BaseType)(ByVal identifier As String) _
      As IWorksheet(Of BaseType)
    ReadOnly Property Identifier() As String
    Default Property Item(ByVal identifier As String) As IWorksheetBase
End Interface
```

In this modified declaration, the method GetSheet() acts like the Get part of the default property, but notice where the .NET generics parameter BaseType is declared. The declaration is after the method identifier and before the first bracket. In the case of IWorkbook, we use the method-level .NET generics parameter to allow the caller to determine the type of the worksheet instances. The implementation of IWorkbook has to do nothing other than perform the appropriate cast. Method-level .NET generics parameters are great when you are dealing with mixed types, as in the case of IWorkbook.

The code to retrieve a worksheet that previously needed a cast is rewritten as follows:

```
Dim workbook As IWorkbook
Dim worksheet As IWorksheet(Of String) = _
    workbook.GetSheet(Of String)(WorksheetIdentifiers.Configuration)
```

The cast has not disappeared completely. It is done for us in the implementation of the GetSheet(Of BaseType)() method, as demonstrated by the following code.

```
Friend Class Workbook
    Implements IWorkbook, IDebug

    Private _worksheets As IDictionary(Of String, IWorksheetBase) = _
      New Dictionary(Of String, IWorksheetBase)()

    . . .

    Public Function GetSheet(Of BaseType)(ByVal identifier As String) _
      As IWorksheet(Of BaseType) Implements IWorkbook.GetSheet
      SyncLock _worksheets
          Dim retval As IWorksheet(Of BaseType) = Nothing
          If _worksheets.ContainsKey(identifier) Then
              retval = TryCast(_worksheets.Item(identifier), _
                               IWorksheet(Of BaseType))
          Else
              retval = New Worksheet(Of BaseType)(identifier)
              _worksheets.Add(identifier, retval)
          End If
```

```
        Return retval
    End SyncLock
End FunctionEnd Class
```

The bolded code shows that there is still a cast, but the type cast is in the method, and it uses the .NET generics parameter declared at the method level.

■**Note** The SyncLock keyword ensures that the code in this method is not executed by more than one thread at a time. That way, the calling code always gets back the correct sheet.

Implementing the Server Spreadsheet

Now let's look at how the workbook and worksheet are implemented. I will explain only the important pieces, but all of the code is available for download from the Source/Downloads area of the Apress web site (http://www.apress.com). The class Worksheet(Of BaseType) implements the interface IWorksheet, but does not specify on which type the worksheet should be based. In this application, we also have a class called TraderBaseClass. In most applications, there is some functionality that most classes will need. That common functionality is what I call a domain-specific base class. In the case of TraderBaseClass, that is the implementation of the IDebug interface.

Using Lambda Expressions in the Spreadsheet

The data members of Worksheet(Of BaseType) are very similar to the previously defined spreadsheet class, except the declarations are lambda-ready. *Lambda-ready* means that you use the Func(Of) type whenever you want to declare a variable that references a lambda expression. The following three data members are used to store the state of the cell, cell calculations that will calculate the state of a cell, and cell calculations that calculate the state of cells for an entire column.

```
Private Cells As Func(Of IWorksheet(Of BaseType), Integer, Integer, BaseType)(,)
Private CellState As BaseType(,)
Private ColCells As Func(Of IWorksheet(Of BaseType), Integer, Integer, BaseType)()
```

The data member CellState contains the state of the worksheet cell, and its type is BaseType, meaning that the type of the worksheet cell is whatever BaseType is declared as. The data members Cells and ColCells are declared as lambda expression references, where there are three parameters and a return value.

Before I continue with the lambda expression explanation, I want to shift focus to illustrate a problem. We are going to play a game of what animal am I, where we'll use lambda expressions in conjunction with a closure. The idea is to store the identifier of the animal in a closure and then return it when it's requested.

```vbnet
Dim animals(1) As Func(Of String)
Dim animal As String

animal = "cow"
animals(0) = Function() animal

animal = "horse"
animals(1) = Function() animal

For Each callAnimal In animals
    Console.Write ("(" & callAnimal() & ")")
Next
```

The example creates an array of lambda expressions (`animals`) where space for two lambda expressions is allocated. The individual lambda expressions will reference a variable `animal`, which contains the animal of the lambda expression. In the code, the lambda expressions are assigned when the state of `animal` changes from `cow` to `horse`.

Let's say you run the code, and `Console.WriteLine()` generates its output. What do you think the animals will be? Do you expect `cow` and `horse`, respectively? Here's the output:

```
(horse) (horse)
```

The generated output is not what you would expect. This demonstrates that lambda expressions are *stateless*. Yet in earlier explanations of lambda expressions and closures, I said that variables can be stored in lambda expressions. Since `animal` is a value type, you would expect two copies of `animal`, right? Wrong.

Closures do work, and variable state is kept across lambda expressions. The mistake in this code is that the same variable is referenced by two lambda expressions. Thus, when the two lambda expressions execute, they will reference the same animal, which was last assigned to be a horse.

The code that solves the problem uses two unique variables, as follows:

```vbnet
Dim animals(1) As Func(Of String)

Dim animal1 = "cow"
animals(0) = Function() animal1

Dim animal2 = "horse"
animals(1) = Function() animal2

For Each callAnimal In animals
    Console.WriteLine(callAnimal())
Next
```

This time when you run the code, you get the following output.

```
cow
horse
```

Returning to the spreadsheet example, the problem is that the behavior just described means this code won't work:

```
Dim myWorksheet As IWorksheet(Of Double)
For row As Integer = 0 To 10
    myWorksheet.AssignCellCalculation(row, 1, _
        Function(worksheet, cellRow, cellCol) _
            myWorksheet.GetCellState(row, 0) - _
            myWorksheet.Calculate(10, 0))
Next
```

whereas this code would work:

```
Dim myWorksheet As IWorksheet(Of Double)
For row As Integer = 0 To 10
    Dim temp = row
    myWorksheet.AssignCellCalculation(row, 1, _
        Function(worksheet, cellRow, cellCol) _
            myWorksheet.GetCellState(temp, 0) - _
            myWorksheet.Calculate(10, 0))
Next
```

The difference between the two pieces of code is that the second one has the lambda expression that uses the variable declared temp in the context of a loop. For each iteration of the loop, a new instance of temp is allocated, and hence each lambda expression has its own instance of the row.

Assigning State Without Knowing the Type

When using .NET generics types, one of the most common problems occurs when you need to work with proper types. In the implementation of the IWorksheet interface, it is necessary to implement the AssignCellState() method defined in the interface IWorksheetSerialize.

The explanation of IWorksheetSerialize is slightly complicated and relates to the problem of loading an IWorksheet without knowing the type. Say that you are saving an IWorkbook with multiple IWorksheet instances. Each IWorksheet instance is a specific type. When you want to load an IWorkbook, how does the loader know which types there are? The answer is that the loader does not, and thus must first load a general type, and then make a specific cast. Take a look at the serialization source code in the project Devspace.Trader.Common and the namespace Devspace.Trader.Common.ServerSpreadsheet.SerializerImpls, available as part of the downloadable code.

```
Public Interface IWorksheetSerialize
    Sub AssignCellState(Of ValueType)(ByVal row As Integer, _
      ByVal col As Integer, ByVal value As ValueType)

    Sub AssignCellState(ByVal row As Integer, ByVal col As Integer, _
                            ByVal value As Object)
End Interface
```

The problem is that the function passes in as a parameter of one type and is assigned to CellState, which is another undefined .NET generics type. The implementation of the AssignCellState() method is as follows:

```
Public Sub AssignCellState(ByVal row As Integer, ByVal col As Integer, _
  ByVal value As Object) Implements IWorksheetSerialize.AssignCellState
    CellState(row, col) = DirectCast(value, BaseType)
End Sub
```

The code looks so simple and innocent, but it is actually masking many potential problems. Here, the value of the parameter value is of type Object. Then to convert the value to type BaseType—because that is what CellState is defined to be—you use a cast. For the most part, this code will work, if value is the correct type.

Consider the following code, which would generate an exception.

```
Dim worksheet As Worksheet(Of Double) = New Worksheet(Of Double)()
worksheet.Dimension(10, 10)Dim buffer As String = "hello, world"
worksheet.AssignCellState(1, 2, buffer)
```

The variable worksheet is declared to be of type Worksheet(Of Double). When the method AssignCellState() is called, the cell 1, 2 is assigned to be type String. Calling AssignCellState() is not a problem, but in the implementation, the assignment will fail. You can't willy-nilly assign a String to a Double. Of course, this begs the question, "Why have a function of type Object?" Sometimes you can't get around it, and you need to write a general object method. The proper way to call the method would be as follows:

```
Dim worksheet As Worksheet(Of Double) = New Worksheet(Of Double)()
worksheet.Dimension(10, 10)
Dim buffer As String = "hello, world"
worksheet.AssignCellState(1, 2, Double.Parse(buffer))
```

The bolded code shows that the string buffer is parsed by the Double.Parse() method, converting a string buffer into a Double value. Of course, the conversion will fail, since the string buffer represents a string, but that is another problem.

Another way of solving the problem is to avoid the object altogether and declare the method as being a .NET generics method. The advantage of the .NET generics method is that you could execute in a type-safe manner without explicitly forcing the user to implement parsing routines. Consider the following modified .NET generics method declaration of AssignCellState().

```
Public Sub AssignCellState(Of ValueType)(ByVal row As Integer, _
                                         ByVal col As Integer, _
                                         ByVal value As ValueType) _
    Implements IWorksheetSerialize.AssignCellState
    If GetType(BaseType).IsAssignableFrom(GetType(ValueType)) Then
        CellState(row, col) = DirectCast(DirectCast(value, Object), BaseType)
    ElseIf TypeOf (value) Is String And _
            GetType(Double).IsAssignableFrom(GetType(BaseType)) Then
        Dim obj As Object = DirectCast(value, Object)
        Dim dValue As Double = Double.Parse(CStr(obj))
        Dim objDValue As Object = CType(dValue, Object)
        CellState(row, col) = DirectCast(objDValue, BaseType)
    Else
        Throw New InvalidCastException("Could not perform conversion")
    End If
End Sub
```

The cell state to be assigned is a .NET generics parameter and defined to be the type ValueType. You can only guess what ValueType is; it is determined when the method AssignCellState(Of)() is called. For example, suppose this method call is made:

```
Dim buffer As String = "hello, world"
worksheet.AssignCellState(1, 2, buffer)
```

The type for ValueType will be String, even though you have not explicitly specified it. One of the things that is possible with .NET generics methods is that types can be deduced implicitly. The following would be an explicit usage of AssignCellState(Of)().

```
Dim buffer As String = "hello, world"
worksheet.AssignCellState(Of String)(1, 2, buffer)
```

Knowing that ValueType is String, AssignCellState(Of)() will then first check if ValueType can be assigned to BaseType:

```
If GetType(BaseType).IsAssignableFrom(GetType(ValueType)) Then
```

This code is rather clever, because it uses what is known as *reflection* to determine if one type can be assigned to another type. Essentially, it asks if it is OK via a cast to assign value to CellState. You could try to do this without the If statement, but then you risk an unnecessary exception. If it is permissible to assign, then the assignment is done via a two-step casting:

```
CellState(row, col) = DirectCast(DirectCast(value, Object), BaseType)
```

Here, you first convert the type to an Object, and then convert the type to BaseType, which happens to be the type that the spreadsheet is declared as. It is absolutely imperative that the cast to the object is added; otherwise, the Visual Basic compiler will complain that the cast is not possible.

But suppose that the type cannot be directly assigned. Let's say that value references a String that contains a number. Then, using reflection, you can verify what ValueType and BaseType are and perform the conversion yourself:

```
ElseIf TypeOf (value) Is String And _
      GetType(Double).IsAssignableFrom(GetType(BaseType)) Then
```

The first part of the If statement asks if value is of type String. The second part asks if Double can be assigned to BaseType. If both are valid, it means the input is a String and the spreadsheet type is a Double, so to convert, you only need to call Double.Parse().

Providing this automatic conversion functionality for the caller of the code does not save code, but it centralizes it and makes it general. The caller will not generally need to worry about the most common conversions, as they will happen automatically (you will have implemented them). For those conversions that cannot be done, a cast exception is thrown, just as the original object-based AssignCellState() would have thrown an exception.

The assignment is a series of casts and conversions that you need to do so that you can convert one type to another. The main problem when converting types in this way is that the method-level .NET generics parameter is a type that is not related to the type-level .NET generics parameter.

```
Dim obj As Object = DirectCast(value, Object)
Dim dValue As Double = Double.Parse(CStr(obj))
Dim objDValue As Object = CType(dValue, Object)
CellState(row, col) = DirectCast(objDValue, BaseType)
```

The first step is to convert the parameter into an object so that the cast operators that expect objects will work without the Visual Basic compiler generating errors. The If statement said that the input type is a String, and destination type is a Double. Thus, the methods CStr() and Double.Parse() are called to convert the input string to a double number. Once the string-to-double functions have completed, the CellState could be assigned, if it were not for the little problem of the .NET generics-type level parameter. The next steps of casting using CType() and DirectCast() are a boxing and unboxing of a value type. This is necessary because the compiler considers everything as an object, and thus you need to first convert to an object and then convert to the actual type.

■**Note** The steps to convert from one .NET generics type to another .NET generics type would seem cumbersome, and to a degree they are. Although the steps illustrated here are the minimum, they allow you to convert one type to another. The steps are dangerous in that if you don't know ahead of time whether the conversion is allowed, an exception could result. In the example, an exception is almost impossible because the types were checked ahead of time, and an appropriate plan of action was taken.

Overall, the AssignCellState(Of)() method with .NET generics parameters provides the ability to cleanly assign a value to the spreadsheet, and a clean and maintainable method to perform a conversion. This goes back to the original requirement of being able to mix types safely.

Overriding the ToString() Functionality

Debugging a data structure like a spreadsheet is a fairly complex task, because there is too much data. The Worksheet(Of) class implements the ToString() method and generates a string. The string can be retrieved and then displayed using a method like Console.WriteLine().

Here is the implementation of worksheet's ToString() function.

```
Public Overrides Function ToString() As String
    Dim builder As New StringBuilder()
    Dim row As Integer
    For row = 0 To Cells.GetLength(0) - 1
        Dim needComma As Boolean = False
        If _generateRowCounter Then
            needComma = True
            builder.Append(row)
        End If
        Dim col As Integer
        For col = 0 To Cells.GetLength(1) - 1
            If needComma Then
                builder.Append(",")
            Else
                needComma = True
            End If
            If ellState(row, col) IsNot Nothing Then
                builder.Append(CellState(row, col).ToString)
            End If
        Next col
        builder.Append(ChrW(10))
    Next row
    Return builder.ToString
End Function
```

Because the worksheet can be large, StringBuilder is used to incrementally build a string that is returned.

■Note The ToString() method is useful when you're debugging or trying to perform analysis of the state of an object without actually debugging the program. Thus, for improved debugging or runtime analysis, always implement ToString().

Using the Spreadsheet

With the interfaces and implementations complete, it is possible to use the spreadsheet. The sample application is a spreadsheet that calculates the average of a set of numbers and then calculates how far each number is from the average.

Calculating an Average

The spreadsheet calculates the average of a set of numbers, and then subtracts the average from each number. The example demonstrates reading a complete spreadsheet to get a number and reading individual elements to perform a calculation.

Let's use the following numbers to calculate the average.

```
Dim items As Double() = New Double() { 1.0, 2.0, 3.0 }
```

The average number is 2.0, and if you subtract the average from each number, you will get the series –1, 0, and 1.

To make this work for a spreadsheet, the first step is to declare and then populate an IWorksheet(Of BaseType) instance. To instantiate an IWorksheet(Of BaseType) instance, you use a factory that will instantiate the Worksheet(Of BaseType) class. The code looks like this:

```
Dim sheetAverage As IWorksheet(Of Double) = _
  SpreadsheetManager.CreateEmptyWorksheet(Of Double)("")
Dim items As Double() = New Double() {1, 2, 3}
sheetAverage.Dimension((items.Length + 10), 3)
For row = 0 To items.Length - 1
    sheetAverage.SetCellState(row, 0, items(row))
Next row
```

The worksheet is declared as being of type Double (IWorksheet(Of Double)), allowing you to manage a Double value. To populate sheetAverage, the numbers are iterated in a For loop and assigned to the worksheet using the SetCellState() method. The method Dimension() is needed to create a fixed-length worksheet.

With the worksheet populated, to make sure everything looks right, you could call the method ToString() and see if all is as expected.

The next step is to assign the lambda expressions that will be used to calculate the average and then the individual differences from the average. When you assign a calculation to the worksheet, you need to know whether the lambda expression will be stateful or stateless. Remember that lambda expressions have some state. It is just a question of whether you want a shared-state lambda expression or an individual-state lambda expression. In the case of the lambda expressions for the average calculations, a shared state is acceptable.

To calculate the average, you use a technique where the average calculation is the last element in the series of the array calculations. Thus, when the average calculation is called, it knows how many elements there are because of the row in which the average calculation is stored.

```
Function Average(ByVal worksheet As IWorksheet(Of Double), _
                ByVal cellRow As Integer, ByVal cellCol As Integer)
    Dim runningTotal As Double = 0
    Dim row As Integer
    For row = 0 To cellRow - 1
        runningTotal = (runningTotal + worksheet.GetCellState(row, 0))
    Next row
    Return (runningTotal / CDbl(cellRow))
End Function
. . .
sheetAverage.AssignCellCalculation(items.Length, 0, AddressOf Average)
```

In the example, the average is calculated by using the variable cellRow as a maximum row. Every cell (GetCellState()) before cellRow is added to a running total (runningTotal), and then, finally, an average is returned by dividing runningTotal by cellRow.

With the average calculated, the next step is to calculate the difference between the average and the individual items. The result will be stored in a column to the right of the item cell state. This is done by subtracting the average calculation cell state from the item value, as follows:

```
For row = 0 To items.Length - 1
    sheetAverage.AssignCellCalculation(row, 1, _
        Function(worksheet As IWorksheet(Of Double), cellRow As Integer, _
                cellCol As Integer)
          (worksheet.GetCellState(cellRow, 0) - _
          worksheet.Calculate(items.Length, 0)))
Next row
```

The number of cell-state calculations depends on the count of numbers in items. Each cell calculation is assigned a locally declared lambda expression, meaning that the lambda expressions of all cell states will be identical and share the same state. The only shared variable is items.Length. All the lambda expressions expect the same length, and so it is acceptable to share this variable. The average difference is calculated by calculating the average and then subtracting it from the worksheet cell item value that is in the zeroth column.

Finally, when everything is assigned, you can call the worksheet.Calculate() method to calculate the average and difference from the average.

```
sheetAverage.Calculate()
Console.WriteLine(sheetAverage.ToString())
```

Understanding Why the Calculation Worked

The cell calculations work because the spreadsheet has the ability to track what has been calculated and what has not been calculated. In a typical spreadsheet, you can change one cell in a sheet and have everything magically recalculate. There is no such feature for this spreadsheet. However, this simpler spreadsheet version can make sure that when there are dependencies, they are not calculated multiple times.

Look back at the source code to calculate the difference between the average and a number. The only reason the calculation worked is that the cell that contained the average was called using the Calculate() method. Had the GetCellState() method been used, the average might not have been calculated, and thus the difference calculation would have been corrupted.

But having each and every cell calculate the average whenever a small change is made is a waste of resources, since the change might not affect a cell that is recalculated. To avoid this, built into the spreadsheet is a version-control mechanism that calculates a cell to the latest version. Then, if another calculation is called with the same version number, the value is retrieved from the cell state. The following is the code from Worksheet(Of BaseType) that manages the version number.

```
Public Function Calculate(ByVal row As Integer, ByVal col As Integer) As BaseType _
    Implements IWorksheet(Of BaseType).Calculate
        If (CurrVersion > CalculationVersion(row, col)) Then
            CellState(row, col) = Cells(row, col)(Me, row, col)
            CalculationVersion(row, col) = CurrVersion
        End If
        Return CellState(row, col)
End Function
```

```
Public Sub Calculate() Implements IWorksheet(Of BaseType).Calculate
    CurrVersion += 1
    Dim row As Integer
    For row = 0 To Cells.GetLength(0) - 1
        Dim col As Integer
        For col = 0 To Cells.GetLength(1) - 1
            If Cells(row, col) IsNot Nothing Then
                Calculate(row, col)
            End If
        Next col
    Next row
End Sub
```

Calling the method `Calculate()` without parameters indicates a desire to recalculate the entire spreadsheet. In the implementation of `Calculate()`, the variable `CurrVersion`, which represents the version number of the current calculation, is incremented. Then each cell is iterated, and if it exists, the individual cell form of `Calculate()` (`Calculate()` with the parameters `row` and `col`) is called. In the individual cell form of `Calculate()`, a check is made to see if the calculation version number of the cell is the latest of the spreadsheet; if not, the cell's lambda expression is called. After the new `CellState` has been assigned, the cell-state version number is incremented, and the cell state is returned.

■**Note** The calculation of the spreadsheet is nothing earth-shattering, and you might be tempted to argue it is irrelevant to the scope of the book. In fact, the calculation and its side effects are of major relevance. With lambda expressions, you have a form of asynchronous processing, very much like a spreadsheet. The cell calculations of the spreadsheet do not know when they will be called, and they cannot make assumptions about the state. Thus, when a lambda expression is created, the state at the time of the lambda expression may not be the same as when the lambda expression is executed. If you are not acutely aware of this potential pitfall, you could have some major bugs in your code.

The Important Stuff to Remember

In this chapter, you learned how to use .NET generics and also expanded your knowledge of lambda expressions. The main items to remember are as follows:

- .NET generics code can use .NET generics, or it can be code that provides types based on .NET generics.

- Performance and type-safe characteristics are primary reasons for using .NET generics.

- You can use .NET generics at the type level or at the method level. Using .NET generics at the type level implies concretizing the type when the type is instantiated. Using .NET generics at the method level implies concretizing the type when the method is called.

- Lambda expressions may be shared state or individual state, depending on how they are declared and manipulated.

- For complex types, you should always implement ToString() as a way of figuring out the state of an instance.

- Lambda expressions act asynchronously. When you use them, remember to not make assumptions of a particular state.

Some Things for You to Do

The following are some exercises that allow you to apply what you've learned so far.

1. The Worksheet(Of BaseType) class always requires you to dimension the fixed-cell array ahead of time. Change this code so that the number of rows and columns can change dynamically. Remember that the focus is on performance, and the fastest approach is a fixed-dimension array.

2. The average calculation knows how many items there are by the row number. Rewrite the average calculation code so that the user of the average code does not need to deal with the complexities of adding more elements, moving the cell calculation, and so on.

3. The methods Calculate() and GetCellState() seem to do the same thing. So, is there a need to have separate methods? Answer the question, and then make any necessary changes to the source code based on your answer.

■ ■ ■

CHAPTER 12

Learning About Application Configuration and Dynamic Loading

All of the examples in the preceding chapters have demonstrated how to use an application with a specific component. You knew which type to instantiate, which interface to use, and which project to reference. In these cases, you, as the developer, are in complete control, and when your application is built, all of the assemblies pop out as a nice, neat package.

But what works for the developer might not necessarily work for others. Let's go back to the lighting system presented in Chapter 8. We created a kernel that was responsible for turning on and off the lights. The implementations of the individual rooms were in a predetermined project with a specific name. This architecture would not work with a third-party library, because the kernel expected a project of a certain name. You might be thinking, "Heck, that's easy to solve—I just delete the old project and rename my project to match the old name." That technique would work, but it would also be an administrator's nightmare. The solution is to tell the program, "For lighting room implementations, look at this project and these types." And to give the program this information, you define some text in a file. A file that tells a program to do some task is called a runtime *configuration file*.

This chapter focuses on two areas: using application configuration files and dynamically loading code. A related topic is how much dynamically executed code should be configuration and how much should be convention.

Convention over Configuration

The question of how to reference and instantiate classes is both philosophical and pragmatic. Consider the architecture shown in Figure 12-1, which is a modular interface and implementation that was presented as an alternative architecture for the lighting system example in Chapter 8. In this figure, each of the boxes represents a single project: a project that contains the interface definitions, a project that contains the implementations, and a project that contains the kernel. The idea of all of these projects is to make it possible to update a single project without needing to update all of them. However, what is not indicated in the picture is the fact that your application must be able to *reference* all three projects. If one of those projects is missing, you have a problem, because your program cannot function.

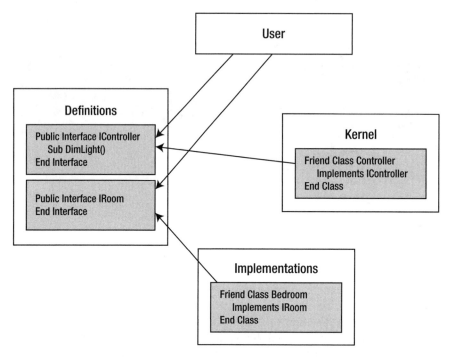

Figure 12-1. *How components can be defined*

The referencing of individual projects is not an issue. The issue is how each project learns about the others. In previous chapters, I said that you should use a factory, because a factory takes away the decision of what implementation to use.

Let's look at this from the perspective of code. Suppose the following interface definition is in a project that contains all interface definitions.

```
Public Interface IMyInterface
End Interface
```

A class that implements the interface is defined in a project called Implementations.

```
Class MyImplementation : Implements IMyInterface
End Class
```

If a class in another project wants to use the functionality of MyImplementation, then this factory is created:

```
Public Module Factory
    Public Function Instantiate() As IMyInterface
        Return New MyImplementation()
    End Function
End Module
```

Because MyImplementation is not declared as Public, the Factory module must be defined in the project Implementations. This implies that the project that uses the functionality has a reference to Implementations.

Using a factory is acceptable and solves the problem of decoupling so that the user of the implementation does not need to know about the implementation. The user does not have to know the name of the implementation, but does need to know in which project the implementation resides. This means when you develop the code, you need to reference the appropriate project while coding. This is called *component architecture*, in that you decouple the interface from the implementation, but you couple the projects.

You want to decouple the components at runtime (when the application runs) to solve the problem illustrated in Chapter 8, where we created a lighting kernel, but did not know the lighting implementations ahead of time. Using configuration, you could have an end user "plug in" lighting implementations that are controlled by the kernel. Developers like to call runtime decoupling a *plug-in* architecture (`http://en.wikipedia.org/wiki/Plugin`). And this is where configuration and convention come into play. "Convention over configuration" is a Ruby on Rails philosophy. The idea is that developers define only the nonconventional parts of their applications.

Decoupling Using a Configuration Architecture

In a runtime configuration scenario, the architecture of Figure 12-1 is not altered; it still has the definitions, implementations, kernel, and user assemblies. What is altered is how the references to each of the pieces are created.

Let's start with a simple situation. You have a question, and you happen to know who would know the answer. You know the person and you know she has a telephone. What you don't know is her telephone number. Translated into programming terms, the telephone acts as an interface to an implementation. The challenge is connecting to the implementation. In the case of the telephone, you can discover the telephone number by using the telephone book.

The telephone book contains the names of individuals at specific addresses and their telephone numbers. Names and addresses are easy to remember; telephone numbers are a bit more complicated. Thus, the telephone book serves the purpose of cross-referencing an easy piece of information with a more complicated piece of information. In programming terms, the cross-referencing is a configuration file that is associated with the .NET application. Once you have cross-referenced the information, you have the location of the project and can then instantiate the cross-referenced type. In programming terms, the configuration file gives you the location and name of the type.

Decoupling Using a Convention Architecture

Configuration files are useful, but they can become too complicated. Some projects have such complicated configuration files that bugs arise due to an improperly configured application.

Convention architecture attempts to simplify complexity by instituting a familiar pattern to the referencing of the type. Consider a telephone number like 1-800-BIG-CARS. The 1 and 800 are easy to remember, as is BIG CARS. This works because of the convention where a digit on the telephone keypad corresponds to three or four letters. So in the case of BIG-CARS, the number is 244-2277.

Conventions are good things as long as you know what they are. For example, if you were not familiar with the telephone system, you would wonder how BIG CARS represents a telephone number. The missing piece of information is the convention of how to convert the letters into the numbers.

What is useful with convention architecture is that you are not limited to what is defined in the configuration file, as there is a general logic. When implementing a convention architecture, you are not discarding configuration, but you are making assumptions for the user and implementation of the code. You will still probably have a configuration file, but the configuration is for specific functionality.

Regardless of whether you use a configuration architecture or a convention architecture, you will dynamically load assemblies, as demonstrated in this chapter.

Setting Up the Dynamic Loading Projects

For this chapter's examples, four projects are defined:

- Definitions: A class library that contains the definition for the interface IDefinition and the class ConfigurationLoader. The class ConfigurationLoader will contain the functionality to dynamically load the assemblies Implementations1 and Implementations2.

- Implementations1: A class library that contains the class Implementation and implements the interface IDefinition. The class Implementation is defined in the namespace Implementations1 and is not declared Public.

- Implementations2: A class library that contains the class Implementation and implements the interface IDefinition. The class Implementation is defined in the namespace Implementations2 and is not declared Public.

- CallRuntimeImplementation: A console application that will be referenced throughout the chapter as the user application.

In the Definitions project, the references are to the standard .NET libraries (System, System.Core, and so on). The unique reference that you need to add is to System.configuration. The System.configuration reference contains the types that you need to read the application configuration file.

Here is the code for IDefinition:

```
Public Interface IDefinition
    Function TranslateWord(ByVal word As String) As String
End Interface
```

The Implementations1 project contains the file Implementation.vb, which is the type Implementation and implements the interface IDefinitions. The implementation of Implementation is as follows (make sure you add a reference to the Definitions project):

```
Imports Definitions
Class Implementation : Implements IDefinition
    Public Function TranslateWord(ByVal word As String) _
      As String Implements IDefinition.TranslateWord
        Return ""
    End Function
End Class
```

The class Implementation has a hard reference to IDefinition, so under the References node in the Implementations1 project is a reference to the Definitions project. Because there is a hard reference to IDefinition, the interface IDefinition is declared as Public, but Implementation is not.

The Implementations2 project has the same implementation and reference to Definitions as Implementations1. What is special about Implementations2 is its use of a strong name, which makes it unique. Thus far, all of your assemblies are not unique. To make them unique, you need to enable signing. You must also enable signing in the Definitions project. The next section describes how to enable signing.

The CallRuntimeImplementation project is the user application and is responsible for calling the functionality in Implementations1 and Implementations2. What you need to consider very carefully in the CallRuntimeImplementation project structure is that in the References node, only the Definitions project is present. It does not contain references to Implementations1 or Implementations2.

It is important to understand that when a project does not have a reference to another project, it does not imply that the functionality cannot be used. To use the functionality of a project that is not referenced, you need to write code that will load the assembly dynamically. With a dynamically loaded assembly, you can do whatever is possible with a hard-linked reference.

Note Remember that assemblies are the results of compiling a project. A code library will produce a DLL file, while an executable project will produce an EXE file.

Signing an Assembly

Signing an assembly is giving the assembly a strong name, which is a unique name. Think of it as follows. My name is Christian Gross, and on this planet we call Earth, there are probably a few dozen people with the name Christian Gross. Our governments distinguish between the various people with my name by way of a passport. A passport is a unique identifier that converts my common name into a strong name. This is exactly what happens when you use strong names with an assembly. A strong name is required when you want to add the assembly to the global assembly cache (GAC). The GAC is where you can place an assembly to make it available for global shared access. You'll learn more about the GAC in the "Loading a Strongly Named Assembly" section later in this chapter.

By default, signing is not used. To enable signing, you need to alter the properties of the project. Follow these steps to enable signing for the Implementations2 project and the Definitions project:

1. Right-click the project in the Solution Explorer and select Properties.

2. Click the Signing tab.

3. Check the Sign the Assembly check box.

4. Select <New...> from the combo box, which pops up a dialog box allowing you to specify the file name.

5. Type in a key file name and a password, and then click OK.

6. Save your project.

Setting the Output Path

The aim of the chapter is to demonstrate two things: configuration files and the dynamic abilities of .NET. Explaining, debugging, and running the configuration source code is simple, because everything is laid out for you in the Visual Basic IDE. You will not run into any problems running the configuration code. However, for the dynamic loading, there is a complication.

As you've seen, the CallRuntimeImplementation project does not have explicit references to Implementations1 and Implementations2. This means that if the code from Implementations1 or Implementations2 is referenced from CallRuntimeImplementations using dynamic techniques, Visual Basic Express will have no clue as to what you are doing. You might argue that there is one Visual Basic Express solution, and Implementations1 and Implementations2 are part of the overall project, but unless an explicit reference is made, Visual Basic Express does not know about this.

However, you can overcome this problem fairly easily by changing where the projects place their compiled output. As a habit, I often make all projects build to a central directory. You can set the output directory in the Compile tab of a project's Properties window, as shown in Figure 12-2.

Figure 12-2. *Setting the build output path to a common path (..\bin\)*

You need to set the Build Output Path field to a common location for all projects. When you do that, a build will result in a directory structure like that shown in Figure 12-3 (in the next section). With all of the files in a common directory, running the dynamic-loading routines becomes trivial.

Defining and Processing a Configuration File

A configuration file is a file that contains information about how a program should behave. Configuration files by themselves do not control how a program behaves. For a configuration file to influence the behavior of a program, the program needs to read and act on the information in the configuration file.

Using a configuration file is not as easy as you may think it is. Yes, it is easy to define a configuration file and read the configuration file. What is difficult is how to define where the configuration file is located.

Suppose you have an application that is installed on the hard disk, and the application must make an assumption about where the configuration file is stored. One assumption could be the root directory of the C: drive. Yet that could be incorrect, because some computers don't have C: as the root drive.

.NET solves this problem in an interesting way: whatever the executing application is called, the configuration file has the same name with a .config extension. Figure 12-3 shows an example, in which the console application is CallRuntimeImplementation.exe. The configuration file is CallRuntimeImplementation.exe.config. A configuration file and the assembly that it relates to are located in the same directory.

Figure 12-3. *A console application and its associated configuration file*

■**Note** Naming the configuration file using a combination of the assembly's application name with the .config extension is an example of a convention architecture.

In this section, you'll see how to write a configuration file and then reference it within an application. This setup will use the configuration file whenever a request for a certain piece of functionality is made and supply the exact location of the assembly.

Creating an XML-Based Configuration File

The configuration file contains Extensible Markup Language (XML). XML is a way of structuring a text file.

Consider the following text structure using spaces.

```
First Element
    Second Element
    Third Element
```

First Element is a parent, and Second Element and Third Element are subelements of the parent. The structuring of the parent and child elements is fragile, to say the least. We need a more robust way of structuring the data, which is where XML comes in. Think of XML as having the ability to define folders and folders within folders.

Let's define the XML that makes up a .NET application configuration file. All .NET application configuration files can be created using Visual Basic Express, as follows:

1. Right-click the CallRuntimeImplementation project and select Add ➤ New Item.

2. Select Text File.

3. Name the file App.config and click Add. The App.config file is created.

It is fine to leave the name as is, because when your .NET application is compiled, the .NET application configuration file will be renamed and placed beside the .NET application.

■**Note** .NET application configuration files apply to.NET assemblies. Thus, if an assembly uses the configuration API, the configuration file applied will be the one associated with the calling application.

Open the new App.config file and add the following XML:

```
<?xml version="1.0" encoding="utf-8" ?>
<configuration>
</configuration>
```

The first line is called an *XML declaration*, and it can specify the encoding that will be used (plus other information, which we won't need to concern ourselves with here). The second and third lines define a *root XML node* (also called an *XML element*). Think of a root XML node as analogous to a root folder where all of the other folders will be stored.

The root node is started with the identifier configuration surrounded by angle brackets. The node is terminated by the same identifier and angle brackets, with the addition of a slash prefix to the identifier. The only place where another XML node can be placed is between the beginning and ending XML nodes. For example, this XML is invalid:

```
<configuration>
<item>
</configuration>
</item>
```

In the example, <item> is started inside the declaration of <configuration>, but its termination, </item>, is outside the declaration of <configuration>.

Adding the Dynamic Loading Configuration Items

After you've added a configuration file, the next step is to add the elements that will be used by the dynamic loader. The idea will be to define some abstract identifier that will be cross-referenced to a type and assembly. Thus, to load `Implementations1.Implementation`, we'll use the identifier `Impl1`, type `Implementations1.Implementation`, and assembly `Implementations1.dll`. Similarly, `Impl2` will cross-reference to the type `Implementations2.Implementation` and the assembly `Implementations2.dll`.

Modify the configuration file as shown here, adding the bolded code.

```
<?xml version="1.0" encoding="utf-8" ?>
<configuration>
  <appSettings>
    <add key="Assemblies"
        value="Impl1,Implementations1.Implementation,Implementations1.dll,
               Impl2,Implementations2.Implementation,Implementations2.dll" />
  </appSettings>

</configuration>
```

The XML node `<appSettings>`, which you could think of as adding the folder `appSettings`, contains XML nodes with the identifier `<add>`. This node defines a section in the configuration file that contains application settings expressed as key/value pairs. Each key/value pair is defined in the XML node using the XML attributes `key` and `value`.

Notice that the XML node `<add>` has a starting element, but not an ending element. This is because the `<add>` node is terminated with an angle bracket prefixed with a slash. This means that the ending element is not necessary.

The configuration file defines a key `Assemblies` and a value that contains a buffer of comma-separated identifiers. The identifiers represent the identifier, type, and assembly of supported dynamically loaded assemblies.

The configuration file is complete, but will not influence the behavior of the application, because source code must be added to the application that reads the configuration file settings, as described in the next section.

■**Note** For the examples in this chapter, use the XML shown in the listings. XML is not difficult to learn, but for now, you'll get by with what I show you here. For more information about XML, visit the MSDN XML Developer Center at `http://msdn2.microsoft.com/en-us/xml/default.aspx`.

Reading a Configuration File

Reading a configuration file is very simple because the .NET Framework comes with an easy-to-use configuration API. For example, to read the value for the key `Assemblies`, use the following code, which would be added to your application when the application first starts, such as in the `Main()` method of a console program.

```
Dim value As String = _
  System.Configuration.ConfigurationManager.AppSettings("Assemblies")
```

ConfigurationManager is a shared class that provides the entry point to reading items from a configuration file.

In this example, a couple assumptions have been made. The first assumption is that you want to read the configuration settings from the application that is currently executing. The second assumption is that you want to read the configuration items stored within the XML node <appSettings>. Based on those two assumptions, the settings are stored in a shared property named AppSettings, which returns an instance of type NameValueCollection. (The way that AppSettings is referenced makes it appear as if AppSettings were an indexer, which it is not.)

When retrieving the buffer of comma-separated identifiers using ConfigurationManager, you need to parse the buffer and then make sense of the information, as described in the next section.

Dynamically Loading an Assembly

In .NET terms, to use the configuration file with a dynamically loaded application, you need to load the assembly, and from the assembly, instantiate the type. You can reference assemblies locally and also reference them from the GAC.

Dynamically Instantiating a Type

The code to dynamically instantiate a type requires parsing the comma-separated buffer into its respective identifiers. To keep things organized, the three pieces of information are stored in a class. This can be called a *data class* because it has only data members.

The data class is a placeholder, needed only by the code used to dynamically load the type. This makes it possible to define the data class as a private class, because a private class implies only the parent class can instantiate it.

With the ConfigurationLoader class defined as the class used to dynamically instantiate other types, the private class is declared as follows (added to the Definitions project):

```
Public Class ConfigurationLoader
    Private _availableTypes As Dictionary(Of String, ConfigurationInfo) = _
        New Dictionary(Of String, ConfigurationInfo)

    Private Class ConfigurationInfo
        Public AssemblyName As String
        Public EasyName As String
        Public TypeName As String
    End Class
End Class
```

ConfigurationInfo contains three data members: AssemblyName, EasyName, and TypeName. The class is prefixed with Private, indicating that nothing external to the ConfigurationLoader class can see the configuration. Had ConfigurationInfo been declared with the Public keyword, the following code would have been legal.

```
Dim cls As ConfigurationLoader.ConfigurationInfo = _
    New ConfigurationLoader.ConfigurationInfo()
```

ConfigurationInfo is used to store the information from the configuration file. The configuration information is cross-referenced using a Dictionary, where the key is the EasyName data member.

To parse the configuration information and create the individual instances of ConfigurationInfo, the following code (part of ConfigurationLoader) is used.

```
Imports System.Configuration

Public Sub Load()
    Dim value As String = ConfigurationManager.AppSettings("assemblies")
    Dim values As String() = value.Split(","c)
    Dim c1 As Integer = 0

    Do While (c1 < values.Length)
        Dim configInfo As New ConfigurationInfo()
        configInfo.EasyName = values(c1)
        configInfo.TypeName = values((c1 + 1))
        configInfo.AssemblyName = values((c1 + 2))
        _availableTypes.Add(values(c1), configInfo)
        c1 = (c1 + 3)
    Loop
End Sub
```

The configuration is read using AppSettings, and then split into an array of string element values. Processing three array elements at a time iterates the array. With every iteration, an instance of ConfigurationInfo is created. Once the buffer has been processed, it is possible to dynamically instantiate a type using the following ConfigurationLoader method.

```
Imports System.Reflection
. . .

    Public Function Instantiate(Of RequestedType)(ByVal identifier As String) _
        As RequestedType
        If Not _availableTypes.ContainsKey(identifier) Then
            Throw New ArgumentException(("identifier (" & identifier & _
                                    ") is not a listed type"))
        End If
        Dim info As ConfigurationInfo = _availableTypes.Item(identifier)
        Dim assemblyName As AssemblyName = _
          AssemblyName.GetAssemblyName(info.AssemblyName)
        Console.WriteLine(("assemblyname(" & assemblyName.ToString() & ")"))
        Return DirectCast( _
          Assembly.Load(assemblyName).CreateInstance(info.TypeName), _
          RequestedType)
    End Function
```

Look at the declaration of the method Instantiate(), and you will see that it is a .NET generics method (discussed in Chapter 11). The idea is to instantiate a type and perform an automatic cast to the request type. It avoids needing to define Instantiate() using the Object type. The parameter identifier is a string that is used to search the Dictionary data member _availableTypes. If the identifier exists in _availableTypes, the ConfigurationInfo instance is retrieved and used to instantiate the type. If the identifier does not exist, an exception is thrown.

The bolded code is the special code because it is unlike what you have encountered thus far in the book. Built into .NET is the ability to dynamically execute code, as illustrated here. The first bolded line makes the reflection ability available, and the second is used to load the assembly. So, for example, if the parameter identifier equaled Impl1 (remember, this is one of the keys in the configuration file <appSettings> element), the first bolded line would reference and dynamically load the assembly Implementations1.dll. However, and here is the catch, the assembly can be loaded dynamically only if Implementations1.dll exists in the local directory or the GAC. As an alternative, you could specify the entire path in the definition of the assembly. The downside to this strategy is that your assembly must always be located at the same place on different machines.

When the code assigns the variable assemblyName, it is to a reference of a loaded .NET assembly. The assembly will be parsed, and from there, it is possible to instantiate a type. The second bolded line calls the method CreateInstance(), with the name of the type that you want to instantiate, including the namespace. So, for example, if Implementations1.dll has been loaded, you could instantiate the type Implementations1.Implementation. The instantiation will work even though Implementations1.Implementation is a private class, because you are using dynamic programming principles.

However, being able to instantiate the type does not imply being able to use the type. To be able to use the instantiated type, you need to be able to cast to a type that has been declared publicly.

We will continue the Implementations1.Implementation example and figure out how to instantiate and manipulate the instantiated object. But before we get to that code, we need to talk about an additional programming feature: singletons.

Using Singletons

The class ConfigurationManager is a shared class in .NET terms, which means that you cannot instantiate the class. In Visual Basic-speak, a shared class is a module, and a shared method is a method marked Shared. A module, shared methods, and shared data members result in a single-instance class. Another way to get the same effect is to create a *singleton*. A singleton behaves like a shared class, except that the class is instantiated. An advantage of using the singleton approach is that you can have multiple singletons of the same type, whereas with the shared class, there can be only a single shared class.

Consider that locks have keys, and sometimes a lock has a single key. Think of the single key as a shared class. If that key is to open a vault, you will most likely want only one person to have a key. But what if the key is to your house door? You would probably want multiple copies, but you will want to control who has those keys. So, maybe you will have a single house key, or maybe you will have multiple house keys, but you will always be in control. The house key example is analogous to the use of a singleton. You could argue that a singleton could just as well be used to open a vault, since you can create a single key. But the problem with a singleton is that using properly written source code, you could instantiate a second or third instance of the singleton. If you use a shared class, then source code cannot instantiate a second instance, thus enforcing a certain programming style.

Let's define the class ConfigurationLoader as a singleton, which implies two things:

- The creation of a property called Instance that references a single instance of ConfigurationLoader.

- The constructor of ConfigurationLoader as private, implying that only ConfigurationLoader can instantiate an instance of ConfigurationLoader. This ensures that ConfigurationLoader has similar behavior to a shared class in that the consumer cannot instantiate an instance of the type.

The following is the singleton code for ConfigurationLoader (placed in the Definitions assembly).

```
Public Class ConfigurationLoader
    Public Shared ReadOnly Property Instance() As ConfigurationLoader
        Get
            Return ConfigurationLoader._instance
        End Get
    End Property

    Private Sub New()
        _availableTypes = New Dictionary(Of String, ConfigurationInfo)()
    End Sub

    Private Shared _instance As ConfigurationLoader

    Shared Sub New()
        _instance = New ConfigurationLoader()
    End Sub

    . . .
```

The singleton property Instance is declared as Shared, allowing a reference of ConfigurationLoader.Instance. The implementation of the shared property must reference a shared data member, which is the data member _instance in this example. The data member _instance is instantiated by the shared constructor Shared New(). The instance constructor will instantiate the Dictionary _availableTypes.

■**Note** The shared constructor is called before the instance constructor and therefore before any client code has a chance to access members of the class.

Using the Instantiated Type

Now that we've covered the singleton aspect, we need to get back to the original problem of writing the code to instantiate a type dynamically. The following code is used to instantiate Impl1 in the Main() method of CallRuntimeImplementation's principal module.

```
ConfigurationLoader.Instance.Load()
Dim definition as IDefinition = _
  ConfigurationLoader.Instance.Instantiate(Of IDefinition)("Impl1")
Console.WriteLine(definition.TranslateWord("hello"))
```

■**Note** You might get errors running the code. If you do, it is because the assemblies are not in the same path and the dynamic loading methods cannot find the assemblies. Solve this by copying all of the assemblies into a single directory and running the code.

The first line is used to retrieve the assembly and type information from the configuration file. The second line is used to instantiate Impl1 and then cast Implementations1. Implementation to type IDefinition. The cast will work because the IDefinition interface has been implemented by Implementations1.Implementation. The assigned variable definition will reference a valid object instance that implements IDefinition and the method TranslateWord().

At this point, we need to step back and reflect on what has occurred. We have defined within a configuration file the location of a type. Some source code in the application read the configuration file at runtime and stored the available types. The calling code knew about only the abstract type made available under the label Impl1 and knew it implemented the interface IDefinition. Then, using some .NET magic involving dynamic techniques, the type's assembly is loaded and instantiated. This process is unique because an administrator has the ability to update where and what type should be instantiated and called, without needing to recompile or update the infrastructure. That flexibility makes it much simpler for you to update functionality without having to update the caller of the functionality.

■**Note** The ability to dynamically update the functionality is of benefit to the administrator of the application. There is minimal benefit to the developer, because the developer has already converted the architecture to use components. In general, developers consider this approach to components as building a plug-in architecture.

Enhancing the Configuration File

The configuration file is a bit of a clumsy definition because all of the available types are stored in a single key/value pair. It would be preferable to be able to define custom items in the configuration file, as follows:

```
<loader easyname="Impl1"
        typename="Implementations1.Implementation"
        assemblyname="Implementations1.dll" />
```

This approach is preferable because it is easier to read and understand, thus reducing the chances that you will have an error. Additionally, because the various identifiers are broken up, you don't need to build a lengthy single-line string.

■**Note** For simplicity, we will have only a single dynamic type, represented by the `<loader>` XML element. In a complete solution, you would use the same approach with different interfaces and types.

If you were to add the sample XML into the configuration file and run the .NET application, you would get a configuration initialization failure. That's because the XML node `<loader>` is not a standard configuration item and thus needs custom parsing. And when you want custom parsing, you need to tell the .NET configuration infrastructure what code to execute. The following is the complete .NET configuration file with custom processing tags.

```
<?xml version="1.0" encoding="utf-8" ?>
<configuration>
  <configSections>
    <section name="loader" type="Definitions.LoaderSection,Definitions" />
  </configSections>
  <appSettings>
    <add key="Assemblies"
        value="Impl1,Implementations1.Implementation,Implementations1.dll,
               Impl2,Implementations2.Implementation,Implementations2.dll" />
  </appSettings>
  <loader easyname="Impl1"
        typename="Implementations1.Implementation"
        assemblyname="Implementations1.dll" />

</configuration>
```

The bolded section represents a new part of the configuration file that could be called "configuring the configuration." Any XML node that is within the `<configSections>` section is used to customize the configuration-parsing infrastructure. In the example, the XML node `<section>` has two attributes that refer to what the configuration infrastructure should do when it encounters a specific XML node. The attribute `name` specifies the name of the XML node, and the attribute `type` references a type (`Definitions.LoaderSection`) and assembly (`Definitions`) that will process the XML node.

Step back and think about what is happening here. The XML node `<section>` is used to configure the configuration processor using dynamically loaded types. This demonstrates that the process of dynamically loading and executing pieces of code is not rocket science, but a daily part of developing components in .NET.

Marshaling the Configuration File Data

When you want to use a custom node in a configuration file, you need to implement a class that subclasses `System.Configuration.ConfigurationSection`. The purpose of the custom class is to process and structure the data in the configuration file into something that the application can manipulate. In other words, we are marshaling the data from the configuration file to the .NET environment. Here's the start of our class, which belongs in the `Definitions` assembly:

```
Public Class LoaderSection
    Inherits ConfigurationSection
```

The .NET infrastructure helps you implement the marshaling routines by providing class types that allow you to explicitly associate an XML attribute or keyword with some variable. For example, suppose you want to cross-reference the XML attribute easyname with a .NET type. To do so, first define the nature and type of the property using the type ConfigurationProperty (this code goes in the LoaderSection class):

```
Dim _propEasyName As ConfigurationProperty = _
  New ConfigurationProperty("easyname", GetType(String), Nothing, _
                            ConfigurationPropertyOptions.IsRequired)
```

This example uses the ConfigurationProperty constructor that has four parameters:

- "easyname": Identifies the XML attribute identifier that will be used.

- GetType(String): Identifies the type of the attribute, which could also include Double and Integer to indicate a number.

- Nothing: Identifies the default value of the attribute if the attribute is not present in the XML configuration file.

- ConfigurationPropertyOptions.IsRequired: Identifies some characteristics of the attribute; in the case of this example, the attribute is required.

■Note There are multiple constructors for ConfigurationProperty. For more information, check out the MSDN documentation (http://msdn2.microsoft.com/en-us/library/system.configuration. configurationproperty.configurationproperty.aspx).

Once you have defined a property, you need to cross-reference it with a property and the base class ConfigurationSection (again, this code goes in the LoaderSection class):

```
<ConfigurationProperty("easyname", IsRequired := True)> _
Public ReadOnly Property EasyName() As String
    Get
        Return CStr(MyBase.Item(_propEasyName))
    End Get
End Property
```

Whenever you reference the property EasyName, the attributes associated with the property provide a cross-reference with the configuration file. Whenever the property is called, the base indexer with data member that references ConfigurationProperty is called and marshals the data from the configuration file to the .NET type.

The complete implementation used to process the XML node <loader> is as follows (added to the Definitions assembly):

```vbnet
Imports System.Configuration

Public Class LoaderSection
    Inherits ConfigurationSection

    Private Shared _propAssemblyName As ConfigurationProperty = _
      New ConfigurationProperty("assemblyname", GetType(String), Nothing, _
                          ConfigurationPropertyOptions.IsRequired)
    Private Shared _propEasyName As ConfigurationProperty = _
      New ConfigurationProperty("easyname", GetType(String), Nothing, _
                          ConfigurationPropertyOptions.IsRequired)
    Private Shared _properties As ConfigurationPropertyCollection = _
      New ConfigurationPropertyCollection()
    Private Shared _propTypeName As ConfigurationProperty = _
      New ConfigurationProperty("typename", GetType(String), Nothing, _
                          ConfigurationPropertyOptions.IsRequired)

    Shared Sub New()
        _properties.Add(_propAssemblyName)
        _properties.Add(_propEasyName)
        _properties.Add(_propTypeName)
    End Sub

    <ConfigurationProperty("assemblyname", IsRequired:=True)> _
    Public ReadOnly Property AssemblyName() As String
        Get
            Return CStr(MyBase.Item(_propAssemblyName))
        End Get
    End Property

    <ConfigurationProperty("easyname", IsRequired:=True)> _
    Public ReadOnly Property EasyName() As String
        Get
            Return CStr(MyBase.Item(_propEasyName))
        End Get
    End Property

    <ConfigurationProperty("typename", IsRequired:=True)> _
    Public ReadOnly Property TypeName() As String
        Get
            Return CStr(MyBase.Item(_propTypeName))
        End Get
    End Property
End Class
```

The LoaderSection class does two jobs: it tells the underlying configuration infrastructure what LoaderSection is interested in, and it provides an easy-to-use API to the configuration data. The first job is nice to have done, but the second is absolutely essential.

To understand what happens, let's see an example of retrieving the values from a configuration file.

Reading the Enhanced Configuration File

As you've seen, the <configSections> element declares a custom XML node that, when encountered, instantiates a specific type—LoaderSection is instantiated in this example.

The values are retrieved from the custom configuration as follows:

- The configuration infrastructure reads the various attributes, such as <ConfigurationProperty("easyname", IsRequired:=True)>.

- The configuration infrastructure does a cross-reference of which attributes exist and if they are required. Think of this step as the bookkeeping of the custom configuration information.

- The configuration infrastructure waits for the application code to call the properties EasyName, TypeName, or AssemblyName. In the implementation of the individual properties, the MyBase indexer (such as MyBase.Item(_propTypeName) from LoaderSection.TypeName) is referenced, and the value of the configuration item is retrieved using the property descriptors declared as shared members.

We can use the following code to read the custom configuration item (added to the Definitions assembly). This code is an example of replacing the previously declared Load() functionality.

```
Public Sub Load()
    Dim loader As LoaderSection = _
      CType(ConfigurationManager.GetSection("loader"), LoaderSection)
    If loader IsNot Nothing Then
        Dim configInfo As ConfigurationInfo = _
          New ConfigurationInfo() With { _
                            .EasyName = loader.EasyName, _
                            .TypeName = loader.TypeName, _
                            .AssemblyName = loader.AssemblyName}

        _availableTypes.Add(loader.EasyName, configInfo)

    End If
End Sub
```

The only major difference between this code and the previous Load() code is the ConfigurationManager reference. In the previous Load() implementation, it was assumed that all configuration settings were stored in the <appSettings> section. This time, we retrieve the <loader> section, which is defined to be the type LoaderSection. We still create all available types using the _availableTypes dictionary collection, but the parsing and breaking apart of the various buffers are not necessary.

■**Note** Writing your own configuration section is not that difficult, but it is tedious. It is tedious because you need to explicitly tell the configuration infrastructure what every item means and how you will use it. There is no simple way to get around this, because the configuration infrastructure needs to know which configuration items should be processed and how they should be processed. Thus, to implement a configuration section with multiple items, you will need to use more pieces of the predefined configuration infrastructure in the same manner as illustrated by this simple example. See the .NET configuration infrastructure documentation, at `http://support.microsoft.com/kb/313405/EN-US/`, for more information.

Loading a Strongly Named Assembly

In the previous section, the example demonstrated the dynamic loading technique in which you explicitly define where the assembly is and then instantiate a type in that assembly. Another approach to instantiating an assembly involves using the formal declaration of a type.

In .NET, there is an easy way to reference an assembly and a more difficult way to reference an assembly. This is analogous to the easy way to identify a person and the more complicated way. The easy way to identify me is to use my name, Christian Gross, and that works to a degree. The problem is that I'm not the only Christian Gross on this planet. The precise way to find me is to look at my passport. The passport approach works, but it has a long, ugly number that is hard to remember.

The assembly name `Implementations2.dll` is a simple assembly identifier like Christian Gross. The following is the precise .NET identifier of the assembly.

```
Implementations2, Version=1.0.0.0, Culture=neutral, PublicKeyToken=6bc4c8c27c08ba48
```

The identifier is quite a mouthful, but it says everything you need to know. This specifies the name as `Implementations2`, the version number, the culture (combination of language and country), and a fixed-signed identifier. When culture is defined as `neutral`, it means that only the language is taken into account and not the country-specific bit. For example, if the culture is `en-CA`, with `neutral`, the `CA` bit will be ignored, which means a neutral form of English, known in this context as international English, will be used.

Using all of these attributes, you can uniquely identify an assembly. This lets you load a specific version of the assembly, allowing multiple similar assemblies to be loaded simultaneously. This specific referencing lets you to use components according to version and language.

The extra information is specified in the source code file `AssemblyInfo.vb`. If you want to edit this file, select the project and then choose Project ➤ Show All Files. You'll find the `AssemblyInfo.vb` file under the My Project node in the Solution Explorer. Following is the complete implementation for `Implementations2.dll`.

```
Imports System
Imports System.Reflection
Imports System.Runtime.InteropServices

' General Information about an assembly is controlled through the following
' set of attributes. Change these attribute values to modify the information
' associated with an assembly.
```

```vbnet
' Review the values of the assembly attributes

<Assembly: AssemblyTitle("Implementations2")>
<Assembly: AssemblyDescription("")>
<Assembly: AssemblyCompany("devspace.com")>
<Assembly: AssemblyProduct("Implementations2")>
<Assembly: AssemblyCopyright("Copyright © devspace.com 2008")>
<Assembly: AssemblyTrademark("")>

<Assembly: ComVisible(False)>

'The following GUID is for the ID of the typelib if this project is exposed to COM
<Assembly: Guid("be93515c-5ab6-4f17-8fcb-3a9b1578e8bd")>

' Version information for an assembly consists of the following four values:
'
'       Major Version
'       Minor Version
'       Build Number
'       Revision
'
' You can specify all the values or you can default the Build and Revision Numbers
' by using the '*' as shown here:
' <Assembly: AssemblyVersion("1.0.*")>

<Assembly: AssemblyVersion("1.0.0.0")>
<Assembly: AssemblyFileVersion("1.0.0.0")>
```

Notice that all of the assembly descriptors are declared as .NET attributes. The bolded attributes reference the version of the assembly. By adjusting these attributes, you can tweak which assembly is loaded, as explained in more detail in the upcoming "Versioning Assemblies" section.

To load a specific assembly, you need to create an assembly name, like this:

```vbnet
Dim assemblyName As AssemblyName = New AssemblyName(value)
Dim assembly As Assembly = Assembly.Load(assemblyName)
Dim obj As Object = assembly.CreateInstance(info.TypeName)
```

The variable value contains the precise .NET identifier of the assembly and is passed as a constructor parameter to AssemblyName. The resulting AssemblyName instance is passed to the method Assembly.Load(), which loads the assembly. The instantiation of the type follows the same sequence as previously outlined.

Note that there is no indication of where the assembly is located. The default locations that are probed are the local working directory of the executing process and the GAC.

■**Note** For more details about assembly loading, see *Pro VB 2008 and the .NET 3.5 Platform, Third Edition* by Andrew Troelsen (Apress, 2008).

Relocating a Strongly Named Assembly to the GAC

Besides having the ability to tweak which assembly is loaded, another reason to use the precise assembly name is to have the ability to load an assembly from the GAC. The GAC is a place where assemblies can be placed to have global shared access. Think of the GAC as the `Windows\System32` directory of the .NET environment. The precise location for the GAC is `c:\windows\assembly`.

Even though the GAC is just another directory, you should not just delete and add assemblies there, as you would with any other directory. To delete a file from the GAC, use the context-sensitive Uninstall menu item (in Windows Explorer right-click the assembly you want to uninstall and select Uninstall).

To add an assembly to the GAC, use the utility `gacutil`, which is distributed with the .NET SDK (not with Visual Basic Express). You can locate it at `C:\Program Files\Microsoft SDKs\Windows\v6.0\Bin` or similar. Add this directory to your path so that you can run `gacutil` anywhere.

The following command lines demonstrate how to add the `Definitions` and `Implementations2` assemblies to the GAC (assuming the files `implementations2.dll` and `definitions.dll` reside in the current directory).

```
gacutil /I definitions.dll
gacutil /I implementations2.dll
```

Remember to add `Definitions`, because `Implementations2` depends on `Definitions`. Failing to add `Definitions` will generate `gacutil` errors.

ORGANIZING DYNAMIC CODE

If you are going to place files in the GAC, don't use the techniques demonstrated in this book when doing a production release. The techniques discussed in this book are meant for developers, and only developers. The techniques are shortcuts that assume you know what the dependencies are and are aware of what you are doing. For distribution purposes, use the Microsoft Windows Installer application to install files into the GAC.

When writing dynamic code, the idea is to separate and completely compartmentalize the development of the component and the caller of the component. Thus, you should not develop both pieces in the same project. Create separate projects and have them working with test routines. Then, at runtime, combine the functionalities, and everything should work (that is, if you properly tested your code).

Using Version Numbers

Version numbers are a way of being able to control the features and robustness of an application. In the packaged software market, the concept of the version number has nearly disappeared. For example, consider Microsoft's operating system versions: Windows 95, Window 98, Windows XP, Windows 2000, Windows Vista, and so on.

In open source software, version numbers are used extensively and are considered very important. Yes, the version numbers resemble a lottery ticket, but they do follow a convention. Understanding the convention makes it easier to select open source packages. And more important, applying this versioning strategy makes it simpler to understand your assemblies.

Understanding Version Numbers

Let's say you want to download the open source program Capivara (a Java file manager and synchronization program). You see the version number 0.8.3. The version number contains three parts:

Major number: The major number is 0 in the example. If the software has not reached the number 1, the version is considered a beta. But often, a beta identifier does not mean the version is unusable. Changing the major version number indicates a major change of functionality. This means what worked in version 1 may not work with version 2. An example is the Apache HTTPD server project, where the 1.*x* and 2.*x* series are two different implementations.

Minor number: The minor number is 8 in the example. It is used to define minor functionality changes in a piece of software. Changing the minor number (such as 7 to 8) indicates new features, but old functionality is supported. A change may include bug fixes or patches.

Patch number: The path number is 3 in the example. It is used to define a patched version of the software that has bug fixes or other changes. The changes do not include features, and the functionality does not change.

When you attempt to download an open source package, you are typically confronted with multiple versions. For example, you might see the version numbers 4.23 and 4.29 (beta). Because most people want the latest and greatest, they might be tempted to download 4.29. But remember that open source projects make multiple versions available. In the example, you should download version 4.23, because 4.29 is a beta that may or may not work. Version 4.23 is considered stable and therefore usable.

The open source community will often use the following terminology when releasing software.

- *Stable*: A version that can be used in a production environment and should not crash.

- *Unstable*: A version that should not be used in production. It will probably work, but have some crashes.

- *Nightly*: A version with all bets off, meaning that the version may or may not work. The reason for using a nightly build is to monitor progress and check specific issues. Such a version is not intended for consumer consumption; it is intended solely for developers.

- *Alpha*: A version that demonstrates the concepts that will make up a future version of the software. However, in alpha versions, what was available one day might be gone the next day.

Versioning Assemblies

.NET assembly version numbers are different from those used for open source packages. The following is an example of versioning an assembly.

```
<Assembly: AssemblyVersion("1.1.0.0")>
<Assembly: AssemblyFileVersion("1.1.0.0")>
```

The attributes AssemblyVersion and AssemblyFileVersion can be added anywhere in the assembly or application. In Visual Basic Express, most likely the attributes are added to the file AssemblyInfo.vb.

The versions of the file have four significant parts. From left to right, these are major version, minor version, build number, and revision. The build number can represent a daily build number, but this is not required. The revision identifier can represent a random number, but this is not required either. For my assemblies, I use a revision number of 0, and consider the build number as a patch number.

Visual Basic Express has a built-in mechanism that automatically updates the build and revision numbers. Here, the asterisk represents the auto-increment:

```
<Assembly: AssemblyVersion("1.0.*")>
```

Alternatively, you can use a versioning tool, or you can increment the numbers manually. The gacutil tool can be executed multiple times with multiple versions, as shown in Figure 12-4.

■Note For more information about using versioning tools, see this blog entry about auto-incrementing assembly versions: http://weblogs.asp.net/bradleyb/archive/2005/12/02/432150.aspx.

Figure 12-4. *An assembly added three times to the GAC with three different versions*

In Figure 12-4, the assembly VersioningAssembly has been added three times to the GAC with three different versions (1.0.0.0, 1.1.0.0, and 1.2.0.0). With the GAC in this state, an application or another assembly has the option to reference three different versions of the same assembly.

For an application or assembly to use another assembly, you create a reference. When the application or assembly is compiled, a specific version number of the assembly is referenced. For example, if a reference to the version 1.1.0.0 of VersioningAssembly is defined, then version 1.1.0.0 of the assembly is loaded.

Adding an Assembly Redirection to a Configuration File

Let's say an application or assembly needs to use a new version of the VersioningAssembly assembly. To make the application or assembly aware of the new assembly, you update the application or assembly configuration file that references the old assembly. The configuration file update includes an assembly redirection. Essentially, what the redirection says is that if a certain version of an assembly is requested, the new version should be loaded. The following is an example of an assembly redirection.

```xml
<?xml version="1.0"?>
<configuration>
  <runtime>
    <assemblyBinding
        xmlns="urn:schemas-microsoft-com:asm.v1">
      <dependentAssembly>
        <assemblyIdentity name="VersioningAssembly"
          publicKeyToken="bd42f9cb12b40d1b"
          culture="neutral" />
        <bindingRedirect oldVersion="1.1.0.0"
          newVersion="1.2.0.0"/>
      </dependentAssembly>
    </assemblyBinding>
  </runtime>
</configuration>
```

This configuration file includes an assemblyBinding XML element that defines a collection of assemblies that will be affected. The collection of assemblies is embedded within the dependentAssembly element. Within the dependentAssembly element are two child elements: assemblyIdentity and bindingRedirect. The assemblyIdentity element is used to identity the assembly for which a reference will be redirected.

The bindingRedirect element contains two attributes: oldVersion and newVersion. The oldVersion attribute identifies the version of the old assembly in the calling assembly or application. If the specified version of the old assembly is found, the newVersion attribute is used to identify which assembly version should be used instead. In the example, the old version is 1.1.0.0, and the new version is 1.2.0.0. The new version has an incremented minor number, indicating a new version of an assembly. However, the binding redirection does not care whether the newVersion attribute references a newer version or an older version. The version identifiers identified by the attributes newVersion and oldVersion are just that: identifiers.

Implementing a Shared Typed Convention-Based Architecture

There has been quite a bit of talk in the software community about convention over configuration. Most of this talk began in earnest with the development of Ruby on Rails (http://www.rubyonrails.org/). Ruby on Rails (Rails for short) is a tool that allows people to very quickly create web sites that provide useful functionality.

Many attribute the success of Rails to its use of convention over configuration. Some say it is the Ruby language. Others say it is because Rails is a professional product. I believe it's a combination of factors, but the convention over configuration angle does play an important role.

Let's go back to the problem of loading code dynamically, or for that matter, executing code dynamically. How much do you expect the programmer to know, and how much do you expect the programmer to guess? Consider this code:

```
Interface IDefinition
End Interface

Sub DoIt(ByVal def As IDefinition)
    ' Do Something with def
End Sub
```

In the code, you can see an interface IDefinition and a method DoIt(), with a parameter of type IDefinition. This creates a contract where to call DoIt(), you need to pass an instance of type IDefinition.

Is it correct to assume that the dynamic loading of a type can fulfill the contract of DoIt()? Can you assume that the type even supports IDefinition?

What convention over configuration attempts to do is create pockets of self-contained functionality that can take care of themselves. That self-contained functionality may require configuration file settings, and it may require other assemblies. But what it does not require is a directive that includes source code that explicitly states what to do when.

Consider a workplace scenario. Instead of having a manager tell the workers what to do at every step, a certain amount of peer-to-peer intelligence and self-reliance are assumed. The self-reliance is both good and bad. It is good in that there are fewer moving parts, but bad in that the peers might be doing something that they should not.

The following code shows an example of convention.

```
Interface ICommand
    Sub Run()
End Interface
. . .
ConfigurationLoader.Instance.Load()
Dim definition As IDefinition = _
  ConfigurationLoader.Instance.Instantiate(Of ICommand)("Impl1")
definition.Run()
```

The code runs some other code via the Run() method and does not have any return values or parameters. The code doing the executing is hoping that everything will work out, because it cannot check a return value. And that is the gist of convention over configuration—the calling code hopes everything will work out.

For the most part, convention works out quite nicely because it is easier to extend and maintain a convention-based system, since there are fewer moving parts. For any complex system, the fewer moving parts the better. The downside is that the administrator needs to understand what the moving parts are.

People have a tendency to make everything configurable and leave nothing to the computer program. Whether or not something works depends on how the configuration is written. In a convention architecture, the called functionality will make decisions about what it deems appropriate.

Here is an example of configuration:

```
<ConfigurationProperty("typename", IsRequired:=True)> _
Public Property TypeName() As String
    Get
        Return CStr(MyBase.Item(_propTypeName))
    End Get
End Property
```

The code should look familiar, as it reassembles the configuration code you saw earlier. But this code is overconstrained and requires too many moving parts. It would be great to simplify it to the following code (which does not compile because you cannot change the code base of the .NET library).

```
<ConfigurationProperty()> _
Public ReadOnly Property TypeName() As String
    Get
        Return CStr(MyBase.Item(_propTypeName))
    End Get
End Property
```

The difference between the two code pieces is the missing parameters in the .NET attributes. The parameters are not necessary because they are already defined by the data member _propTypeName, and you can use the identifier of the property as that extra piece of information. So the property identifier TypeName could be used as an identifier for an XML attribute.

Some may argue that by having a cross-reference between the property identifier and configuration identifier, you are creating a hard-coded dependency. That's a valid argument. But is the code's assumption a common-sense assumption? Is it an extreme proposition to say that your property identifier is the name of your XML attribute? The answer is that it is not an extreme proposition, and the Ruby on Rails creators said the same when creating their own architecture.

Let's now consider the ability to indicate whether a configuration item is required. By specifying whether or not an attribute is required, you can avoid an exception at a later point. However, think about the bigger context. The .NET IsRequired attribute is processed when the program is started. The validity of the configuration file is not processed at compile time, and thus the only thing that IsRequired does is generate an exception earlier. Maybe you want to avoid any runtime errors that could bring down a program during processing. I don't think it is a big advantage, but I am sure others will think it is, and thus using the IsRequired property is a judgment call.

■**Note** The aim of convention-based architecture is to make as many assumptions as possible, without sacrificing the bigger goal of the application. A good convention-based architecture is not easy to create because it requires completely understanding the needs of the developers and those who run the application. My personal rule of thumb is to solve the problem first, and then decide what should be configured and what should be a convention.

Dynamically Loading Base Class or Interface Types

This chapter demonstrated two categories of code that were dynamically loaded. The first category was a type that implemented an interface (Implementation and IDefinition). The second type was a class that subclassed another class (LoaderSection, ConfigurationSection). Each approach has its advantages and disadvantages, but there is a single rule that you can use.

Whether to use an interface or class depends on how much responsibility you want to delegate to the implementation. In the configuration processing example, the .NET infrastructure specifically indicated that the only responsibility of the dynamically loaded class is to indicate which identifiers should be processed. How the value of the identifiers are extracted and converted into .NET types is the responsibility of the base class.

When you instantiate a type and use an interface, you are delegating complete control to the dynamically instantiated type. The calling code is explicitly saying, "Here is your contract. How you deal with it is your responsibility. Just make sure to implement the contract properly." By delegating all the responsibility, you are, in a sense, asking for trouble, because developers might implement a contract incorrectly.

The Important Stuff to Remember

In this chapter, you learned about configuring an application and dynamically loading code that is executed. The main items to remember are as follows:

- A .NET application configuration file works only because there is code in the application that uses the specified items in the configuration file.

- Applications have .NET application configuration files where the name of the file is the name of the executing application appended with a .config.

- A .NET application configuration file is a specially formatted XML file.

- A .NET application configuration file applies to a specific assembly loaded by the application.

- The default scenario for a .NET application configuration file is to store the settings as key/value pairs in the <appSettings> section.

- You can enhance the .NET application configuration file, but that implies implementing types that specifically outline which XML nodes and attributes are to be present in the XML.

- When processing data, you sometimes need a type (such as `ConfigurationInfo`) that is used to store information in a structured manner for a specific reason.

- .NET has plenty of functionality that allows a developer to dynamically execute code.

- One way of dynamically executing code is to load an assembly, instantiate a type, and then cast the instance to a specific known type.

- You can instantiate private types declared in an assembly.

- You can use the GAC to store assemblies that will be shared by multiple applications.

- Use the GAC only if you must. If you do use the GAC, you need to create strongly named assemblies using signing.

- Regardless of how an assembly is versioned, a version number should exist and be used.

- In convention-based coding, your code makes assumptions about its behavior. Convention-based coding is more compact, but because assumptions are made, the code is less flexible. However, do not confuse flexibility with being the best way to do something. You should have flexible code when you need it, not just because it can be written that way.

Some Things for You to Do

The following are some exercises for you to do to apply what you've learned in this chapter.

1. Rewrite the configuration code so that the configuration file specifies a directory where all assemblies in that directory are loaded.

2. Having read all of the assemblies with the rewritten configuration, call a predefined type that will tell the caller which types are available and their appropriate types.

3. Modify `ConfigurationLoader` so that it uses the new configuration architecture to instantiate types.

■■■

CHAPTER 13

Learning About Multithreading

Your brain allows you to multitask. For example, you can prepare dinner while talking on the telephone. However, this multitasking has limits, and you can do only two or three things simultaneously. But suppose you could put down the work, start another piece of work, then put that down, and then switch to the original work. How many tasks could you handle at the same time? Probably a few hundred, because what you are doing is *serializing* the multitasking.

Now suppose you and another person are preparing dinner in the kitchen, but you are not communicating with each other. What is the likelihood that you will run into the other person? Probably pretty high. What I am trying to get across here is the difference between multitasking with a single brain and multitasking with multiple brains. Multitasking always has a cost, which is orchestration. And sometimes doing more multitasking is not going to speed things up. There is a limit to how many brains are required to run an efficient kitchen.

The focus of this chapter is how to write code that is capable of multitasking. The operating system multitasks, by default, but whether or not your program multitasks depends on how you write your code. For example, suppose the lighting controller introduced in Chapter 8 had to control 3,000 rooms? To be able to process such a large number of rooms, you would use the same code, except run it in parallel. And therein lies the problem of code that needs to multitask. It's more difficult to make code run efficiently in parallel. A common problem in multitasking applications is the dreaded deadlock. A deadlock occurs when two tasks need data from each other to continue, which means neither can continue.

Running code in parallel requires coding discipline, as you will learn in this chapter. We will use only a single project, named JugglingTasks, which is a console application that implements the techniques demonstrated in this chapter.

Understanding Multitasking

One of the biggest jumps in computing history was when the computer went from a machine that carried out a single task to a multitasking machine. The old Commodore 64 and VIC-20 were single-tasking machines. You started the computer, and then the computer waited for you to do something. If you decided to make the computer run a loop saying "hello" millions of times, that is all the computer would do. The computer could not do one thing and then do something else while waiting for an answer from the executing task. How could anyone get anything done? (On the other hand, you could argue that people might be more productive if they could work in only a single program, and not also check their e-mail, look at the latest blog entry from their favorite author, and so on.)

Things changed quite dramatically when computers could multitask. Server computers running operating systems like Unix were multitasking from day one. Operating systems like Windows were not 100% preemptive multitasking until Windows NT and Windows 95. Notice that I used the term *preemptive*, which makes a big difference.

Plain-vanilla multitasking is multitasking where individual tasks cooperate and allocate resources as a collective. It is essentially a dead-end idea, and the best example of how it worked is Windows 3.0 and Windows 3.1 (but these were full of hacks). Now let's see what preemptive multitasking means.

Preemptive Multitasking

Preemptive multitasking is when the operating system controls which application does what and when. Realize that you can run an application because applications are treated as components. You don't believe me? Create a console application and rename the method Main() to Mains(). See what happens. The reality is that the Main() method, as it is declared, is an API used by the operating system to run your component, which masquerades as a program.

So we have this program called the operating system that runs components called programs. The next question is how can multiple programs run at the same time? The answer is that the operating system program is no ordinary program. It is the foundation upon which applications can be launched and managed. The operating system hooks into special features of the microprocessor that allow the operating system to time slice the individual programs. Because your .NET programs are components, they will never need to access the microprocessor directly.

Time Slicing

Time slicing is when an operating system can dictate for how much time a program is allowed to execute. Between the times of execution, the program is in a state of deep freeze and does nothing. You, as a user, are not aware of the time slices, because a time slice operates on the order of microseconds. Because time slicing is so fast, you think your program is running continuously. To see the time slicing in action, open the Windows Task Manager and select the Processes tab.

Look closely at the Task Manager window shown in Figure 13-1, and you'll see that explorer.exe has 6% of the CPU. You can say that the explorer.exe application is using the appropriate amount of time slices that equals 6% of the CPU time. How the CPU slices the 6% is a detail of the operating system.

Say you have a program that runs two tasks: task 1 and task 2. The microprocessor is a single core, and thus when running two separate tasks, there will be two time slices, as illustrated in Figure 13-2. In the figure, the entire processing cycle is represented as a pie, and each time slice is a slice of the pie.

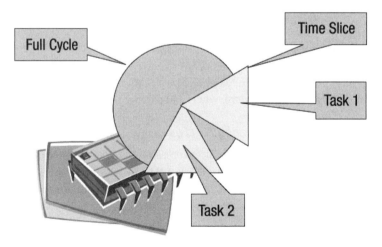

Figure 13-1. *Windows time slicing in action*

Figure 13-2. *Single-core microprocessor running two tasks*

Notice how task 1 and task 2 run in a serial manner, rather than concurrently. This is because the microprocessor is a single-task device made to look like a multitask device. You would run multiple tasks on a single-core microprocessor when you want to have application background tasks that should not affect the foreground task of the application. For example, when running a word processor, you don't want the spell checker slowing down your typing. The operating system will still allocate time slices in this case and use preemptive multitasking.

Figure 13-3 illustrates how the same application executes on a multiple-core microprocessor. Did you notice what happened? The operating system, in a bid to make more efficient use of the microprocessor, has put one task on one core and another task on the other core. Now both tasks are running in parallel. And now it's possible that both tasks would want to manipulate the same piece of data at the same time. In a single-core microprocessor, that is not physically possible. However, with a single processor, it is still possible for one task to be interrupted mid-flight while accessing some data, and for the other task to step in and use inconsistent data.

Figure 13-3. *Multiple-core microprocessor running two tasks*

If you have a multitasking application, you must be careful how you manipulate global state in the application. If you are not careful, you could corrupt the state of your program.

■**Note** As companies like Intel and AMD introduce microprocessors with more and more cores, it is your job as a software developer to write software that can make use of those cores. This is not always easy and requires some forethought, since you need to work out the logic. For example, if you are processing data that is sent to a file, you can't read the file before the data has been processed.

Using Threads

Tasks can run in two ways on the Windows operating system: via threads and via processes. A *process* is when you start a program, causing the operating system to instantiate resources and time slices for the program. A *thread* can be seen as a lightweight process that executes in the context of a process.

All processes will start a single thread. The thread that is executed as part of the process is the main thread, and when it exits, so does your application. If the main thread creates other threads, when the main thread exits, so do the created background threads. From an architectural perspective, when multitasking, the main thread will execute and coordinate the threads that run your code. Two processes cannot reference each other. This is so that if one process crashes, it does not cause the other process to crash. Threads executing in the context of a process have the ability to bring down an entire process.

■**Note** You could run multiple processes and then use interprocess communication mechanisms to communicate. However, I can't recommend that solution, since you can get the same effect of a process by using a .NET application domain (AppDomain). For the most part, you don't need to concern yourself with AppDomains. You will use threads, since they are lightweight (compared to a process), easy to manage, and easy to program.

Creating a New Thread

You can create a new thread that will run independently of its originating thread. In the following example, the main thread creates two other threads. Each of the threads outputs some text to the console. Note that the type `Thread` and other related types used in this chapter's examples are in the `System.Threading` namespace.

```
Imports System.Threading

Module Module1

    Sub Main()
        SimpleThread()
    End Sub

    Sub SimpleThreadTask1()
        Console.WriteLine("hello there")
    End Sub

    Sub SimpleThreadTask2()
        Console.WriteLine("Well then goodbye")
    End Sub

    Private Sub SimpleThread()
        Dim thread1 As New Thread(AddressOf SimpleThreadTask1)
        Dim thread2 As New Thread(AddressOf SimpleThreadTask2)
        thread1.Start()
        thread2.Start()
    End Sub

End Module
```

To create a thread, you instantiate the Thread type and call the Start() method. The Thread type is a class that contains all of the functionality necessary to start and control a multitasking thread.

When running a thread, the Thread type needs code to execute. The solution used by Thread is a delegate, which is passed to Thread via the constructor. The name of the delegate type is ThreadStart. The example here does not use the ThreadStart type explicitly, because both threads use programming constructs that do not need a delegate declaration. Here's the explicit syntax for completeness:

```
Dim thread1 As New Thread(New ThreadStart(AddressOf SimpleThreadTask1))
Dim thread2 As New Thread(New ThreadStart(AddressOf SimpleThreadTask2))
```

Running the thread example, you may see this output:

```
well then goodbye
hello there
```

Notice how hello there is after well then goodbye. The output implies that the second thread (thread2) starts before the first thread (thread1). However, your output might be the opposite, which demonstrates the true nature of threading, concurrency, and why threading is so difficult.

Imagine for a moment that the sample thread code were not multithreaded, but executed in a serial manner. Calling thread1.Start() and then thread2.Start() results in the text hello there being first. The serial behavior is easy to understand for humans. Things become complicated when you need to think of multiple tasks at the same time. While the computer has no problem with threads, a human who is thinking in a serial manner codes the logic, and thus the logic could be wrong.

Writing a good threading application should remind you of herding cats or dogs. If you are not careful with your threads and synchronization, then it is like herding ten cats into a single corner—a nearly impossible task, since cats do not respond well to commands. But if you are careful and conscientious, then it is like herding ten dogs into a corner—fairly easy if the dogs are trained.

Waiting for the Thread to End

Calling Start() will start a thread, causing a task to be executed. The caller of the thread does not wait for the created thread to end, because the created thread is independent of the caller. So if you were running a batch process, you would need to wait until all threads have completed. The caller logic only needs to start the threads, and thus its work requires a fraction of the time that the threads require.

There is a way for the caller thread to know when a created thread has exited. This technique involves using the Join() method, like this:

```
Sub ThreadWaitingTask()
    Console.WriteLine("hello there")
    Thread.Sleep(2000)
End Sub
```

```
    Private Sub ThreadWaiting()
        Dim thread As New Thread(AddressOf ThreadWaitingTask)
        thread.Start()
        thread.Join()
    End Sub
```

The line at the end of the code calls the Join() method, which means that the thread calling Join() is blocked until the thread referenced by the instance ends. A Thread.Sleep() call is used to put the other thread to sleep for the time specified by the parameter—2000 milliseconds, or 2 seconds, in this example.

This code solves the problem of the premature exit of the calling thread, but if the calling thread is going to wait until the created thread exits, what's the benefit? In this simple example, using Join() adds no benefit. However, when the caller thread executes many threads, the caller wants to continue only when all threads have finished executing. So in a multithreading situation, you would want to call Join() on each and every thread.

Another variation of Join() is where a parameter specifies a timeout. Imagine starting a thread, and in the worst-case scenario, you predict a processing time of 5 minutes. If the processing time is exceeded, the logic is to forcibly exit the thread. Here's the code to implement that logic:

```
If Not thread.Join(300000) Then
    thread.Abort()
End If
```

In the example, calling Join() will cause the executing thread to wait 300,000 milliseconds (5 minutes) before continuing. If the timeout occurred, the Join() method would return False, and the code would forcibly exit the thread using the Abort() method.

■**Note** It is wise to avoid using Abort() except in the most dire of situations, because data will be corrupted.

Creating a Thread with State

In the threading example, the threads did not manage any state. In most cases, your threads will reference some state.

Implementing a ThreadStart Delegate

One way to run a thread with state is to define a type that implements a delegate of the type ThreadStart. The following example defines a class with a method that will be called by a thread. The technique used is where a delegate from another class instance is passed to the Thread type.

```
Class ThreadedTask
    Private whatToSay As String

    Public Sub New(ByVal whattosay As String)
        _whatToSay = whattosay
    End Sub
```

```
    Public Sub MethodToRun()
        Console.WriteLine("I am babbling (" & _whatToSay & ")")
    End Sub
End Class
```

To use the method, the threading code is changed as follows:

```
Dim task As ThreadedTask = New ThreadedTask("hello")

Dim thread As Thread = _
  New Thread(AddressOf task.MethodToRun)
thread.Start()
```

In the example, the `ThreadedTask` type is instantiated with a state, and then `Thread` is instantiated with the stateful `task.MethodToRun()` method. When the thread starts, the data member `_whatToSay` will have some associated state. The code is logical and has no surprises. But what if you were to use the stateful method twice, like this:

```
Dim task As ThreadedTask = New ThreadedTask("hello")

Dim thread1 As Thread = New Thread(AddressOf task.MethodToRun)
Dim thread2 As Thread = New Thread(AddressOf task.MethodToRun)
thread1.Start()
thread2.Start()
```

Here, there are two `Thread` instances, but a single `task` instance. There will be two threads doing the same thing, and even worse, two threads sharing the same state. It is not wrong to share state, but sharing state requires special treatment to ensure that state remains consistent. You need to instantiate a single `ThreadedTask` and associate it with a single `Thread` instance, like this:

```
Dim task1 As ThreadedTask = New ThreadedTask("hello")
Dim task2 As ThreadedTask = New ThreadedTask("goodbye")

Dim thread1 As Thread = New Thread(AddressOf task1.MethodToRun)
Dim thread2 As Thread = New Thread(AddressOf task2.MethodToRun)
thread1.Start()
thread2.Start()
```

If you are running a stateful method, you need to associate a task instance with a thread instance.

Using a Thread Parameter

Suppose that you want to create a stateful thread. You can do this by using a thread parameter. In other words, the method that you invoke on another thread takes a parameter. Here's an example:

```
Sub SimpleThreadWithStateTask(ByVal buffer As Object)
    Console.WriteLine("You said (" & buffer.ToString() & ")")
End Sub

Private Sub SimpleThreadWithState()
    Dim thread1 As New Thread(AddressOf SimpleThreadWithStateTask)
    thread1.Start("my text")
End Sub
```

The major difference with a thread parameter is that you declare the function that is executed with a parameter, and the Start() method has a parameter.

Two restrictions apply to using a thread parameter: you can send only a single parameter, and that parameter must be an object.

Synchronizing Between Threads

When you have two threads and both share state (such as a variable), a concurrency situation may arise. Sharing state between two independent threads is not a problem if both threads consider the data as read-only. What does the reading thread read? Is the state consistent? It is probably not consistent, and that is why you need to synchronize access to state.

Let's consider a simple .NET collection class example. The following source code executes in the calling thread, instantiates a list collection, and then adds two numbers to the collection.

```
Dim elements As List(Of Integer)= New List(Of Integer)()
elements.Add(10)
elements.Add(20)
```

In the next step, we define a method that iterates the elements collection (which is declared at a higher scope).

```
Sub Task1()
    Thread.Sleep(1000)
    Dim item As Integer
    For Each item In elements
        Console.WriteLine("Item (" & item & ")")
        Thread.Sleep(1000)
    Next
End Sub
```

This thread iterates the data, and the two Thread.Sleep() calls put the threads to sleep for 1000 milliseconds, or 1 second. By putting the thread to sleep, we can artificially construct a situation where another thread adds to the collection while the collection is being iterated.

The method that adds an element to the collection is defined as follows:

```
Sub Task2()
    Thread.Sleep(1500)
    elements.Add(30)
End Sub
```

The Task1() and Task2() methods are started in separate threads as follows::

```
elements.Add(10)
elements.Add(20)
Dim thread1 As New Thread(AddressOf Task1)
Dim thread2 As New Thread(AddressOf Task2)
thread1.Start()
thread2.Start()
```

Running the threaded code will generate an exception, but not immediately. First, the caller thread creates and starts thread1 and thread2. thread1 goes to sleep for 1 second, and thread2 goes to sleep for 1.5 seconds. After thread1 awakens, one item in the collection is iterated, and thread1 goes to sleep for another second. But before thread1 reawakens, thread2 awakens and adds an element to the collection. When thread1 reawakens and attempts to iterate another element in the collection, an exception is generated, as shown in Figure 13-4.

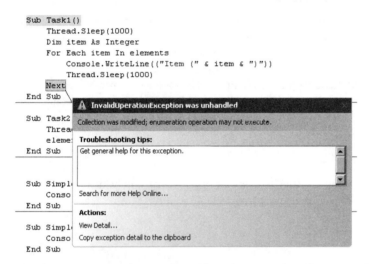

Figure 13-4. *Exception thrown after adding element to the collection, as shown in the Visual Basic IDE*

The InvalidOperationException is thrown to indicate that you can't add elements to a collection while iterating a collection. The collection classes think it is a bad idea to modify and iterate a collection at the same time. I agree with the collection classes, because doing so could give unpredictable results.

The problem in the source code is how to use the collection classes in a multithreaded context. In the example, items are added to the collection while the collection is being iterated. A commonly suggested approach is to use the type System.Collections.ObjectModel. ReadOnlyCollection, as in the following example.

```
Imports System.Collections.ObjectModel
Imports System.Threading
```

```vbnet
Module ThreadProblem
    Dim elements As List(Of Integer) = New List(Of Integer)()

    Sub Task1()
        Thread.Sleep(1000)
        Dim item As Integer

        Dim listElements As New ReadOnlyCollection(Of Integer)(elements)
        For Each item In listElements
            Console.WriteLine("Item (" & item & ")")
            Thread.Sleep(1000)
        Next
    End Sub

    Sub Task2()
        Thread.Sleep(1500)
        elements.Add(30)
    End Sub

    Sub Main()
        elements.Add(10)
        elements.Add(20)
        Dim thread1 As New Thread(AddressOf Task1)
        Dim thread2 As New Thread(AddressOf Task2)
        thread1.Start()
        thread2.Start()
    End Sub

End Module
```

The change is the bolded code, which instantiates the type System.Collections. ReadOnlyCollection, to which we pass the elements list. The ReadOnlyCollection provides the base class for a generic read-only collection. The For Each iterator then iterates a collection that is read-only, but based on the original collection. However, running the code will result in the same exception. This demonstrates that ReadOnlyCollection does not take a snapshot, but masks the collection. The mask disables the addition of items to the collection, but because the other thread is taking a shortcut and editing the original collection, the read-only collection is modified as well.

Let's say that converting the collection into a read-only collection had worked. It would not have solved anything. A read-only collection means that the second thread would generate an exception because you can't add elements to a collection that is read-only. The point is that when writing multithreaded code that shares variables, you don't have an easy solution, because you are trying to solve the problem of how to keep multiple cooks productive in a single kitchen.

We are trying to solve a classic reader/writer problem, where some threads are interested only in reading the data, and other threads are interested only in modifying the data. One way to synchronize the readers and writers is to use an exclusive lock, so that only one thread may read or write.

Using Exclusive Locks

When using exclusive locks in .NET, you are saying, "Only one thread may execute this piece of code." If two threads want to execute a particular piece of code, one will be granted access, while the other thread waits until the granted thread has exited the code block. It is important to understand that an exclusive lock grants access to code, not data, but that code could access data. And because only one thread is accessing the code, it is implied that only one thread can access the data.

The following is an example of code that uses exclusive locks.

```
. . .
Module ThreadProblem
    Dim elements As List(Of Integer) = New List(Of Integer)()

    Sub Task1()
        Thread.Sleep(1000)
        SyncLock elements
            Dim item As Integer
            For Each item In elements
                Console.WriteLine("Item (" & item & ")")
                Thread.Sleep(1000)
            Next
        End SyncLock
    End Sub

    Sub Task2()
        Thread.Sleep(1500)
        SyncLock elements
            elements.Add(30)
        End SyncLock
    End Sub

    Sub Main()
        elements.Add(10)
        elements.Add(20)
        Dim thread1 As New Thread(AddressOf Task1)
        Dim thread2 As New Thread(AddressOf Task2)
        thread1.Start()
        thread2.Start()
    End Sub

End Module
```

The bolded lines use the SyncLock and End SyncLock keywords, which represent a code block of exclusive access. The thread is granted access to only a single code block in each instance. Looking at the code within the block, you can see that the collection is accessed in two locations. Using the exclusive SyncLock argument where a single thread can access only a single code block, one thread will write to the collection, and another thread will read from the collection.

The SyncLock statement has a parameter that is a reference to lock against. In both threads, the reference is elements. The common reference synchronizes access to code. At any given point in time, the code contained within the SyncLock block will have only a single thread executing. This implements the desired feature, where only one thread is accessing code that reads or writes to the collection. The flow of the program is as follows:

1. Both threads wait.

2. After a 1 second, thread 1 acquires a lock because no other thread has done so.

3. Thread 1 executes its code.

4. Once thread 1 has started executing the synchronized code, no other code can acquire the lock that is associated with the variable elements.

5. When thread 2 wakes up after a sleep of 1.5 seconds, it will attempt to acquire the lock, but it can't because thread 1 is still holding the lock. So the second thread must wait.

6. Thread 1 eventually exits the synchronized code block, allowing the second thread to add an element to the collection. This time, no exception is thrown.

The reference to lock against does not need to be the reference that is manipulated within the code block. The reference is just that: an arbitrary reference. You could use a different object instance, and even instantiate an object like this:

```
Dim _syncRoot As Object = New Object()
. . .
SyncLock _syncRoot
    . . .
End SyncLock
```

When using exclusive blocks, you need to use them when reading or writing the object. Don't think that you need an exclusive lock only when modifying the data, because a reader might be reading a state that is being modified. As the example of the collection demonstrated, modifying a collection while it is being read causes an inconsistency and an exception. The following code does not have a lock for the reading of the collection, and it results in an exception being thrown.

. . .

```
Module ThreadProblem
    Dim elements As List(Of Integer) = New List(Of Integer)()

    Sub Task1()
        Thread.Sleep(1000)
        Dim item As Integer
        For Each item In elements
            Console.WriteLine("Item (" & item & ")")
            Thread.Sleep(1000)
        Next
    End Sub
```

```
    Sub Task2()
        Thread.Sleep(1500)
        SyncLock elements
            elements.Add(30)
        End SyncLock
    End Sub

    Sub Main()
        elements.Add(10)
        elements.Add(20)
        Dim thread1 As New Thread(AddressOf Task1)
        Dim thread2 As New Thread(AddressOf Task2)
        thread1.Start()
        thread2.Start()
    End Sub

End Module
```

Getting back to the code that worked, it would seem that all is OK. From a code-execution perspective, that's true. But from an execution-efficiency perspective, everything is not OK, because the reading of the collection is causing the writer to wait unnecessarily.

Again, this collection example illustrates the difficulty with writing multithreaded code. You want to be able to add elements to a collection without needing to wait for other threads to iterate a collection. You want to be efficient, as well as being logically correct.

Synchronizing with Cloning

One way of making a lock more efficient is to clone the object so that the local copy that you read from does not lock and hinder another thread. The two-thread example could be rewritten as follows:

```
. . .
Module ThreadProblem
    Dim elements As List(Of Integer) = New List(Of Integer)()

    Sub Task1()
        Dim items As Integer()
        Thread.Sleep(1000)
        SyncLock elements
            items = elements.ToArray()
        End SyncLock
        Dim item As Integer
        For Each item In items
            Console.WriteLine("Item (" & item & ")")
            Thread.Sleep(&H3E8)
        Next
    End Sub
```

```
    Sub Task2()
        Thread.Sleep(1500)
        SyncLock elements
            elements.Add(30)
        End SyncLock
    End Sub

    Sub Main()
        elements.Add(10)
        elements.Add(20)
        Dim thread1 As New Thread(AddressOf Task1)
        Dim thread2 As New Thread(AddressOf Task2)
        thread1.Start()
        thread2.Start()
    End Sub

End Module
```

The code still uses a lock, but only in the places where it is necessary. When the collection is being iterated, the lock is applied to the operation of copying the collection to an array (ToArray()). For the array iteration itself, there is no lock. When writing to the collection, there is a lock.

So, how can it be more efficient to take a snapshot of the collection, since taking a snapshot takes time? The answer is that normally it is not more efficient, but it is more time-slice-effective.

Consider a word processor that loads some text. When Microsoft Word loads text, it immediately displays the first page, allowing you to edit right away. In the background, you see the other pages being loaded and prepared for editing. Using the snapshot approach, you get the same effect.

As a general threading rule, use locks as sparingly as possible, but use them whenever necessary. If you do use them, use them for as little code as possible. Locks synchronize access to resources, and thus only a single thread can be executing for a locked piece of code. The less time code is locked, the faster your code will be.

How Not to Deadlock Your Code (Mostly)

A *deadlock* makes code stop executing. A deadlock occurs when one piece of code has a lock and waits for some information to become available. However, the information does not become available, because another thread that could provide that information is waiting for a lock to become free.

I've said that if you are using locked code, you should use it as sparingly as possible. That's because using locks can lead to deadlocks. Deadlocks are a royal pain in the butt.

Consider the following two-thread collection example.

```
. . .
Module ThreadProblem
    Dim elements As List(Of Integer) = New List(Of Integer)()
```

```
Sub Task1()
    Dim items As Integer()
    Thread.Sleep(1000)
    SyncLock elements
        Do While (elements.Count < 3)
            Thread.Sleep(1000)
        Loop
        items = elements.ToArray()
    End SyncLock
    Dim item As Integer
    For Each item In items
    Console.WriteLine("Item (" & item & ")")
        Thread.Sleep(1000)
    Next
End Sub

Sub Task2()
    Thread.Sleep(1500)
    SyncLock elements
        elements.Add(30)
    End SyncLock
End Sub

Sub Main()
    elements.Add(10)
    elements.Add(20)
    Dim thread1 As New Thread(AddressOf Task1)
    Dim thread2 As New Thread(AddressOf Task2)
    thread1.Start()
    thread2.Start()
End Sub
End Module
```

The iteration code waits until the collection count is 3. However, this never happens, because the thread that could make the collection count 3 is waiting for the lock to become free. The bolded code is the waiting code that queries whether the collection count is 3. If it is not, the thread waits for 1 second and asks again. But throughout all of this waiting, the lock is never given up, and thus the second thread that could add an element is waiting. The code will deadlock.

Without modifying the locks, here is a tweak that will avoid the deadlock (the thread sleeps for only 0.5 seconds instead of 1.5 seconds, so the writing thread can get in first before the reader thread gets in):

```
Sub Task2()
    Thread.Sleep(500)
    SyncLock elements
        elements.Add(30)
    End SyncLock
End Sub
```

The single change (shown in bold) makes the code work. In the first version, the timing of the code was such that the reading thread went first. In this version, the writing thread goes first. This shows that deadlocks are often timing-related.

The annoying part of deadlocks is that your code's behavior is not deterministic. Deterministic behavior is when an action will result in a single result, as in the case with most source code. Typically, when you have a bug, you didn't think far enough ahead and can work through the error systematically. However, with threading, your code ceases to be deterministic, because timing can change the behavior. Timing can be an influence in many ways: resource swapping, debuggers, microprocessor speed, and a host of other features.

To make the code deterministic, you need to fix the part of the code that hung onto the lock when it should not have. Remember the cardinal rule: keep a lock for as short a time as possible.

You need to use a more advanced lock construct that allows you to wait for data to become available. .NET has quite a few constructs related to threading and synchronization, and each construct is specific to the type of problem you are trying to solve. In the case of a deadlock, you want to use the Monitor type. The Monitor type is an advanced synchronization type that allows locking and pulsing of trigger signals for those threads that are waiting.

Let's return to our multiple cooks in the kitchen analogy. Say one cook needs a particular fish pan, which is already being used by another cook. Does the waiting cook tap her foot beside the cook doing the cooking? Or does the waiting cook do something else and ask the cook using the pan to inform her when the pan is free? Most likely, the cook will do something else and wait to be informed that the pan is free.

This concept of working together and being able to notify other lock users is a powerful feature programmed into the Monitor type. Monitor has the ability to take a lock, give it up so others can get the lock, and then take it back again.

When using the Monitor type, you do not declare a block of code that is protected, because Monitor is much more flexible than that. For example, you could define a class that has an instance-level lock mechanism, like this:

```
Class DoSomething
    Public Sub GetLock()
        Monitor.Enter(Me)
    End Sub
    Public Sub ReleaseLock()
        Monitor.Exit(Me)
    End Sub
End Class
```

Any code that uses a Monitor is not restricted to where it's placed in the code, but a Monitor is bound to a thread. So if a thread grabs a Monitor (by calling the Enter() method on the Monitor object), it has control until the thread dies or the thread gives up control (by calling the Exit() method on the Monitor object). This has the added benefit that, once having acquired a lock, a Monitor can get it over and over again. However, if the same thread locked the Monitor five times, the same thread needs to release it five times before another thread can be granted access to the lock.

The following is the rewritten two-thread source code that uses a Monitor.

```
Sub Task1()
    Dim items As Integer()
    Thread.Sleep(1000)
    Monitor.Enter(elements)
    Do While (elements.Count < 3)
        Monitor.Wait(elements, 1000)
    Loop
    items = elements.ToArray()
    Monitor.Exit(elements)
    Dim item As Integer
    For Each item In items
        Console.WriteLine("Item (" & item & ")")
        Thread.Sleep(1000)
    Next
End Sub

Sub Task2()
    Monitor.Enter(elements)
    elements.Add(30)
    Monitor.Pulse(elements)
    Monitor.Exit(elements)
End Sub
```

The bolded code lines are the new pieces that use the Monitor type. In the definition of the first thread to get the lock, the Monitor.Enter() method is called with the parameter elements, which, as in the earlier SyncLock example, defines the lock reference handle. Once the lock has been acquired, the thread checks to see if the list count is greater or equal to 3. If the counter is less than 3, the Monitor.Wait() method is called. The behavior of Monitor.Wait() is similar to Thread.Sleep(), except that the Monitor lock is given up.

Releasing the lock is a unique feature of a Monitor. The lock is given up only during the time that the caller is in Monitor.Wait(). When the Monitor.Wait() method returns, the lock is acquired again. The code says that the thread is reawakened after 1 second. After that second, the thread does not have the lock and needs to wait before it can acquire the lock. If another thread is holding onto the lock for a long time, it could take a while to get the lock back again.

Another way for the Monitor.Wait() method to awaken is if a signal is sent by another thread. The code for the second thread uses Enter() and Exit(), but also Pulse(). The Monitor.Pulse() method triggers a signal that awakens the first thread, but the first thread will execute only after the second thread has released control of the lock.

The big advantages of a Monitor in comparison to SyncLock are that the Monitor can be used anywhere in the code and that the Monitor will release a lock while waiting for an answer. You would use SyncLock when you want to control access to a block of code. If the access goes beyond method boundaries, then it is preferable to use Monitor. It is not that you could not use a SyncLock that spanned boundaries, but if you need to add code that could produce a deadlock, it is easier to control that code using a Monitor.

Now that we've covered the fundamentals of multithreading, the next sections focus on more advanced threading architectures—reader/writer and producer/consumer—and using asynchronous calls.

Implementing a Reader/Writer Threaded Architecture

The reader/writer threaded architecture is based on the idea that if one thread is reading and another thread would like to read as well, why not let it? However, if one thread wants to write, then only that thread can write. In other words, multiple threads are allowed to read data simultaneously, but to write, a thread must have an exclusive lock.

.NET implements a System.Threading.ReaderWriterLock class, which contains the reader/writer functionality. This class is like a Monitor, in that it gives you the control to manage how data is accessed but does not determine what you are accessing. The ReaderWriterLock type has a number of methods and properties. The most important ones are listed in Table 13-1.

Table 13-1. *Important ReaderWriterLock Methods*

Method	Description
AcquireReaderLock()	Acquires a reader lock. Multiple threads can acquire a reader lock.
AcquireWriterLock()	Acquires a writer lock. Only a single thread can acquire a writer lock.
DowngradeFromWriterLock()	Converts a writer lock into a reader lock. Using this method avoids the need to call ReleaseWriterLock() and AcquireReaderLock().
UpgradeToWriterLock()	Converts a reader lock into a writer lock. Using this method avoids the need to call ReleaseReaderLock() and AcquireWriterLock().
ReleaseLock()	Releases all locks, regardless how many times you have called to acquire the reader or writer locks.
ReleaseReaderLock()	Decrements the reader lock a single count. To completely release a reader lock, you need to make sure the number of times you called ReleaseReaderLock() is equal to the number of times you called AcquireReaderLock().
ReleaseWriterLock()	Decrements the writer lock a single count. To completely release a reader lock, you need to make sure the number of times you called ReleaseWriterLock() is equal to the number of times you called AcquireWriterLock().

Let's look at a collection example that has four threads: three readers and one writer. The example uses Thread.Sleep() strategically, so that you can see how a reader thread and writer thread interact with each other.

```
Imports System.Threading

Friend Module TestMoreTopics
    Private rwlock As New ReaderWriterLock()
    Private elements As New List(Of Integer)()
```

```vb
Sub Task1()
    Thread.Sleep(1000)
    Console.WriteLine("Thread 1 waiting for read lock")
    rwlock.AcquireReaderLock(-1)
    Console.WriteLine("Thread 1 has read lock")
    Dim item As Integer
    For Each item In elements
        Console.WriteLine("Thread 1 Item (" & item & ")")
        Thread.Sleep(1000)
    Next
    Console.WriteLine("Thread 1 releasing read lock")
    rwlock.ReleaseLock()
End Sub

Sub Task2()
    Thread.Sleep(1250)
    Console.WriteLine("Thread 2 waiting for read lock")
    rwlock.AcquireReaderLock(-1)
    Console.WriteLine("Thread 2 has read lock")
    Dim item As Integer
    For Each item In elements
        Console.WriteLine("Thread 2 Item (" & item & ")")
        Thread.Sleep(1000)
    Next
    Console.WriteLine("Thread 2 releasing read lock")
    rwlock.ReleaseLock()
End Sub

Sub Task3()
    Thread.Sleep(1750)
    Console.WriteLine("Thread 3 waiting for read lock")
    rwlock.AcquireReaderLock(-1)
    Console.WriteLine("Thread 3 has read lock")
    Dim item As Integer
    For Each item In elements
        Console.WriteLine("Thread 3 Item (" & item & ")")
        Thread.Sleep(1000)
    Next
    Console.WriteLine("Thread 3 releasing read lock")
    rwlock.ReleaseLock()
End Sub

Sub Task4()
    Thread.Sleep(1500)
    Console.WriteLine("Thread 4 waiting for write lock")
    rwlock.AcquireWriterLock(-1)
    Console.WriteLine("Thread 4 has write Lock")
```

```
        elements.Add(30)
        Console.WriteLine("Thread 4 releasing write lock")
        rwlock.ReleaseLock()
    End Sub

    Private Sub ReaderWriter()
        elements.Add(10)
        elements.Add(20)
        Dim thread1 As New Thread(AddressOf Task1)
        Dim thread2 As New Thread(AddressOf Task2)
        Dim thread3 As New Thread(AddressOf Task3)
        Dim thread4 As New Thread(AddressOf Task4)
        thread1.Start()
        thread2.Start()
        thread3.Start()
        thread4.Start()
    End Sub

    Public Sub RunAll()
        TestMoreTopics.ReaderWriter()
    End Sub

End Module
```

The bolded code contains all of the references to the reader/writer .NET class implementation. Unlike the keyword SyncLock or the type Monitor, the ReaderWriterLock type is instantiated and the instance is shared between threads.

The code to acquire a reader lock or writer lock has a parameter of value -1, which means to wait until the lock is acquired. A positive value means to wait for a number of milliseconds, and if the lock has not been acquired, then return from the method call. If you do use a timeout, before you attempt to manipulate shared code, you need to reference the property IsReaderLockHeld or IsWriterLockHeld to ensure that you have acquired the lock. In the reader threads, after having acquired the reader locks, the items are iterated.

■**Note** The example seems to break the rule regarding keeping locks for as short a time possible, since it holds onto the lock while iterating. In the case of a reader/writer implementation, you have a unique situation in that you should be manipulating data that is mostly to be read, which implies that most of the time, you will be treating the shared data as read-only. For those times when you are writing to the shared data, it is fine if the thread must wait a moment or two. A reader/writer lock does not make sense if you do not have data that is essentially read-only. In other situations, you should use the Monitor approach, as described in the previous section.

The example demonstrates handling data that is mostly to be read, since it has three threads reading and one thread writing. It is important to make sure that you don't end up writing while holding a read-only lock.

Running the code results in the following output.

```
Thread 1 waiting for read lock
Thread 1 has read lock
Thread 1 Item (10)
Thread 2 waiting for read lock
Thread 2 has read lock
Thread 2 Item (10)
Thread 4 waiting for write lock
Thread 3 waiting for read lock
Thread 1 Item (20)
Thread 2 Item (20)
Thread 1 releasing read lock
Thread 2 releasing read lock
Thread 4 has write Lock
Thread 4 releasing write lock
Thread 3 has read lock
Thread 3 Item (10)
Thread 3 Item (20)
Thread 3 Item (30)
Thread 3 releasing read lock
```

In the generated output, the sequence of events is as follows:

1. Thread 1 wants and acquires a read-only lock.

2. Thread 1 outputs the first number in the collection. Thread 1 then sleeps, which lets in another thread for execution.

3. Thread 2 wants and acquires another read-only lock.

4. Thread 2 outputs the first number in the collection. Thread 2 then sleeps, which lets in another thread for execution.

5. Thread 4 wants a writer lock and is kept on hold.

6. Thread 3 wants a read-only lock, but because thread 4 has asked for a writer lock and is queued, thread 3 is put on hold. At this step, threads 3 and 4 are put on hold and are waiting for the read-only locks of threads 1 and 2 to be released.

7. Threads 1 and 2 output the remaining numbers in the collection.

8. Threads 1 and 2 release the read-only locks.

9. Thread 4 is given a writer lock, and thread 3 is still on hold.

10. Thread 4 writes to the collection and releases the writer lock.

11. Thread 3 acquires a read-only lock and iterates the individual numbers, including the number added by thread 4.

Notice that the reader/writer lock makes the sequence of reading and writing events orderly, so that the shared state is always consistent. The reader/writer lock does not hinder or stop deadlocks, which can occur if you are not careful with how you write your code. The reader/writer lock is concerned about only the code that is used to manage data.

Implementing a Producer/Consumer Architecture

The producer/consumer technique has never been defined as a type, but it is used throughout many multithreaded applications. The idea behind a producer/consumer architecture is to split the problem into two parts. One side is the producer of data, information, and tasks. The producer wraps up the information into a task to be executed. The other side is the consumer, and it is responsible for unwrapping the information and doing something with it.

Using a Hidden Producer/Consumer Implementation

In Windows GUIs, multithreaded applications are not allowed to access UI components if they are not the thread that created the UI element. To get around that problem, the `Windows.Forms` library uses the `Invoke()` method. To demonstrate, we'll create a GUI application that uses another thread to periodically increment a counter that is displayed in a text box.

Follow these steps:

1. Create a new Windows Forms application, and set it as the startup project if it isn't already (right-click its name and select Set as StartUp Project).

2. Drag a TextBox control onto Form1 in the design window.

3. Select the TextBox control. If the Properties window isn't visible, right-click the control and select Properties.

4. Change the TextBox's `Name` property to `txtMessage`.

5. Right-click the form and select View Code.

6. Add the following code.

```
Imports System.Threading

Public Class Form1

    Private _counter As Integer

    Private Sub IncrementCounter()
        Me.txtMessage.Text = "Counter (" & _counter & ")"
        _counter += 1
    End Sub

    Delegate Sub DelegateIncrementCounter()
```

```
Private Sub PeriodicIncrement()
    Do While True
        Invoke(New DelegateIncrementCounter(AddressOf IncrementCounter))
        ' You can't call the GUI using a thread other than the GUI thread
        'IncrementCounter()
        Thread.Sleep(1000)
    Loop
End Sub
Private _thread As Thread

End Class
```

7. Switch back to the design view and double-click the form, which should take you back to the code view in the Form1_Load() method.

8. Add the following code to the Form1_Load() method.

```
Private Sub Form1_Load(ByVal sender As System.Object, _
                        ByVal e As System.EventArgs) Handles MyBase.Load
    _thread = New Thread(AddressOf PeriodicIncrement)
    _thread.Start()
End Sub
```

When Form1 is loaded, the Form1_Load() method is executed, which instantiates a new thread, which then executes the PeriodicIncrement() method. Within the implementation of PeriodicIncrement() is a never-ending loop, which calls the Form.Invoke() method, to which we pass a delegate. The delegate is the method IncrementCounter(), which increments a counter and outputs the result to the text box txtMessage.

From a user perspective, it would seem obvious to call the method IncrementCounter() directly from the other thread (_thread). However, hidden in the implementation of Invoke() is a producer/consumer implementation. The producer is the Invoke() method, which adds a delegate that needs to be called to a queue. The consumer is the Windows.Forms.Form class, which periodically checks its Invoke() queue and executes the delegates contained within.

In a nutshell, a producer/consumer implementation is nothing more than a handoff of information from one thread to another thread. This is effective because the producer and consumer are separate and manage their own concerns. The only common information between the producer and consumer is a queue, or list, which is synchronized and contains information of interest to both the producer and consumer.

Implementing a Generic Producer/Consumer Architecture

The architecture implemented by Windows.Forms is elegant and self-containing. You can implement a generic producer/consumer architecture using a delegate, as shown in the following source code. In this case, we use the System.Action class, which encapsulates a Sub that doesn't take any parameters (it is shorthand for Public Delegate Sub Action()).

```
Imports System.Threading

Class ThreadPoolProducerConsumer

    Private _queue As Queue(Of Action) = New Queue(Of Action)()

    Private Sub QueueProcessor(Byval obj As Object)
        Monitor.Enter(_queue)
        Do While _queue.Count = 0
            Monitor.Wait(_queue, -1)
        Loop
        Dim action As Action = _queue.Dequeue()
        Monitor.Exit(_queue)
        ThreadPool.QueueUserWorkItem(AddressOf QueueProcessor)
        action()
    End Sub

    Public Sub New()
        ThreadPool.QueueUserWorkItem(AddressOf QueueProcessor)
    End Sub

    Public Sub Invoke(ByVal toExec As Action)
        Monitor.Enter(_queue)
        _queue.Enqueue(toExec)
        Monitor.Pulse(_queue)
        Monitor.Exit(_queue)
    End Sub
End Class
```

ThreadPoolProducerConsumer has a single public method, Invoke(), which is used in the same fashion as the Windows.Forms Invoke() method. What makes the generic producer/consumer work is its use of the Monitor synchronization class.

To understand how Monitor works in the producer/consumer context, consider the overall producer/consumer implementation. The consumer thread (QueueProcessor()) executes constantly, waiting for items in the queue (_queue). To check the queue, the Monitor.Enter() method is called, which says, "I want exclusive control for a code block that ends with the method call Monitor.Exit()." To check the queue, a Do While loop is started. The loop waits until there is something in the queue. The thread could execute constantly, waiting for something to be added, but while the thread is looping, it has control of the lock. This means a producer thread cannot add anything to the queue.

The consumer needs to give up the lock, but also needs to check if anything is available in the queue. The solution is to call Monitor.Wait(), which causes the consumer thread to release the lock and say, "Hey, I'm giving up the lock temporarily until somebody gives me a signal to continue processing." When the consumer thread releases its lock temporarily, it goes to sleep waiting for a pulse.

The producer thread (Invoke()) also enters a protected block using the Monitor.Enter() method. Within the protected block, an item is added to the queue using the Enqueue() method. Because an item has been added to the queue, the producer thread sends a signal using the Monitor.Pulse() method to indicate an item is available. This will cause the thread that gave up the lock temporarily (the consumer thread) to wake up. However, the consumer thread executes when the producer thread calls Monitor.Exit(). Until then, the consumer thread is in ready-to-execute mode.

In the simplest case of this implementation, a single thread would constantly execute QueueProcessor(). An optimization is to create and use a *thread pool*. A thread pool is a collection of ready-to-execute threads. As tasks arrive, threads are taken from the pool and used to execute the tasks. Once the thread has completed executing, it is returned to the thread pool in ready-to-execute mode. In the ThreadPoolProducerConsumer constructor, the method ThreadPool.QueueUserWorkItem() uses thread pooling to execute the method QueueProcessor(). In the implementation of QueueProcessor(), the method ThreadPool.QueueUserWorkItem() is called again before calling the delegate. The result is that one thread is always waiting for an item in the queue, but there may be multiple threads executing concurrently, processing items from the queue.

Using the generic producer/consumer is nearly identical to using the Windows.Forms Invoke() method. The following is a sample implementation.

```
Imports System.Threading

Public Class TestProducerConsumer
    Delegate Sub TestMethod()

    Sub Method()
        Console.WriteLine("Processed in thread id (" & _
            Thread.CurrentThread.ManagedThreadId & ")")
    End Sub

    Public Sub TestSimple()
        Dim producer As ThreadPoolProducerConsumer = _
          New ThreadPoolProducerConsumer()
        Console.WriteLine("Sent in thread id (" & _
            Thread.CurrentThread.ManagedThreadId()& ")")
        producer.Invoke(AddressOf Method)
    End Sub
End Class
```

The TestSimple() method instantiates the ThreadPoolProducerConsumer type. Then the Invoke() method is called using the delegate TestMethod, which executes the Method() method.

■**Note** The Thread.ManagedThreadId property uniquely identifies the managed thread to which it belongs.

Using an Asynchronous Approach

Using asynchronous techniques means to perform a task, such as read a file or database result, and then rather than wait for the results, let some other code handle the results. The asynchronous interaction is an example of the producer/consumer architecture, where the consumer makes a request of the producer and carries on until it gets a response to that request.

The asynchronous technique used throughout the .NET API is consistent and is easily demonstrated by reading a file asynchronously. In Chapter 10, you learned how to read a file or console stream using synchronous techniques. You could just as well have read that file or stream asynchronously.

You would use asynchronous techniques when you don't want to wait around for the task to complete. To read a file asynchronously, the following source code is used.

```vb
Imports System.IO
Imports System.Text

Friend Module TestAsynchronousFile
    Dim data As Byte() = New Byte(200000) {}
    Private filename As String = "threads.vb"

    Public Sub RunAll()
        TestAsynchronousFile.LoadFileAsynchronously()
    End Sub

    Private Sub LoadFileAsynchronously()
        Dim fs As New FileStream(TestAsynchronousFile.filename, FileMode.Open)
        fs.BeginRead(Data , 0, Data .Length, _
                    AddressOf DoAsyncRead, fs).AsyncWaitHandle.WaitOne()
     End Sub

    Sub DoAsyncRead(ByVal result As IAsyncResult)
        Dim localFS As FileStream = DirectCast(result.AsyncState, FileStream)
        Dim bytesRead As Integer = localFS.EndRead(result)
        Dim buffer As String = Encoding.ASCII.GetString(data)
        Console.WriteLine("Buffer bytes read (" & bytesRead & ")")
        localFS.Close()
    End Sub
End Module
```

To read a file, you need to open a file stream, just as in Chapter 10's examples. However, instead of reading the data directly, the BeginRead() method is called, and it starts a read operation. What distinguishes the asynchronous operation is that BeginRead() returns immediately. Think of it as starting the producer.

When you call BeginRead(), the first three parameters represent the variable that contains the read bytes. The first parameter is the byte array where the data should be written. The second and third parameters are the starting and ending locations of the write operation in the byte array. The fourth parameter to BeginRead() is the delegate that will be called when the data is ready to be processed. The last parameter is like a thread parameter and is assigned to the

IAsyncResult.AsyncState data member. IAsyncResult is in the System namespace and is therefore part of the .NET API.

When you call BeginRead(), you are saying, "Please fill up as many bytes as possible in the byte array. When you have read the bytes, call my consumer code." The filling of the array and calling of the consumer code occur in a separate thread.

For illustration purposes, the AsyncWaitHandle.WaitOne() method is called so that the main calling thread continues only after the data has been read and processed. It is a superfluous method call, since doing this would make the file-reading behavior resemble a synchronous operation.

The consumer code (that is, the DoAsyncRead() method)is executed on another thread and is responsible for reading all the bytes. The method receives an IAsyncResult parameter, which has an AsyncState property and is the value that we passed in as the fifth parameter to BeginRead() (the file stream). DoAsyncRead() then converts this parameter into a FileStream and reads the remaining bytes from the stream. The byte stream is then converted into a string buffer. When all the data has been read, the file stream is closed.

When using this asynchronous approach, you are really writing producer/consumer code. The use of IAsyncResult, BeginRead(), and EndRead() is quite common. The purpose of the asynchronous interface is to convert a synchronous operation into an asynchronous operation.

The Important Stuff to Remember

In this chapter, you learned the essentials of using threads and how to write multithreaded code. The main items to remember are as follows:

- The operating system assigns time slices to your application.

- A time slice is a predefined amount of time in which your program can execute and has full control of the microprocessor.

- To implement tasks that you want to run separately from the main program, you use threads.

- Each program that is started is a task and has a main thread from which you can start other threads.

- Threading is not difficult and easily implemented. What is more difficult is synchronization between the threads.

- Synchronization is not about the data, but about synchronizing access to code that modifies data that is shared. If your data is not shared, you don't need synchronization.

- In the context of a single application, you will use either the exclusive lock or the Monitor for synchronization.

- Locking code slows down the code. You should keep the locks for the shortest time possible.

- To improve throughput, you can take a snapshot of the data.

- Higher-level synchronization abstractions are the reader/writer and producer/consumer architectures.

- Reader/writer locks are exclusive locks, but they separate code that reads from code that writes. To improve code efficiency, reader/writer locks allow multiple readers, but only a single writer. Reader/writer locks are effective only if, for the most part, you are reading data.

- Producer/consumer locks split the task of producing and consuming data into two separate steps. The .NET API uses the producer/consumer concept extensively; examples are `Windows.Forms` and `IAsyncResult`.

- Deadlocks occur because timing changes cause your code to not be deterministic.

- Deadlocks can be partially avoided using `Monitors`, but the most effective way of avoiding deadlocks is to use the producer/consumer development technique. This is because the producer/consumer architecture takes the approach of handing off data, rather than sharing data.

- Applications that multitask effectively are applications that have been designed using logic, rather than development techniques where you think up the code as you go along.

Some Things for You to Do

The following is an exercise to help you apply what you learned in this chapter.

1. Write a general architecture that generates a series using multiple threads. For the first series, generate the square of all numbers between 1 and 100. For the second series, generate the Fibonacci series. That is, after two starting values, each number is the sum of the two preceding numbers. The first Fibonacci numbers are 0, 1, 1, 2, 3, 5, 8, 13, 21, 34, 55, 89, 144, 233, 377, 610, 987, 1597, 2584, 4181, 6765, 10946, 17711, 28657, 46368, 75025, 121393, 196418, and 317811. Outline the limits of multithreading when generating a series.

CHAPTER 14

■■■

Learning About Relational Database Data

Literally hundreds of techniques, tips, tricks, and libraries are associated with relational databases. Covering relational databases would take an entire a book, and in fact, many books are devoted to that subject. This chapter will cover the basics and give you enough knowledge to read and write to a database.

The focus of this chapter is to demonstrate accessing relational databases with ADO.NET and the Visual Studio Dataset Designer. Since we'll need a database to work with, you'll also learn how to create a database with Visual Basic Express.

A relational database stores data, such as the lottery numbers in Chapter 10's example. Building on that lottery-prediction example, in this chapter, you'll see how to create a database application that reads and writes the lottery numbers, and associates winners with a particular lottery drawing.

Understanding Relational Databases

As a beginner developer, one of your greatest challenges will be how to manage relational database data. A *relational database* is an old piece of technology. The relational model on which it is based was written in about 1969 (according to the relational model entry at http://en.wikipedia.org/wiki/Relational_model). A relational database is defined as follows (http://en.wikipedia.org/wiki/Relational_database):

> Strictly, a relational database is merely a collection of relations (frequently called tables). Other items are frequently considered part of the database, as they help to organize and structure the data, in addition to forcing the database to conform to a set of requirements.

Relational Database Tables

A relational database is a collection of tables. When you were reading and writing a file in Chapter 10's example, you were actually reading and writing a table of lottery numbers, which looked something like this:

```
2000.05.31 5 6 13 23 25 37 43
2000.06.03 7 10 11 18 32 41 5
2000.06.07 15 23 24 28 38 39 45
2000.06.10 1 3 12 23 29 33 27
2000.06.14 2 4 13 19 39 45 26
2000.06.17 3 8 17 19 21 25 35
```

The data is arranged as a table, and thus could be easily converted into a relational database table. In relational database-speak, each row in the file corresponds to a row of data. But to create a row of data, you need fields, each of which is also in a column. A relational database table is a grid of rows and columns. When working with a relational database, you don't manipulate columns; you manipulate individual rows.

What distinguishes a relational database is that you can combine tables and create more complicated data structures. It is the relationships (called *relations*) between pieces of data that make a relational database so powerful. For the lottery data, a relation could be who won the jackpot on the draw dates. Modifying the table to include the person who won would look this:

```
2000.05.31 nobody 5 6 13 23 25 37 43
2000.06.03 nobody 7 10 11 18 32 41 5
2000.06.07 nobody 15 23 24 28 38 39 45
2000.06.10 jack 1 3 12 23 29 33 27
2000.06.14 nobody 2 4 13 19 39 45 26
2000.06.17 nobody 3 8 17 19 21 25 35
```

For the most part, no one won the jackpot. But on June 10, 2000 (2000.06.10), a person named Jack won the jackpot. You might know a Jack. I might know a Jack. But would he be the same Jack? Probably not. So to distinguish winner Jack from another Jack, you would need his full name, address, and other details. But where do you put this extra information?

Do you put the information about Jack into the lottery data table? Or do you create another table? The answer is that you create another table. But since you are working with files, it will be a file, not a table. The file will be called `jack.txt` because the winner of the lottery jackpot was Jack. The `jack.txt` file could contain the following information.

```
Jack Smith
Address
City
Country
```

The information in `jack.txt` and the information in the lottery data file have a relation. The relation is the winner of the jackpot. This is what a relational database is all about. The reason you use a relational database and not files that cross-reference each other is because a relational database is extremely efficient at managing tables and relations. The techniques demonstrated in Chapter 10 are nowhere near as efficient and effective as using a relational database.

Relational databases are quite capable of handling terabytes of data. Additionally, relational databases are capable of building efficient relations that span terabytes of data.

Database Relations

Relations are very powerful, but they can also make things extremely complicated. When you split tables and create relations between the tables, you are *normalizing* the data. Database normalization is defined as follows (http://en.wikipedia.org/wiki/Database_normalization):

> *Database normalization is a technique for designing relational database tables to minimize duplication of information and, in so doing, to safeguard the database against certain types of logical or structural problems, namely data anomalies. For example, when multiple instances of a given piece of information occur in a table, the possibility exists that these instances will not be kept consistent when the data within the table is updated, leading to a loss of data integrity. A table that is sufficiently normalized is less vulnerable to problems of this kind, because its structure reflects the basic assumptions for when multiple instances of the same information should be represented by a single instance only.*

For example, the data on the winner and the data on the lottery ticket are kept in separate tables, making the overall data structure more efficient from a maintenance and performance point of view.

Creating relations between tables is a form of referencing, where one table says information here references information in another table. The referencing is carried out using columns of one table that are cross-referenced with columns of another table.

The lottery ticket example is interesting because of the relations between the lottery draws and the winners, which could be of two types:

- *One draw to many winners*: When a lottery ticket is drawn, there can be many winners.

- *One winner to many draws*: Even though it is improbable, one winner could win multiple draws.

In the file example, you saw the one-winner-to-many-draws relation. You probably did not think it was that type of relation, and more likely thought it was a one-draw-to-one-winner relation. But consider the following text file, where jack is referenced twice.

```
2000.05.31 nobody 5 6 13 23 25 37 43
2000.06.03 jack 7 10 11 18 32 41 5
2000.06.07 nobody 15 23 24 28 38 39 45
2000.06.10 jack 1 3 12 23 29 33 27
2000.06.14 nobody 2 4 13 19 39 45 26
2000.06.17 nobody 3 8 17 19 21 25 35
```

The table of draws has the ability to reference the same winner twice, which means the relation of one winner to many draws is possible. To add the relation of one draw to many winners, the table would need to be modified like this:

```
2000.05.31 nobody 5 6 13 23 25 37 43
2000.06.03 jack jill 7 10 11 18 32 41 5
2000.06.07 nobody 15 23 24 28 38 39 45
2000.06.10 jack 1 3 12 23 29 33 27
2000.06.14 nobody 2 4 13 19 39 45 26
2000.06.17 nobody 3 8 17 19 21 25 35
```

Here, another field indicates Jill as the second winner of the draw. Adding another field throws a monkey wrench into the entire table structure and makes processing much more complicated, because the parsing routines will need to verify if another field is present. This breaks the nice grid structure and is plain wrong.

Another approach using the text file would be to create a third file that cross-references the winners with the dates. So the lottery file would go back to the original version:

```
2000.05.31 5 6 13 23 25 37 43
2000.06.03 7 10 11 18 32 41 5
2000.06.07 15 23 24 28 38 39 45
2000.06.10 1 3 12 23 29 33 27
2000.06.14 2 4 13 19 39 45 26
2000.06.17 3 8 17 19 21 25 35
```

And a winners table would be created:

```
2000.06.03 jack
2000.06.03 jill
2000.06.10 jack
```

The winners table is a grid of draw dates and winners on those dates. Notice how there is no entry for nobody, so only draw dates with winners are included.

■**Note** These three tables are an example of correctly normalized data. When the data is well normalized, each table contains unique data. In this example, one table contains all of the lottery drawings, but who the winners are is stored in another table. Using database relations, the winners and lottery data are related, yet neither table needs to know about the other table.

Now what happens if two different people named Jack are lottery winners? The data might look like this:

```
2000.05.31 nobody 5 6 13 23 25 37 43
2000.06.03 nobody 7 10 11 18 32 41 5
2000.06.07 nobody 15 23 24 28 38 39 45
2000.06.10 jack 1 3 12 23 29 33 27
2000.06.14 jack 2 4 13 19 39 45 26
2000.06.17 nobody 3 8 17 19 21 25 35
```

We know the two jack entries are not for the same Jack. So now we have an additional problem of uniqueness. Uniqueness is not unusual when dealing with relational databases, and the common technique is to identify each Jack with a unique key. For example, a unique key could be jack_1 or jack_2. The problem with using jack_1 and jack_2 is that you need to search the database to see if there is a jack entry, and then find out the last jack entry. Those steps are resource-intensive and typically avoided. Another solution is to use a database-provided field that generates a unique key, which could be a row number or globally unique identifier (GUID). If the unique identifier were to be computer-generated, the table might look as follows:

```
2000.05.31 1877_ds 5 6 13 23 25 37 43
2000.06.03 1877_ds 7 10 11 18 32 41 5
2000.06.07 1877_ds 15 23 24 28 38 39 45
2000.06.10 1023_ad 1 3 12 23 29 33 27
2000.06.14 1022_xy 4 13 19 39 45 26
2000.06.17 1877_ds 3 8 17 19 21 25 35
```

In the modified table, you would have no idea who the identifiers represent. The way to find out is to take a key and open its associated field—say 1877_ds and the file 1877_ds.txt. Upon opening the file, you would know that the winner is nobody. The process of finding out who the winner is involves more steps, but a relational database knows how to manage these types of relations quite effectively.

WHY THE THOUSANDS OF APIS, LIBRARIES, AND TECHNIQUES?

In the space of 12 years, the following data-access technologies have emerged: Open Database Connectivity (ODBC), Remote Data Objects (RDO), the Jet Database Engine, Data Access Object (DAO), ActiveX Data Object (ADO), Object Linking and Embedding, Database (OLE DB), ADO.NET, and Language Integrated Query (LINQ). This means that every 2 years, a new database technology is introduced. Each database technology has libraries to make it easier to write code. The result is an amazing number of ways to access a piece of technology that is nearly 40 years old.

So why do we have so many ways to access and manipulate the database? Wouldn't we, as developers, get our act together and work toward a common approach to manipulating a relational database? I can't give a logical and accepted answer as to why there are so many data-access technologies. But I can tell you what I think.

For any real production application, it is not uncommon to have tables that have 30 columns. When writing code to add, delete, and modify a row in a table that has 30 fields, you are, for the most part, trying to figure out which field goes to which piece of data. Thus, people try to automate the job. After all, it is more interesting to work through a threading bug than an incorrect-field-placement bug.

Another issue is a technology mismatch between a programming language and a relational database. A relational database treats data as a set. There are no individual pieces of data in a relational database. Programming languages treat data as individuals. Even in a collection class, you have an individual class managing a set of individual references. This causes a mismatch, and trying to bind to the two technologies is difficult.

So when you are writing database code, you are trying to automate the fitting of a square peg into a round hole. You get many extremely creative ideas and results, but at the end of the day, you are still fitting a square peg into a round hole.

The essence of the problem when dealing with sets of data in a programming language is how to integrate the two. There is light at the end of the tunnel, in the form of programming language alterations such as LINQ. LINQ will be discussed in the next chapter.

Accessing Relational Databases

Regardless of the database implementation that you use, a common architecture is employed, as illustrated in Figure 14-1.

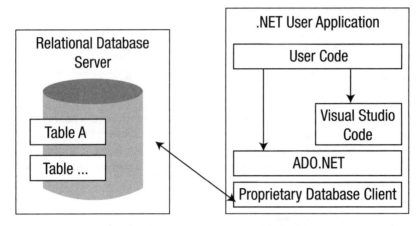

Figure 14-1. *Common database architecture*

Most relational database servers are separate applications that run on their own. To interact with a running relational database, the database vendor provides a database driver. In .NET, a database driver is a piece of proprietary code that talks to the relational database server, but exposes its functionality using the ADO.NET layer.

The ADO.NET layer is a technology that abstracts the database client into a neutral set of interfaces. By itself, ADO.NET does not implement any technologies, but it defines the interfaces that a database needs to have implemented. ADO.NET is similar to the lighting manager application introduced in Chapter 8, where specific lighting implementations need to implement interfaces.

The ADO.NET code can be accessed directly in your application by your code. However, doing that means accessing the individual rows, columns, and database tables. It is not a difficult undertaking, but it means you need to do everything manually. With respect to the lottery example, it means manipulating the lottery winners and the lottery draws tables.

Visual Basic Express and other Visual Studio editions have a number of tools that will generate code that automatically binds to tables and rows, reducing the amount of work that you need to do. In Figure 14-1, the user code has arrows pointing to both the Visual Studio–generated code and the ADO.NET code. These arrows indicate that your code does not need to use the Visual Studio–generated code; it is optional. But the advantage of using the Visual Studio code is that it reduces the amount of grunt work that your code needs to do. The Visual Studio–generated code is a thin functional layer on top of the ADO.NET code that maps directly to the tables that you are manipulating.

When you are developing an application that accesses a relational database, you need to consider the following issues:

ADO.NET drivers: When you write ADO.NET code, you will need an ADO.NET driver for each database. Thus, if you wish to use MySQL, you will need a MySQL driver. However, for the most part, the code that you write in your application will remain identical, regardless of which type of database you are using.

Abstraction: There will always be differences in the code used to access different relational databases. Be prepared to abstract your database code if you access the database directly using ADO.NET.

Designing a Database Using Visual Basic Express

Visual Basic Express is very helpful when designing and building database applications. It provides interface-based tools for designing the database, managing connections, and managing data access.

With Visual Basic Express, you can directly integrate the ADO.NET drivers for only Microsoft SQL Server. (This does not mean you cannot use a different ADO.NET driver using code.) If you want to use the GUI tools for a database driver other than for SQL Server, you will need to upgrade your Visual Studio edition. For this chapter's examples, we'll use the SQL Server Express Edition driver (http://msdn.microsoft.com/vstudio/express/sql/).

You can add the GUI tool-based database support to any Visual Basic project type. For this chapter, we'll use a console project called DatabaseConsoleEx.

After you have created the DatabaseConsoleEx console project in Visual Basic Express (using the procedure outlined in Chapter 1), you can set up the database, and then add tables to your new database.

Configuring the Data Source

Using the Visual Basic Express Data Source Configuration Wizard, you can add a database as your data source, set up the database connection, and select database objects to include in the project. Follow these steps to use the wizard:

1. Select Data ➤ Add New Data Source to start the Data Source Configuration Wizard.

2. Choose Database as the data source and click Next.

3. You're asked to choose a data connection. When choosing the data connection, you are defining the connection settings to your relational database. Since we are creating a new database in this example, click the New Connection button.

4. Choose Microsoft SQL Server Database File and click Continue.

5. In the Add Connection dialog box, fill in the database file name. For this example, enter the name lottery. Visual Basic Express will automatically add an .mdf extension to the file name to indicate that it is a SQL Server file and save it in your My Documents folder by default. Click OK to add the connection and select Yes when asked to choose to create the file if it doesn't exist.

6. The Choose Your Data Connection screen reappears with your data connection filled in. Click Next.

7. Since we're using a SQL Server Express Edition driver for this example, the dialog box shown in Figure 14-2 appears. It asks if the database file can be copied into the project. Click Yes.

8. You are asked if you want the application configuration information added to the project. Click Next to add the information.

9. The Choose Your Database Objects screen appears. Since this is a SQL Server Express Edition file, it doesn't have any tables. If the database connection referenced a relational database that already existed, database objects would be available. Click Finish.

Figure 14-2. *Adding the SQL Server Express Edition file to the local project*

Visual Basic Express will rebuild your project. When it is finished, the result will be similar to the project structure shown in Figure 14-3.

Figure 14-3. *Modifications made to the Visual Basic Express project*

The Visual Basic Express project contains a reference to a file that is provided by Microsoft SQL Server Express Edition. The diagram shown earlier in Figure 14-1 indicates that a database server is another process that you access using a client library. In about 80% of the cases, this is true, but some database servers are file-based. These types of databases are used in simpler single-user database applications. From a programming perspective, nothing changes, and the source code should not even be aware of whether the database is a file or server process.

Adding the Tables

In Visual Basic Express, you can add tables to your database using the Database Explorer. Through the Database Explorer, you can modify all of the data objects available within the database. Here are the general steps for adding a table:

1. Right-click the `lottery.mdf` file in the Solution Explorer and select Open to open the Database Explorer. The Database Explorer displays information about the database.

2. Right-click the Tables node and select Add New Table to open a window for creating the new table, as shown in Figure 14-4.

3. Specify the column name and type for each column in the table. You can also specify other details about each column, such as its length and whether it must be unique.

4. Once you have entered the column information, save the table (Ctrl+S) and give it a name. For this example, we will add three tables: `draws`, `persons`, and `winners`. The following sections describe the columns and types for these tables.

Figure 14-4. *Creating a new table*

Each column of a table must have a name and type. Just as Visual Basic has types, so does a database. What is frustrating about database types is that they are similar but not identical to Visual Basic types. To make things even more frustrating, not all database implementations have the exact same types. Fortunately, if you use the Visual Studio tools, the wizard will map a specific database type to a Visual Basic type.

■**Tip** The Microsoft Visual Studio documentation has an excellent reference on the various data types and their accuracy. See the "Data Types" section of the Microsoft SQL Server Books Online documentation (http://msdn2.microsoft.com/en-us/library/ms130214.aspx).

Draws Table

The draws table contains all of the drawn lottery numbers. Table 14-1 shows the column names and types for this table.

Table 14-1. *Draws Table Columns*

Name	Type
draw_date	datetime
first_number	int
second_number	int
third_number	int
fourth_number	int
fifth_number	int
sixth_number	int
bonus	int

The draw_date column holds the date of the draw. The declared type is datetime, which is like the datetime type in .NET. However, you will need to be careful in mapping types, as explained in Chapter 3.

The rest of the columns represent a number in the winning draw, including the bonus number. As in Visual Basic, SQL Server includes various numeric types. The number columns in the draws table are declared as the int type.

■**Note** The one SQL Server numeric type that does not exist in .NET is numeric. This type behaves like the decimal type in .NET, except for the precision. With numeric, you can specify the number of digits before and after the decimal point.

Persons Table

The persons table lists all of the people who have won a lottery drawing. Table 14-2 shows the column names and types for the persons table.

Table 14-2. *Persons Table Columns*

Name	Type
id	uniqueidentifier
first_name	nvarchar(100)
last_name	nvarchar(100)

The persons table is a collection of people with their first names and last names. The challenge in a relational database is uniquely identifying a user. Think of it as trying to define a unique hash code. The solution most databases use is a number. When you have millions of records, a number might not be adequate as a unique identifier. In that case, you can use the SQL Server uniqueidentifier type, as we're doing for the id column of the persons table.

The first_name and last_name columns both have the type nvarchar(100). A string in a database behaves like a number type, in that strings have length limits. In the example, we use the nvarchar type, for a variable-length string with a maximum length of 100 characters. In contrast, specifying char(100) would give you a string 100 characters long, regardless of how many bytes contain letters. If the entry in a char column has fewer characters than specified, the remainder of the char string is filled with space characters, by default.

Winners Table

The winners table matches the winning people to their lottery drawing. Table 14-3 shows the column names and types for the winners table.

Table 14-3. *Winners Table Columns*

Name	Type
id	uniqueidentifier
draw_date	datetime

Both columns are the types of the specific columns in the tables being referenced. The idea is to use the winners table in conjunction with the persons table and the draws table to create the list that shows who won which lottery drawing and their numbers.

After you've created the three tables, your Database Explorer will resemble Figure 14-5.

Figure 14-5. *Modified database structure with the added tables*

Now that we have a database with some tables, let's see how to access that database directly, using ADO.NET.

Accessing the Database Using ADO.NET

Accessing the database directly using ADO.NET involves using the ADO.NET interfaces. The first step is to define a connection. Once the connection has been established, you can manipulate the tables in the database—to add, remove, and update records.

Now we will continue with the sample lottery database created in the previous section. We'll write code to add, select, and delete records.

Connecting to a Database

Define a database connection with the following code, which illustrates a general approach (added to the DatabaseConsoleEx application).

```
Imports System.Data.SqlClient
. . .
Dim connection As IDbConnection = _
  New SqlConnection(DatabaseConsoleEx.My.Settings.Default.lotteryConnectionString)
```

We need to import the System.Data.SqlClient namespace because it contains the classes to access and use SQL Server (that is, the ADO.NET driver).

The variable connection is a SqlConnection object, which is specifically for accessing SQL Server. Think of it as picking up the telephone and hearing the telephone tone. The connection requires a username, password, and the name of the database to which you want to connect, which are bundled into a connection string. That information is stored in lotteryConnectionString, which was defined when you configured the data source in Visual Basic Express.

Once you have a connection instance, you can create a live connection, which is akin to dialing a telephone number and hearing that telephone ring. Here is the code for opening the connection:

```
connection.Open()
```

Now you can work with the tables in the database.

Closing a Database Connection

After having processed your SQL statements, you should close the connection to indicate that you are finished using the database. Here's how:

```
connection.Close()
```

It is good practice to open and close database connections as quickly as possible. You should open a connection only when you are absolutely ready, and close it as soon as you are finished with it.

Adding Table Data

The draws database table you created earlier is empty. Now we will add some content. To add data to a database using SQL, use the SQL INSERT command, as follows:

```
Imports System.Data.SqlClient
. . .
    Dim cmd As IDbCommand = _
      New SqlCommand("INSERT INTO draws (draw_date, first_number, second_number, " _
                                 & "third_number, fourth_number, " _
                                 & "fifth_number, sixth_number, bonus) " _
               & "VALUES (@pDrawDate, @pFirstNumber, @pSecondNumber, " _
          & "@pThirdNumber, @pFourthNumber, @pFifthNumber, @pSixthNumber, @pBonus)")

    cmd.Connection = connection

    Dim paramDate As IDbDataParameter = New SqlParameter()
    paramDate.ParameterName = "@pDrawDate"
    paramDate.DbType = System.Data.DbType.DateTime
    paramDate.Size = 8
    paramDate.SourceColumn = "draw_date"
    paramDate.Value = DateTime.Now
    cmd.Parameters.Add(paramDate)

    Dim param As IDbDataParameter = New SqlParameter()
    param.ParameterName = "@pFirstNumber"
    param.DbType = System.Data.DbType.Int32
    param.Size = 4
    param.SourceColumn = "first_number"
    param.Value = 1
    cmd.Parameters.Add(param)

    . . .

    param = New SqlParameter()
    param.ParameterName = "@pBonus"
    param.DbType = System.Data.DbType.Int32
    param.Size = 4
    param.SourceColumn = "bonus"
    param.Value = 1
    cmd.Parameters.Add(param)

    Dim retval As Integer = cmd.ExecuteNonQuery()
    Console.WriteLine("retval (" & retval & ")")
    connection.Close()
```

To execute a command, you need to instantiate a class that implements the IDbCommand interface, where the constructor parameter is the SQL statement that you want to execute. The SQL statement contains SQL parameters. How a SQL parameter is defined often depends on the ADO.NET implementation. The command is associated with the database connection using the cmd.Connection property.

Each parameter, regardless of the database driver used, is of type IDataParameter or IDbDataParameter (which implements IDataParameter). The type associated with IDbDataParameter is SqlParameter in this case, because we are using SQL Server.

The properties of IDbDataParameter are as follows:

- ParameterName: Specifies the name of the parameter and must be prefixed with an at sign (@) character.

- DbType: Specifies the type of the parameter.

- Size: Specifies the size of the parameter (in bytes).

- SourceColumn: Specifies in which column the parameter will be stored.

- Value: Specifies the value for the parameter.

■**Note** As a general rule of thumb, stick to using and manipulating the standard ADO.NET interfaces, rather than the types specific to the ADO.NET driver.

The example shows code that you would write when you want to explicitly define the attributes of every parameter. This was to allow you to see what is happening when parameters are converted and stored in a table. A simpler notation is as follows:

```
Dim connection As IDbConnection = _
  New SqlConnection(DatabaseConsoleEx.My.Settings.Default.lotteryConnectionString)
connection.Open()

Dim cmd As IDbCommand = New SqlCommand("INSERT INTO draws (draw_date, " _
        & "first_number, second_number, third_number, fourth_number, " _
                & "fifth_number, sixth_number, bonus) VALUES (@pDrawDate, " _
                & "@pFirstNumber, @pSecondNumber, @pThirdNumber," _
                & "@pFourthNumber,@pFifthNumber,@pSixthNumber,@pBonus)")

cmd.Connection = connection

cmd.Parameters.Add(New SqlParameter("@pDrawDate", DateTime.Now))
cmd.Parameters.Add(New SqlParameter("@pFirstNumber", 10))
cmd.Parameters.Add(New SqlParameter("@pSecondNumber", 1))
cmd.Parameters.Add(New SqlParameter("@pThirdNumber", 30))
cmd.Parameters.Add(New SqlParameter("@pFourthNumber", 19))
cmd.Parameters.Add(New SqlParameter("@pFifthNumber", 2))
cmd.Parameters.Add(New SqlParameter("@pSixthNumber", 21))
cmd.Parameters.Add(new SqlParameter("@pBonus", 5))
```

Once you have defined the parameters and assigned them with a value, the SQL query can be executed. In the case of a SQL INSERT statement, no data will be returned, because you are sending data from the application to the database. Thus, you will need to execute the method that does not expect any return data, which is ExecuteNonQuery(), like this:

```
Dim retval As Integer = cmd.ExecuteNonQuery()
Console.WriteLine("retval (" & retval & ")")
```

ExecuteNonQuery() returns the number of rows affected by the statement (which should be 1, because we've inserted one row).

Selecting Data from a Table

After your tables have some data, you probably will want to retrieve the data. To do that, you use the SELECT statement. Here is the code for viewing data in the draws table:

```
Dim connection As IDbConnection = _
   New SqlConnection(DatabaseConsoleEx.My.Settings.Default.lotteryConnectionString)
connection.Open()

Dim cmd As IDbCommand = New SqlCommand("SELECT * FROM draws")
cmd.Connection = connection
Dim reader As IDataReader = cmd.ExecuteReader()
While reader.Read()
    Console.WriteLine("(" & reader.GetDateTime(0).ToString() & ") " _
       & reader.GetInt32(1))
End While

reader.Close()
connection.Close()
```

To select data, the steps are to open a connection, create a command, and execute the command. In the example, the SELECT statement did not have any parameters. SELECT * means to select all columns. Alternatively, you could define identifiers to select specific columns.

When you are using a SELECT statement, the server will return data. To read the returned data, you call the method ExecuteReader(), which will also execute the command. This is different from the ExecuteNonQuery() method you use to insert data, mainly in that ExecuteReader() returns an instance of IDataReader. IDataReader is an interface used to iterate individual records, which gives you the chance to retrieve the individual fields of the records, and you can examine the data in the columns for each record.

To access the fields, use the appropriate GetNNN() method, with the index of the field. Knowing which index to use is a bit perplexing. The index of the appropriate field is related to the position of the column in the SELECT command (though, in this case, we've selected all the data with *, so it depends on the position of the column in the table). For example, the following code retrieves the fourth column from a result set.

```
reader.GetDouble(3)
```

In our example, we obtain the date and the first draw number.

Deleting Data from the Database

Of course, you may need to delete data from table. The SQL statement for removing data from a table is DELETE. The following example deletes a particular lottery drawing entry from the draws table.

```
Dim cmd As IDbCommand = _
   New SqlCommand("DELETE FROM draws WHERE draw_date=@pDrawDate", _
                  CType(connection, SqlConnection))

Dim paramDate As IDbDataParameter = New SqlParameter()
paramDate.ParameterName = "@pDrawDate"
paramDate.DbType = System.Data.DbType.DateTime
paramDate.Size = 8
paramDate.SourceColumn = "draw_date"
paramDate.Value = DateTime.Now
cmd.Parameters.Add(paramDate)

cmd.ExecuteNonQuery()
connection.Close()
```

As with the INSERT statement, you use ExecuteNonQuery() with DELETE, which does not return any results (except for the number of rows affected by the command).

Recapping ADO.NET Usage

Looking at all of the code presented in this section, you should notice the following points about using ADO.NET directly:

- There are general interfaces, implemented by a specific library.

- The IDbConnection and IDbCommand interfaces are implemented by all ADO.NET drivers.

- SqlConnection, SqlCommand, and SqlParameter are specific classes from the database driver.

- The database code involves opening a connection; defining a SQL command such as INSERT, SELECT, and so on; assigning the SQL parameters; executing the SQL command; and then closing the connection.

■**Note** For more details on SQL, see Wikipedia's SQL entry (http://en.wikipedia.org/wiki/SQL) and W3School's SQL tutorial (http://www.w3schools.com/sql/default.asp). These provide a good explanation of the basics of SQL. The MSDN documentation is fairly good as well.

Next, let's take a look at another Visual Studio tool for working with database applications.

Using the Dataset Designer

The Dataset Designer is a utility provided by Visual Basic Express to help you write database applications. MSDN provides a detailed tutorial on how to create client data applications (http://msdn2.microsoft.com/en-us/library/h0y4a0f6.aspx). The tutorial describes how to click options and use the wizards, but it does not explain some of the underlying details. Here, we'll use the Dataset Designer to set up the relations between the lottery database tables, and take a look at the code that is generated automatically to create those relations.

A *dataset* is an in-memory representation of the data in the database. It is used for manipulating the data away from the database server before you update the database. This disconnected form of working with the data improves performance, because you reduce the number of times you need to query the database server.

Building Relations Between Tables

The first step in using the Dataset Designer is to convert the tables in the Database Explorer to something that the Dataset Designer can use. To do this, from the Solution Explorer, double-click the file that has the extension .xsd—lotteryDataSet.xsd in our example. The .xsd file is the XML Schema Definition file, which translates the database's datasets into XML files.

The lotteryDataSet.xsd file has a number of child files, which you can open and inspect. These files are part of a collection that is used by the Dataset Designer. The only file that you can modify is lotteryDataSet.vb (which you can view by right-clicking lotteryDataSet.xsd and selecting View Code). The other files are managed by the Dataset Designer.

We want to build relations between the three tables. Relations are important because they allow you to maintain database consistency. For example, imagine adding a winner to the winners table for a lottery drawing date that does not exist. Using relations, you can enforce a consistency check, so that the drawing date must exist in the database before you can add a winner for that date. We will define two relations: winners with draws and winners with persons. Remember that the winners table is a cross-reference between the persons and draws table.

Follow these steps to define the relations:

1. Double-click lotteryDataSet.xsd in the Solution Explorer. You will see a message indicating that the Dataset Designer has no data.

2. Drag and drop each of the three tables you created earlier from the Database Explorer onto the surface of the Dataset Designer, as shown in Figure 14-6. This automatically adds default support for the three tables.

Figure 14-6. *Dataset Designer with the three tables*

3. To build a relation, right-click the data generator surface and choose Add ➤ Relation. The Relation dialog box appears. This dialog box allows you to associate two tables via a specific field.

4. As shown in Figure 14-7, specify winners as the parent table and persons as the child. The key column is id. Click OK to create the relation.

Figure 14-7. *Creating the winners and persons relation*

The winners and draws relation is created in the same way as the winners and persons relation, except that the columns linked are draw_date, as shown in Figure 14-8.

After you have created both relations, the Dataset Designer surface should look like Figure 14-9.

Figure 14-9 illustrates a well-defined database structure that includes relations. The structure is very important for the Dataset Designer, because it defines how the generated code will appear. Look closely at Figure 14-9 and notice how each table representation shows Fill, GetData() at the bottom. The Fill() and GetData() methods are used to retrieve the data from the database and convert it into data that Visual Basic can process.

Figure 14-8. *Creating the winners and draws relation*

Figure 14-9. *Dataset Designer surface with all tables and relations*

If you were to click the table adapter, the Dataset Designer would display the properties, similar to Figure 14-10.

Figure 14-10. *Properties of Dataset Designer table structure*

The properties show the exact syntax of the SQL INSERT and SELECT commands. Remember these two statements are used to add and select data from database tables. This illustrates that the Dataset Designer code is no different than the ADO.NET code (except the dataset is a cache).

Now consider the following code, generated by the Dataset Designer, to bind the columns of the draws table to the generated data structure (in lotteryDataSet.Designer.vb).

```
<Global.System.Diagnostics.DebuggerNonUserCodeAttribute()> _
Private Sub InitAdapter()
    Me._adapter = New Global.System.Data.SqlClient.SqlDataAdapter
    Dim tableMapping As Global.System.Data.Common.DataTableMapping = ➡
      New Global.System.Data.Common.DataTableMapping
    tableMapping.SourceTable = "Table"
    tableMapping.DataSetTable = "draws"
    tableMapping.ColumnMappings.Add("draw_date", "draw_date")
    tableMapping.ColumnMappings.Add("first_number", "first_number")
    tableMapping.ColumnMappings.Add("second_number", "second_number")
    tableMapping.ColumnMappings.Add("third_number", "third_number")
    tableMapping.ColumnMappings.Add("fourth_number", "fourth_number")
    tableMapping.ColumnMappings.Add("fifth_number", "fifth_number")
    tableMapping.ColumnMappings.Add("sixth_number", "sixth_number")
    tableMapping.ColumnMappings.Add("bonus", "bonus")
    Me._adapter.TableMappings.Add(tableMapping)
    Me._adapter.InsertCommand = New Global.System.Data.SqlClient.SqlCommand
    Me._adapter.InsertCommand.Connection = Me.Connection
    Me._adapter.InsertCommand.CommandText = "INSERT INTO [dbo].[draws] ➡
([draw_date], [first_number], [second_number], [third_n"& _
      "umber], [fourth_number], [fifth_number], [sixth_number], [bonus]) ➡
```

```
VALUES (@draw_"& _
    "date, @first_number, @second_number, @third_number, @fourth_number, ➡
@fifth_numbe"& _
    "r, @sixth_number, @bonus)"
    Me._adapter.InsertCommand.CommandType = Global.System.Data.CommandType.Text
    Me._adapter.InsertCommand.Parameters.Add(New ➡
Global.System.Data.SqlClient.SqlParameter("@draw_date", ➡
Global.System.Data.SqlDbType.DateTime, 0, ➡
Global.System.Data.ParameterDirection.Input, 0, 0, "draw_date", ➡
Global.System.Data.DataRowVersion.Current, false, Nothing, "", "", ""))
    Me._adapter.InsertCommand.Parameters.Add(New ➡
Global.System.Data.SqlClient.SqlParameter("@first_number", ➡
Global.System.Data.SqlDbType.Int, 0, ➡
Global.System.Data.ParameterDirection.Input, 0, 0, "first_number", ➡
Global.System.Data.DataRowVersion.Current, false, Nothing, "", "", ""))
    .  .  .
End Sub
```

The bolded code shows how close the generated code is to a variation of the code used to insert data in the ADO.NET section. The generated code is more explicit and verbose than the previous code, but that does not matter, since you are not supposed to edit the generated code. You are supposed to use the Dataset Designer.

■**Note** The Dataset Designer gives you the advantage of not having to provide bindings between Visual Basic and a database, and an easy binding between a user interface and the database. By providing a GUI where you can drag, drop, and so on, the Dataset Designer just makes it much simpler to write that code.

Using the Generated Code

Using the code generated by the Dataset Designer is easy, as long as you know what is going on. The Dataset Designer generates two major pieces of code: a table adapter and a dataset. The table adapter is code used to interact with the table directly and is the link between your code and the database. If you wanted to add, select, or delete items, use the table adapter. When you select data, the data will fill a dataset.

The following is the code to insert a record into the draws table (in the DatabaseConsoleEx application).

```
Dim table As DatabaseConsoleEx.lotteryDataSetTableAdapters.drawsTableAdapter = _
  New DatabaseConsoleEx.lotteryDataSetTableAdapters.drawsTableAdapter()
table.Insert(DateTime.Now, 2, 12, 14, 31, 18, 4, 20)
```

The code is a trivial two-liner. It instantiates the drawsTableAdapter, and then calls the Insert() method to add a record. Connecting to the database, executing the command, and assigning the parameters are done automatically.

Note   Generated code is both a blessing and a curse. Generated code hides complexity and makes it simpler for you to get your job done. But as you saw in the code excerpts, there is quite a bit going on behind the scenes, and if you don't understand ADO.NET, you will not know what to do when things go wrong. For example, when is a connection to the database made? The only way to know that is to look at the generated source code and follow the ADO.NET calls. A connection to a database is made the first time you call one of the SQL methods (for example, `Insert()`), not when the adapter is initialized.

To retrieve and iterate the data in the table, use the following code.

```
Dim dataset As DatabaseConsoleEx.lotteryDataSet = _
    New DatabaseConsoleEx.lotteryDataSet()

Dim table As DatabaseConsoleEx.lotteryDataSetTableAdapters.drawsTableAdapter = _
    New DatabaseConsoleEx.lotteryDataSetTableAdapters.drawsTableAdapter()

Dim count As Integer = table.Fill(dataset.draws)
Console.WriteLine("Record count is (" & dataset.draws.Count & ")(" & count & ")")
For Each row As DatabaseConsoleEx.lotteryDataSet.drawsRow In dataset.draws
    Console.Writeline("Date (" + row.draw_date.ToString() & ") (" _
        & row.first_number & ")")
Next
```

The variable `table` is initialized to an adapter that connects to the draws table. The variable `dataset` is an empty collection ready for the draws table.

To fill the data table in the dataset, the method `table.Fill()` is called, and the destination is the `dataset.draws` data table. After having called `Fill()`, the number of records read is returned and assigned to `count`.

To iterate the individual rows, a `For Each` loop is used. It references the type `drawsRow`, and each instance of `drawsRow` has data members that represent the `draw_date`, `first_number`, and other columns. The iteration of the individual rows resembles the iteration of a collection. The ADO.NET example used a `While` loop and required you to know which column was associated with which `SELECT` field.

The Important Stuff to Remember

In this chapter, you learned about the basics of ADO.NET and the Dataset Designer. Here are the main points to remember:

- The real problem when using a relational database and a programming language like Visual Basic is the mismatch of set-based operations and individual object operations.

- To access a relational database, you can use ADO.NET. There is an ADO.NET database driver for each relational database.

- The Dataset Designer code is based on ADO.NET, and thus if you understand ADO.NET, you will be able to understand how the Dataset Designer works and how it can be optimized.

- When using ADO.NET, the steps are typically to connect to a database, create a command, populate the parameters, execute the command, retrieve the data (if necessary), close the command, and close the connection.

- SQL is a language used to manipulate the tables of a relational database. You need to learn SQL on top of learning how to use ADO.NET.

Some Things for You to Do

The following are two exercises for applying what you've learned in this chapter.

1. The basis of the lottery application is defined in terms of a database, tables, and data. Write a console application that populates the `draws` table using a lottery file. Write a console application that dumps the contents of the `draws` table as a lottery file.

2. Create a console application that accepts as command-line arguments a winner and the date of the draw. Your console application must account for doubles and populate both the `persons` and `winners` tables.

CHAPTER 15

■ ■ ■

Learning About LINQ

In the previous chapter, you learned about how to access a database using the traditional ADO.NET technologies. When you make ADO.NET requests, you are making SQL calls and organizing the result set data using SQL.

Language Integrated Query (LINQ) is a technology that lets you organize your results in a consistent manner, regardless of the underlying source of the data. Why yet another technology to query information? The answer is related to XML.

XML is a technology used to represent information in a hierarchical manner. You saw an example of XML in Chapter 12. XML has solved many problems in an elegant and understandable manner. One of the solutions proposed by XML is the ability to reference information in an XML structure with XPath, which is a way of referencing an object structure using a set of filters. Using XPath, you can find any node, and the filters can include the presence of dependent elements, which is not easily possible in other technologies. Put simply, XPath and XML are very powerful techniques used to find information.

You can consider XML and XPath as inspiration for LINQ. Where LINQ and XML XPath deviate is that LINQ can be used to query Visual Basic collection objects, XML documents, and relational databases. Think of LINQ as a general mechanism used to search a collection of information. The focus of this chapter will be to explain the mechanics of LINQ, and demonstrate how to write queries and use the methods associated with the LINQ library.

Finding the Frequency of Winning Numbers

The lottery application we've been working with in previous chapters collects information about lottery drawings to predict the next set of winning lottery numbers. The idea is to find patterns. Again, the reality is that lottery drawings are random, so even if you could identify patterns, that wouldn't mean you could predict winning numbers. However, what is interesting about this problem is that you can use LINQ to slice and dice the data. LINQ lets you keep the data as objects, and to perform SQL- and XPath-like operations, as you'll see in this chapter.

In Chapter 10, you saw a streaming architecture, where a console application read in text data and spat out text data. You also saw examples of text-to-binary and binary-to-text conversions. The application in this chapter (in the FrequencyProcessor project) will read in text, process the data, and then generate text describing the frequency of lottery numbers. Thus, we need to use the text-to-text interface, which was defined in Chapter 10 as follows:

```
Public Interface IProcessor
    Function Process(ByVal input As String) As String
End Interface
```

The input is a text stream that looks like this:

```
2006.03.11 3 7 15 28 30 38 44
2006.03.15 10 18 30 34 41 43 5
2006.03.18 3 11 12 16 20 40 9
2006.03.22 2 3 7 13 42 43 41
2006.03.25 3 10 36 40 43 44 35
2006.03.29 3 4 8 16 34 39 45
```

If you want to find the frequency of the individual numbers, you could parse each individual number, and then increment the count of the individual number as an array, like this:

```
Dim frequency As Integer = 0
Dim splitUpText() As String = lineOfText.Split(New Char() {" "c})
frequency(Integer.Parse(splitUpText(0))) += 1
frequency(Integer.Parse(splitUpText(1))) += 1
. . .
```

The split line of text contains the list of numbers, separated by spaces, which is then converted to a series of numbers, each of which is used as an index for the frequency. The solution is fast and works, but it has a big problem: it is not extendable. The solution solves a single problem and only a single problem.

For example, let's say that you want to figure out other statistical information, such as which numeric combinations occur most often. Using the previous solution, that would require reparsing the text stream again. That is an expensive and tedious solution. The better solution would be to convert the stream into a series of objects that could be processed.

However, the problem at hand is calculating the frequency of individual numbers. So why exert the extra effort if the solution that solves the single problem works? Writing good code means solving problems using a generic but specific approach. You want to write specific code so that you do not get bogged down in thinking about details in the future, and you want to write generic code so that any future requirement does not cause you to completely rewrite the old application. Knowing when to write specific code and when to write generic code is really a matter of experience—the only way to learn is to write code.

Extending the Lottery-Prediction System

In Chapter 10, the IProcessor interface was a good first step because it solved the problem at hand. The problem was to convert each line of text into another line of text. However, in this chapter's example, that interface is not enough. We need to add two other methods: Initialize() and Destroy().

We want to find the frequencies of an individual number in the drawn lotteries. The original interface method IProcessor.Process() is used to process an individual line of text, and the frequencies can be calculated only after all of the draws have been processed. Thus, we add Destroy(), which is called after all of the lines of text have been read. Common coding convention says that if you have a Destroy() method, you should have an Initialize() method that is called before the lines of text are processed.

Having extra requirements is not a problem and is fairly common. But you want to add the extra requirements without disrupting existing functionality. After all, if some code works, you don't want to break it because of additional requirements. Thus, you don't want to add the methods to the IProcessor interface like this:

```
Public Interface IProcessor
    Function Initialize() As String
    Function Destroy() As String
    Function Process(ByVal input As String) As String
End Interface
```

This code is a no-no because you are breaking existing functionality. Any class that implements IProcessor must now implement the methods Initialize() and Destroy(), even though those classes don't need those methods.

Thus, when adding requirements, you should not change existing interfaces. You create new interfaces and subclass the existing interfaces, like this:

```
Public Interface IExtendedProcessor
    Inherits IProcessor
    Function Destroy() As String
    Function Initialize() As String
End Interface
```

The new interface IExtendedProcessor has the new methods Initialize() and Destroy(), but inherits the method Process(). The old functionality still has only a single method, and the new functionality is free to implement either interface.

Adding new interfaces and new methods does not mean everything will work as is. If you go back and look at the source code from Chapter 10, you'll see that the IProcessor interface was used by the Bootstrap class. So, if you want the IExtendedProcessor interface to be recognized, you must update Bootstrap. Updating Bootstrap is fine, because it does not mean that IProcessor implementations must be updated (or, at least, Bootstrap should not require that IProcessor implementations be updated).

The original abbreviated implementation of Bootstrap is as follows:

```
Imports System.IO

Public Module Bootstrap
    Public Sub DisplayHelp()
        Console.WriteLine("You need help? Right now?")
    End Sub

    Public Sub Start(ByVal args As String(), _
        ByVal processor As IProcessor)
        Dim reader As TextReader = Nothing
        Dim writer As TextWriter = Nothing
```

```vbnet
        If (args.Length = 0) Then
            reader = Console.In
            writer = Console.Out
        ElseIf (args.Length = 1) Then
            If (args(0) = "-help") Then
                Bootstrap.DisplayHelp()
                Return
            End If
            reader = File.OpenText(args(0))
            writer = Console.Out
        End If
        ' Abbreviated
        writer.Write(processor.Process(reader.ReadToEnd()))
    End Sub

End Module
```

In the original implementation, the method Process() is called to read an input and write an output stream. Since Initialize() and Destroy() should be called before and after the string is processed, the most logical location of each method would be before and after the processor.Process() method, like this:

```vbnet
Imports System.IO

Public Module Bootstrap
    Public Sub DisplayHelp()
        Console.WriteLine("You need help? Right now?")
    End Sub

    Public Sub Start(ByVal args As String(), _
        ByVal processor As IProcessor)
        Dim reader As TextReader = Nothing
        Dim writer As TextWriter = Nothing
        If (args.Length = 0) Then
            reader = Console.In
            writer = Console.Out
        ElseIf (args.Length = 1) Then
            If (args(0) = "-help") Then
                Bootstrap.DisplayHelp()
                Return
            End If
            reader = File.OpenText(args(0))
            writer = Console.Out
        End If
        ' Abbreviated
        If TypeOf processor Is IExtendedProcessor Then
            writer.Write( _
            DirectCast(processor, IExtendedProcessor).Initialize())
        End If
```

```
    writer.Write(processor.Process(reader.ReadToEnd()))
    If TypeOf processor Is IExtendedProcessor Then
        writer.Write(DirectCast(processor, IExtendedProcessor).Destroy())
    End If
End Sub

End Module
```

In the solution, the processor interface is tested to see if the interface is an instance of IExtendedProcessor. If so, then the Initialize() and Destroy() methods can be called.

Extending interfaces and extending those classes that consume the old and new interfaces at the same time is keeping *backward-compatibility*. Backward-compatibility is an important concept, because it implies you can gradually introduce new functionality into a working application without breaking old functionality.

Keeping backward-compatibility without breaking working functionality is difficult, and there is a point where adding new functionality becomes too complicated. Once you reach this stage, you need to break backward-compatibility by doing the following:

```
Public Interface IExtendedProcessor
    Function Initialize() As String
    Function Destroy() As String
    Function Process(ByVal input As String) As String
End Interface

<Obsolete("IProcessor is obsolete, please use IExtendedProcessor ", _
    true)> _
Public Interface IProcessor
    Function Process(ByVal input As String) As String
End Interface
```

The example will break backward-compatibility due to the Obsolete attribute being associated with the IProcessor interface. Thus, when any class or interface references the IProcessor interface, a compile error results. The second parameter of Obsolete is true, which forces the compiler error. If you left out that parameter, when the interface is referenced, a compiler warning, rather than a warning, is generated.

The IExtendedProcessor interface does not subclass IProcessor and includes the method Process(). Thus, there are no dependencies between IExtendedProcessor and IProcessor, and all functionality in the application must use IExtendedProcessor rather than IProcessor.

■**Note** Breaking backward-compatibility is a major step, because your code cries that some code is broken and requires alteration. However, sometimes you will need to break code, and when you do, make sure that the code cries "broken!" very loud. Otherwise, you might get unexpected errors.

Now that we've updated the Bootstrap class and added the IExtendedProcessor interface, all of the samples in Chapter 10 will continue to function, and we can implement the frequency solution.

Implementing a Frequency Solution

The solution that we want to use is to read in the text, convert the text into binary objects, calculate some statistics, and finally write out the text. The interesting part of this solution is that pieces of it have already been written. If you remember in Chapter 10, there was a requirement to convert the lottery draws into binary form. That code will be borrowed to implement the statistics functionality.

The statistics console application (FrequencyProcessor) requires an IExtendedProcessor implementation. The following is the complete implementation (note the imports from Chapter 10's example).

```
Imports LottoLibrary
Imports ReaderWriter
Imports System
Imports System.Collections.Generic
Imports System.IO
Imports System.Linq
Imports System.Text

Friend Class LottoTicketProcessor
    Implements IExtendedProcessor

    Private _tickets As List(Of Ticket) = New List(Of Ticket)()

    Public Function Destroy() As String Implements IExtendedProcessor.Destroy
        Dim builder As New StringBuilder()
        Dim c1 As Integer
        For c1 = 1 To 46 - 1
            builder.Append("Number (" & c1 & ") Found (")
            Dim foundCount As Integer = 0
            builder.Append(((foundCount + FrequencyOfANumber(c1)) & ")" & ChrW(10)))
        Next c1
        Return builder.ToString()
    End Function

    Private Function FrequencyOfANumber(ByVal numberToSearch As Integer) As Integer
        Dim query = From ticket In _tickets _
                    Where ticket.Numbers(0) = numberToSearch _
                    Or ticket.Numbers(1) = numberToSearch _
                    Or ticket.Numbers(2) = numberToSearch _
                    Or ticket.Numbers(3) = numberToSearch _
                    Or ticket.Numbers(4) = numberToSearch _
                    Or ticket.Numbers(5) = numberToSearch _
                    Select ticket.Numbers
        Return query.Count()
    End Function
```

```
Public Function Initialize() As String Implements IExtendedProcessor.Initialize
    Return ""
End Function

Public Function Process(ByVal input As String) As String _
  Implements IProcessor.Process
    Dim reader As TextReader = New StringReader(input)
    Do While reader.Peek <> -1
        Dim splitUpText As String() = reader.ReadLine.Split(New Char() {" "c})
        Dim dateSplit As String() = splitUpText(0).Split(New Char() {"."c})
        Dim ticket As New Ticket( _
                            New DateTime( _
                              Integer.Parse(dateSplit(0)), _
                              Integer.Parse(dateSplit(1)), _
                              Integer.Parse(dateSplit(2))), _
                              New Integer() { _
                              Integer.Parse(splitUpText(1)), _
                              Integer.Parse(splitUpText(2)), _
                              Integer.Parse(splitUpText(3)), _
                              Integer.Parse(splitUpText(4)), _
                              Integer.Parse(splitUpText(5)), _
                              Integer.Parse(splitUpText(6))}, _
                              Integer.Parse(splitUpText(7)))
        _tickets.Add(ticket)
    Loop
    Return ""
End Function
End Class
```

Let's examine how the implementation works.

Borrowing Code to Solve Another Problem

The borrowed code is the implementation of the Process() method, shown here in abbreviated form:

```
Public Function Process(ByVal input As String) _
    As String Implements IProcessor.Process
    Dim reader As TextReader = New StringReader(input)
    Do While reader.Peek <> -1
        Dim splitUpText As String() = reader.ReadLine.Split(New Char() {" "c})
        Dim dateSplit As String() = splitUpText(0).Split(New Char() {"."c})
        Dim ticket As New Ticket( _
          ' . . .
    Loop
    Return ""
End Function
```

Other than the new _tickets.Add(ticket) line, the code is identical to the Text2Binary. Process() implementation. The bolded code adds the lottery draw to the list of drawn numbers. Once the tickets have been instantiated, they can be added to the list of tickets that will be queried and searched.

CODE REUSE

The borrowed code demonstrates code reuse through copy and paste. Realize that code that was used to process binary objects is now being used in a completely new context.

The copied and pasted code reuses classes and functionality from another problem context. You copied and pasted the functionality to parse and instantiate the Ticket type, but reused the Ticket type itself.

When we worked on the code for the Ticket type, you probably had no idea that we would reuse the same code. In fact, even *I* had no idea that we would reuse the code. I find this happens a lot in my projects.

So how does this work? I write code to fulfill two criteria: minimal to solve the task and general enough to not restrict further usage. So I don't actually design for code reuse, and I don't have code reuse on my mind. What I have on my mind is to design code in such a way that it could potentially be reused.

Let's look at that code that could have solved the frequency problem previously.

```
Dim splitUpText() as String = lineOfText.Split(New Char() { " "c })
frequency(Integer.Parse(splitUpText(0))) += 1
frequency(Integer.Parse(splitUpText(1))) += 1
. . .
```

Is this code efficient? No, even though the lines of code are minimal, the code itself is not efficient. If I wanted to use the same code to perform another frequency analysis, which could happen, I would need to copy and paste yet again, and thus the code is not efficient.

Is this code general enough to be used in another context? Absolutely not, because to reuse the code, you would need to copy and paste it, and do some slight alterations.

This is an excellent example of code that can be written very quickly and is very effectively used by copying and pasting it everywhere. You are productive and can solve a problem quickly, but it cannot be easily extended or maintained. Imagine finding a bug and having copied and pasted the code ten times. That would mean you would need to find the ten different locations and see if the bug exists in those different locations.

Using LINQ

To find the frequency of a specific number, you don't need to use LINQ. In fact, LINQ can always be avoided by using Visual Basic code. So then why use LINQ? The reason is that LINQ makes it easier for you to write complicated search queries that are agnostic of the source. An example is two versions of the code used to solve the frequency problem: one that is not reusable and one that is reusable. The code that is not reusable is the query without LINQ, and the reusable code is the query with LINQ.

So let's look at the frequency code that is not reusable.

```
Function FrequencyOfANumberNotReusable(ByVal numberToSearch As Integer) _
  As Integer
    Dim runningTotal As Integer = 0
    For Each aTicket as Ticket in _tickets
        If aTicket.Numbers(0) = numberToSearch OrElse _
          aTicket.Numbers(1) = numberToSearch OrElse _
          aTicket.Numbers(2) = numberToSearch OrElse _
          aTicket.Numbers(3) = numberToSearch OrElse _
          aTicket.Numbers(4) = numberToSearch OrElse _
          aTicket.Numbers(5) = numberToSearch Then
             runningTotal += 1
        End If
    Next
    Return runningTotal
End Function
```

Notice the similarity of the code to the code presented in Chapter 9. The problem with this code is that you are iterating and solving a particular problem. The code cannot be easily adapted to solving another problem.

The reusable code is in the form of a LINQ expression:

```
Private Function FrequencyOfANumber(ByVal numberToSearch As Integer) As Integer
    Dim query = From ticket In _tickets _
                    Where ticket.Numbers(0) = numberToSearch _
                    Or ticket.Numbers(1) = numberToSearch _
                    Or ticket.Numbers(2) = numberToSearch _
                    Or ticket.Numbers(3) = numberToSearch _
                    Or ticket.Numbers(4) = numberToSearch _
                    Or ticket.Numbers(5) = numberToSearch _
                    Select ticket.Numbers
    Return query.Count()
End Function
```

The LINQ expression uses many constructs similar to a SQL SELECT statement. Here are the basic rules of LINQ:

- All LINQ queries must have a data source (From).

- All LINQ queries must have a filter (Where); however, if the filter does not exist, an automatic include-everything filter is implied.

- All LINQ queries must have a resulting dataset creator (Select).

To execute a LINQ expression, you need a data source. The data source could be an object list, an XML document, or even a relational database table. In the example, the data source is an object list and is defined using the From statement:

```
From ticket In _tickets
```

Looking at the From statement, you could get the idea that it is a For Each statement without the types. Indeed, the iteration happens only when you actually try to use the result of the LINQ query. The From statement is saying to iterate the data source and assign each element (a Ticket) to the variable ticket. Note, however, that there is no explicit type information, which is one of the strengths of LINQ—you have the ability to easily slice and dice data to suit your needs.

As you retrieve each item, you want to verify whether the item matches your needs. If you look at the code that isn't reusable, you'll see that it checks this with an If statement. In LINQ, you use the Where statement, which is similar to its SQL equivalent. With the Where statement, you test to see if the item matches your criteria. In our case, we check each number in the Ticket instance to see if it matches the number we're currently seeking.

If the Where returns True, we have a match and we will want to do something. In the code that isn't reusable, that means incrementing the runningTotal integer. In LINQ, the aim is to filter the data source (_tickets in our case), and thus the Select statement is used to create a new result set of drawn numbers. This result set contains all of the draws with the number we're looking for (numberToSearch), and if the draws are counted, we can get the frequency of that number, which we then return.

Let's look at the LINQ that could be used to find the frequency of two numbers being drawn.

```
Function FrequencyOfTwoNumbers(ByVal number1ToSearch As Integer, _
                              ByVal number2ToSearch As Integer) As Integer
    Dim query = From ticket2 In _
                (From ticket In _tickets _
                Where ticket.Numbers(0) = number1ToSearch _
                Or ticket.Numbers(1) = number1ToSearch _
                Or ticket.Numbers(2) = number1ToSearch _
                Or ticket.Numbers(3) = number1ToSearch _
                Or ticket.Numbers(4) = number1ToSearch _
                Or ticket.Numbers(5) = number1ToSearch _
                Select ticket) _
                Where ticket2.Numbers(0) = number2ToSearch _
                Or ticket2.Numbers(1) = number2ToSearch _
                Or ticket2.Numbers(2) = number2ToSearch _
                Or ticket2.Numbers(3) = number2ToSearch _
                Or ticket2.Numbers(4) = number2ToSearch _
                Or ticket2.Numbers(5) = number2ToSearch _
                Select ticket2.Numbers
    Return query.Count()
End Function
```

The LINQ statement is a concatenation of two LINQ queries, where one LINQ query is bolded. When the query is executed, the embedded query is executed and generates a result set. The result set is a data source on which the outer and second query operates, which then generates another result set.

You do not need to embed LINQ queries as in the preceding code. You could write functions and embed the result of a LINQ query as the data source of another LINQ query. The power of LINQ is that you can, in theory, arbitrarily embed many queries within other queries, since you are creating a filtering mechanism where one result set is the data source of another query.

■**Note** LINQ's strength is in its ability to slice and dice data to find the information that you want (which is easy because it is data source–agnostic). LINQ requires more resources than similar Visual Basic code in longhand format. But the benefit you get with LINQ is reusable code that you can maintain.

In the preceding section, we used LINQ to solve the frequency problem in a manner that promoted reusability. For example, if you wanted to find out more statistics of the lottery draws, all you would need to do is write more LINQ statements that sliced and diced the existing list of lottery draws. It would require adding only the method calls to the IExtendedProcessor. Destroy() method. However, let's consider the problem solved and think about what else can be done with LINQ.

Learning More LINQ Tricks

LINQ is not the only way to filter data. Associated with LINQ are a number of extension methods that can be applied to lists. For example, to filter for the frequency of a particular number, the following code could also have been used.

```
Function FrequencyOfANumber(ByVal numberToSearch As Integer) As Integer
    Dim query = _tickets.Where( _
                            Function(ticket, index) _
            ticket.Numbers(0) = numberToSearch _
            Or ticket.Numbers(1) = numberToSearch _
            Or ticket.Numbers(2) = numberToSearch _
            Or ticket.Numbers(3) = numberToSearch _
            Or ticket.Numbers(4) = numberToSearch _
            Or ticket.Numbers(5) = numberToSearch)
    Return query.Count()
End Function
```

The ideas of LINQ that include From, Where, and Select are not lost; they just have not been used. The From part is the _tickets variable itself. The Where part is the method Where(), and the Select part is a default selection of the currently selected node.

To specify an action with Where(), you use a lambda expression, which has two parameters: the object and the index of the object. The lambda expression expects that you return a Boolean value indicating whether the ticket item should be added to a returned list.

LINQ is a syntax that wraps SQL-like text. LINQ is much easier to understand and program than using the method-call syntax of the previous example. Using the methods gives you more flexibility, but they also are more complicated to write.

For example, if you wanted to find the frequency of two numbers in a list, you could use this code:

```
Function FrequencyOfTwoNumbersList(ByVal number1ToSearch As Integer , _
                                    ByVal number2ToSearch As Integer) As Integer
    Dim query = _tickets.Where( _
                         Function(ticket, index) _
            ticket.Numbers(0) = number1ToSearch _
            Or ticket.Numbers(1) = number1ToSearch _
            Or ticket.Numbers(2) = number1ToSearch _
            Or ticket.Numbers(3) = number1ToSearch _
            Or ticket.Numbers(4) = number1ToSearch _
            Or ticket.Numbers(5) = number1ToSearch).Where( _
                         Function(ticket, index) _
            ticket.Numbers(0) = number2ToSearch _
            Or ticket.Numbers(1) = number2ToSearch _
            Or ticket.Numbers(2) = number2ToSearch _
            Or ticket.Numbers(3) = number2ToSearch _
            Or ticket.Numbers(4) = number2ToSearch _
            Or ticket.Numbers(5) = number2ToSearch)
    Return query.Count()
End Function
```

In the code, the bolded line demonstrates how the output of one method can serve as the input for another method. This chaining of methods works because the list method returns other lists. Thus, you could add multiple criteria by concatenating multiple Where() method calls.

The methods are used to filter or manipulate the set where the details of the method are provided by a lambda expression. Table 15-1 briefly describes some of the useful methods that you can use to filter and manipulate a list. The best way to learn about all of the methods is to use Visual Basic Express, declare a list, and use IntelliSense to discover the different methods available. Also, see http://msdn2.microsoft.com/en-us/vbasic/bb688088.aspx for many examples that demonstrate the various list-manipulation methods.

Table 15-1. *Some Methods for Filtering and Manipulating Lists*

Method	Description
Aggregate()	Returns a fact about the list. A fact could be how many even numbers there are or the frequency of a particular number. All of the elements in the list are iterated and returned as a single fact, not as a list.
All()	Iterates all elements of the list and tests according to a lambda expression, where a True or False is returned. For example, the test could be to find out if all objects have a value greater than 10. The test needs to return only a True or False value for the individual object, where the All() method will correlate the results and return a True or False.
Any()	Like All(), except that the question is changed to test if any of the objects meet the criteria, such as having a value greater than 10. If so, then a True value is returned; otherwise, a False value is returned.
Average()	Calculates the average of a sequence of values. The average value returned is a numeric Decimal value. This method is a bit odd, because to calculate an average, you need numbers, even though the lambda expression could calculate the average of objects.

Table 15-1. *Some Methods for Filtering and Manipulating Lists (Continued)*

Method	Description
Cast()	Returns a list where each item is converted from the list type to another type. This is a good method to use when you need to perform bulk conversions of instance types in a list.
Concat()	Concatenates two lists.
Contains()	Verifies whether an item is present in the list. The method uses a lambda expression to determine whether the specified item is in the list, and returns True or False accordingly.
ConvertAll()	Returns a list where each item is converted from the list type to another type. This is a good method to use when you need to perform bulk conversions of instance types in a list.
Distinct()	Removes all duplicates from a list. By default, the implementation of Distinct() checks for equality by calling GetHashCode() first, and then calling Equals() if necessary. A variation of the Distinct() method is to supply an IEqualityComparer interface instance that can be used to determine whether two types are equal. However, a better approach would be to implement GetHashCode() and Equals().
Except()	Takes the current list and a passed-in list and performs a difference between the two sets, which is returned to the caller as a new dataset. The equality tests are identical to Distinct().
Find()	Finds an element of a particular list. Note that the lambda expression you use when it has found an element will cause the Find() method to stop processing the list and return what you marked as found.
FindAll()	Like Find(), except you can find multiple elements in a list. This is like the Where() method.
FindLast()	Like Find(), except the search starts at the end of the list.
ForEach()	An iterator that uses a lambda expression to process each element. The ForEach() method is a simplification of the code illustrated in Chapter 9.
GroupBy()	Takes a list and splits it into specific groupings as per the provided lambda expression. For example, you could use it to split the earnings of individuals into brackets.
Intersect()	Takes the current list and a provided list and determines the elements that are common to both lists. Uses the same equality tests as Distinct().
Max()	Finds the maximum value of a list.
Min()	Finds the minimum value of a list.
Reverse()	Reverses the order of the list.
Select()	Selects from the iteration being executed.
SelectMany()	Selects many items from a list where the selected items form another list.
Sum()	Calculates the sum of a list.
Union()	Takes the list and the passed-in list and calculates the union of the two lists. Uses the equality test as defined in the Distinct() method.

■**Note** With Visual Basic 2008, lists and the manipulation of lists have dramatically changed for the better. The general structure is to define methods that allow a developer to specify a lambda expression that is then chained together with other methods. Take some time to learn about all of the possibilities.

As an example of the power of the various methods, consider the following code, which compacts the frequency code into a couple of lines of source code.

```
Function FrequencyOfANumberFunc(ByVal numberToSearch As Integer) As Integer
    Return _tickets.SelectMany( _
        Function(ticket) ticket.Numbers).Where( _
            Function(num) num = numberToSearch).Count()
End Function
```

Here, each ticket is iterated by calling the SelectMany() method. This returns an array of numbers, which represents the drawn numbers. The purpose of SelectMany() is to combine the individual arrays of numbers into a large array of numbers. The code then calls Where() to filter out only those numbers that equal the number to search for, and finally the Count() method is called to return the number of found values.

The following sections present examples of using the extension methods with LINQ. They are in the LINQExamples project, which is a console application.

■**Note** In all of the examples, I have taken shortcuts for simplicity. So you will see some coding practices that are not recommended, such as creating public data members and not using properties.

Selecting and Altering Data

When running a LINQ query, the data that you filter and manipulate does not need to stay in its original form. Let's say that you have a list of customers, and you have identified a set of customers who deserve more loyalty points. You want to select those customers, increment their points, and then return the list of altered customers. To do that, you can mix LINQ with the extension methods.

Consider the following simplified customer declaration.

```
Class Customer
    Public Identifier As String
    Public Points As Integer
    Public Overrides Function ToString() As String
        Return "Identifier (" & Identifier & ") Points (" & Points & ")"
    End Function
End Class
```

A list will be created with two customers, where one customer has no points and the other one does. Here is the source code to create that list:

```
    Private Function CreateList() As Customer()
        Return New Customer() { _
            New Customer() With {.Identifier = "Person 1", .Points = 0}, _
            New Customer() With {.Identifier = "Person 2", .Points = 10}}
    End Function
```

The customers that have enough points are selected and rewarded with extra points. To do that, use the following LINQ statement.

```
    Function Increment(ByVal pCustomer As Customer, ByVal index As Integer) _
       As Customer
          pCustomer.Points += 5
          Return pCustomer
    End Function

    Sub CountCustomers()
        Dim points = (From customer In CreateList() _
                      Where customer.Points > 5 _
                      Select customer).Select(AddressOf Increment)
        Console.WriteLine("Count is (" & points.Count() & ")")
    End Sub
```

The LINQ query is combined with a modification operation. The LINQ statement that uses `From`, `Where`, and `Select` is not new. New are the parentheses enclosing the LINQ statement. By using a set of parentheses, you are identifying the LINQ statement as an object that references a result set.

In the example, the method called on the LINQ statement is `Select()`. Using the `Select()` method, each item in the result set is iterated and passed as a parameter (`pCustomer`) to the lambda expression (`Increment()`). Passed with the item is the index of the item in the list. The role of the lambda expression is to do something with the item and return what should be used as a basis for another list. In the example, an instance of the type `Customer` is passed in to `Increment()`, and an instance of type `Customer` is passed out. But before the instance is returned, it is manipulated to get an additional five bonus points.

What might concern you is that there is no test to check if the customer actually warrants earning five bonus points. That would be a concern if you were not using the LINQ expression. The LINQ expression is responsible for filtering out only those customers who should get the additional bonus points. Thus, when the method `Select()` is called, you are 100% sure that only the customers who should get bonus points actually get bonus points. Think of this as building a pipeline of manipulations.

Selecting with Anonymous Types

The `Select()` method and statement are used to generate a result set after finding a particular element. As demonstrated in the previous section, a `Select` statement is used to generate a new result set. For example, what if you want to find all of the customers who fulfill a certain criterion, but do not want to copy all of the associated data? You might want only the customer identifier and accumulated points. To do that, you could modify the `Select()` part of the LINQ statement to return a new type that you declare dynamically. The following is the previous example rewritten to use an anonymous type.

```
Function Increment2(ByVal pCustomer As Customer, ByVal index As Integer)
    pCustomer.Points += 5
    Return New With {.identifier = pCustomer.Identifier, _
            .points = pCustomer.Points}
End Function

Sub CountCustomers2()
    Dim points = (From customer In CreateList() _
                    Where customer.Points > 5 _
                    Select customer).Select(AddressOf Increment2)
    Console.WriteLine("Count is (" & points.Count() & ")")
End Sub
```

In the example, the `Return` statement in the `Increment2()` method uses the keyword `New` without a type identifier, but with the syntax of an object initializer. This is defining an anonymous type. An *anonymous type* is an object instance that has no explicitly named type. The anonymous type has properties, but it does not have methods.

Anonymous types are useful only in the context of the method in which they are declared. The variable `points` in the `CountCustomers2()` method is a collection of anonymous-type objects that could be iterated as follows:

```
For Each customer in points
    Console.WriteLine("Customer (" & _
        customer.identifier & ")(" & _
        customer.points & ")")
Next
```

The compiler that translates the LINQ expression knows that the final result set contains anonymous-type objects with the properties `identifier` and `points`.

Processing Multiple Streams

In all of the LINQ examples so far, a single result set has been manipulated, processed, and filtered. You can process multiple inputs at the same time, but you will get a combinatorial type answer.

For example, suppose you had this LINQ:

```
Dim set1 As Integer() = New Integer() {1, 2, 3, 4, 5}
Dim set2 As Integer() = New Integer() {1, 2, 3, 4, 5}
Dim set3 As Integer() = New Integer() {1, 2, 3, 4, 5}
Dim triples = _
    From a In set1 _
    From b In set2 _
    From c In set3 _
    Select New With {a, b, c}
```

In pseudo-code, the following would be identical.

```
Dim items As List (Of Object) = New List(Of Object)()
For Each a In set1
    For Each b In set2
        For Each c In set3
            items.Add(New With { a, b, c })
        Next
    Next
Next
```

When you specify multiple From clauses, you are creating a looping mechanism where each item is iterated against the other elements. This sounds useful, but it can have a disastrous side effect: a seemingly innocent query can take much longer than it should. After having written the individual From statements, you can use Where and Select as usual.

Sorting the Results

After having selected elements, you will probably want to sort the result set. Using LINQ, you can sort by anything you deem important. The obvious approach is to sort according to a number or letter, but you could also sort according to length of the word.

Regardless of how you sort, in LINQ you use the keywords Order By or the method OrderBy(). The following is a LINQ example that does an alphabetic sort.

```
Dim words As String() = { "cherry", "apple", "blueberry" }

Dim sortedWords = _
    From w In words _
    Order By w _
    Select w
```

The phrase Order By is inserted before Select. In this case, it will sort the words in ascending alphabetical order. The way that the Order By works is that the *value* of the variable is compared, rather than the actual variable.If you want to sort in reverse order, you can use the keyword Descending, as follows:

```
Dim sortedWords = _
    From w In words _
    Order By w Descending _
    Select w
```

This approach allows you to perform sorts according to other values. For example, you could sort by the length of word, like this:

```
Dim sortedWords = _
    From w In words _
    Order By w.Length _
    Select w
```

The `Order By` queries for the value of `w.Length`, which returns a number. If that number happens to be longer or shorter than another word, it is placed after or before the other word.

You could also sort according to multiple criteria. For example, you could sort the words alphabetically and then by length:

```
Dim sortedWords = _
    From w In words _
    Order By w, w.Length _
    Select w
```

To sort by multiple criteria, append them to the `Order By` keywords, each separated by a comma.

Note The alphabetical and length sort is fruitless, because when you sort alphabetically, you will automatically sort by length. The example is just for illustrative purposes.

Performing Set Operations

The last major topic that you need to know about when using LINQ is the ability to perform set operations on a collection. The major downside, however, to performing set operations is that you must use the methods, and at the time of this writing, no LINQ command syntax existed for set operations.

Knowing about set operations is useful because they enable you to sort and organize multiple result sets. The examples in this section involve the `Customer` type again. However, to make sure that the set operations function properly, you need to implement the `Equals()` and `GetHashCode()` methods, like this:

```
Friend Class Customer
    Public Overrides Function Equals(ByVal obj As Object) As Boolean
        If TypeOf obj Is Customer Then
            Dim otherObj As Customer = TryCast(obj, Customer)
            If otherObj.Identifier.CompareTo(Identifier) = 0 Then
                Return True
            End If
        End If
        Return False
    End Function

    Public Overrides Function GetHashCode() As Integer
        Return Identifier.GetHashCode()
    End Function

    Public Overrides Function ToString() As String
        Return String.Concat(New Object() _
            {"Identifier (", Me.Identifier, ") Points (", Me.Points, ")"})
    End Function
```

```
    Public Identifier As String
    Public Points As Integer
End Class
```

Note The GetHashCode() implementation here is rudimentary. In the source code that comes with this book, you will find a GetHashCode library class, which makes it simpler to implement GetHashCode(). The source code is in the project ServerSideSpreadsheet/Devspace.Trader.Common/Automators.

Look at how GetHashCode() and Equals() are implemented. Notice that the points data member is ignored. In the case of a customer, this is acceptable, because a customer with identical identifiers but unequal points does not imply two separate customers.

Implementing Equals() and GetHashCode() for custom types is absolutely imperative, because the set operations use that information to determine whether two objects are identical. If you don't implement either method, the set operations will use the default implementations of Equals() and GetHashCode(), which are incomplete and will give you the wrong results.

The next step is to create two separate lists of customers. In this example, both lists contain the same valued customer. Realize that the identical customer is not the same object instance, but contains the same values.

```
    Dim customers1 As Customer() = New Customer() { _
        New Customer() With {.Identifier = "Person 1", .Points = 0}, _
        New Customer() With {.Identifier = "Person 2", .Points = 10}}
    Dim customers2 As Customer() = New Customer() { _
        New Customer() With {.Identifier = "Person 3", .Points = 0}, _
        New Customer() With {.Identifier = "Person 2", .Points = 10}}
```

To get a list of all unique customers, you can use Union(), as follows:

```
Dim uniqueCustomers = customers1.Union(customers2)
```

Contained within the list represented by the variable uniqueCustomers will be the three customers of the two lists.

Using LINQ in Other Contexts

So far, all of the examples in this chapter involved using LINQ and objects. However, LINQ is not just an object-searching technology. It is also usable with XML and relational databases. Using LINQ with these other data sources is not a problem, since the querying is identical. What is a problem is getting the query to work in the first place.

Consider Figure 15-1, which illustrates the LINQ architecture.

As you can see in Figure 15-1, all .NET programming languages can access the LINQ library. The data manipulated by the LINQ library comes from what is called a LINQ-enabled data source. The examples that you've seen use the LINQ to objects data source.

Figure 15-1. *LINQ architecture (based on an image in MSDN Magazine, http://msdn.microsoft.com/ msdnmag/issues/07/06/csharp30/default.aspx)*

However, there is also the possibility to use a LINQ-enabled ADO.NET connection. The good news is that you can use LINQ with a relational database. The bad news is that the relational database's ADO.NET driver must support the special LINQ characteristics. At the time of this writing, only the Microsoft SQL Server driver supports LINQ. Currently, the drivers for Microsoft Access, MySQL, and other relational databases do not support LINQ.

Consider this LINQ query:

```
Dim northwind As NorthwindDataContext = _
  New NorthwindDataContext()
Dim products = From p In northwind.Products _
    Where p.OrderDetails.Count = 0 And p.UnitPrice > 100 _
    Select p
```

Notice the code in the From statement. The data source is an object that references the relational database Products table. If a database driver is optimized for LINQ, it will understand the LINQ query and optimize it as if it were a SQL statement.

If your database driver does not support LINQ, then you have a problem because, in theory, you would need to download all the data from the table, and then execute the LINQ query. That would waste resources and is not recommended.

■**Note** For examples of LINQ using relational databases, see *Beginning VB 2008 Databases* by Vidya Vrat Agarwal and James Huddleston (Apress, 2008).

Let's say that you want to execute LINQ on an XML document. Consider the following XML LINQ code (from `http://www.hookedonlinq.com/LINQtoXML5MinuteOverview.ashx`).

```
Dim loaded As XDocument = XDocument.Load("C:\contacts.xml")

' Query the data and write out a subset of contacts
Dim q = From c In loaded.Descendants("contact") _
        Where CType(c.Attribute("contactId").Value, Integer) < 4 _
        Select c.Element("firstName").ToString() & " " & _
               c.Element("lastName").ToString()
```

Notice how the same LINQ syntax that you've seen in the previous examples is used, but the source of the data that is to be manipulated by LINQ is different. Keep in mind that when you are manipulating data using LINQ, you are manipulating objects that may point to XML files, relational databases, or plain-vanilla data objects.

The Important Stuff to Remember

In this chapter, you learned about the basics of LINQ and how to write queries. Here are the key points to remember:

- LINQ is an API that sits on top of other technologies such as Visual Basic objects, relational databases, and XML documents.

- LINQ can work effectively only if the underlying data source technology has been optimized for LINQ. Otherwise, you are left with having to load a single record set and then manipulate that record set.

- Regardless of the data source, the techniques used to query and write LINQ are identical.

- When manipulating LINQ objects, the methods and properties associated with the various data sources are different. For example, when searching XML documents, you can use XML Document Object Model (DOM) methods and properties that are not available when manipulating plain-vanilla objects.

- LINQ is not just a syntax, but a series of extension methods associated with sets of data. The methods allow for more sophisticated data pipelining and processing of information.

Some Things for You to Do

The following are two exercises to help you apply what you've learned in this chapter.

1. The solution for finding a frequency presented in this chapter went from text to text to calculate the statistics. Can you think of another approach that would require minimal changes in the interface structure? Hint: the way the objects were parsed into objects borrowed code from another application. Could that other application be used somehow?

2. You saw a LINQ query embedding another LINQ query when finding the frequency of two numbers. Rewrite the code to generate the frequency of all combinations of single, pairs, and triples.

■ ■ ■

Learning About Other Visual Basic Techniques

This last chapter in the book is about tying up loose ends. The techniques discussed in this chapter are those that you will use in specific situations. This chapter covers the following topics:

- How to use arithmetic operators to manipulate numbers

- How to overload operators

- When you might use the `GoTo` statement

- How to use .NET generics constraints

- How to use nullable types

- How to use partial classes and methods

Operators

You have seen various operators used in examples throughout the book, such as the assignment operator (a = 3), and the logical operators (If(a = b)). Visual Basic has many more arithmetic operators that you can use to process types. You can also define custom operators.

Using Arithmetic Operators

The subtraction (-), multiplication (*), and division (/) operators are typically applicable to only numeric values. These operators are directly comparable to the mathematical operators you learned about in elementary school. Let's look at what the other arithmetic operators do.

Addition

The addition (+) operator is used to indicate the addition of two values, like this:

```
a = c + 1
```

The addition has a left-hand side and right-hand side, separated by the equal sign (=). On the right-hand side, the variable c is added to 1 and assigned to the variable a.

The notion of a left-hand side and a right-hand side as two separate parts is important when you consider this code:

```
a = a + 1
```

In the example, the variable a is added with the value 1 and assigned to the variable a, but these operations do not happen at the same time; they happen sequentially. First, the right-hand side is executed, and then the left-hand side is executed. By executing the left-hand side, the existing value of the variable a is overwritten.

Let's consider another example:

```
b = a = a + 1
```

If you were to run this code, b would not be assigned, because the example has mixed operators, which translates to this:

```
Dim b As Integer = CInt(-((a = (a + 1)) > False))
```

The result is not what you expected, and not even close to what you were trying to achieve (and isn't even allowed with Option Strict set to On). What this illustrates is that you need to be careful with operators.

Bitwise Operators

Bitwise operators are used to access and manipulate individual bits in a whole number.

As you learned in Chapter 2, the computer sees numbers as binary, with only two unique identifiers. Thus, whole numbers could be viewed as arrays of Boolean values, as there are only two valid values: 1 and 0 or True and False.

Let's look at example of using the bitwise operators. Say that you want to know whether a person is tall, wears hats, and runs slowly. Using Boolean data members, you would write the following code.

```
Class PersonWithAttributes
    Public IsPersonTall As Boolean
    Public WearsHats As Boolean
    Public RunsSlowly As Boolean
End Class
```

In this definition, each attribute of PersonWithAttributes is its own data member. Another way to achieve the same effect is to consider each attribute as its own binary flag that is encoded into PersonWithAttributes. The class would be rewritten as follows:

```
Class PersonWithAttributes
    Public Attributes As Integer
End Class
```

In the rewritten example, the Boolean attributes are encoded into the data member Attributes using bitwise operators.

To encode a flag in a number means to tweak the individual binary bits of a number. To access the individual bits, you need to create constant numbers that are a power of 2. We use a power of 2 convention because binary is a counting system based on the power of 2. Thus, the three Boolean data members are converted to constants:

```
Const isTall As Integer = 1
Const wearsHats As Integer = 2
Const runsSlow As Integer = 4
```

Now you could create a person that is tall and runs slowly, like this:

```
Dim person As PersonWithAttributes = New PersonWithAttributes()
person.Attributes = isTall Or runsSlow
```

The variable person.Attributes is assigned the operations of isTall and runsSlow. So if isTall is 0001, and runsSlow is 0100, taking the bitwise OR (Or) of the two values results in 0101.

A bitwise OR is when you compare two values, and if either value is nonzero, then the answer is nonzero. If you were to convert the binary number into a decimal number, you would get the value of 5. You could verify that the person isTall like this:

```
If (person.Attributes And isTall) <> 0 Then
    Console.WriteLine("Person is tall")
Else
    Console.WriteLine("Person is not tall")
End If
```

A bitwise shift is the shifting of the bits to the left or to the right by the number of places indicated by the shift. The following code demonstrates shifting the bits two places to the left (<<).

```
Dim shifted As Integer = 8
shifted = shifted << 2
```

When the code is executed, the value held in shifted is 32. The value 8 has the binary representation 1000. Shifting two places to the right is 32, which has the binary representation 100000.

Here's an example of shifting to the right (>>):

```
Dim shifted As Integer = 8
shifted = shifted >> 2
```

The result is 2, which has the binary value 10.

For the most part, you probably will not use the binary shift operators. Unless you are dealing with hardware-related programming (such as GUI interactions), whatever you can do with flags can be replicated using a combination of Boolean types and structures. However, when you do encounter bitwise operators, you will recognize what they are doing.

Modulus

The modulus operator (Mod) is very useful when you want to perform division operations and need to know how much is left over. For example, the following calculation yields a value of 3.

```
Dim a As Integer = 17 / 5
```

Yet because it is an integer division, you don't know if the value is evenly divided by 5. The following calculation lets you figure out the remainder for the division.

```
Dim remainder As Integer = 17 Mod 5
```

Increment and Decrement

The increment (+=) and decrement (-=) operators are useful in place of the addition and subtraction operators. Visual Basic also has the *= and /= operators, which you can use in place of the multiplication and division operators. The idea behind these operators is to perform an operation on the variable itself.

Let's say you execute this code:

```
Dim a As Integer = 2
a += 1
```

Then after the increment operation, the variable a will have a value of 3.

Overloading Operators

Suppose you want to implement a special type, such as a complex number type, and want to support the + sign. To do so, you would need to implement the + operator, which, in turn, overloads the + operator.

As an example, let's walk through implementing the + operator for the complex number type. Complex numbers are numbers that have two parts: real and imaginary. For example, a + b is a complex number, where a is the real part and b is the imaginary part. To add a complex number, you add the real parts, and then add the imaginary parts, and that gives you the new number. The following is the complex number type, ComplexType, declaration.

```
Public NotInheritable Class ComplexType
    Private ReadOnly _imaginary As Double
    Private ReadOnly _real As Double

    Public Sub New(ByVal real As Double, ByVal imaginary As Double)
        _real = real
        _imaginary = imaginary
    End Sub

    Public Overrides Function ToString() As String
        Return String.Concat(New Object() {"(", _real, ") (", _imaginary, ")i"})
    End Function

    Public ReadOnly Property Imaginary() As Double
        Get
            Return _imaginary
        End Get
    End Property
```

```
    Public ReadOnly Property Real() As Double
        Get
            Return _real
        End Get
        Set(ByVal value As Double)
            _real = value
        End Set
    End Property
End Class
```

ComplexType is an immutable type that has two data members representing the real and imaginary number parts.

The goal is to define the + operator so that the following code can be compiled.

```
Dim a As ComplexType = New ComplexType(1.0, 10.0)
Dim b As ComplexType = New ComplexType(2.0, 20.0)

Dim c As ComplexType = a + b
```

Overloading the + operator means to add a method that has a special notation. The following is the modified ComplexType type with the overloaded operator implemented (bolded).

```
Public NotInheritable Class ComplexType
    Private ReadOnly _imaginary As Double
    Private ReadOnly _real As Double

    Public Sub New(ByVal real As Double, ByVal imaginary As Double)
        _real = real
        _imaginary = imaginary
    End Sub

    Public Shared Operator +(ByVal a As ComplexType, ByVal b As ComplexType) _
      As ComplexType
        Return New ComplexType((a.Real + b.Real), (a.Imaginary + b.Imaginary))
    End Operator

    Public Overrides Function ToString() As String
        Return String.Concat(New Object() {"(", _real, ") (", _imaginary, ")i"})
    End Function

    Public ReadOnly Property Imaginary() As Double
        Get
            Return _imaginary
        End Get
    End Property
```

```
    Public ReadOnly Property Real() As Double
        Get
            Return _real
        End Get
    End Property

End Class
```

The declaration of the overloaded operator is a specially defined function, which follows these rules:

- The method is always declared as Shared in the context of the type.

- The method has a return type, which should be the type that you want to construct. In most cases, it is the type of the declaration (except where a Boolean is required).

- The method identifier starts with the keyword Operator, followed by a space, and then the operator being overloaded (+, -, and so on).

The GoTo Statement

The GoTo statement allows you to jump from one spot in the code to another. In the past, when we did not have objects, methods, and other advanced programming constructs, developers used the GoTo statement because they had no other choice. Currently, many in the software industry dislike the GoTo statement. They think that the GoTo statement is a sign of poor programming, and that you never need to use it. The Channel 9 forum (http://channel9.msdn.com/ShowPost.aspx?PageIndex=1&PostTD=14652) has a good discussion on the use of GoTo statements. In this discussion, a person who was against the GoTo statement said this:

> *The only possible exception would be if you are doing some sort of computer graphics app, where I would tolerate a (for y) (for x) nesting, because the inner loop is likely to be quite simple and the structure makes more sense as an entirety.*

So, he would tolerate the GoTo statement in a specific situation, and that means that one can't argue that GoTo is all bad.

What I like about how Visual Basic implemented GoTo is that it is designed to solve a particular problem, but not raise the old problems of spaghetti code making a mess of things. So if you need to use a GoTo statement, go ahead; just don't use it excessively.

One example where it is not easily possible to avoid using a GoTo statement is in the following pseudo-code.

```
Do While FirstActionLoop()
    Do While SecondActionLoop()
        If BreakOutOfLoops() Then
            GoTo EXIT_ALL
        End If
    Loop
Loop
EXIT_ALL:
```

This code has two loops. If the code is executing the second loop and decides to end processing, then exiting the loop becomes a bit tricky, as you can break execution only one loop at a time using the Exit Do statement. Thus, one solution is to use the GoTo statement, as shown.

The GoTo statement is associated with an identifier that represents a label. The label can be placed almost anywhere in the declared method. An exception is that you can't place a label in a Select statement. However, you can place the label before or after the GoTo keyword.

.NET Generics Constraints

.NET generics have been covered in several chapters. An additional aspect of .NET generics is *constraints*, which can be optionally used to optimize programming. Constraints limit the types that the parameter can be.

Three types of constraints are Class, New, and a specific type. As a general rule, a constraint is added in the form of an As statement, as follows:

```
Class Example(Of DataType As {New})
End Class
```

This example limits DataType to types that have a default constructor.

Using the Type Constraint

Type constraints allow you to associate a minimal type with the .NET generics parameter. For example, suppose this interface is defined:

```
Interface IExample
    Sub Method()
End Interface
```

Adding an IExample constraint to the .NET generics parameter allows you to define a class as follows:

```
Class ExampleMgr(Of DataType As { IExample})
    Private _inst As DataType

    Public Sub New(ByVal inst As DataType)
        _inst = inst
    End Sub

    Public Sub DoSomething()
        _inst.Method()
    End Sub
End Class
```

In the example, the constraint of IExample allows a developer to call Method(). If the constraint were not there, the reference to Method would generate a compiler error, because Method() is not a method of DataType.

But is this ability to reference a method an advantage? After all, you could write the ExampleMgr code without using .NET generics, like this:

```
Class ExampleMgr
    Dim _inst As IExample

    Public Sub New(ByVal inst As IExample)
        Me._inst = inst
    End Sub

    Public Sub DoSomething()
        _inst.Method()
    End Sub
End Class
```

The .NET generics code and the interface-based code do the exact same thing, and using .NET generics offers no advantage in this example. But that is not always the case. Consider the following modified example of ExampleMgr.

```
Class ExampleMgr(Of DataType As { IExample })
    Dim _inst As DataType

    Public Sub New(ByVal inst As IExample)
        Me._inst = CType(inst, DataType)
    End Sub

    Public Sub DoSomething()
        _inst.Method()
    End Sub

    Public ReadOnly Property Inst() As DataType
        Get
            Return _inst
        End Get
    End Property
End Class
```

With .NET generics, you can write a property that contains a reference to the base type. Had you used the pure interface-based code, the Inst property would need to be of type IExample, and to get the same effect as the .NET generics example, a cast would be involved. A cast is not the end of the world, but it is inconvenient and not type-safe, since you don't know if a cast will work until you execute the code.

You can add multiple interfaces and classes as constraints, although you are limited. The limitations are identical to the limitations when subclassing a class or interface:

- You can subclass only a single class.

- You can subclass as many interfaces as desired, but they must be declared after the class.

Using the New Constraint

The purpose of the New constraint is to limit the data type to one that has a default constructor, as in this example:

```
Class Example(Of DataType As {New})
    Private _value As DataType

    Public Sub New()
        _value = New DataType()
    End Sub
End Class
```

Without the New constraint, the bolded code cannot be compiled.

The constructor that is defined with the New constraint does not take parameters, and it would seem that this is a bother. After all, you might want to instantiate the type with some state. What you can do is constrain DataType, and then instantiate the type using object initializers. For example, the following is an interface that has a single property.

```
Interface IBase
    Property Value() As Integer
End Interface
```

Combining the IBase interface and the New keyword as constraints, you could write the following code.

```
Class Example(Of DataType As {IBase, New})
    Private _value As DataType

    Public Sub New()
        _value = New DataType() With {.Value = 10}
    End Sub
End Class
```

In the modified example, the bolded code instantiates DataType, and then using the constraints, the object initializer that defines _value is possible.

Using the Class Constraint

The main purpose of the Class constraint is to indicate whether the .NET generics type is a value type or a reference type. Here is an example of a type that wants to manage only reference types:

```
Class AssumeReferenceType(Of DataType As {Class})
    Private _value As DataType

    Public Sub New(ByVal value As DataType)
    End Sub
End Class
```

If you were to declare the AssumeReferenceType using an Integer, as shown in the following example, the code would not compile.

```
Dim cls As AssumeReferenceType(Of Integer) = _
  New AssumeReferenceType(Of Integer)(Nothing)
```

Nullable Types

In .NET, Nothing means no value, and we all understand what it represents, right? For example, the following code shows how to use Nothing.

```
Dim value As Object = Nothing

If value Is Nothing Then
    Console.WriteLine("Yup a Nothing")
End If
```

The example is obvious and does nothing useful. If you attempted to call the Object.ToString() method on value, an exception would be generated. So, what the code has created is a variable value that references nothing and is nothing. This works because the example uses a .NET reference type. Let's see what happens when you assign a value to a value type that we equate to no real value.

```
Dim value As Integer = 0

If value = 0 Then
    Console.WriteLine("Yup a Nothing???")
End If
```

This time, value is not of the type Object, but is of the type Integer. And value is assigned a value of 0 to indicate no real value. Now many of you will be saying, "Hey, wait a minute—0 <> Nothing." Yet, in the programming languages C++ and C, Nothing and 0 have the same contextual meaning, so it's not so outlandish.

Visual Basic has a programming construct called the *nullable type*. The nullable type solves the problem of knowing whether or not a value type has been assigned. This is needed when interacting with relational databases. For example, there is no way to indicate that an integer value is not assigned, since declaring a value type means declaring a stack variable, and it will have a default value. In other words, there is no chance a value type will have a null reference.

A nullable type in Visual Basic is used to define a value-type variable that might have a null state. In the value type example, the integer value was assigned a value of 0, but a value of Nothing would have been more appropriate. However, value types cannot be assigned a value of Nothing; they must be assigned some valid value.

To further demonstrate the restrictions of a value type, the following is a Structure declaration.

```
Structure ExampleStructure
    Public value As Integer
End Structure
```

Here's how we might use it:

```
Dim ex As ExampleStructure = Nothing
```

The structure ExampleStructure is defined using the Structure keyword, which means that ExampleStructure is a value type. The next line, where the variable ex is assigned a value of Nothing, will result in an action where nothing happens other than resetting the variable ex to 0. And as was illustrated earlier, 0 is not Nothing.

The inability to assign Nothing is odd, because structures behave similarly to reference types in many ways. Instantiating a default value of a structure is not always the right answer, since the data members might not have a default value.

The nullable type makes it possible for value types (for example, structures) to be nothing. In Visual Basic, you define a nullable type by using the .NET generics class Nullable or the nullable type notation, as follows:

```
Dim ex As Nullable(Of ExampleStructure) = Nothing
```

or

```
Dim ex As ExampleStructure? = Nothing
```

Using nullable types, it is possible to assign a Nothing value to a value type. To assign a value to a nullable type, you need to explicitly assign the variable, as in the following example.

```
ex = New ExampleStructure() With {.value = 10}
```

And then to reference the structure—in particular, the property value—use the following code.

```
Console.WriteLine("(" & ex.Value.value & ")")
```

The additional reference of Value is the link between the reference type Nullable and the value type ExampleStructure.

■**Note** Nullable types are not intended to be used in conjunction with reference types. If you attempt to use a nullable type with a reference type, you will get a Visual Basic compiler error. Nullable types are designed for use by value types, and there is no other mystical or magical reason to use a nullable type.

Partial Classes and Methods

By default, whenever you create a type, you must declare the complete type in one file and as one entity. For example, the following class would need to be declared in the context of a single file.

```
Class Example
    Const BaseValue as Integer = 10
    Public Sub AddNumbers(ByVal value1 As Integer, _
                          ByVal value2 As Integer, _
                          ByRef response As Integer)
        response = BaseValue + value1 + value2
    End Sub
End Class
```

The Example class has a single method AddNumbers, and the method implementation adds two numbers to a base value (BaseValue). Everything is in a single file. But suppose you wanted to automatically generate Example, and have it generate the data member BaseValue, but not the method AddNumbers. To do that, you would need to split the class into two separate classes, where one class subclasses the other:

```
Class BaseGenerated
    Protected Const BaseValue As Integer = 10
End Class

Class Example : Inherits BaseGenerated
    Public Sub AddNumbers(ByVal value1 As Integer, _
                          ByVal value2 As Integer, _
                          ByRef response As Integer)
        response = BaseValue + value1 + value2
    End Sub
End Class
```

Having one class subclass the other is fine, and it works. The class BaseGenerated could be stored in one file, and Example could be stored in another file. But that approach can be a bit problematic, as it implies a specific architecture where one class subclasses the other. Another approach would be to use the Partial keyword in the context of a class, as follows:

```
Class Example
    Const BaseValue As Integer = 10
End Class

Partial Class Example
    Public Sub AddNumbers(ByVal value1 As Integer, _
                          ByVal value2 As Integer, _
                          ByRef response As Integer)
        response = BaseValue + value1 + value2
    End Sub
End Class
```

When you use the Partial keyword, you are defining a partial class. The complete class is the sum of all the separate partial class definitions for the class (which could, and typically would, reside in separate files). Thus, one part of the class could be autogenerated, and the other piece could be hand-coded.

A requirement of partial classes is that they must be wholly defined in an assembly. The partial class is of relevance only to the Visual Basic compiler, and not to the .NET language.

Another usage of the `Partial` keyword is to have methods that are defined in one place but implemented in another. Think of partial methods as defining an abstract class method and implementing it within the same class. The following is an example of using a partial method.

```
Class Example
    Partial Private Sub AddNumbers(ByVal value1 As Integer, _
                                   ByVal value2 As Integer, _
                                   ByRef response As Integer)
    End Sub

    Public Sub Method()
        Dim response As Integer = 0

        AddNumbers(1, 2, response)
        Console.WriteLine("Added numbers (" & response & ")")
    End Sub
End Class

Partial Class Example
    Private Sub AddNumbers(ByVal value1 As Integer, _
                           ByVal value2 As Integer, _
                           ByRef response As Integer)
        response = value1 + value2
    End Sub
End Class
```

Partial methods are defined in the context of a partial class. In one part of your class, you would prefix the identifier `Partial` to the method and declare it. In the other part of the class, you would implement the method.

Partial methods, like partial classes, have some restrictions:

- They must be declared as a `Sub`.

- They must be declared to be `Private`.

- The methods can be shared and use extension methods.

Overall, partial methods and classes should not be used as a general programming practice, because they are intended to be employed in the context of autogenerated code (such as `Form1.vb` in Windows forms). When used in that context, partial methods and classes are an excellent solution.

Partial methods are also useful substitutes for conditional compilation constants, because if you don't implement a partial method, any mention of it is removed from the compiled class. This means, for example, that you can wrap the implementation with a single `#If`, rather than littering many instances of `#If` in your code. Here's an example:

```
    Partial Private Sub Display(ByVal message As String)
    End Sub

#If DEBUG Then
    Private Sub Display(ByVal message As String)
        Console.WriteLine(message)
    End Sub
#End If

    Sub RunAll()
        RunFirst()
        Display("Done RunFirst()")
        RunSecond()
        Display("Done RunSecond()")
        RunThird()
        Display("Done RunThird()")
    End Sub
```

The Important Stuff to Remember

In this chapter, you learned about some Visual Basic techniques that are useful in specific situations. Here are the points you should keep in mind:

- You will need to use the arithmetic operators. Some are obvious; others are not. Take the time to get used to coding with them.

- Overloading operators makes sense when you need to define custom types and you want them to support basic operators such as add, subtract, and so on. When implementing the operators, be careful to do a logically correct implementation.

- To be able to use methods or properties on .NET generics parameters, they need to be constrained. Constraints are an effective way of indicating basic functionality possessed by .NET generics types. Even though you could usually achieve the same results using interfaces, that approach is not as elegant.

- Visual Basic has the GoTo keyword, even though some consider the use of GoTo as poor programming. Visual Basic has ensured that you can't easily shoot yourself in the foot.

- The nullable type is used to indicate whether or not a value type has been assigned. You will use this type when interacting with a database type.

- Partial methods and classes are useful in the context of autogenerated source code. They make it easier to split apart the functionality that is autogenerated and store it in one file, while the hand-coded part is stored in another file. They can also be used in place of conditional compilation constants.

Some Things for You to Do

The following two exercises are the final ones this book.

1. Build a two-dimensional matrix class that supports the + and - operators.

2. Write a question to the author asking him to solve two problems that you have encountered. Send the e-mail to christianhgross@gmail.com.

Index

You Need the Companion eBook

Your purchase of this book entitles you to buy the companion PDF-version eBook for only $10. Take the weightless companion with you anywhere.

We believe this Apress title will prove so indispensable that you'll want to carry it with you everywhere, which is why we are offering the companion eBook (in PDF format) for $10 to customers who purchase this book now. Convenient and fully searchable, the PDF version of any content-rich, page-heavy Apress book makes a valuable addition to your programming library. You can easily find and copy code—or perform examples by quickly toggling between instructions and the application. Even simultaneously tackling a donut, diet soda, and complex code becomes simplified with hands-free eBooks!

Once you purchase your book, getting the $10 companion cBook is simple:

❶ Visit **www.apress.com/promo/tendollars/**.

❷ Complete a basic registration form to receive a randomly generated question about this title.

❸ Answer the question correctly in 60 seconds, and you will receive a promotional code to redeem for the $10.00 eBook.

THE EXPERT'S VOICE™

2855 TELEGRAPH AVENUE | SUITE 600 | BERKELEY, CA 94705

Offer valid through 8/11/08.